Mastering

Psychology

MACMILLAN MASTER SERIES

Accounting
Arabic
Astronomy
Australian History
Background to Business
Banking
Basic Management
Biology
British Politics
Business Communication
Business Law
Business Microcomputing
C Programming
Catering Science
Catering Theory
Chemistry
COBOL Programming
Commerce
Computer Programming
Computers
Economic and Social History
Economics
Electrical Engineering
Electronics
English as a Foreign Language
English Grammar
English Language
English Literature
Financial Accounting
French 1
French 2

German 1
German 2
Hairdressing
Human Biology
Italian 1
Italian 2
Japanese
Manufacturing
Marketing
Mathematics
Modern British History
Modern European History
Modern World History
Nutrition
Pascal Programming
Philosophy
Physics
Practical Writing
Psychology
Restaurant Service
Science
Secretarial Procedures
Social Welfare
Sociology
Spanish 1
Spanish 2
Spreadsheets
Statistics
Study Skills
Typewriting Skills
Word Processing

Mastering

Psychology

Roger Davies and Peter Houghton

MACMILLAN

First published 1991 by
THE MACMILLAN PRESS LTD
Houndmills, Basingstoke, Hampshire RG21 2XS
and London
Companies and representatives
throughout the world

ISBN 0–333–49709–0

A catalogue record for this book is available
from the British Library.

Printed in China

10 9 8 7 6
00 99 98 97 96 95 94

Contents

List of Figures		ix
List of Tables		xi
Preface		xii
Acknowledgements		xv

1 Development over the lifespan — **1**
1.1 Introduction — 1
1.2 Early social behaviour and the parent–child relationship — 1
1.3 The attachment process — 3
1.4 The childhood years — 5
1.5 Adolescence — 7
1.6 Adulthood — 11
1.7 Questions and exercises — 13

2 Aspects of socialization — **14**
2.1 Introduction — 14
2.2 The acquisition of sex roles — 14
2.3 Theories of sex-role typing — 18
2.4 The development of aggression — 21
2.5 Questions and exercises — 29

3 Social influence — **31**
3.1 Introduction — 31
3.2 Social facilitation — 31
3.3 Conformity — 32
3.4 Criticisms and comments on conformity experiments — 38
3.5 Compliance — 40
3.6 Obedience — 42
3.7 Questions and exercises — 48

4 Attitudes — **49**
4.1 Introduction — 49
4.2 Definitions — 49
4.3 Measuring attitudes — 50
4.4 What you say and what you do: attitudes and behaviour — 52
4.5 The development of attitudes — 54
4.6 Changing attitudes — 56
4.7 Consistency theory — 61
4.8 Questions and exercises — 63

5 Social perception — **64**
5.1 Introduction — 64
5.2 Impression formation — 64
5.3 Prejudice and discrimination — 67

5.4	Causes of prejudice and discrimination	69
5.5	Reducing prejudice and discrimination	72
5.6	Interpersonal attraction	75
5.7	Questions and exercises	80

6 Perception — **81**
6.1	Introduction	81
6.2	Classification of sensory receptor systems	82
6.3	Principles common to sensory systems	82
6.4	The human visual system	85
6.5	Visual processing by the brain	90
6.6	Sensation and perception	92
6.7	Perceiving is believing	94
6.8	Is perception innate or learnt?	105
6.9	*Gestalt* theory of perception	106
6.10	Questions and exercises	108

7 Attention — **109**
7.1	Introduction	109
7.2	Selective attention	111
7.3	Divided attention	116
7.4	Automatic and conscious processing	118
7.5	Questions and exercises	119

8 Memory — **120**
8.1	Introduction	120
8.2	Sensory memory	120
8.3	The Atkinson–Shiffrin model of memory	120
8.4	Research and evidence	122
8.5	Criticisms of laboratory studies of memory	124
8.6	Eyewitness testimony	125
8.7	Levels of processing	125
8.8	Semantic memory	129
8.9	Questions and exercises	131

9 Intelligence — **132**
9.1	Introduction	132
9.2	The development of IQ testing	133
9.3	Construction of modern IQ tests	136
9.4	Theories of intelligence	138
9.5	Determinants of IQ test performance	141
9.6	Artificial intelligence	145
9.7	Current intelligence research	147
9.8	Questions and exercises	147

10 Cognitive development — **148**
10.1	Introduction	148
10.2	The work of Jean Piaget	148
10.3	The development of the intellect	149
10.4	Piaget's stage theory	150
10.5	Piaget on moral development	158

10.6 Piaget's theory: a critical evaluation   160
10.7 Questions and exercises   165

11 Language and communication   **166**
11.1 Introduction   166
11.2 The structure of language   166
11.3 From sounds to words: the acquisition of language   168
11.4 Beyond simple sentences   171
11.5 Impaired language development   172
11.6 Theories of language acquisition   173
11.7 Language in other animals   177
11.8 Questions and exercises   179

12 Animal learning   **180**
12.1 Introduction   180
12.2 Ivan Pavlov and classical conditioning   180
12.3 Instrumental or operant conditioning   182
12.4 Thorndike and the law of effect   182
12.5 Skinner and reinforcement   183
12.6 Positive and negative reinforcement   183
12.7 Punishment versus negative reinforcement   184
12.8 Primary and secondary reinforcement   185
12.9 Partial and continuous reinforcement   185
12.10 Schedules of reinforcement   185
12.11 Comparison between the different schedules   187
12.12 Applications of learning theory   189
12.13 The competence–performance issue   194
12.14 Latent learning   195
12.15 Questions and exercises   196

13 Animal behaviour   **197**
13.1 Ethology   197
13.2 Basic ethological concepts   198
13.3 Evolution and behaviour   200
13.4 Evolution and predator-prey relationships   202
13.5 Genetics and behaviour   203
13.6 Maturation and behaviour   205
13.7 Imprinting   206
13.8 Sociobiology   209
13.9 Kinship   210
13.10 Inclusive fitness   211
13.11 Questions and exercises   211

14 Abnormal behaviour   **212**
14.1 Introduction   212
14.2 The medical model of abnormal behaviour   212
14.3 Neuroses and psychoses   213
14.4 Psychological perspectives on mental disorders   213
14.5 Schizophrenia   215
14.6 Depression   219
14.7 Learned helplessness   220

14.8   Community care   222
14.9   Questions and exercises   223

15 Neuropsychology   **224**
15.1   Introduction   224
15.2   The neurone   224
15.3   The synapse   226
15.4   The human nervous system   227
15.5   Language and the brain   233
15.6   Split-brain studies   233
15.7   Questions and exercises   236

16 Personality theory   **237**
16.1   Introduction   237
16.2   Psychoanalytic theory   237
16.3   Role theory and personality   238
16.4   Humanism and personality theory   240
16.5   Trait and type approaches to personality   240
16.6   Freud's psychoanalytical theory   241
16.7   Jung's theory of personality   248
16.8   Questions and exercises   251

17 Methods of research   **252**
17.1   Introduction   252
17.2   Experiments   252
17.3   Observation studies   258
17.4   Case studies   259
17.5   Large-scale social research   261
17.6   Correlation   261
17.7   Computer simulation   262

18 The work of the psychologist   **263**
18.1   Introduction   263
18.2   The clinical psychologist   263
18.3   The occupational psychologist   264
18.4   The educational psychologist   264
18.5   The criminological psychologist   265
18.6   The psychology teacher   265
18.7   Other specialist and non-specialist careers   266
18.8   Questions and exercises   267

19 Historical issues in psychology   **268**
19.1   Introduction   268
19.2   The nature–nurture debate   268
19.3   Reductionism in psychology   269
19.4   Mind–body dualism   270
19.5   Historical perspectives on psychology   271
19.6   Questions and answers   275

Bibliography   277
Glossary of terms   291
Index   296

List of Figures

1.1   The infant smile   2
2.1   Child with Bobo doll   23
2.2   Representation of the drive theory of aggression   25
2.3   An interpretation of the revised model of the
      frustration–aggression hypothesis   26
3.1   Children working together   31
3.2   Example of material presented to subjects in conformity
      experiments   34
3.3   Arrangement used by Asch in studies of conformity   35
3.4   Example of material used by Asch in a subsequent experiment   37
3.5   Example of material used in Crutchfield in conformity
      experiments   39
3.6   Set-up used by Milgram in his study of obedience   43
4.1   Questionnaire in progress   55
4.2   Persuasive communication?   58
6.1   The visible spectrum   84
6.2   The human eye   85
6.3   The structure of the human retina   86
6.4   The visual pathways from the eyes to the brain   87
6.5   The blind spot   88
6.6   The 'receptive field' of one RGC   90
6.7   The single neurone   91
6.8   The pathway of the 'second visual system' to the inferotemporal
      cortex   92
6.9   What do you perceive here?   93
6.10 The Müller–Lyer illusion   93
6.11 Identifying objects from the barest amount of information   95
6.12 Which of the straight lines is longer?   95
6.13 The Ponzo illusion   95
6.14 A picture incorporating the idea of the Ponzo illusion   96
6.15 Impossible objects   97
6.16 Other types of illusion   98
6.17 Perceiving circles   99
6.18 Perceiving lines   99
6.19 The Necker cube   100
6.20 The Schröeder staircase   100
6.21 More optical illusions   101
6.22 Perceiving an ambiguous stimulus – 1   103
6.23 Perceiving an ambiguous stimulus – 2   105
7.1   The dichotic listening task   110
7.2   Broadbent's filter model of selective attention   113

7.3   Stimuli used in Sutherland and Holgate's study on the effects
      of presenting a compound stimulus on learning   114
7.4   Treisman's attenuator model of selective attention   115
7.5   Results of the study by Posner and Boies illustrating their
      resource allocation model of attention   117
8.1   The Atkinson–Shiffrin model of memory   121
8.2   The serial position effect   122
8.3   The effects of rehearsal time on STM   124
8.4   Task 'depth' and recall ability in a hypothetical experiment   126
8.5   The 'level of processing' model of memory   127
8.6   Hierarchical network model   130
8.7   Sentence verification task   131
9.1   Binet test item for $2\frac{1}{2}$–3-year-olds   134
9.2   The standard normal distribution for IQ   138
9.3   Spearman's model of intelligence structures   140
9.4   Vernon's hierarchical model of the structure of human abilities 142
10.1 Child and 'Three Mountains' model   153
10.2 The falling sticks problem   154
10.3 Piaget's conservation tasks: area and substance   155
10.4 Piaget's conservation tasks: liquid and number   156
10.5 Display used by Borke (1975) to demonstrate decentration
      in 3–4-year-olds   162
10.6 Hughes's policeman doll study   163
11.1 The 'parts' of a sentence   167
11.2 Mother and infant in 'conversation'   169
12.1 The generalization curve   181
12.2 The Skinner Box   183
12.3 Extract from a linear program   192
12.4 Learning with computers   193
12.5 Latent learning by rats   195
13.1 The double concentric runway used by Hess and others to
      investigate imprinting phenomena   208
14.1 The number of hospital beds and admissions to mental health
      institutions in the period 1950–90   223
15.1 The neurone   225
15.2 The synapse   227
15.3 The structure of the brain   228
15.4 The lobes of the brain   232
15.5 Language functions localized in the left hemisphere of the brain 234
17.1 Methods of research in psychology   253
17.2 Experimental method   254
17.3 Example of a schedule for a systematic observation study   260

List of Tables

1.1 Some primary and secondary sexual characteristics of males
     and females   8
1.2 Erikson's eight stages of psychosocial development   10
2.1 Sex-role stereotypes in Western society   15
2.2 Simplified summary of three approaches to acquisition of
     sex roles (boys)   21
5.1 Variables in experiment by Aronson *et al.* (1966)   80
10.1 Piaget's stage theory of cognitive development   151
12.1 Example of a VR5 schedule   186
12.2 Example of a VI10 schedule   187
14.1 Medical model of mental disorders   216
14.2 Drug treatments of mental disorders   218
16.1 Freud's stages of development and the approximate ages
     at which they emerge   247
17.1 Counter-balancing the subject order in a repeated-measures design   257
17.2 Summary of the advantages and disadvantages of using the
     two main experimental designs   258

Preface

Each of us is a student of human behaviour. From the earliest hours of life an infant becomes curious about what those strange large adults all around are up to. It soon learns that they may bring comfort and nourishment, inflict pain or show interest; they are sometimes tender and soothing, and sometimes ill-tempered; they come in numerous shapes and sizes and are never still for long; they are infinitely complex and subtle and ever changeable. From infancy to old age we continue actively probing and searching our own and others' behaviours, trying to make some sense of it all. Sometimes we may want to understand each other for selfish reasons so we may know how to prosper from the foibles and mistakes of others. At other times we may need to place our trust and confidence in someone and so we evaluate them for this motive. Yet there is always the desire to understand ourselves as individuals: how we are like other people and in what ways we are unique.

Psychology is the formal science of studying people. Those few of us who earn our living from such an activity which is as natural as breathing are very fortunate indeed. And yet the science of psychology goes far beyond that which deals with the intuitive, superficial level of explanation. The many popular questionnaires published on a regular basis in magazines entreating you to uncover the darkest secrets of your mind, or to discover how to make yourself a 'successful person' or a wonderful lover, have nothing to do with psychology. In much the same way as tribal witchdoctors rely upon the superstitious beliefs and faith of their patients, so too do authors and astrologers in the Press depend on the fallible curiosity in all of us to understand more about ourselves and others.

As the scientific discipline of psychology is relatively new there are few things which can be said about the subject matter which are certain and known, in the sense that any scientific understanding can be certain or knowable. Psychology is at the stage where its knowledge is contained more in the pages of research articles than it is in textbooks. Whereas many of the early theories in the subject have already been discarded, and progress in our particular era seems slow and laborious, this is an inevitable process in the development of any science.

What, then, does the modern psychology textbook have to offer that the Press articles do not? Well, the first point is that no rash promises are, or can be, made that you will come to understand your mind or become a better person after reading it. Rather, the aim of this and every other introductory textbook is to provide a condensed and yet comprehensive account of the major theories which make up the area of study. In this sense this book is a tribute to the generations of psychologists who have already contributed to human knowledge about humans. Second, since psychology is a scientific discipline, discussion concerning the methods of enquiry and how data is collected and evaluated are inevitable inclusions even at the commencement of your study of the subject. Finally, we hope to infect the reader with a germ of enthusiasm with which to continue the study of psychology. Although we have already said that there is no one comprehensive explanation for the workings of the human mind or behaviour, there is a corporate wisdom contained in the many approaches and in the mass of knowledge which has been acquired over the past century since psychology was first inaugurated as a science.

As a scientific endeavour, one of the things that psychology is trying to establish is knowledge structures. Each piece of established 'truth' becomes the starting point for further research. Psychology's 'truths' are simply its theories which have been verified through its research investigations. Understanding how theories are devised and tested is essential to the scientist, and so this practical side of the subject is an inevitable part of any book or course in psychology. Yet there is no one logical order of study: the way in which you tackle this book depends upon your own interests and background. After all, the point of studying psychology is to reach some level of understanding of the entire person and so attempts to study fragments of human existence are merely to be thought of as milestones on the road to knowledge of the integrated being. Although all psychological theorists agree on the intended destination they often disagree about the best means of travel and also on the exact route which should be followed. The student should therefore learn to cope with the conflicting theories that will sometimes arise in any one study area. In fact the ability to evaluate and distinguish between the various theories and approaches to the subject is highly regarded by psychologists and is something to be aimed at, even by students beginning their courses and reading.

This book begins by covering aspects of the developing individual from infancy through to senescence (old age). In the early chapters this is discussed with the intention of giving the reader an overview of the social and emotional development of the child and how early experience may influence later adult behaviour and thought. These opening chapters are often referred to as 'social and development processes' in courses of psychology.

From Chapter 6 begins a discussion of what are treated in psychology as 'individual processes'; that is, facets of behaviour which may be understood regarding the structure of the individual person, such as perception, attention, memory and intelligence.

Chapter 10 continues with the theme of intellectual ability but looks at it from a developmental perspective (i.e., how the human capacity for thought and intelligence grows through childhood). The topic of language in Chapter 11 is given a similar perspective.

Chapters 12 and 13 are normally treated as a specialism within the subject, known as 'comparative psychology', which generally means the study of animal behaviour with the intention of throwing light on human behaviour. This is approached in Chapter 12. The following chapter is more concerned with the discipline of *ethology*, which is the study of animal behaviour in the animals' natural habitat. Chapter 14 is about another specialism within psychology and deals with abnormal behaviour.

The biological bases of human behaviour are an essential component of any psychology course and this is covered in Chapter 15 under the heading of neuropsychology, since its main concern is with the functioning of the nervous system in relation to behaviour. Personality theory (covered in Chapter 16) provides a discussion of some major theories. In the final chapters some selected historical issues are traced back to their nineteenth-century origins. The authors hope to prompt the student to treat historical contributions to the subject respectfully, whatever the current vogue regarding their status. For one thing, many current research views owe not only their roots to an earlier theorist but also (in some cases) the original views have been resurrected for a fresh look. Sometimes the grave-robbers concede their debt to the forerunners but regrettably such tributes are often overlooked.

The book concludes with an extensive bibliography and glossary of terms: words defined in the glossary are printed in bold type on their first appearance in the text. It is unfortunate for the student that psychology has evolved such a large amount of technical jargon and we hope this section helps to overcome this potential obstacle. And so from two committed students to another, we welcome you aboard the enterprise!

ROGER DAVIES
PETER HOUGHTON

Acknowledgements

The authors wish to thank Dorothy Brooks and David Jordan for their help with the manuscript and illustrations. Thanks are also due to Andy Hooton, the staff and pupils of Mabs Cross Primary School, Wigan, and to the Photography Department of Wigan College of Technology. We also appreciate the advice and encouragement given to us by Jane Wightwick, Publisher at Macmillan Education. We have benefited from the assistance of Iain Garner, Sarah Johnson and Simon Smith who helped to make the text more readable than it otherwise would have been. Finally, we warmly acknowledge the help, encouragement and forbearance of Christine and Jane, to whom we dedicate this book.

ROGER DAVIES
PETER HOUGHTON

Development over the Lifespan

1.1 Introduction

When the human infant enters the world he or she is totally dependent on others for the provision of food, warmth and protection. With maturation comes increasing confidence in motor coordination, and by 14 months most infants are able to walk unaided even though it will be several years before they gain independence and acquire the many skills and abilities which most adults take for granted.

From birth onwards the presence of a principal caretaker (usually, but not always, the mother) is perhaps of greatest importance, both physically and psychologically. Not only is an infant's survival dependent on the care afforded by those around them, but the establishment of an affectional bond in the early formative years may influence the individual's subsequent social and emotional behaviour with other people.

As a young child the individual's experience and abilities rapidly increase; basic linguistic skills are mastered, and the social influence of **peers** becomes apparent when, for example, the child begins playgroup or nursery school.

During the school years further cognitive advances are made and often the first significant friendships are formed. It is around this period that the individual enters adolescence, which is effectively a bridge between childhood and adulthood. This is also a time of rapid change, not only physically but also in social and intellectual terms.

By early adulthood commitment and security tend to become priorities and this is reflected in career ambitions and in the move towards more enduring personal relationships. For many people middle adulthood represents a transition when a shift of direction may occur, possibly stemming from disappointment with earlier achievements. With the approach of old age the individual may reflect on past successes and failures and then consider the necessary readjustments which this time of life brings. Although this is usually a period of stability and contemplation the onset of old age, like other aspects of the lifespan, has its own particular psychological characteristics.

In this chapter we will explore some of the major features of the lifespan from a psychological viewpoint, in particular referring to empirical studies of the respective age groups that are available.

We begin with the earliest interactions that take place between human beings: those between parents and their offspring.

1.2 Early Social Behaviour and the Parent–Child Relationship

Within the first few weeks of life infants will readily engage in interactive behaviour with the people around them. The human face, in particular, appears highly effective in eliciting an infant's attention. Several studies have documented the perceptual world of the child, especially the kind of things they prefer to look at.

Fantz (1961) reasoned that if infants are given a choice of stimuli and spend more time looking at one than the other then this shows their ability to discriminate between such stimuli. In a series of now-famous experiments he was able to show that infants even as young as one week old preferred complex patterns to simpler ones, and in a related study he demonstrated what appeared to be infants' preference for patterns which resembled faces. Evidence of such abilities in very young infants suggests that this attraction towards human faces is present at birth.

If this is so what particular features of faces is it which elicits the most interest from infants? Ahrens (1954) found that initially face-like shapes in which only eyes featured were sufficient to gain a smiling response, but that more and more detail in the face was required to elicit smiling in older infants. Smiling itself is a significant developmental display and it provides an example of an early form of interaction between parent and infant.

Initially the smile may be a simple reflex or an indication of a state of pleasure or contentment (see Figure 1.1). But at around seven or eight weeks infants produce a social smile (i.e., one which is given as an active response to another person).

Smiling occurs at around the same time in all infants, even in babies who are blind at birth. Blind babies will smile at a familiar voice, as opposed to a familiar

Figure 1.1 The infant smile

face. This point provides support for the view that the smile is innate in humans (i.e., it is not something which requires learning in order for it to occur), although once the social smile has emerged its frequency can be modified by environmental conditions. For example, Gewirtz (1965) found that the amount of smiling exhibited by infants reared in institutions gradually decreased compared with that shown by non-institutionalized groups. This may be explained by considering the reciprocal nature of the smile: if someone smiles at us we usually smile back at them in return. In the case of these infants reared in institutions there was less opportunity to smile because there were relatively fewer people at whom to smile.

Reciprocity is also important in other aspects of parent–child interaction, such as mutual gazing and looking, whereby an exchange is 'set up' between the two people which both find rewarding. Of course, such exchanges also represent a significant step in terms of laying the foundations for linguistics development since they involve the kind of turn-taking which is associated with conversations (see Chapter 11). Perhaps more importantly, though, these interactions provide opportunities to strengthen the bond of affection that exists as the relationship between parent and child develops, which in turn leads to **attachment** behaviours.

1.3 The Attachment Process

We have already stated that the infant is highly vulnerable at birth and therefore requires the attention of specific others for their care and upbringing. This individual may be described as the principal caregiver, and it is the infant's efforts to seek closeness to this person which reveals itself as attachment.

The infant's attempts to remain in close proximity to the caregiver are certainly one indication of attachment; other behaviours include the ease with which this figure is able to calm the infant when distressed, and the tendency to be less afraid of unfamiliar objects or people when the caretaker is present. Conversely, the infant's attachment may be displayed through various signals of distress (for instance, upon separation). The most obvious of these is crying, a highly effective 'trigger' for the caregiver's attentions.

Attachment, then, has an intrinsic value, serving to ensure the infant's survival. This is especially so in the early formative years, but is obviously much more than a requirement to be near to someone. The establishment of a strong affectional bond provides for the infant's psychological well-being as well as satisfying physical needs, since it (naturally) implies an emotional involvement. Psychologists such as John Bowlby believe that the experience of attachment forms the basis for subsequent interpersonal development, and that maternal deprivation (separation) could have dire consequences for social, emotional and intellectual development (see the spotlight Box).

SPOTLIGHT Breaking the bond: what are the consequences?

In 1951, John Bowlby presented a report highlighting the consequences for social and emotional development in young children who experienced a separation from their mothers. In it, he claimed that 'mother love in infancy and childhood is as important for mental health as are vitamins and proteins for physical health'. His findings were based largely on studies of children who had undergone either long or short-term separation (e.g., a period of hospitalization) early in life, with apparently drastic results on their personalities and behaviour.

Many of Bowlby's conclusions on the effects of 'maternal deprivation' have since been re-interpreted by other researchers (e.g. Rutter). However, his observations regarding the psychological distress of such events have been widely accepted.

- What are the implications of the quote from Bowlby's report shown above?

- The symptoms of distress upon separation involved a sequence of three phrases: protest, despair and finally an emotional detachment shown by the child to those around them. How might this sequence be prevented?

- What advice would you give to parents whose young child was about to go into hospital for a few weeks?

Are all infants similar, though, in eliciting care and affection and, furthermore, does the quality of attachment vary? Infants differ in terms of disposition of temperament: some babies are placid, quiet and easily soothed, whereas others tend to be noisy, unsettled and difficult to console. Such variations in temperament can also influence the nature of the early relationship between the child and caregiver. Although these differences represent individuality and infant personality, some evidence suggests that early contact between mother and baby can have important consequences.

Klaus and Kennell (1982) suggested that mothers who were able to have close bodily contact with their babies immediately after birth were less likely to experience difficulties later, and in addition their children tended to display 'better' development compared with those who were deprived of this early opportunity for closeness.

However, although the findings of researchers such as Klaus and Kennell seems to imply that a critical period was involved in attachment formation (i.e., that if an infant did not become attached by a certain time then it never would), they did acknowledge that this immediate contact is not essential for bonding to occur; strong affectional bonds between mother and infant may develop without this initial degree of intimacy between the two.

Thus it appears there is little evidence to support the existence of a critical period in human attachment formation. However, Ainsworth (1989) cites a number of animal studies which present a different picture; in some animal species if the infant and mother are separated even for a brief period shortly after birth then the mother may reject her baby.

Although it is always difficult to draw comparisons between human and animal examples, Ainsworth points out that human mothers who experience lengthy separation following birth often do experience difficulty in displaying affection and devotedness to their infant when contact is restored.

However, with human beings other factors are involved which make early separations tolerable. It has, for instance, been suggested that mothers may mentally 'prime' themselves in readiness before the birth so that unforeseen difficulties are more easily resolved.

An indication of attachment is the infant's ability to cope with separations once the bond has been established (which may be several months after birth). In this respect the infant needs not only to derive comfort and security from the caregiver, but also to have the assurance or confidence to explore his or her surroundings, which suggests a sense of trust in the relationship.

An investigation of this aspect of attachment behaviour was conducted by Bretherton and Ainsworth (1974) using a procedure known as the *strange situation*, which allowed them to observe mother, infant and stranger interactions. Typically, the mother and child are first observed playing together, following which the mother may leave the infant alone, and their subsequent reaction is recorded. In another 'episode' a stranger enters while the mother is absent and again the infant's behaviour is observed. As a result, some infants were described as *securely attached* if they were content to use the mother as a base to explore unfamiliar surroundings, returning to her at regular intervals for reassurance. In contrast, other infants were referred to as having an *insecure avoidant attachment*, whereby they avoided or ignored their mother even following a separation period. Another group had *insecure ambivalent attachment*, and showed much distress upon the mother's departure, but reacted with anger or frustration upon being reunited with her.

It is apparent from studies such as these that the relationship between infant and caregiver is dependent upon much more than simple physical care; love, sensitivity and responsiveness to the infant's requirements must also be provided so that secure attachment can be promoted.

Finally in our brief discussion of attachment we will consider the role of the father in the process. Research in this area tends to imply that the 'primary caregiver' and 'mother' are synonymous terms, and that whatever contribution the father brings to the relationship can never be as meaningful as that provided by the mother. However, Ainsworth (1989) cites several studies which illustrate that, given the opportunity for interaction, fathers can play an active role in caregiving and bond formation. By using mainly animal studies as evidence for this, Ainsworth suggests a tentative comparison may be drawn between species, whilst also advocating the need for more research into the area of paternal involvement in the attachment process. Many of the human studies to date, she claims, concerned fathers who had already demonstrated a sense of commitment, and as such may be an unrepresentative sample.

Next we will turn our attention to the developing child, and particularly to the influence of peers upon behaviour.

1.4 The Childhood Years

The immediate family obviously plays an important role in children's early development but what about the influence of other children? At what ages do peer interactions begin to have significance? What do children learn from such interactions? In this section we shall consider some of the issues that have been examined regarding peer influences.

The word 'peer' comes from the Latin for 'equal', and so may be used to refer to an individual who is the same as oneself with regard to particular character-istics, although the term is generally taken to refer to people of the same age. Of course, individuals of the same or similar age-group to oneself tend to share in other characteristics merely by definition. For example, two children of the same age may be in the same class at school, be at similar cognitive levels and so on.

Whilst it is difficult to pinpoint precicely when peer influences become important, it is quite apparent that even very young children notice each other. On first being confronted with another toddler a child will regard the other with intense fascination, and often this looking may be accompanied by physical contact and vocalizations (young children appear able to communicate with each other even if they are of different nationalities and where a language barrier exists between them).

At the age of around 2–3 years children can be seen to engage much more in social play (i.e., with others) which they will often initiate themselves. During these interactions they may show an appreciation of turn-taking, together with an element of cooperation based around the activity in which they are involved. Furthermore, children are able to undergo longer separations from parents as their independence gradually increases. Workers such as Ainsworth established an important link between securely attached infants and their later interactions with peers, finding that such infants generally relate better to their peers in terms of, for example, being cooperative and initiating routines in social and intellectual activities.

The pre-school period provides further opportunities for interaction, as encounters with larger numbers of peers may occur: for example, when children attend playgroups or nursery. In the next chapter we shall refer to various 'agents' in the socialization process, of which peers represent a significant contribution (i.e., peers may influence a range of behaviours in others). The nursery school setting provides perhaps the first substantial opportunity for this outside the family unit. One example is aggression which may be learned via observation and imitation of models, namely, other children. Sylva and Lunt (1982) point out that nursery groups are frequently arranged to provide opportunities for free (rather than highly-structured) play activities, enabling youngsters to become familiar with social skills and the development of relationships, in controlling aggression and acting in a **prosocial** manner, for instance. In addition, the child develops a growing self-awareness and sense of identity; cognitive abilities are also enhanced and children become more proficient in their use of language.

In terms of the development of the child, perhaps of greatest importance is the degree of *independence* which children acquire at nursery school. Sylva and Lunt (1982) cite examples of mothers who claim this aspect to be one of the most beneficial, because after all it reflects a marked improvement in the child's self-confidence, and shows that they are able and willing to do things without the constant attention or presence of parents.

SPOTLIGHT   Is play valuable?

If you watch young children playing they often appear to have endless energy. Indeed such an activity may, to an observer, appear quite futile. However, research suggests that play serves a very useful purpose in a child's development. For example, children learn the social skills required to interact with others and, furthermore, play provides an outlet for creative expression and imagination.

- Make a list of the main characteristics involved in play.

- Ask children to explain some of the games they play, and note down what they appear to be learning from such activities.

- Try to observe a group of children at play, and make a list of the different behaviours involved. Consider any sex difference which may be apparent in the types of activities involved.

- Visit a local playgroup and find out the kind of facilities they provide.

Nursery school settings, then, provide an invaluable source of opportunity to develop a wide range of skills: social, intellectual and emotional. Furthermore, the transition into school may be made easier for children who have had regular playgroup or nursery experience.

On beginning school the socializing influence of peers continues. Aspects such as aggression, sex-role typing, morality and prosocial behaviours, which emerged in parental interactions and throughout the pre-school years, are further developed. School-mates and teachers can serve as significant dispensers of reinforcement or disapproval whilst also acting as **models**. In this respect teachers may be effective **role** models for behaviours such as those associated with the sex role, whereby children may identify with same-sex teacher figures to a similar extent as with same-sex parents.

In addition, teachers may provide a source of encouragement, thereby influencing the child's self-concept and confidence levels; the use of praise or disapproval, together with the expectations that teachers place upon individual students, can also contribute significantly to performance. (An example of this **self-fulfilling prophecy** is described in Chapter 9 in the section on teachers' expectations.)

1.5 Adolescence

The period of development which starts with the onset of puberty and ends with physical and psychological maturity is called *adolescence*. Long regarded as being an unsettled time when the individual comes to terms with the end of childhood and the approach of adulthood, it has been labelled in various ways by workers over the years. Most of these have tended to emphasize the difficulties encountered, with descriptions including 'inner turmoil' and periods of 'storm and stress'. However, although a great many young people do experience problems, others do not: their transition into adulthood often passes without fuss. What happens during this period which may result in such potential confusion? Most significant is the fact that during adolescence rapid changes occur in physical, emotional, cognitive and social development. Furthermore, as this period is taken to signify an important step towards adulthood, and the responsibilities which this entails, the individual often appraises their sense of identity ('Who am I?', 'What do I want from life?').

We will now briefly consider some of the aspects of these changes, starting with the physical changes which occur at this time.

Physical development during adolescence

The road to physical maturity begins with the influence of hormones found in the pituitary gland of the brain. They act upon the sex organs in each sex (i.e., female ovaries and male testes) and as a result they induce the physical changes of the primary and secondary sexual characteristics (see Table 1.1).

Table 1.1 *Some primary and secondary sexual characteristics of males and females*

	Males	Females
Primary sexual characteristics	Testes and scrotum enlarge	Vagina and clitoris increase in size
	Penis size increases	Uterus increases in size
	Increase in amount of sperm produced	Menstruation begins (menarche)
Secondary sexual characteristics	Pubic hair appears	Pubic hair appears
	Voice becomes deeper	Development of breasts
	Muscular development	Rounder hips
	Facial and underarm hair appears	

Another significant aspect of physical development in adolescence is known as the 'growth spurt', characterized by substantial gains in height and weight. For girls this usually begins at around $10\frac{1}{2}$ years of age, and around 12 years for boys, although these figures may vary among different individuals. At the point when the growth spurt slows down menstruation commences in females, and males become fertile as sperm production rises. The point at which both males and females become able to reproduce (which varies between the sexes and between individuals) is known as puberty, although the various other physical changes and development tend to be regarded as signs of puberty too.

Psychological development during adolescence

A major problem which stems from physical development concerns **maturation** rates. As male and female adolescents mature at different rates the consequences of 'early' or 'late' development can play an important role in the individual's self-esteem and confidence.

Generally speaking, early-maturing males are at an advantage since being bigger and looking 'older' may gain them more respect from others. In contrast, late-maturing boys tend to feel quite self-conscious and inferior in comparison with others. These observations have been confirmed in studies of personality differences. Mussen and Jones (1957), for example, found that late-maturing boys tended to feel more dominated by others, and had much lower self-esteem than early-maturers, who by comparison were often more confident and had a higher status in their peer group. In a follow-up study of the same group as adults, many of the differences were still apparent (Jones, 1957).

The differences between early- and late-maturing females are not as marked as with males. Although to some extent early-maturing females may display greater confidence, it often depends on the time of puberty. For instance, a girl of 10 years who begins to menstruate earlier than her friends may become anxious and self-conscious, considering herself to be 'the odd one out'.

Related to the aspect of early maturation comes a deep concern with physical appearance. Adolescents are bombarded with an entire 'sub-culture' from magazines and other media. These influences, together with peer pressures, mean keeping up with fashions in an attempt to present a good image to one's friends. A distorted self-image is often one of the causes in girls of eating disorders such as *anorexia nervosa*, an intense fear of becoming obese, in which anorexics believe themselves to be overweight, when in fact this is not the case. This can result in menstruation ceasing (known as amenorrhoea).

The increase in importance of the peer group at this time may also result in disharmony in the relationship with parents. Parents may expect certain standards and principles, but there is often a strong desire for independence from such a regime on the adolescents' part; they wish to try out things for themselves, thereby incurring parental disapproval.

Adolescence is also characterized by the young people's attempts to develop a sense of their own identity (i.e., separate from the wishes and aspirations of parents). Whereas in the past (and in many poorer countries of the present day) the period of adolescence was short, and often individuals started work immediately upon leaving school, modern Western culture provides individuals with an extended period in which to consider their future ambitions, hopes and aims. In this sense establishing an identity may be delayed, and the adolescent may 'try out' various roles, although economic factors mean that responsibility cannot be delayed for long.

An important theory which encompasses the notion of identity formation and role confusion was proposed by Erik Erikson (1968). His theory incorporates eight psychosocial stages which in effect cover the entire life span (see Table 1.2). Each stage consists of a conflict of 'opposites' or crises which, he claims, needs to be successfully negotiated in order to develop as a stable, well-balanced individual.

Regarding adolescence, the individual undergoes an *identity crisis* which may be successfully resolved so long as the preceding crises are met with favourable outcomes. Erikson also recognized that identity crises could occur in adult years; it is common for adults to develop fresh interests and skills and have a wish to try something new, which in turn will affect their sense of identity.

One possible explanation for the adolescent's desire to search for their own personal identity may stem from a rejection of parental ideals, as we have already stated. To what extent is the view of a 'generation gap' justified?

It is certainly true that in our rapidly developing society standards shift to some extent, so that parents of adolescents may feel 'out of touch' with their world. Today's teenagers are more open about many 'taboo' issues and are more likely to discuss problems amongst themselves which arise in their lives. As one example, concern about the spread of the AIDS virus led to a greater responsibility shown

Table 1.2 *Erikson's eight stages of psychosocial development*

Stage	Psychosocial crisis	Favourable outcome*
First year	Trust versus mistrust	Gain in trust of others and environment
Second year	Autonomy versus shame and doubt	Exercise of control and will
Third to fifth year	Initiative versus guilt	Gain in sense of purpose, and ability to initiate activities
Sixth year to puberty	Industry versus inferiority	Sense of competence confidence and industriousness
Adolescence	Identity versus role confusion	Develop view of self as integrated individual with strong sense of identity
Early adult years	Intimacy versus isolation	Develop commitment to other individual; career progressing
Middle adulthood	Generativity versus stagnation	Show concern for others, e.g., family, society
Late adulthood (old age)	Integrity versus despair	Develop sense of fulfilment and contentment with one's achievements

*NB: unfavourable outcomes, which in theory are equally likely, involve the virtual opposite of favourable outcomes. For adolescence this would entail confusion over one's role and identity as a person.

Source: Erikson (1968)

by many people in their use of contraceptives. However, although changes in attitude are inevitable to some extent in a modern society, several studies report a high frequency of agreement between parents and their adolescent offspring: for example, in one survey Kandel and Lesser (1972) observed similar priorities to exist in activities and aspirations between mothers and their adolescent children.

In a comprehensive study of American adolescents' attitudes, Sorenson (1973) reported that approximately 88 per cent of the sample of 13–19 year olds questioned held their parents in high esteem, and 78 per cent expressed an opinion that the relationship between them was warm and affectionate.

Although for some, adolescence is a time of anguish and stress, the transition into adulthood can be relatively smooth for others. At best, parents of adolescents can display a sense of understanding and tolerance towards their youngsters, whilst also being aware of the need for their offspring's independence and privacy.

1.6 Adulthood

We may consider the period of adulthood in terms of three phases: early, middle and late. Each of these is characterized by specific aspects of social and psychological change; and we will conclude this chapter by examining each in turn.

Early adulthood

According to Erikson (1968) this period of development consists of a conflict between intimacy and isolation, in which the young adult is concerned with building a meaningful relationship with another individual as a 'life partner'. In many ways this seems a natural progression following on from the experiences of adolescence, when enduring relationships with particular individuals were considered less of a priority, at least early on. Certainly young people at this stage (twenties to thirties) tend to look more towards stability, and desire a settled and intimate commitment with another person.

Another major consideration is that of career ambitions as young adults consider an occupation which will ideally provide a foundation upon which to build their future plans. Working fulfils needs other than financial ones, although for many people money is a priority. However, a sense of fulfilment often comes from the satisfaction provided by the job itself: for example, the responsibility it entails or the feeling of achievement gained.

Early adulthood is also a time when people contemplate what the future may hold. For some, this may lead to feelings of excitement, while for others it is a time of insecurity, without clear goals at which to aim. Neugarten (1968) refers to important milestones in the life span which occur at specific age ranges. These include leaving home, embarking on a career, getting married, and so on. According to Neugarten, the sequence of such events takes the form of a 'social clock', which marks out an individual's life. Furthermore, unsuccessful attainment of these milestones at appropriate stages is associated with stress often brought about by outside pressure, such as the concerned parent who continually reminds a son or daughter of the importance of getting a 'good' job, or of getting married and settling down. It is also worth mentioning that what is considered an important marker may vary from culture to culture, and also that within any given society the values may change over time.

Middle adulthood

This is generally the period from around the age of forty to the early sixties, and is often described as 'middle age'. However, although for many this use of the term often implies depressing connotations (e.g., the advance of old age, and 'time running out') as typified in the phrase 'mid-life crisis', other adults in contrast take the opportunity to change careers, or adopt new interests with great enthusiasm.

Erikson's model describes this era as concerning *generativity versus stagnation*, when adults show a willingness for productivity and creativity, often in the form of rearing children, but also with the idea of making a contribution to society and leaving an aspect of themselves behind, and so on. Failure to negotiate this psychological crisis results in a tendency to become withdrawn, self-centred and inactive. An aspect of our society which is detrimental to the feeling of contentment and generativity is the threat of unemployment or redundancy which often looms in many areas of today's workforce. Unfortunately, society aodpts the view that middle adulthood is a time when re-training, for instance, is impractical, with the result that redundant workers find themselves 'on the scrapheap', so to speak. Once people become unemployed at this time of life they soon develop feelings of inadequacy, and their self-esteem decreases as they come to terms with their position, resigning themselves to the poor prospect of regaining work.

Late adulthood

Old age is no such uncomfortable thing, if one gives oneself up to it with good grace. (H. Walpole in a letter to the Countess of Aylesbury, November, 1774)

The concept of old age is relative and depends often on the age of the 'beholder.' For instance, a young child's view of 'old' may be twenty or so whilst, at the other extreme, people in their seventies may not feel particularly 'old' as such.

Usually, 'old age' is considered to be the mid-sixties onwards, as around this time (and in some cases earlier), certain degenerative processes are underway. Simply put, individuals reach the end of their life span because vital organs cease to function as well as they did in earlier years. Organs such as the brain, heart and kidneys become less efficient, and illnesses which might have only minor consequences for a young adult may result in an old person's death.

The process of 'getting old' (senescence) is also apparent during middle adulthood: the skin loses its elastic properties, and wrinkles are visible.The lens of the eye also becomes less elastic and is unable to accommodate to near objects. Body stature and muscular power also tend to diminish with age.

What of the psychological aspects of ageing? According to Erikson (1968), the main issue during old age is that of 'integrity versus despair'. Individuals reflect on their life's achievements with the satisfactory outcome being a confident assuredness in what they have accomplished, and old people may accept death with a dignified manner. However, for the old person who has difficulty with this 'crisis', regret is often experienced over what might have been, accompanied by a sense of despondency, despair and a fear of dying.

With the onset of old age a number of skills and abilities noticeably change. The extent to which people are able to learn unfamiliar tasks is affected, together with the ability to understand and to process complicated information. Generally, by around the age of fifty, adverse effects begin to make an appearance, all the more so if individuals are required to work to the peak of their mental (or even physical) capabilities.

One reason for the difficulty with learning new skills is the decline in 'short-term memory' (see Chapter 8 for a discussion) which comes with old age. Studies have also found that reaction time is poorer, often because the *decision time* taken to process and respond to information slows down (Welford, 1958).

Intelligence levels may to some extent decline with age but this often reflects how intelligence is measured: for example, tests which require quick thinking and dextrous performance may not allow the old person an opportunity to demonstrate other capabilities. Furthermore, individual differences are evident; many old people continue to pursue interests which allow them to remain mentally active, such as attending evening classes at their local college.

An important aspect also is society's view of the elderly. Many people tend to harbour misconceptions and generally treat old persons in a patronizing manner. For the elderly themselves, adjustment may or may not be a problem, depending largely on how they choose to adapt to it.

The majority of people in Western societies now live well into their seventies, and many still view life with enthusiastic vigour. Even people in their eighties may have their mental faculties intact (only about 20 per cent of the population suffer from senile dementia which is a loss of intellectual capacity), as often do those who are older still. Thus the prospect of old age ought not to be a daunting one.

A significant milestone for most people is the age of retirement which is often regarded as signalling the onset of age. A number of theories have been proposed on this issue. Cumming and Henry (1961) refer to the process of 'disengagement' to describe the gradual withdrawal from society which many embark upon. One reason for this is that when the individual retires he or she may regard his or her contribution to society as at an end. Further, it is more likely that with old age their circle of friends decreases, either through death or serious illness. Again, this contributes to people's negative perceptions of life and their lack of active participation in it.

A second approach, which was originally proposed by Havighurst (1964), is called *activity theory*. Here, successful adaptation to ageing comes from retaining an active existence, even perhaps taking up new interests and ventures following retirement. Thus, the individual has a renewed sense of purpose which brings with it self-confidence, a feeling of active involvement and, perhaps most importantly, a perception of being in control of one's life.

1.7 Questions and Exercises

1. List the ways in which parents and infants interact.
2. Discuss what is meant by attachment, with reference to empirical studies.
3. Design a questionnaire to investigate one aspect of the life span, such as attitudes of the elderly or adolescents, and their career ambitions, etc.
4. Compare and contrast two aspects of the life span with reference to Erikson's psychosocial theory of development.
5. Discuss the contention that adolescence is a period fraught with difficulties.

② Aspects of socialization

2.1 Introduction

Socialization is the process which commences from birth onwards whereby we learn the norms expected in our society. Within any given culture there exists an unwritten set of guidelines for various behaviours such as those involving morality, aggression and the different roles assigned to the sexes.

Although a child's parents or guardians tend to provide the main influence in this process, so to some extent do siblings, peers (age-mates), teachers and the media. Collectively, these are referred to as *agents of socialization*. These respective agents may exert a greater or lesser influence depending upon their relative importance at any particular time.

In this chapter we will discuss the variety of explanations which have been proposed for the development of two central aspects in the socialization process, those of sex roles and aggression. There are three broad theories which contribute to an understanding of the socialization process, although none of them offers a complete picture.

1. The **cognitive development theory** views the various aspects of socialization in the wider context of continuing changes in mental processes such as thinking and intelligence. Supporters include Piaget and Kohlberg (see Chapter 10).

2. **Social learning theory** is an approach which reflects the principles of learning theory (see Chapter 12) and advocates that behaviours are acquired by means of selective reward and **punishment**. It places great emphasis on the role of observational learning and modelling (a 'model' in this context is any influential figure whose behaviour may be emulated). Proponents of this approach include Bandura, Walters and Mischel.

3. **Psychoanalytic theory** is based on the work of Sigmund Freud, and stresses the underlying importance of basic drives, such as sex, together with the influence of the unconscious in affecting and determining our behaviour and personality. It will be discussed in more detail in Chapter 16.

2.2 The Acquisition of Sex Roles

Sex and gender

A person's sex is determined biologically by the arrangement of sex chromosomes present in the cells of the offspring. Normally an individual has 23 pairs of chromosomes and it is one of these pairs which influences the sex of the child.

Genetically, a female has two X chromosomes while a male has one X and one Y. In sexual reproduction the mother contributes one of her two Xs to the offspring and the father either his single X or his single Y. Thus it is the father who determines whether the sex of the child is male or female.

There are, however, a number of abnormalities which may result from the loss or addition of a single sex chromosome. For example, in Turner's syndrome (XO), a chromosome is absent with the result that the individual has normal female appearance although short and lacking ovaries. Another variation, XXY, is known as Klinefelter's syndrome. Such individuals are male in appearance, although their sexual organs are unusually small and there may be female characteristics (such as breast development).

Advances in the field of sex and sexual identity have been made by the 'sexologist' John Money, who for several years has researched the determinants of human sexuality, and in particular the influence of sex hormones. Money says that a series of **critical periods** exist which are important in influencing the child's sex. For example, one critical period is found in pre-natal development when sex hormones exert their influence, resulting in either a male or female offspring. However, even here variations may occur because, if a female foetus is flooded with an excess of the male hormone androgen during this period, this can bring about characteristic physical and behavioural features such as an enlarged clitoris or tomboyishness (Money and Erdhardt, 1972).

However, although the sex of the offspring is determined by chromosomal and hormonal factors, the way in which an individual behaves with respect to masculinity or femininity is very much influenced by the society and culture in which they are reared. Studies suggest that sex roles are learnt and that within any society or culture there exist rigid stereotyped ideas governing appropriate behaviour for each sex. Definitions of sex-appropriate behaviour may also change over time within a culture, as what was considered appropriate masculine and feminine behaviour a few decades ago no longer applies, or at least not to the same extent (see Table 2.1).

Table 2.1 *Sex-role stereotypes in Western society*

Masculine	*Feminine*
Aggressive	Non-aggressive
Dominant	Submissive
Independent	Dependent
Strong	Weak
Competitive	Non-competitive
Ambitious	Unambitious

With the advent of sexual equality these differences are gradually breaking down. For instance, women are no longer expected to be submissive or dependent, and men take a much more active part in looking after children, sharing domestic duties and expressing tender feelings. Unfortunately, however, stereotyping and discrimination still exists at many levels of society.

Sex-role typing

A person's feelings with regard to their sexuality, known as gender, develops through an interaction between physical make-up and various socializing factors. Here we may distinguish between gender identity (an individual's inner sense or awareness of being either male or female) and gender role, which concerns a person's outward expression of behaviour. It is this latter aspect which may be particularly influenced by what our society considers appropriate.

Sex-role typing may be defined as the process by which children acquire the values, motives and behaviours appropriate to either males or females in a specific culture. This process commences at birth when infants are given the 'blue or pink treatment' depending upon their sex, and continues through childhood with the provision of sex-appropriate toys, clothes, hairstyles, play activities and so on (Bandura, 1969).

Parents play a large part in the sex-role typing process: fathers may handle boys more roughly than girls, for example, and parents become a child's first models of feminine and masculine behaviour. In this role they serve to strengthen and reinforce desired behaviours, and research has shown that parents react more positively when their children engage in sex-appropriate behaviours (Fagot, 1978).

In various settings children themselves display some knowledge of sex-typed behaviour. In one study of pre-school children, paper dolls representing male and female were used in a game in which children had to assign one of the dolls to particular situations and descriptive statements. For example, they would be asked whether the male or female doll would 'like to build things' or would 'grow up to be a nurse'. The results showed that even very young children have some notion of sex-appropriate activities and sex-role stereotypes, presumably acquired through primary agents of socialization (Kuhn *et al.*, 1978).

As children grow older they tend to increase their sex-typed preferences in many aspects of behaviour such as choice of playmates and toys. However, even very young children have been influenced by their parents for a number of years and therefore it is difficult to isolate the contributing factors.

SPOTLIGHT   Boys don't cry

As we have already mentioned, within each society there exist fairly rigid views concerning the appropriate behaviour for girls and boys. Western culture, for example, long maintained a notion of females as being the 'weaker' sex, the term implying much more than a reference to their physical strength. Even nursery rhymes portrayed the two sexes with unambiguous clarity; little girls, we were told, were made of 'sugar and spice and all things nice', while in stark contrast little boys consisted of 'frogs and snails and puppy dogs' tails'. It is perhaps hardly surprising, then, that many children, especially when young, begin to form clear ideas themselves regarding their sex role, what they can wear and even which toys to play with.

- Collect a number of magazines (old catalogues are especially useful), and cut out the pictures of toys. Paste them individually to sheets of card or strong paper. Then show them, one at a time, to children of varying ages, and ask them to say for each picture whether it is a boy's or a girl's toy, and why it is so. Try this with as wide an age group as possible, and also compare the responses of boys and girls for each toy.

Siblings, too, may influence the process of sex-typing as, like parents, they act as role models. Boys with older sisters tend to behave less aggressively than those with older brothers, while girls with older brothers tend to be more competitive and often tomboyish compared to girls with older sisters.

Outside the family, a child's peers play a major role in shaping sex roles and attitudes. Peers may continue the influence which parents have begun by showing approval or disapproval for certain behaviours and actions. Peer pressure at school, for instance, may be very influential in reinforcing sex-appropriate behaviour, even when parents attempt to rear their children without adhering to social and cultural stereotypes.

The portrayal of masculine and feminine behaviour in books, magazines and television may also serve to promote and reinforce sex-role **stereotypes**. Together with the other influential figures mentioned, they can have an important effect upon what the child considers appropriate for males and females. Children's literature up until quite recently vividly presented boy and girl characters very much in a stereotyped fashion, with the boys being daring and adventurous while the girls were seen as passive and dependent.

Despite trends towards equality of the sexes, advertisements in magazines and on television regularly portray characters in situations that only serve to strengthen stereotyped sex roles. For instance, males are usually seen as car drivers, with females being passengers, and cookery or household items are frequently directed solely at females.

Children are likely to be more susceptible than adults to advertisements and characters presented on television, but to some extent the effects of stereotyped portrayals can be reversed. One study with a degree of success presented programmes to children which depicted role reversals, and included girls being seen as competitive and ambitious, traits traditionally associated with male stereotypes (Davidson *et al.*, 1979).

Sex reassignment in childhood

A pertinent illustration of the important contribution of social factors in determining gender roles is provided by studies of sex reassignment. In some instances a child may have ambiguous sexual organs or, through hormonal influence, have chromosomal characteristics of one sex, but external genitalia of the other.

One case involved a child with male chromosomes and testes, but external organs more similar to a female. Assigned as male at birth, the decision was later reversed and the child underwent corrective surgery. Following this reassignment the child was reared as a girl and treated accordingly by those around her (Money and Ehrhardt, 1972).

Another case concerned two male identical twins, one of whom was involved in a surgical accident when only a few months old, resulting in the amputation of his penis. Following medical advice, the parents decided on sex reassignment and their 'son' was subsequently given extensive hormone treatment, accompanied intricate plastic surgery in order to produce female sexual organs. Over the next few years the twins were treated very differently, with the girl being dressed appropriately and encouraged to grow long hair and help with domestic duties. She was also discouraged from being rough and aggressive, although for the male twin this kind of behaviour was considered quite acceptable.

Both these examples demonstrate that sexual identity and behaviour involves much more than physical make-up, and that the socializing influence of those around us is largely responsible for the learning of sex roles.

Cross-cultural studies

Cross-cultural studies are useful in that they allow a comparison to be made between the practices and behaviours of different societies throughout the world. It also enables us to establish the extent to which particular characteristics are universal.

With regard to sex roles, studies have shown that there are enormous cultural differences in what is considered appropriate behaviour for males and females. Mead (1935), observed three New Guinea tribes and found there to be different roles for each sex. In the Arapesh tribe, both men and women were mild-mannered, gentle and caring, and both shared the responsibilities of looking after children, whereas in the Mundugumor tribe men and women were aggressive and highly competitive towards each other, tending to keep any caring side of their nature to a minimum. Men and women in the third tribe, the Tchambuli, had different roles from each other, with their behaviour being almost the opposite of those in traditional Western society. The women were the assertive, dominant sex who took charge of managing the family, while the men had less responsibility, were dependent upon the females and tended to spend most of their time carving, painting, practising dancing and looking after their ornate hair styles.

In each of these three societies, children were raised according to cultural expectations, which demonstrates that sex roles are not the result of biological differences but instead are determined by the culture or society in which one is reared. However, this study is not without faults as researchers have argued that Mead may have placed subjective interpretations on her findings.

2.3   Theories of Sex-role Typing

Psychoanalytic theory

This approach centres around the complex process of **identification**, in which an individual takes on the behaviour and attitudes of another person in order to be like them. With respect to sex roles, the young child is said to identify with the same-sex parent to the extent that they acquire the appropriate behaviours for either males or females. According to Freud, identification is forged within the phallic stage (see Chapter 16) and is the end product of either the Oedipus complex (for boys) or the Electra complex (for girls).

In both cases, the young child is thought to develop an unconscious wish to possess the opposite-sexed parent. Thus, a boy desires his mother but is also aware that his father is a rival for his affection towards her, and fears that his father will retaliate when he discovers these feelings. Furthermore the boy, having observed that women lack penises, fears that retaliation will take the form of castration. This results in a state which Freud refers to as *castration anxiety*, which forces the boy to repress these feelings for his mother, and instead defensively identify with his father on the basis that the father has qualities which his mother is attracted to. It is thus through identification that the boy acquires values and beliefs attributed to the masculine role.

The Electra complex in girls involves the girl realizing that she has already been castrated. Blaming her mother for this, she develops penis envy and becomes attracted to her father because he has a penis. However, just as for boys, this situation produces conflict (in this case in the mother and daughter relationship), so the girl represses her feelings for her father and identifies with her mother in order that the conflict be resolved. The concept of the Electra complex as a whole is less clear than the equivalent process in boys, and Freud himself considered his explanation far from satisfactory.

Although both processes have some support (e.g., the **case study** of 'little Hans', a young boy whose extreme fear of being bitten by horses was interpreted by Freud to symbolize his fear of being castrated by his (own) father!) in that empirical evidence does support same-sex parent and child conflict in the early years, critics point out that the theory is limited in its universality and thus applicability.

Social learning theory

In its simplest form, this theory of sex role acquisition centres on the importance of observation and imitation. Children observe and imitate influential models, usually the same-sex parent, and learn appropriate behaviour through reward through reward and punishment. Thus a little boy acquires masculine behaviour by imitating his father, and in addition by being rewarded for doing things expected of boys whilst also being punished for behaviour considered inappropriate. The equivalent process takes place for girls who learn their sex role through imitation of a same-sex model and by reinforcement (Mischel, 1970). In this way the expectations which society places upon sex-role behaviour are largely responsible for shaping the child, who is basically seen as a passive receiver of information from external sources. Is there evidence available in support of this position? Certainly young children do copy behaviour and actions that go on around them, but the question is whether or not the process of differential rewarding and observation, advocated by social learning theorists, is solely responsible for the acquisition of sex role behaviour.

Fagot (1978) found that parents behaved quite differently in their treatment of sons and daughters; boys were given encouragement for vigorous actions (such as climbing) while these activities were frowned upon for girls, who in contrast were encouraged for 'feminine' behaviours such as playing with dolls and prettifying themselves.

The process of modelling was demonstrated by Carlsmith (1964), who found that boys whose father was absent in their early childhood years due to military service tended to follow less masculine interests; presumably this was due to lack of a male role-model.

More recent work on social learning theory has revealed that children are not merely passive recipients who 'take in' everything which they observe. Fagot (1985), for instance, found that while **reinforcement** is effective, children are selective in their responses. For example, in a study of nursery school children, boys did not respond to reinforcement provided by girls.

Cognitive development theory

The emphasis in this approach is that sex roles develop from an increasing understanding and awareness of gender identity on the part of the child. That is, the child comes to terms with their being male or female in just the same way as they begin to comprehend many other aspects involved in cognitive development.

According to Kohlberg (1966), an important concept for children to grasp is *gender constancy*, and he claims that they have difficulty with the notion of gender up until they are 6 years old. Children younger than this are unclear as to what determines the difference between males and females, anatomically or otherwise.

Evidence for this came from a study by Katcher (1955) who gave children figures of boys, girls, men and women that could be divided into three sections: head/shoulders, trunk and below the waist. Sometimes the figures were shown clothed and other times unclothed.

The children were required to assemble the sections together correctly, and then state the gender. Katcher found that 3 and 4 year olds were reasonably competent at this when the figures were clothed, but experienced some difficulty if they were not. This suggests that the children were using the clothing as the main clues for gender identity and failed to understand how the differences related to genital anatomy.

By the same token, it has also been demonstrated that very young children have no idea that gender identity is a permanent attribute of the self, and would claim, for instance, that a boy could just as easily be a girl if he wore a different hairstyle and girls' clothes.

The difficulty which young chilren have with the concept of gender constancy when considered in relation to cognitive development represents one of the many problems associated with this period of childhood. Cognitive development, and particularly the work of Piaget,, will be examined in detail in Chapter 10.

Table 2.2 represents a simplified summary of the three approaches considered here as they relate to boys. Finally, although these approaches represent the most significant account for the development of sex role behaviour, a recent viable alternative lies in gender **scheme** theory. Originally proposed by Bem (1981), this basically provides a variation on the cognitive theme, and points to the existence of gender schemas: frameworks which guide children in processing new information specifically to do with gender.

Although this represents a new direction in research, psychologists are acknowledging it as an area worthy of detailed investigation. Indeed, Jacklin (1989) suggests that our present understanding of the socialization process in general may be altered as a consequence.

Table 2.2 *Simplified summary of three approaches to acquisition of sex roles (boys)*

	Psychoanalytic theory	Social learning theory	Cognitive developmental theory
Arises from:	Sex drive	Social and cultural factors	Growing cognitive awareness
Important figures:	Opposite and same-sex parents	Teachers, parents, peers, media	Self and own experiences and interactions within environment
Processes involved:	Erotic attraction to opposite-sex parent; fear of father	Observation imitation, reinforcement	Gradual appreciation of many constancies; including those of gender
Outcome	Identification with father and male role	Identification with father and male role	Identification with father and male role

2.4 The Development of Aggression

Definitions

Aggression is often defined as any behaviour carried out with the intention of harming another person, whether it be physical or verbal. Some researchers also distinguish between hostile and instrumental aggression. Hostile aggression involves behaviour carried out solely with the intention of harming another individual (e.g. when someone attacks an innocent passer-by purely for the sake of it). Instrumental aggression, on the other hand, involves behaviour which, although carried out with intention, has an underlying motive. An example of this would be fighting for a cause, such as defending one's family.

Eron (1987) chooses to define aggression as an act which injures or irritates another person, arguing that previous definitions are unacceptable since it is very difficult actually to measure intentionality.

The term 'aggression' is also used in a variety of other contexts, especially regarding comparative psychology and animal behaviour where researchers distinguish between territorial aggression, maternal aggression, altruistic aggression, and so on.

Theories of aggression

The range of uses and terms becomes apparent when considering the major theoretical accounts of aggression, with proponents of each theory tending to favour a particular definition. Some researchers argue that aggression is innately determined and influenced by biological factors, while others claim that the main influence is that of learning. We shall briefly consider four approaches.

The ethological approach

Ethologists study animal behaviour in its natural environment (See Chapter 13) and consider aggression to be an inborn, instinctive characteristic that is triggered or released by specific stimuli. An early demonstration by Tinbergen (1951) for example, showed that in male sticklebacks the display of aggression is released by the red colouring on the rival male's belly. Konrad Lorenz, one of the founders of **ethology**, considers human aggression to be an instinctive and natural feature of human behaviour. Although his account is based largely on findings from the animal kingdom, he claims that it is justifiable to make such comparisons on evolutionary grounds. In men and animals aggression serves a purpose: that of adaptation to the environment. Is such a comparison justfiable? Within many animal species, ritualized threat displays (such as locking antlers), or appeasement gestures (such as adopting a sexual posture) seem to have evolved, according to ethologists, which prevent serious injury during conflicts. To a certain extent, human parallels do exist. In aggressive situations people will stand bolt upright in order to appear larger, and direct eye contact in aggressive confrontations is usually perceived as a threat. In contrast avoiding or averting eye contact in such situations is a submissive signal.

Essentially, Lorenz believes that humans, just like animals, are naturally aggressive, although they appear to differ in at least one respect: namely, the extent of the destruction of which humans are capable. Advances in military technology, for instance, have meant that large-scale destruction is possible within aggressive confrontations.

Critics of Lorenz's position argue, amongst other things, that humans are not unique with regard to killing their own kind. Several examples are provided in which animals intentionally kill others of their species. Jane Goodall (1978), for example, has carried out extensive research on non-human primates, and reported one incident in which an entire group of male chimpanzees was killed by a rival colony. Similarly male lions, in usurping the place of another male within a pride, will kill any cubs that are not their own. This is often found in other species of primate: male langurs and baboons which successfully 'take over' a harem of females will kill the infants present.

The position of ethologists, then, is that human aggression is innate within each of us, but whilst there is evidence (from physiological studies) that biological mechanisms – specifially, areas of the brain – play a role in the control of aggression (Mark and Ervin, 1970), human behaviour is influenced to a large extent by learning and social factors.

Social learning theory

This approach emphasizes the role of reinforcement, observation and imitation in the acquisition of aggressive behaviour. In this way a child may observe an aggressive act, attempt to imitate it and, if subsequently reinforced for this behaviour, will be more likely to use aggression in the future (i.e., aggressive behaviour may acquire reinforcing properties).

The presence of a reinforcing adult may be influential in this process, particularly if this person is a parent. As mentioned earlier, aggression may be expected of boys as being sex-appropriate and so may be looked upon favourably by parents. The Newson study (1965), in interviewing several hundred British families, found that some parents encouraged their children to use aggression as a means of response if provoked by others.

The mere observation of aggressive models can also be effective. In a famous experiment by Bandura, Ross and Ross (1961, 1963) children were allowed to observe an adult model under several conditions, one of which involved the adult being aggressive towards a Bobo doll (an inflatable clown). Children were then taken to a room which contained toys such as a tea set, crayons, a hammer and a Bobo doll, and given the opportunity to play for a while (see Figure 2.1). The results showed that children who had watched an aggressive model were more aggressive than those children who had observed a non-aggressive model or those who had watched no model at all, and then been given the same play materials.

Critics of these experiments have pointed out that the situation is an unrealistic and artificial one, and as such has no relevance in explaining real-life aggression. However, more recent studies have suggested that behaviour in one setting may transfer to another. For example, Johnston *et al.* (1977) noticed a link between the amount of aggression children show at play and their aggressiveness in other situations.

Important in the social learning theory approach is the notion that aggressive behaviour is seen to be rewarding. Bandura (1977) admits that aggression is not a

Figure 2.1 Child with Bobo doll

natural outcome of frustration (see frustration–aggression hypothesis below), but will become so if an individual learns that such behaviour is reinforcing. Thus, if a child uses aggression on one occasion and by its use succeeds in obtaining a desired outcome, they will then be more likely to use aggression as a means to an end in future situations.

Parents may have an influential effect on the development of children's aggression by their display of approval or non-approval of such conduct. However, peer interaction tends to be the focus of more aggressive behaviour, in that during childhood such behaviour tends to be directed towards other children rather than adults. It is in contact with age-mates that children fully comprehend the consequences of aggression. This was clearly demonstrated in a study which observed nursery-school children over a period of ten weeks, and in particular recorded the interactions involving aggressive behaviour (Patterson *et al.*, 1967). It was noticed that when children used aggression to get what they wanted, with the result that the victims submitted to their demands (e.g., gave up their sweets), then this provided positive reinforcement, and so the aggressor was much more likely to use a similar strategy again. Even those children who had previously been victims of such encounters, but who later succeeded by counter-attacking, learnt to use aggression in their behaviour, and on occasion were noticed actually to imitate attacks themselves! However, it may be that disposition played some role here, as children who appeared to be passive and showed little interest in interacting did not increase their aggressive tendencies; neither did those who were unsuccessful in retaliating. So it would appear that the consequence which the aggressive behaviour has is important in determining future behaviour.

SPOTLIGHT   Television and aggression

Apart from parents and peers, the influence of television has received interest as a potential factor concerning imitation of violence and aggression.

Research has pointed to a relationship between viewing television violence and aggressive behaviour, but this is largely evidence gathered from **correlations**, and so does not allow for cause-and-effect interpretations.

Nevertheless, some studies have indicated that the level of aggressive behaviour could be predicted in young adults by using a knowledge of the kinds of television programmes they viewed as children (Eron *et al.*, 1972).

However, it is difficult to separate the effects of other confounding variables such as a child's disposition and the environment in which they are raised. Not only can it be shown that children who watch more violence on television are more aggressive, but it is also the case that children with an aggressive disposition are more likely to watch violent television programmes (Eron, 1987), and furthermore that 'aggression-prone' children are likely to become even more aggressive when watching programmes with a violent content (Stein and Friedrich, 1975).

Certainly television is an influential medium, particularly as regards young children, and although there appears to be tentative evidence for the potentially harmful effects of some programmes, other studies have been conducted into the positive effects. Pro social behaviours, such as helping and sharing, can be learnt from various sources, including television. Stein and Friedrich (1975), for example, observed increases in pro social types of play in young children who watched programmes in which behaviours such as sharing were emphasized.

- Choose a number of television programmes (including cartoons, films, etc.) and note the number of aggressive incidents which occur. Consider factors such as the age of the programme; the approximate age of the viewers for which it is intended; whether aggression is punished or glorified, etc.

- List the ways in which the programmes you have chosen could be influencing the viewer.

In summary, social learning theory argues that aggression may be learnt just like any other behaviour, but stresses that individuals will only become aggressive if they find it rewarding. Furthermore, people differ in their responses to frustration; aggression may be one response, given reinforcement, whereas in similar circumstances another person may be reinforced for withdrawing, attempting to be constructive and rational or turning to drugs and alcohol (Bandura, 1977).

Motivational or drive theory
Essentially this view centres around the frustration–aggression hypothesis (Dollard *et al.*, 1939) which asserts that frustration leads to aggression, and also that aggression is a natural outlet from frustrating stimuli (see Figure 2.2).

Many everyday situations provide illustrations of this idea. Hitting the television set if the picture disappears during a favourite programme (which is often reinforced if the picture returns!) or shouting aggressively at the driver who cuts in front amidst a traffic jam are typical examples of aggression arising from forms of frustration. However, this is not to say that any frustrating event automatically leads to aggressive behaviour, but rather that frustration may produce a likelihood that aggression will follow.

In terms of motivational theory aggressive behaviour is considered to bring about what is called drive-reduction, which is considered essential for a balanced internal state. This idea was popular in explaining aggressive acts in which individuals 'flared up' prior to committing a violent crime, presumably releasing their pent-up energies. However, drive theory alone does not provide a completely satisfactory account of such behaviour, which in some cases has been linked to physiological diseases such as brain tumours (Sweet *et al.*, 1969), controversial though this link may be.

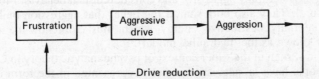

Figure 2.2 Representation of the drive theory of aggression

Although there is experimental evidence that aggression may be caused by frustrating conditions (Azrin *et al.*, 1966), the findings from field research, which involves studying behaviour in natural settings, do not present a clear link. Indeed, many psychologists acknowledge that frustration alone is not sufficient to trigger an aggressive reaction and that, although aggression is one possible response to frustration, there are several others which an individual may carry out.

Berkowitz (1965, 1969) has suggested some influential modifications to the original frustration–aggression hypothesis. Rather than frustration and aggression being seen almost as cause and effect, he introduces the concept of 'readiness' into the sequence of events, and states that frustration does not lead automatically to aggression, but rather sets up a readiness or predisposition to behave aggressively. This readiness may be affected by factors such as past experience and the presence of aggressive 'cues' in the environment, which may then evoke a response of aggression (see Figure 2.3).

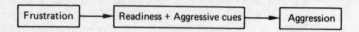

Figure 2.3 An interpretation of the revised model of the frustration–aggression hypothesis

Experimental evidence lends support to this version and Berkowitz and his colleagues have demonstrated that such cues may be very effective. In one study, subjects were first angered by a confederate (usually by being insulted), following which they watched either an aggressive or non-aggressive film. Finally they were given the opportunity to administer electric shocks to the confederate. The results indicated that if, prior to the experiment, the confederate was labelled as being interested in boxing, then the subsequent shocks given by subjects were stronger when compared with a control group who received neutral treatment (Berkowitz, 1965). Apparently, the presence of aggressive cues (film and confederate's label) primed the subjects to respond more aggressively when given the opportunity.

Similar effects have been recorded if weapons are used as cues. For example, subjects will administer more severe shocks if a gun is visible nearby.

There does, then, appear to be a relationship between frustration and aggression, and whilst there are criticisms of this model it offers a logical explanation for aggressive behaviour.

Psychoanalytic theory
In some respects similar to the ethological account, Freud, like Lorenz, believed that each of us is naturally aggressive and considered such behaviour to be part of 'human nature'. They also both shared the belief that aggression builds up as a pool of potentially destructive energy which must somehow be discharged (sometimes known as the 'hydraulic' model).

Freud's view, seen in the wider context of psychoanalytic theory in Chapter 16, was that people have an aggressive instinct represented in the form of what he termed 'Thanatos', or the death instinct, named after the Greek god of death. Freud considered it to be expressed in behaviours such as rejection, hatred and destruction. Furthermore, this destructive force was often thought to be directed against the self where it received an outlet in self-destructive acts such as denial or, more extremely, masochism. However, operating in conflict with death instincts are those involved in self-preservation, which Freud referred to as Eros, after the Greek god of love. Directed away from the self, the accumulated energy is discharged outwards on to objects or people. This was considered an essential process in life-preservation, for as Freud himself put it: 'The living creature preserves its own life . . . by destroying an extraneous one' (Freud, 1963). Seen in such inevitable terms, Freud was able to provide an explanation for the mass destruction of war in that it was one outlet for the human aggressive instinct. Despite this somewhat gloomy view of mankind, more acceptable outlets exist. These include participation in competitive sports and, to some extent, watching such activities, both of which were thought to provide a means of releasing pent-up tensions.

Although it may be tempting to portray aggression in such terms this model remains largely unsupported. One criticism concerns the notion of natural, spontaneous aggressive energy requiring an outlet of some kind. Most psychologists are now generally agreed that an external stimulus is needed (which would seem to indicate support for the approaches discussed earlier). The idea that watching or participating in aggressive sports allows a person to rid themselves of pent-up aggression (known as catharsis), also receives little support. For example, in a discussion of human aggression, Kohn points out that people are likely to become more violent after watching or taking part in such pastimes (Kohn, 1988). In the same article Kohn refers to an attempt which was made to explore the issues surrounding human aggression when a number of eminent scientists met in Spain in 1986 and produced 'The Seville Statement'. Amongst the conclusions arrived at were that the hydraulic model of aggression is inaccurate and that there is no scientific basis for the view that humans are aggressive and warlike in their nature (Kohn, 1988).

Sex differences in aggression

In their extensive review of the literature available on sex differences in behaviour, Maccoby and Jacklin (1974) dispelled some of the popular myths which existed concerning the sexes, and at the same time highlighted some genuine differences which appeared from their studies.

One such area in which pronounced sex differences exist is aggression. Most research confirms that males are more aggressive than females and, furthermore, this tends to be the case in many non-human species, in the majority of cultures and at virtually all age levels. Indeed, the only discrepancy appears to be the relative contribution of biological and social factors.

Observation of animals appears to lend support to the biological explanation. In one study of young monkeys at play during their first year, marked sex differences were recorded in the amount of rough-and-stumble play with males displaying much more of this activity (Harlow, 1962).

With humans, sex differences in aggression begin to appear around the age of 2, as boys show more aggression at play, and appear generally more likely to adopt aggressive behaviour in interactions with other children (both physically and verbally). Studies have also confirmed these differences in a variety of other cultures around the world, including Switzerland, Africa and India (Maccoby and Jacklin, 1974).

Whilst the argument in favour of a biological explanation seems impressive, a major contributing factor lies in the different ways in which children are socialized. Whereas aggression by girls tends to be frowned upon by parents, it is tolerated and, in some cases, encouraged in boys largely because it is seen as an inherent part of the male stereotype. The aggressive behaviour may be accounted for in terms of both biological and social factors; any biological predisposition present in males is further influenced by learning with the result that males may show a greater tendency towards aggression. Certainly, females are capable of aggressive behaviour and individual differences exist in male aggression, but the general pattern suggests that social and cultural expectations play a major role in supplementing any initial differences between the sexes.

Cross-cultural studies of aggression

These studies provide further evidence for the importance of learning with respect to the development of aggression. At the same time they offer valid criticism of those theories which emphasize instinctive, innate factors. If societies founded upon non-aggressive and peaceful behaviour exist, they act as contradictions to the view that aggression is a natural feature of human behaviour.

In fact, many religious groups have developed with precisely these qualities. Deaux and Wrightsman (1984) cite American communities such as the Amish (featured with Harrison Ford in the film 'Witness'), who advocate a non-aggressive and non-competitive way of life. Similarly, followers of Quakerism endorse a life of pacificism and nonviolence.

Kohn (1988) points out that aggression is not a universal characteristic, and refers to the mere existence of peaceful cultures as being evidence which refutes man's inborn aggressiveness. A country such as Sweden, which has changed from being a warlike and aggressive nation to one based on non-violence, also illustrates opposition to the biological determinism of aggression, and instead highlights the important influence of social and cultural factors.

This was also observed in Mead's study of the Arapesh tribe of New Guinea. She found that children were socialized to be gentle and non-aggressive and that these qualities were encouraged in both boys and girls (Mead, 1935).

Even in societies which appear to adopt aggression as a way of life there is often an important reason for its existence. Sampson (1971), for instance, refers to the Iatmul Indians of New Guinea who practised head-hunting and placed great importance on the number of scalps acquired. However, although this tribe (and others like them) may seem to have a system based upon violence, it is often simply a form of religious ritual rather than a life style of aggressiveness for its own sake.

Clearly, then, social and environmental factors play a major role in the expression of aggressive behaviour. Furthermore, cultural norms may be largely influential in determining the overt display of aggression. If humans have an inborn tendency towards aggressive behaviour, standards and models provided by their culture enable it to be modified accordingly.

2.5 Questions and Exercises

1. What is sex-role typing? Describe and compare two theories which attempt to explain it.
2. Collect items from newspapers and magazines which portray sex-role stereo-typing, and suggest how the items could be changed to remove stereotyping.
3. (a) Define aggression and give your own examples of the different forms it takes.
   (b) List ways in which aggression may be reduced.

4. Conduct a survey into children's viewing habits (this could involve both television and video). For example, you could include questions on the types of programme preferred and the reasons given for the preference. Consider also whether the findings indicate a sex difference in viewing preferences.

3 Social influence

3.1 Introduction

Many animals exist in pairs or larger groups for at least some part of their lives, and human beings are no exception. We live in a social world with many of our daily actions being influenced to a large extent by other people.

Although there are occasions when we all value quiet moments of privacy, it is also true that we value the comfort which being amongst others provides. Indeed, the effects of enforced social isolation can be very distressing: for example, when a group of children shun one member who has broken a group rule. This temporary deprivation of belonging is an upsetting form of punishment for children, and even adults may become withdrawn and dejected under conditions such as solitary confinement or being 'sent to Coventry'.

Although as social beings we place considerable importance on friendships and social interactions, the mere presence of other people can affect our behaviour in a variety of ways. Not only do we alter views of ourselves based on comparisons with others and their reactions to us, but under certain conditions our performance of tasks may be made better or worse as a direct consequence of others being present: athletes running a race in competition may often improve their performance in comparison with someone running alone.

3.2 Social Facilitation

This may be described as the beneficial effect which others produce upon performance by their mere presence. The first systematic study, and indeed the first social psychology **experiment**, was conducted by Norman Triplett in 1897 when he asked cyclists to race a 25-mile course under different conditions. Subjects in the first group cycled alone but attempted to improve on their time against the clock, while those in the second group rode in pairs but were instructed not to compete against each other. Cyclists in the third group were specifically requested to compete with each other.

The important group with respect to social facilitation is group two; although not competing, they had faster times than those racing alone. In this case the mere presence of another cyclist brought about a better performance. This phenomenon is known as the co-action effect, and occurs when pairs or groups perform the same task but without direct interaction.

Similar studies by Triplett in which children worked, alone or in pairs, on tasks such as winding a fishing reel confirmed his original findings: the sight of others working on the same exercise/task improves performance (see Figure 3.1).

Later evidence by other researchers demosntrated that even working within sight of others is not necessary, and that the mere knowledge that others are doing the same task nearby is sufficient.

Figure 3.1 Children working together

Another form of social facilitation is found when a task is performed in front of an audience, and is known as the audience effect. For example, a professional musician may give a better performance before an audience, whereas a novice or amateur may be hindered by others watching. This brings us to the conditions under which social facilitation is likely to take place, an aspect which has also been investigated. Just as performance may be improved by the presence of others, they can also have a detrimental effect. When performance worsens or is prevented by the presence of others, this is referred to as social inhibition. Zajonc (1965) has proposed that an audience will bring about an improvement if the task is familiar and well learnt, but will hinder performance if the task is new or less familiar.

Support for this claim comes from an observational study of pool players by Michaels *et al.* (1982), in which they first of all assessed players' levels of skill by watching them during a number of games. Then, having rated individuals as being either good or below average in ability, the researchers stood in small groups next to a pool table as play was in progress, in order to find out if their presence would influence the players.

The findings confirmed the relationship between social facilitation and skill level. Those players initially rated above average improved their games, showing a significant increase in shot accuracy, whereas for the poorer players accuracy decreased.

Certainly many of us may remember occasions when we have been 'put off' a task because other people were watching nearby. Why does this happen? According to Zajonc (1965), both facilitation and inhibition may be explained by a single process, namely arousal: the presence of others increases an individual's general level of arousal (alertness or motivational drive).

Onlookers may thus make an individual more conscious of what they are doing, whilst at the same time creating an expectancy that the audience will be judgemental. With easy or well-learnt activities (often referred to as dominant responses) the increase in arousal produces an improvement in performance, but if the task is difficult or unfamiliar for the individual concerned, then performance is hindered because the person's level of arousal is increased beyond that which is optimal for the performance of the task.

SPOTLIGHT　To help or not to help?

The mere presence of other people can, as we have seen, greatly influence our own behaviour. Another aspect of this influence concerns what social psychologists term the 'bystander effect'; which originated from a horrendous incident in New York in 1964 in which a woman called Kitty Genovese was brutally slain. Furthermore, the crime was apparently witnessed by at least 40 people, none of whom intervened or raised help. Alarmed at this apathy, psychologists conducted several studies in order to discover the possible causes. It was suggested, for instance, that in such 'emergency' situations, the responsibility for helping is spread amongst those present.

This 'diffusion of responsibility' may certainly provide one explanation for bystander apathy, although it is likely that several factors tend to operate together rather than one in isolation. Attempting to understand and perhaps even explain the complex relationship which exists between a person and their environment in these and other situations is certainly a formidable task, and one which lies at the centre of a relatively new field called **environmental psychology**.

- Imagine that you are walking home with two friends when you notice a man slumped in a shop doorway. Other people are simply walking past with an occasional glance at the figure. Would you stop to offer assistance? If not, why not?

- List any other reasons which might influence your decision, e.g. the appearance of the man, whether he was well-dressed, etc.

3.3　Conformity

Whereas social facilitation looks at how the mere presence of others may have an effect on our behaviour and opinions, conformity focuses upon the ways in which other people exert their influence upon us in such a way that we go along with them. For example, some teenagers may accept the decision of their group of friends to go to the cinema when they themselves would have preferred to go elsewhere. Although this example illustrates only one type, conformity normally involves some kind of social pressure in which the individual's intentions conflict with those of the group. This kind of social pressure is known as conformity.

Definitions of conformity

Aronson (1988): 'a change in a person's behaviour or opinions as a result of real or imagined pressure from a person or group of people'

Crutchfield (1955): 'yielding to group pressures or expectations'

Reber (1985): 'the tendency to allow one's opinions, attitudes, actions and perceptions to be affected by prevailing opinions, attitudes and actions'

These definitions have a common theme: namely, that other people bring about a change in an individual or at least induce a situation of conflict. Since the 1930s this form of social influence has been studied experimentally using a variety of techniques.

Sherif (1935) made use of visual illusion known as the 'Autokinetic Effect'. This occurs when a tiny point of light is seen in an otherwise completely dark room; after a few moments of concentrating on the spot of light it appears to flicker and move. Subjects in this experiment were first brought individually into the room and asked to estimate how far the light moved, for several trials. Following this they were allowed to hear the other subjects' estimates (i.e., a group influence was introduced) and Sherif noted that the subsequent estimates tended to become more alike.

It seemed, therefore, that a shift of opinion had occurred as a result of knowing what others had estimated. However, this study used an ambiguous stimulus because it did not have an absolute answer against which to compare the extent of conformity, and each individual's estimates were completely subjective. Providing subjects with an opportunity to give an 'obvious' clear correct response takes away any sense of ambiguity, and this was previously the basis of the studies by Solomon Asch in the 1950s.

In the basic procedure of Asch's experiment subjects were invited to participate in a study of visual perception which involved judging the lengths of lines against a comparison (see figure 3.2). A group of subjects (usually seven to nine) entered a room in which seats had been set out for each of them. The experimenter explained the procedure and then subjects were asked, in order of seating, to give their answer aloud to problems such as that shown in Figure 3.2.

However, only one unsuspecting individual was a true subject, the others in fact being accomplices (also known as confederates or stooges) of the experimenter. By ensuring that the genuine subject was seated at the end (see figure 3.3), and so was last to answer, a conformity situation could be created and a 'group norm' established.

As the experiment proceeded, and for the first two trials, everyone gave the same (obviously correct) response, in order not to arouse the suspicions of the genuine subject. However, from the subsequent trial onwards the confederates

34

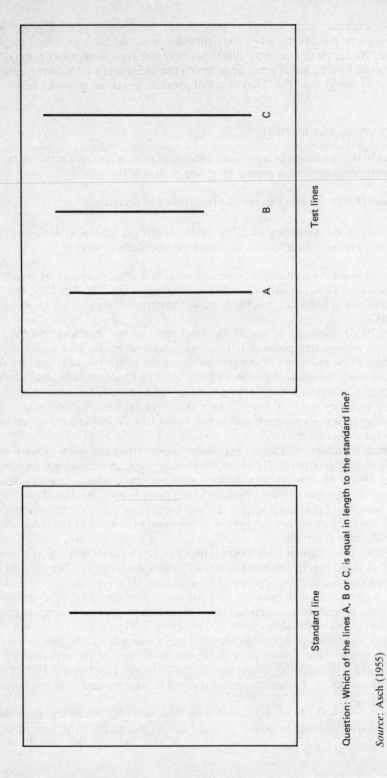

Test lines

Standard line

Question: Which of the lines A, B or C, is equal in length to the standard line?

Source: Asch (1955)

Figure 3.2 Example of material presented to subjects in conformity experiments

Source: Asch (1955)

Figure 3.3 Typical seating arrangement used by Asch in studies of conformity

had all been pre-instructed to give the same incorrect answer which would then present the real subject with a conflict situation: either to go along with the others by giving the wrong answer, or to be independent and give a different, separate response from the group.

In this experiment any question of ambiguity was removed; the answer was quite apparent, and control trials prior to the proper experiment supported this. When tested individually, without group influence, more than 95 per cent of subjects gave correct responses. During the 'critical trials', though, 32 per cent of the subjects were noted to conform with the others by giving the wrong answer.

This figure, whilst not being very high, does nonetheless demonstrate that conformity did take place under circumstances involving unambiguous stimuli (74 per cent conformed on at least one trial). However, further investigation of the findings revealed widespread individual differences betwen subjects; several of them reported that they conformed because that was what they thought the experimenter wanted and, not wishing to appear the odd one out, they gave the same response as the others. Significantly some subjects never yielded to group pressure and remained independent throughout the critical trials.

Factors influencing conformity

In an effort to ascertain the important variables affecting conformity a number of subsequent studies have been performed, and several factors emerged.

First, group size appears to have some significance with regard to the number of confederates present that all give a unanimous response. The question of most interest was whether the level of conformity would rise in proportion to the size of the majority (with a 1:1 ratio very low levels are obtained).

Asch (1955) varied the number of confederates up to about fifteen, but found no significant increase in conformity rate beyond that found for just three or four confederates; a genuine subject was therefore no more likely to conform in a situation with fifteen confederates than with three or four of them. If anything, we might expect conformity levels to decrease with such a large 'opposition' because the true subject may become suspicious of such a unanimous response.

However, other experiments have actually found a use in conformity with a majority larger than three or four confederates. Wilder (1977) suggests that a contributing factor is how the other members of the group are *perceived*. If, for instance, each person's response is judged independently by the genuine subject, then conformity may increase, but only so long as the answers given by stooges are perceived to be independent ones. It is argued that only these responses will influence the subject's own opinion. The number of group members thus perceived as all acting independently is called the *psychological size*. Exactly what might influence a subject's **perceptions** in such a way is not clear (although it may include some combination of the other factors outlined below), but presumably the size of the 'psychological majority' could increase conformity rates indefinitely.

Second, the influence of the majority in a conformity experiment suggests that if the subject was allowed to give their answer away from the group – that is, anonymously – then the levels of conformity could decrease. If people are allowed to give answers in private then they ought to be less likely to be swayed by others' views.

Deutsch and Gerard (1955) allowed subjects to respond in complete privacy by using partition slides to separate them from the subjects, thereby removing any 'face-to-face' effect. Using this method the researchers discovered a drop in conformity level, although it was not entirely eliminated. This would suggest that we are subject to the influence of others even when asked for our 'private' views. Voting behaviour may provide one demonstration of this; although voting in an election, for instance, is an individual and personal response carried out privately, our views may still have been influenced by friends, television, broadcasting and the media and so on, prior to reaching a decision.

Third, several researchers including Asch have found that if the task is ambiguous or the problem made more difficult, then conformity increases. Under conditions in which the answer is not obvious then subjects appear more likely to go along with the group decision and rely on others' opinions. In a variation of his original experiment, Asch (1956) altered the length of the test lines so that the judging of them was made more difficult (see Figure 3.4).

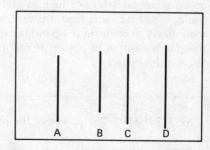

Source: Asch (1956)

Figure 3.4 Example of material used by Asch in a subsequent experiment

In these circumstances conformity levels rose significantly.

At this point it should be noted that the subjects were not allowed 'thinking time'; had they been, this might have led to a more accurate judgement being given. Similarly in everyday situations people often use the behaviour of others in order to assist in their own decision-making where they may be unsure themselves.

Fourth, as stated earlier, unanimity was found to be an important factor. This point is further demonstrated when the effects of the majority are weakened by having another person disagree with the group prior to the true subject giving their response. This has been investigated in the laboratory by providing social support in the form of a dissenter who, although a confederate, is instructed on this occasion to give a different answer from the majority. Even if the answer given is still obviously incorrect, the genuine subject is less likely to conform to the group; presumably because the dissenting confederate appears as someone else willing to go against the majority, thereby giving the subject confidence to do the same. Asch (1958) found that conformity rates dropped to under 10 per cent when one confederate disagreed with the majority view.

That a small proportion of subjects still conformed is interesting, however. Conflict is present on this occasion because the true subject is given a choice of sides with which to agree. Again, for a possible variety of reasons, the subject may perceive the majority as being better informed and, not wanting to stand out from the rest (like the dissenter), will conform to the larger group.

Fifth, personal qualities – such as the need to be liked, the perceived status of the group members and the extent to which an individual is attracted to the group – are also factors which influence conformity. Studies show that subjects tend to conform more when they like the people in the group. If a number of people have attractive characteristics then an individual may go along with their decision in order to be like them. Similarly, people may be more likely to conform when they like the group because they feel that by doing so they will gain the group's approval or liking and so strive to do what they hope is correct. This 'need to be liked' is particularly apparent in individuals rated as having low self-esteem, and this personality characteristic may make them more likely to conform, whereas individuals high in self-esteem may also be more confident and sure of themselves, thereby being less likely to conform.

Factors associated with the group dynamics are also influences upon conformity, especially those relating to leadership and status. Generally speaking, those group members who are high in status relative to the others tend to conform while, less at the same time, the reverse usually applies; low status individuals are more likely to conform to opinions expressed by those of high status, particularly those in a position of power. (Conformity to authority figures will be examined later in this chapter.)

SPOTLIGHT   The power of the majority

We all conform to some extent to various situations which arise in our lives, although the reasons for doing so may depend upon a wide variety of factors. If you consider yourself to be a fairly independent individual and one who is not easily swayed by the wishes of others, imagine being in the following situation. Then consider all the other occasions in which you have conformed (for whatever reason).

At a restaurant with three friends you have just finished dessert when the waiter approaches and asks if anyone would like coffee. Each of your companions, when asked in turn, declines and then the waiter looks to you for your reply.

- Are you likely to request a coffee or not?

- What factors (according to conformity research) will influence your decision? For instance, if you were with seven companions, each of whom declined coffee, would you be more or less likely to accept?

3.4 Criticisms and Comments on Conformity Experiments

The work of Asch and others has shed light on an important aspect of group behaviour which has implications regarding decision-making and social interaction. However, a number of criticisms of these experiments have been raised.

One is that the experiments have a questionable relevance to real life, in that an 'instant' answer was required in the Asch studies. Critics argue that under most circumstances where an individual is not sure what response to give, he or she will say nothing, but this was not a choice that subjects were given in the Asch studies.

Second, the widespread individual differences which occurred make it difficult to generalize these findings to the world at large: although some subjects yielded to the group view, many showed little or no conformity at all.

Third, replications and variations of the experiments have yielded inconclusive findings. Crutchfield (1955) devised a situation which enabled up to five subjects to be tested simultaneously. He presented various tasks to subjects ranging from perceptual judgements (see Figure 3.5) to those which involved giving statements of attitudes and beliefs: for example, army subjects were asked if they agreed with the statement, 'I doubt whether I would make a good leader.' When tested on the 'star-circle problem', approximately 46 per cent of subjects conformed with the 'incorrect' response. As regards the military officers, 37 per cent agreed with the statement in the conformity situation, although none did when asked individually.

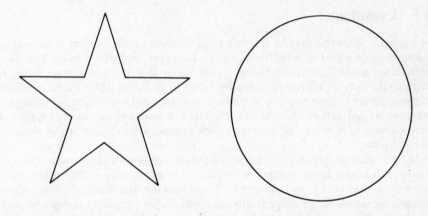

Question: Which is larger, the star or the circle?

Source: Crutchfield (1955)

Figure 3.5 Example of material used by Crutchfield in conformity experiments

In many cases the findings were similar to those of Asch (e.g., difficult items lead to increased conformity), but once again some individuals were not influenced by the supposed views of 'others'.

Nearly two decades later, Larsen (1974) investigated conformity rates in an Asch-type situation but found much lower levels in the extent to which subjects conformed. This was explained with respect to a growing trend for independence which was prevalent at that time (and which is perhaps even more pronounced today), in which people were encouraged to stand up for themselves rather than go along with others.

Trends such as these may also indicate how cultural variations can affect conformity, in that particular cultures and peoples are more likely to conform, and differences along these lines have been found by several researchers.

There are also different types of conformity, including public acceptance, identification and compliance (see below), and it is difficult to isolate which forms are involved in many cases because of the numerous confounding variables present, such as personality.

Another criticism is that the orginal experiments by Asch implied that the tendency to conform to a larger group was a negative or weak characteristic among individuals. Whilst there are certain occasions when independent judgements are more valued, conformity also has beneficial effects. Throughout life group norms provide a standard of guidelines for behaviour, and conformity to many of these societal norms brings rewards, while non-conformity may result in punishment, such as imprisonment.

Thus one view of conformity is that, rather than being an inferior quality, it is essentially fundamental to social stability. This is not to suggest that everyone should conform all the time and in precisely the same way because this would lead to a monotonous and perhaps tedious existence; but a degree of conformity ensures a structure and cohesiveness for social groups (Bernstein *et al.*, 1988).

3.5   Compliance

In a general sense this may be referred to as 'yielding to others', and is often used synonymously with the term 'conformity'. However, a distinction made is that compliance usually involves a change in behaviour as a result of a direct request. With conformity an individual feels pressured to go along with others, although often no direct request to do so is made. There are numerous everyday examples whereby we 'go along' with a direct request. For instance, an elderly neighbour may ask you to help out, or a door-to-door salesperson to buy items in order to aid a charity.

Indeed, such examples provided social psychologists with ideas upon which to base experimental investigations of this area. Bernstein *et al.* (1988) refer to the process of 'getting X by asking for Y' to sum up the various forms which compliance involves. In other words, one way to get people to comply to your wishes is often to ask for something else first, and then subsequently alter the request. This process may take one of three forms.

The foot-in-the-door technique

This effect works on the basis of initially making a small request which, when accepted, is increased to a more substantial one. Once the foot is in the door, so to speak, subsequent requests will be more readily granted.

This was put to the test by an American study carried out in a suburban area of California. Freedman and Fraser (1966) had subjects approached under one of two conditions. In one, homeowners were requested to display a large, somewhat ugly sign proclaiming 'Drive Carefully' (under the pretence of concern about traffic accidents). This represented the control condition, and about 17 per cent of subjects complied with the request to have the sign displayed.

In the experimental condition, homeowners were first asked if they would sign a petition about road safety, and two weeks later a different person returned and requested them to have the large sign on their lawn. The foot-in-the-door technique would predict that subjects would be more likely to comply to the second request in this condition as they have already conceded to the original request and, significantly, 55 per cent agreed to erect the sign.

Many companies employ similar tactics in an effort to sell their products. Working on the basis of 'giving a quote' or estimate without obligation to buy, salespersons often have a better chance of making a sale once inside someone's home.

Explanations for the foot-in-the-door technique tend to reflect the individual's self-image. Essentially, if someone agrees to a request, however small, then this may influence their self-concept (i.e., 'I am helpful'). Therefore a second substantial request may be complied with in order that the individual maintain or live up to this helpful image.

Two factors appear to be important, however: individuals have to think that they have reached the decision themselves, without coercion, and second, the first request must be significant enough to affect people's self-perception if they go along with it. Going out of your way to give a colleague a lift to work would contribute towards a helpful self-image, whereas merely telling someone the time would not (Deaux and Wrightsman, 1984).

The door-in-the-face effect

As the name implies, this involves completely rejecting an initial request, but often with the result that a later demand will be accepted. For this to work properly a substantial request is made to begin with, which is subsequently modified to a smaller, more reasonable one.

Adapted as a sales technique for customers who may have expressed an interest in buying a car, this works as follows. After being offered a luxurious and expensive model, they may be more likely to purchase a more basic and economical version. The important point to stress here is that the latter choice was the intended target of the salesperson, even though the particular customer is pleased with his or her purchase.

Similarly, when department stores hold sales and special offers, the effect is that the customer is able to compare the previous price with the reduced one. (Even though the customer may have entered the shop without any specific intention of buying anything, he or she may leave with a handful of 'bargains'.) By comparing the two prices, shoppers will be more likely to purchase an item simply because it is perceived as being a considerable reduction, even if they do not necessarily need it.

Several workers have tested this effect in experimental situations. Cialdini *et al.* (1975) presented students initially with a substantial request involving the students in doing voluntary counselling work with young offenders (at a local centre) for a period of two years. The majority declined but, when a smaller request was later made (to accompany young people on a day-trip), a larger number of the same subjects were willing to help.

What factors appear to be important in order for compliance to occur? If the foot-in-the-door explanation is true (i.e. self-image as helpful) then the door-in-the-face would seem to suggest that the individual on this occasion regards themselves as uncooperative and so should not comply on the second occasion.

We have seen that this is not the case, however. Again, two points appear important. Both the large and later, small request must come from the same source, or be made by the same person. With the car sale example this allows customers to interpret the result as being a 'victory' on their part because the seller has moved from the original offer. Another point is that the first request must be so large that the individual is likely to reason that no one would agree to it, thereby maintaining a good self-image (Deaux and Wrightsman, 1984).

The low-ball effect

This works by inducing the individual into a situation of accepting a request, after which the original terms are increased. Generally the idea is that, once drawn in, the person will accept the higher demand rather than back out of the request. For example, a friend might ask you for help in moving some small items of furniture, which you agree to do. On arriving to help you may find that there are several bulky, heavy items which need moving as well as the small ones. Such a technique of compliance relies considerably upon the helper's good nature, in that the person is willing to help despite the original terms of the agreement being altered.

In terms of self-image, once people say 'yes' they will not say 'no' at a later stage because this may weaken their notion of themselves as helping and they do not wish to be perceived as unreliable by the one making the request.

Many everyday situations provide illustrations of compliance, although the three main forms, together with possible explanations, may involve several other factors which may not be explicit at the time. These include individual motives and reasons for helping. For example, in some cases a person may go along with another's request in the hope that the favour will be returned at a later date. A related form of compliance is that of obedience, which again involves going along with others' wishes, but for completely different reasons. It is to this that we turn next.

3.6   Obedience

Douglas Bernstein *et. al.* (1988) refer to obedience as a form of submissive compliance, in that people comply with a demand because they feel they must or should do so. In many ways failure to obey may have severe consequences, particularly if the request/demand comes from someone who is perceived to be in authority.

Whereas compliance focuses upon a request to do something, obedience implies that the individual is ordered to go along and, for various factors which will be examined, does so.

The study of obedience from a psychological viewpoint stemmed from the atrocities of the Second World War (1939–45) when millions of innocent people were slaughtered by Hitler's Third Reich. At their trials many of the people held responsible for these 'war crimes' reported that they were simply following orders and doing their job.

The scale of destruction led many people to believe that the perpetrators of such horror were different from ordinary men and women, and this interpretation of events seemed the only way to account for the Nazis' behaviour. Just how far people would 'go' without questioning authority was demonstrated very effectively in a series of laboratory studies of obedience conducted in America in the 1960s by Stanley Milgram.

The Milgram Experiment (1963)

Subjects were males aged between twenty and fifty years of age from various backgrounds and occupations (skilled, unskilled and professional). They were recruited by means of advertisements which appeared in the local newspaper.

The standard procedure was as follows: on arriving at the laboratory (situated in Yale University) the subject would meet another man who was in his fifties, presumably another subject. The experimenter would appear and introduce himself and explain that the experiment about to take place was concerned with the effects of punishment on learning. It was then explained that one of the subjects was to be the Teacher and the other the Learner. This was decided by each person drawing a piece of paper upon which were supposedly written 'Teacher' or 'Learner'.

At this point a process of deception was introduced because the 'subject' who was there first was in fact a confederate working with the experimenter according to a pre-arranged plan. The genuine (naive) subject was assigned the role of teacher, while the confederate was given the role of learner. Both people were then taken to a nearby room where the learner was strapped into a chair and electrodes attached to his wrists by the experimenter. Having seen this done, the teacher was then taken to an adjacent room and seated at a table on which was an authentic looking shock generator (see Figure 3.6).

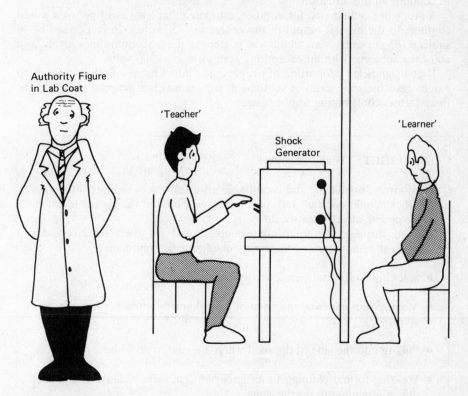

Source: Milgram (1974)

Figure 3.6 Set-up used by Milgram in his study of obedience

The learner was to respond to a list of words read out by the teacher, by pairing two words together correctly. For each incorrect response the teacher was told to administer a shock by throwing a switch on the generator, and to increase the voltage with each successive error. As the test proceeded the learner was heard to moan in pain (although in reality only acting) until at high shock levels (315 volts) he screamed and then went silent. Each time the teacher paused ('That guy's hollering in there'), the experimenter politely urged him to continue. Thus the teacher was not bullied into carrying on, but rather obeyed the calm requests of the 'authority figure' who provided verbal encouragement ('Go on, please teacher') whilst never at any time raising his voice.

At one point, when the learner appeared to be in severe pain, some subjects were heard to laugh; not, as Milgram explained, because they thought the situation amusing, but rather as an expression of 'deeply felt anxiety'. This also occurs when people are put under extreme emotional pressure, as for instance when soldiers go into battle, or when individuals are hysterical as a result of bereavement.

Results

The findings were quite alarming. Some forty subjects were tested in the original experiment and, as a further point of interest. Milgram asked a number of independent groups to estimate how far they thought subjects would be prepared to continue in this situation.

A group of psychiatrists, for instance, estimated that less than 1 per cent would continue to the highest output of the generator (450 volts). In fact 26 out of 40 subjects (65 per cent) went all the way in steps to the maximum shock levels, and all of the subjects, without exception, went as high as 300 volts.

That a significant proportion of people could inflict harm on others to such an extent gave rise to a series of subsequent studies which attempted to isolate the main factors contributing to obedience.

SPOTLIGHT 'That's an order!'

Conformity, obedience and compliance all involve very definite influences of other people upon us and, in a sense, vary only in the *degree* to which other people affect what we do.

Read through the following examples, and for each one, consider whether it demonstrates conformity, obedience or compliance.

- Smoking a cigarette because your friends are.

- Moving your car from the front of a neighbour's house because she asks you to.

- Pulling into the side of the road when directed to do so by a policeman.

- Wearing formal clothing to an important occasion because you expect others attending to do the same.

- Turning the music down at a party because the police tell you to.

- Turning the music down at a party because a neighbour asks you to.

- Leaving a play part way through, because the two friends you are with wish to do so.

- Opening your suitcase at the airport because a customs officer asks you to.

Variations
As the original experiment had been conducted in the much respected and prestigious setting of Yale University (which presumably gave the study added credibility), one of the follow-up studies was carried out in a neglected office building (in another state). Although the rest of the procedure was the same, on this occasion the obedience rate changed to 48 per cent. This suggests that the campus of Yale University may have contributed some influence, but this was by no means of major importance.

Perhaps being able to see one's 'victim' would influence the teacher's performance? In another variation, the learner was seated about two feet away from the teacher but, although the level of obedience fell to 40 per cent, it was clear that other factors were responsible for those who continued to give shocks.

In a further investigation of 'proximity to the learner', the teacher was required actually to press the learner's hand on to a metal plate that gave the shock, thereby being made more responsible for the consequences. However some subjects still continued to administer high voltage shocks, while the overall obedience level dropped to 30 per cent.

The proximity of the authority figure was also manipulated when the experimenter, after giving initial instructions in person, left the teacher and gave further instructions by telephone. This seemed to be one of the most significant factors, as obedience was almost non-existent under these circumstances. However, in a variation on this theme, when the basic procedure was presented either completely by telephone or tape-recorder instructions (i.e., with the experimenter's influence) Milgram found that only about 20 per cent of subjects continued to deliver the maximum output of the generator.

A significant point here is that when subjects could not be 'watched' as they were in the original experiment, then they attempted to deceive the experimenter. For instance, subjects would administer a lower voltage than required, or even fail to give any shock at all.

Another variation entailed the introduction of social support for the teacher (earlier in this chapter we saw how this kind of support brought about decreased conformity rates). Regarding obedience, this took the form of two other 'teachers' who each had roles in the experiment, such that one was responsible for reading out the word-lists (which the learner was to respond to), while the second confederate-teacher indicated to the genuine subject whether or not the response given was correct. The real subject's task was to press the switch on the generator which then supposedly delivered a shock. However, at a pre-arranged moment

(150 volts) the first confederate teacher said that he was not going to conform and left the room. After a few more trials, by which time the voltage delivered was 210, the second confederate complained that the learner was in too much pain and walked out. Under these conditions the level of obedience dropped to 10 per cent.

Criticisms

The main point raised by critics of these studies centred on the ethical aspects of whether or not it is acceptable or justifiable to treat subjects in such a manner. Many subjects suffered conditions of emotional stress, the effects of which were quite apparent as the experiment proceeded. Milgram observed that subjects were seen to 'sweat, stutter, tremble, groan, bite their lips and dig their fingernails into their flesh'. Three of his subjects experienced 'full-blown, uncontrollable seizures' (Milgram, 1963).

A second criticism concerns **generalization**: the extent to which the findings may be applied to a wider population and the real world. It may be that the subject volunteers were not representative of the wider population and that personality characteristics were highly responsible for the obedience shown by the majority of subjects.

However, in reply to his critics, Milgram claimed that great efforts were taken to ensure subjects left the university in no doubt about their actions. Part of their 'debriefing' involved an assurance that no pain was caused to the learner, whom they were allowed to meet when the experiment finished.

Milgram also conducted an extensive survey following the experiments. From interviews and questionnaires he reported that 84 per cent of those taking part had no regrets, and that psychiatrists' findings indicated no long-term psychological harm amongst subjects.

Regarding generalization, although in the original study only forty subjects were tested, the whole total numbered around 1000, a large sample size. Furthermore, Milgram maintained that the actual setting, whether laboratory or otherwise, is not important, as the actual process under observation (i.e., obedience to authority) is exactly the same.

Finally, several researchers have praised Milgram's efforts in highlighting the 'uglier' side of people and in so doing contributing to an important (if somewhat disturbing) aspect of human behaviour. Undoubtedly these experiments raise many issues for consideration, perhaps the greatest being their value in stimulating thought and discussion into an area which still remains of deep interest.

Obedience in non-laboratory settings

The perception of authority was an influential aspect in the Milgram experiments. In many ways the issue is out of the subjects' control even though they inflict the harm ourselves. As we saw earlier, the excuse which perpetrators of atrocity have given is that they were doing as they were told. People will obey orders, it seems, without question as long as they perceive those orders to come from a legitimate authority.

A study by Hofling *et al.* (1966) looked at the perceived authority within the medical profession, and in particular the relationship between nursing staff and doctors. The experiment took place within a number of hospitals. Boxes of a bogus drug named Astrofen had been previously placed in the medicine store. Each bottle was clearly labelled to include the maximum daily dosage (of 10 mgs).

The duty nurse was telephoned by a 'Doctor Smith' (in fact a confederate working for the experimenters) who instructed a *20 mg* dose of Astrofen to be administered to one of his patients and said he would be along shortly after. (In this situation a nurse is required to obtain authorization from another source.) The question was whether or not the nurse would seek confirmation of this request from another source, or just carry out Doctor Smith's wishes, which in fact exceeded the maximum stated dose. Unbeknown to the nurse, the drug was actually a harmless substance. Once the nurse had decided upon a course of action, a nearby observer intervened and provided a debriefing on the experiment.

The results showed that approximately 95 per cent of subjects began to carry out the instructions of the so-called Doctor Smith. Many nurses, when later interviewed, admitted that doctors tended to react angrily if their requests were delayed or instructions not obeyed.

This seems to indicate the differing status between the two groups, with a submissive role for nurses and a dominant, authoritative role for doctors. The results serve to demonstrate further the importance of perceived authority, and that those giving the order, presumably because of characteristics inherent in their role, know what they are doing. Perhaps also as a result of social roles, the need to question the decision is not applied.

Established roles and norms within a society are valuable in providing guides of conduct, and serve to influence our expectations of behaviour. A dramatic illustration of the effectiveness of roles which also conveys the power attributed to prescribed positions in society was conducted by Zimbardo *et al.* (1973), in which they attempted to simulate the psychological effects of imprisonment by role-playing.

The subjects were students who responded to advertisements in a newspaper requesting volunteers to participate in a psychological study of prison life. Those selected by the experimenters were first tested for their suitability, and successful applicants were those considered to be emotionally stable and responsible and having no record of anti-social behaviour.

Those chosen were randomly assigned either to the role of prisoner or prison guard, shortly after which the 'prisoners' were arrested, handcuffed and taken to a nearby police station, charged and then blindfolded, and driven to Stanford University, the basement of which had been reconstructed to resemble a prison.

A person's role is often indicated by clothing and in this case uniforms were provided for both prisoners and guards; prisoners wore large, loose shirts, while guards were given official-looking uniforms together with heavy sticks (although physical harm was not permitted), handcuffs and various other paraphernalia.

Prison conditions were imposed in an effort to make the experiment as realistic as possible, such that prisoners were referred to only by number, restrictions placed on their freedom, and so on, while guards carried out their duties with a ruthless efficiency.

Originally it was intended that the experiment would last for two weeks but it soon became apparent that this was not possible due to the 'transformation' in behaviour of both sets of students. The study ended abruptly after six days.

It appeared that both prisoners and guards had fully entered into their roles to the extent that guards would push and order prisoners around, generally abusing their power, but perhaps doing what they thought was expected of them.

Many prisoners became depressed and withdrawn, several having to be released a few days after the study began; at the end of the experiment the researchers gave several follow-up sessions to those suffering psychological/emotional distress as a consequence of their participation and their experiences.

Obedience to orders, then, is acquired and maintained by the social structure within society which relates to role expectation and our perceptions of those in authority. The Zimbardo study highlights yet again the capabilities which human beings have in their treatment of one another. A more disturbing aspect is that it implies each of us has this potential.

3.7   Questions and Exercises

1. Investigate social facilitation. Devise a range of tasks to include simple (letter cancellation) and difficult (mental arithmetic), and compare the timed performance of (a) individuals, (b) pairs, and (c) effects of audience presence.

2. Design an experiment to test conformity in group decision-making. Compare the effects of simple and difficult problems.

3 Make a list of everyday examples of the three forms of compliance. In groups, discuss ways of testing these types.

4 Critically discuss empirical studies of obedience.

5. Devise an experiment/study to investigate obedience outside the laboratory.

4 Attitudes

4.1 Introduction

As individuals in a social world our interactions and experience lead us to form views and judgements about people, actions and objects around us. This chapter will examine the nature of attitudes and beliefs, together with the ways in which such views, once established, may be changed.

The study of attitudes is claimed by some researchers to lie at the very heart of social psychology, and is undoubtedly an area which has attracted enormous interest and research. Allport (1935) stated that 'the concept of attitude is probably the most distinctive and indispensable concept in contemporary American social psychology'. Despite the fact that this claim was made so long ago, the central concepts of attitudes are just as relevant today.

4.2 Definitions

As with many other topics in psychology the term attitude has proved difficult to define precisely. The word itself has Latin origins, being derived from 'aptitudo' meaning 'fitness' (Reber, 1985). In this context it was used to refer to a fitness to engage in the execution of a task, and in medical terminology it is still used to describe body posture and limb position.

However, ethologists and comparative psychologists extended this usage (and applied the term) to include a notion of intention or readiness to act: thus an animal could be said to adopt a 'submissive attitude'. The modern usage of the term in social psychology still implies this state of readiness or intention. For example, Mednick *et al.* (1975) define 'attitude' as 'a predisposition to act in a certain way towards some aspect of one's environment, including other people'. Similarly, for Bernstein *et al.* (1988), it is described as 'a predisposition towards a particular cognitive, emotion or behavioural reaction to an object, individual, group, situation or action'.

The latter definition is especially significant in that it emphasizes the three components which many workers acknowledge as being inherent in a description of attitude: cognitive, affective and behavioural.

1. Cognitive component: this refers to thoughts or beliefs expressed by an individual regarding an issue (e.g., I believe that animals have rights).
2. Affective component: this concerns the *emotional* feeling people have towards an issue, reflected by their favourable or unfavourable evaluation of it (e.g., I am strongly opposed to the use of animals for experiments).
3. Behavioural component: this refers to the observable behaviour shown by people as a means of expressing their beliefs and feelings on an issue (e.g., sending a donation to an animal rights group, or taking part in a protest demonstration).

It is also worth noting at this point the distinction made between terms like values, beliefs and opinions, which are often used synonymously for 'attitudes'.

☐ *Beliefs* tend to imply trust or confidence and an acceptance of some statement or proposition on the part of the individual, often with an emotional connotation.

☐ *Values* represent a form of committed regard for an issue, in that the individual deems an issue to have some worth. In many cases the value is subjectively imposed by the individual so that what one person holds in high regard, another may not.

☐ *Opinions* can be regarded as the expression of a viewpoint based on known facts or information. It might be suggested that opinions are more susceptible to change and fluctuation, whereas beliefs and values have a tendency to reflect an individual's 'deeper' concerns.

We have seen, in the previous chapter regarding conformity, that these last two aspects can be strongly influenced by the views of others, and often a person's private and public opinions may be quite different.

4.3   Measuring Attitudes

Expressing our views and attitudes and hearing the views of others is something that we experience daily. Everyone has, at some time, been asked to express their views on a topic. Companies spend thousands of pounds on market research each year on surveys and opinion polls to an effort to discover what people think, feel or are likely to do. But measuring attitudes and opinions is, as we shall see, a complex process.

Earlier we stated how attitudes may be considered to have three components, the cognitive, affective and behavioural, each of which may be measured separately. In assessing the cognitive component, for example, an individual could be given a simple paper-and-pencil test such as a questionnaire.

Another form of survey is the interview method. Essentially this differs from a questionnaire in that with an interview the respondent is questioned 'face to face', whereas a questionnaire may be completed by an individual in private. Both methods allow access to a large number of people, however.

The same techniques could be used to measure the affective component by allowing respondents to express their degree of feeling for the issue. It has also been suggested that physiological recordings may also be taken, such as heart rate, pupil dilation, and so on during a person's exposure to, say, a film on the issue concerned.

As the behavioural component, by definition, involves observable characteristics, measurement consists of making direct observations and inferring attitudes from this. For example, we may infer from watching a group of people demonstrating against nuclear arms that they have strong feelings on the matter.

Apart from these methods a number of specialized attitude scales exist that basically consist of a set of statements to which subjects give a response. Usually the statements have a pre-established scale value enabling a quantitative index to be obtained. Three of these scales will be briefly considered.

Likert Scale

This was developed in early 1930s by Rensis Likert. It takes the form of a series of attitude statements, such as 'Smoking should be banned in restaurants', to which respondents are asked to indicate their level of agreement. Normally the scale comprises five options: strongly agree, agree, uncertain, disagree, strongly disagree. On the basis of the subjects' responses their attitude to the statement posed may be evaluated.

Thurstone Scales (1928, 1929)

These actually represent a method or technique for constructing an attitude scale. Based on the work of the American psychometrician, Thurstone, the procedure involves gathering a set of statements which reflect attitudes on particular topics, such as abortion and nuclear arms.

Next, a large number of people (judges) are asked to sort the statements into categories (on an 11-point scale) ranging from most strongly agreeing with the statement (favourable attitude) to most strongly disagreeing with it (unfavourable attitude). The proportion of judges allocating statements to each category is then used to determine the scale values assigned to each statement; if a statement effectively measures an attitude most of the judges will place it in the same category.

This process produces a number of statements, each with a numerical value between 1 and 11. When administered, the individual (subject) indicates those items with which they agree or disagree, and from this a mean attitude score is obtained.

Semantic differential

This is a technique devised by Osgood *et al.* (1957), which may be used to evaluate attitudes and values that people hold with respect to words, objects, issue, and so on. The respondent is asked to rate (the meaning of) each word(s) using pairs of polar opposites such as weak–strong, tense–relaxed, rough–smooth. This is usually done by drawing one short vertical line or cross through the line separating the two polar opposites in order to provide a measurement.

The implied meaning assigned to each word by the subject may be analysed using a statistical procedure known as factor analysis. Typically, this reveals three factors (or clusters) which are taken to underlie the attitude based on subjects' response: the activity factor, the potency factor and the evaluative factor. The subjects' attitudes or values may then be referred from subsequent analysis.

SPOTLIGHT Constructing an attitude scale

We have briefly mentioned three forms of attitude scale that may be used in the measurement of attitudes. In order to familiarize yourself with this technique, as well as to provide an insight into some of the disadvantages and problems involved, a useful exercise is to devise and then test such a scale. Here are some simple steps to follow.

First, think of a number of topics on which people's attitudes could be measured, and then consider upon which of these you could generate the most questions or statements.

For the purposes of this exercise we will use the Likert Scale which, as we have said, comprises a set of statements, and as a topic we will consider 'student attitudes to college life'. One statement is provided as an example.

At the top of the scale a simple instruction is given such as: 'Please read through the following statements, and for each indicate your view by ticking the appropriate box.'

The refectory provides a good choice of meals

Strongly agree	Agree	Don't know	Disagree	Strongly disagree
☐	☐	☐	☐	☐

Some things to bear in mind are the number of people to ask, how representative of the student body they are, the situation in which the scale is administered, etc.

Finally, consider the strengths and weaknesses of this method of attitude measurement.

4.4   What You Say and What You Do: Attitudes and Behaviour

What is the relationship between attitude and behaviour? Attitude scales, like other psychometric tests such as those of intelligence and personality, must fulfil certain criteria if they are to be of any worth. They must, for instance, be reliable and valid; and during their construction great care must be taken with question wording and overall format so as to avoid biasing the answers.

One of the intentions behind attitude scales is to predict how people would be likely to behave in specific situations, as inferred from their verbal or written responses. However, one problem that confounds this area is the extent to which an individual's expressed attitude corresponds to their observable behaviour. For instance, if an individual conveys a negative attitude towards ethnic minorities, we might expect certain behaviours from them in the presence of such groups. Such a conclusion, though, is often completely unfounded.

A classic study which highlighted the disparity between attitudes and behaviour was conducted by Richard LaPiere in 1934. At that time in America the general attitude towards oriental people was unfavourable, and LaPiere toured a large part of the United States with a Chinese couple visiting some 250 restaurants and hotels on their journey (which lasted three months). Only on one occasion was the group refused admission to an establishment and, upon their return, LaPiere wrote to the places visited to ask whether or not they would admit Chinese patrons. Of those proprietors that replied, 90 per cent said they would not serve Chinese customers.

This only appears to illustrate a sharp distinction between attitudes (90 per cent expressing a certain attitude by letter) and behaviour (admitting Chinese to establishments), but critics have suggested otherwise. It is claimed, for instance, that what is being measured here is the difference between actual and intended behaviour, and not attitudes.

Another possible discrepancy is that we cannot be sure whether the proprietors giving a written refusal were the same people who served the Chinese couple when they visited the hotels and restaurants.

In an extensive review of several such studies Wicker (1969) having noticed many inconsistencies, came to the conclusion that there was a' very weak relationship between attitude and behaviour. A number of reasons have subsequently been put forward for this, all of which illustrate the complexity of the subject matter. One problem concerns the difference between general and specific attitudes. Many studies that have produced inconsistent findings have relied upon using a general measure of attitude when investigating a specific aspect of behaviour (e.g., using attitudes towards drugs to predict the likelihood of individuals taking part in a campaign to legalize cannabis). In other words the 'level of specificity' is an important point to consider (Deaux and Wrightsman, 1984).

Another problem related to this again concerns the precise nature of what is being investigated with relation to attitude. In many cases researchers use single cases of behaviour upon which to test their predictions and, subsequently base their conclusions. However, because of the complexities involved, there may be a whole series of attitudes affecting behaviour, including the one being measured. Studies are often confounded by the whole range of attitudes that an individual possesses, and it may be more useful to observe behaviour in a variety of settings, rather than make judgements based on an isolated incident.

Often, also, a conflict of needs may be involved and one attitude is masked by another. For instance, a person may feel a sympathetic concern for a charity but not actually contribute because of a stronger conviction that the government should do more to help. In a demonstration of this, Insko and Schopler (1967) cited an individual with favourable attitudes towards the American civil rights movement but who, given the opportunity, would not donate money to the movement.

In both of these examples a system of priorities may be seen to operate which at first glance appears to represent an inconsistency between attitude and behaviour. However, on further analysis, other values and attitudes have a greater influence and so take precedence, such as personal welfare and financial concerns.

In a recent article, Jaroslovsky (1988) presented several reasons for the inconsistencies between what people think and what they actually do, all of which confirm the complex nature of such research. With specific reference to opinion polls, results can be affected by the question phrasing, the nature of the question preceding the one being asked and the length of the questionnaire. Fatigue by the respondent can be a potential influence because a person may simply say whatever comes into their head first in order to get rid of the questioner.

The appearance, sex, manner and race of the questioner can also affect responses. In one American poll of voting behaviour for the black candidate, Jesse Jackson, the results indicated approximately 50 per cent of black voters going in his favour, but the actual figures showed that Jackson gained over 90 per cent of all black votes. One suggestion was that black respondents did not give their real answer to the poll takers, most of whom were white.

On occasions when the respondent is unsure or has no opinion on the issue at hand, they will often answer a question just to please the interviewer. This represents yet more difficulties for those attempting to make sense of the results (Jaroslovsky, 1988). Despite such problems Jaroslovsky concludes that surveys and polls do have their usefulness and are capable of giving reliable answers, but that caution must be taken when interpreting findings in what is a highly complex field.

Other workers confirm these sentiments. Ajzen and Fishbein (1977), for example, regard attitudes as strong predictors of behaviour where care is taken with the selection and assessment of those characteristics to be measured.

4.5   The Development of Attitudes

Attitudes are gained through experience and contact with the world around us. As individuals develop they acquire a set of beliefs and attitudes which in part influence how they interact with others and may be altered by new experiences and information.

Essentially attitudes are formed through a learning process, and there are a number of ways in which this occurs.

Classical conditioning

Classical conditioning is a type of learning which is discussed in detail in Chapter 12. Basically an association is formed between two stimuli as a consequence of their being paired together, so that the learner gives the same response to the new stimulus as he or she did to the old.

Psychologists consider that attitudes can be acquired in much the same way: a person links an object, group or situation with a specific characteristic so that the object, group or situation is seen to have those properties and an attitude is formed. For example, an individual may develop an unfavourable attitude towards foreign food if it is always experienced in unpleasant circumstances.

Operant conditioning

Simply put, this occurs when a response is followed by a reinforcer, with the consequence that the response is more likely to occur in the future. For instance, if someone expresses their views on abortion and a friend agrees with them (thus providing **positive reinforcement**), then this attitude will be strengthened.

Verbal reinforcement of this kind has been found very effective in shaping behaviour. Insko (1965) attempted to influence attitudes using a verbal reinforcement technique, in a study where students' attitudes (either favourable or unfavourable) were reinforced by the experimenter who followed the view expressed with the word 'Good'. When the students were later given an opportunity to express their views in a questionnaire, those who had been verbally reinforced for favourable attitudes expressed more positive views than those reinforced for unfavourable attitudes.

However, as Deaux and Wrightsman (1984) point out, there are limitations to such findings. The new consideration is that this form of conditioning can only serve to maintain clearly-existing attitudes: the individual must clearly hold an opinion or view which is then strengthened via verbal reinforcement. It is unlikely that an attitude can be created by this procedure.

Figure 4.1 'Excuse me, would you mind answering a few questions?'

Observational learning and imitation

These are the fundamental features upon which social learning theory is based and, according to this approach, are the means by which a wide variety of behaviours are acquired. Attitudes may also develop in this way. For instance, by observing a parent's unfavourable reaction to smoking, a child may acquire a negative attitude towards the habit. Subsequently an individual may imitate or copy the attitude of others, and if this is reinforced it will lead to further development of the attitude. On this occasion the parents act as models in the formation of attitudes, but other sources may exert an influence too. These include peers, teachers and the media, particularly characters portrayed on television.

The tendency for television to present people in certain ways may directly affect how an individual comes to view these people, especially if they have had little personal experience which invalidates what they see on the screen. Ethnic minorities, for example, are often portrayed in a stereotyped fashion, which could lead to distinct attitudes being formed or reinforced about such groups. However, one study attempted to counter-act the formation of both sex and ethnic stereotypes in young children. Following the broadcast of a series in America called 'Freestyle', children were found to express greater acceptance of non-stereotypical activities, such as boys taking part in caring activities. Later observations, though, did not reveal major changes in behaviour (Johnston and Ettema, 1982). As we saw in the previous section, the possible reasons for this discrepancy are many and varied.

4.6 Changing Attitudes

Once developed, the attitudes that a person holds can be highly resistant to change but, under certain conditions, attitudes may be altered. The reasons for attitude change are numerous. For example, we may change a long-held unfavourable attitude towards specific people if we begin to see them in different circumstances (see section 5.5).

Advertising agencies and other groups of people, such as educators and politicians, spend a large part of their time attempting to change other people's attitudes. Psychologists, too, have shown an interest in this aspect of behaviour and, in an effort to explain the processes involved, have identified several factors.

Persuasive communications

How do you persuade someone to change their views, whether they concern a political candidate or new brand of toothpaste? Many of the factors are the same, but the degree to which the attempt is successful has been shown to be influenced by a number of important characteristics.

In an effort to apply the principles of learning theory to attitude change, Hovland, Janis and Kelley (1953) maintained that for a message to be effective it must be attended to, it must be comprehended and it must be accepted. Their model proposes that the message must convey incentives for acceptance, in that the individual assumes there to be some benefit. Furthermore, the acceptance of message is largely influenced by:

(a) the nature of the message itself;
(b) the characteristics of the audience;
(c) the source of the communication;
(d) the context in which the message is delivered.

The nature of the message

How is the message put across? This aspect concentrates on how the argument is organized, the medium used, and what exactly the message consists of (i.e., its content). We shall consider each of these briefly in turn.

Research suggests that an important element concerning the organization and the argument is whether to put forward one or two sides in the communication. For instance, if you were arguing in favour of the return of capital punishment, should you present only those pieces of information which support your claim, or also those which counter it? By putting forward the 'pros' and the 'cons', and at the same time highlighting the weaknesses of the 'cons', you might hope to change attitudes more than if the 'pros' were presented alone.

On this issue, Karlins and Abelson (1970) suggested that several points must be taken into account. Basically, they claim that a one-sided argument may be most effective when the audience is friendly, when your position is the only one that will be presented, or when you want immediate but temporary attitude change. Conversely, if the audience initially disagree with the message, or if it is likely that they will, then a two-sided argument may be more effective.

A final consideration regarding two-sided arguments concerns which side of the issue to present first. Here, there is no conclusive evidence; although the time lapse between the two messages is important, sometimes it is better to present the favourable points first, while at other times presenting the opposing viewpoint first may be more effective (Deaux and Wrightsman, 1984). This effect is known as the 'primacy-recency effect' and will be looked at in more detail in Chapter 5.

Another feature of the message is the medium in which it is delivered. This involves visual, auditory or written methods, although there has been some disagreement over which is most effective. Where the interest centres on getting the audience to yield to an opinion rather than merely understand the issue, it is suggested that videotaped or live messages are best. However, a message which is difficult or complicated may be communicated much better using a written presentation.

The research involving the content of the message has centred around the effectiveness of fear-arousing stimuli. These kinds of message often portray an issue by using 'shock tactics' where the aim is to disturb or shock the audience. Examples of these include recent advertisements on the subject of Acquired Immune Deficiency Syndrome (AIDS), drug addiction and drinking and driving (see Figure 4.2). Do such advertising campaigns work? Although there tends to be some change in, for example, periodic reductions in the number of drink-driving offences, the problems themselves remain. Whilst the disturbing features of a message might make the audience think more about the issue, the 'target audience' (i.e., drug users and drivers who drink) might only be influenced temporarily and, furthermore, may 'justify' their behaviour with a host of other reasons. This individual justification for behaviour will be examined later.

One question that has been asked concerning fear arousal is whether or not it is more effective to induce high fear in the audience or to arouse a low level of fear. Empirical evidence on fear appeals has produced conflicting findings.

Janis and Feshbach (1953) designed an experiment in which the message concerned the penalties of improper dental care. Subjects were allocated to one of two conditions: a low fear condition in which the message explained that small fillings may be needed, and a high fear condition which contained photographs of

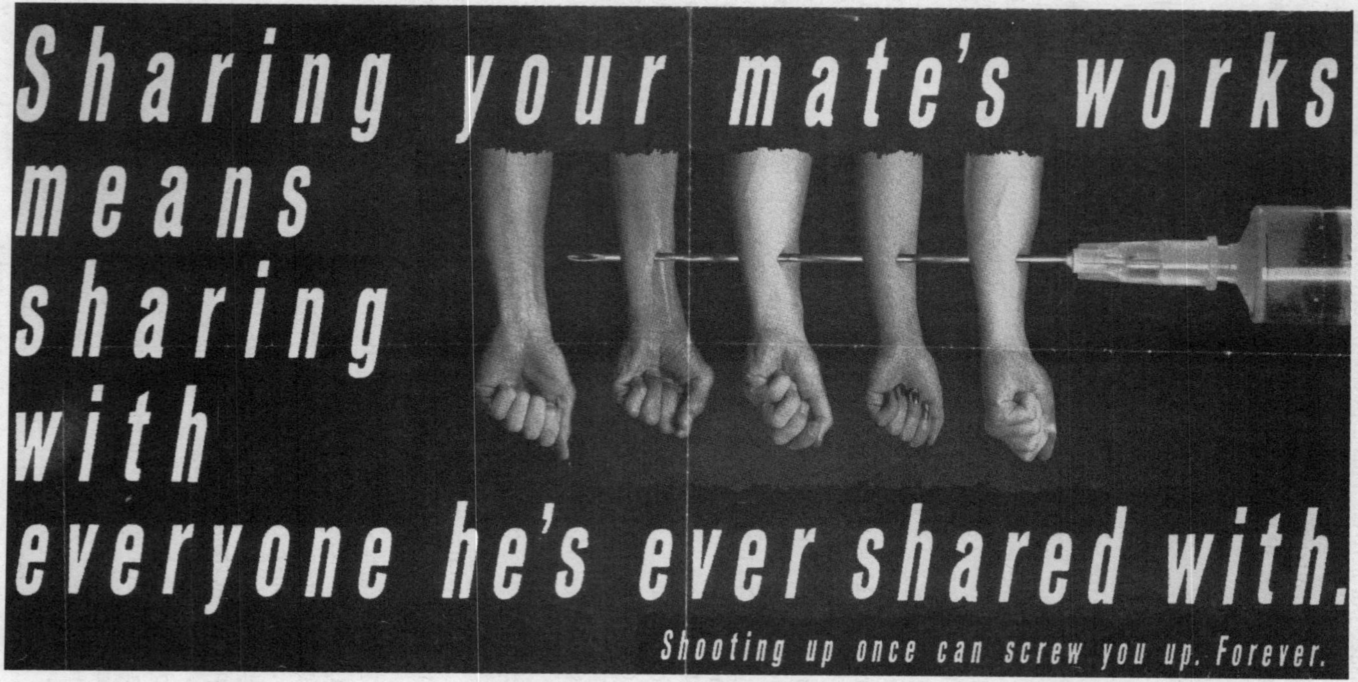

Source: Department of Health

Figure 4.2 Department of Health Aids poster: persuasive communication?

gum diseases. The results showed that subjects in the low fear condition reported the greatest change towards better dental care.

Perhaps too much fear affects the individual's ability to attend to the message and to understand it. However, Aronson (1980) reports that, in the majority of experimental data, the more fear a person experiences from a message the more likely that person is to take positive steps in dealing with it. For example, Leventhal (1970) tried to change people's attitudes to smoking and get them to give up the habit. In one condition subjects were recommended to stop smoking and have a chest X-ray (low fear), while subjects in the moderate fear condition were shown a film in which the character was told he had lung cancer. Subjects in the third condition were exposed to high fear; they watched the same film as subjects in the moderate fear condition, plus an explicit film of a patient having a lung-cancer operation. It was in this latter group that subjects expressed more intentions to stop smoking.

Leventhal and his colleagues went on to show another factor in the effect of high-fear arousal: namely, the people to whom the message is directed.

The characteristics of the audience
In many areas of human behaviour a wide range of individual differences exist, and this is also true of attitude change. Despite the efforts of the communicator and the nature of the message, some people will change their attitudes, but there will also remain others who do not. What makes individuals differ in this respect?

Following on from his experiment on attitudes to smoking, Leventhal (1970) proposed that self-esteem was important and that people with high self-esteem are more likely to act quickly when subjected to high degrees of fear arousal than are people with low self-esteem. One explanation, according to Aronson (1980), is that individuals with a low opinion of themselves feel more threatened by exposure to a high fear message, and tend to need more time before deciding to act.

Other workers have also shown that individual self-esteem is related to the effectiveness of a persuasive communicator. McGuire (1969) claimed that people with low self-esteem are less confident about the basis for their own attitudes and are thus more easily persuaded to adopt another viewpoint. Those with high self-esteem are more sure of themselves and, it seems, less likely to change their attitude once established.

Apart from self-esteem and other personality variables, intelligence has been found to influence susceptibility to persuasive communications. Eagly and Warren (1976) found that when a message is complex, highly intelligent people change their attitudes more easily than less intelligent people. This is presumably because those higher in intelligence are better able to make sense of the message. The effect also seems to occur if a message is largely unsupported or is weak, because then only those of lower intelligence are likely to change their attitudes.

However, highly intelligent individuals may have the ability to weigh up the issues in an argument, spot weaknesses in it, and thus remain convinced that their original view was the correct one. Therefore, although very intelligent people are better able to understand persuasive messages than those of low intelligence, they are also in a better position to counter them. Knowing an individual's level of intelligence would not enable us to predict their likelihood of attitude change.

The source of the communication
A persuasive communication must appear believable, knowledgeable and trust-
worthy: that is, the source must be a credible one. Such messages have been
found more effective in changing attitudes than those with low credibility and
Hovland, Janis and Kelley (1953) proposed that the extent to which a source had
credibility affected a person's incentives to change his or her attitude.

This method of presenting a communication is often used in advertising, where
an 'expert' is seen to endorse a particular product. For example, you may be more
likely to buy a particular brand of bleach if it is seen to be acclaimed by a scientist
in a white coat who appears to know what he or she is talking about, as opposed to
a figure without those characteristics.

Apart from credibility of the source, it is also important that it is seen to be
genuine and sincere. If the communicators are perceived to have no vested
interest in bringing about attitude change, then the audience is more likely to
consider the argument. Again, to use advertisements as an example, many
involve individuals who are apparently just members of the public. When we hear
their opinions about a product or issue we may be more likely to accept it because
they seem genuine. Again though, the extent to which the source is perceived to
be credible and sincere may depend upon factors already outlined, such as
personality and intelligence.

Another way in which the person presenting the message may affect attitude
change concerns how similar they appear to be to the audience. If the communicator is seen to have something in common with us, then we may infer other
positive characteristics as well, such as trustworthiness and attractiveness.
Furthermore, Mills and Aronson (1965) have demonstrated that physical
attractiveness itself is often sufficient to change the opinions of an audience. Such
a characteristic alone, though, whilst it may influence our attitude towards an
unimportant issue, is not considered to be as effective regarding serious issues
such as our attitude to nuclear disarmament, for instance. In other words, liking a
communicator may only affect our opinions and behaviours on trivial matters
(Aronson, 1980).

The context in which the message is delivered
When any message is communicated, whether persuasive or otherwise, an
abundance of distractions may be present. Advertisements on billboards, for
instance, appear in the context of traffic and other noise which influences how
much attention we pay to the message, and thus what we glean from it.

One of the main effects of distractions according to Petty *et al.* (1976) is that
they disrupt mental processing and so interfere with our ability to evaluate an
incoming message fully. Thus it may be that distractions prevent us from
formulating an argument either to back up our views or to contradict an opposing
opinion.

Studies of hecklers (those people who harass and interrupt speakers attempting
to put a viewpoint across) suggest that distraction of this kind generally serves to
reduce the effectiveness and hence persuasiveness of a message if the audience
has a neutral opinion, but has a moderating effect on extreme views. Petty and
Brock (1976) observed that the disruptive effects caused by hecklers can be
cancelled out if the speaker responds by remaining calm and continues to present
his or her argument or viewpoint. Presumably the contrast between the poorly-

presented view of the heckler and the rational argument of the speaker means that the latter view is still communicated effectively to the audience.

4.7 Consistency Theory

Next, we will briefly consider another approach which is often referred to as a consistency theory. This is because it stresses that if individuals experience inconsistencies between their thoughts and their behaviour, then they will take action to alter this state. In terms of attitudes, inconsistency results in attitude change, which consistency theories claim is necessary to justify our actions

---

SPOTLIGHT   Are you easily persuaded?

Take a few moments to glance through a magazine or watch television, and consider some of the advertisements which appear. Each of them puts across a distinctive message in either a brash or a subtle manner, in an effort to persuade the reader or viewer to change cars, hair shampoos, banks or whatever. Indeed a great deal of time and money is invested by advertisers as they attempt to convince us of their products' merits.

A different form of message, but one which often relies on the same technique of communication, sets out to alter attitudes regarding an important social issue. Most of us are familiar with the anti-drinking and driving campaigns which regularly appear, as well as those concerning drug abuse. As we have mentioned, the extent to which such messages are effective in influencing people's attitudes depends on several factors. What approach would you take in attempting to persuade someone to change their views?

- List the factors which you regard as being important in persuasive communications.

- Design a poster which aims to change the reader's attitude on a major issue. Comment on the style of persuasion which you have chosen. What are the disadvantages of this method of communication?

Cognitive dissonance theory

Based on the work of Leon Festinger (1957), this proposes that when individuals hold conflicting **cognitions** about themselves (i.e., their attitudes, beliefs or behaviours), then a state of dissonance is said to exist. According to the theory, this brings about psychological tension and feelings of unease, which then motivate the individual to seek to reduce dissonance. This may be done in a number of ways (Deaux and Wrightsman, 1984).

One way would be to change one of the dissonant aspects so that it is no longer inconsistent with other beliefs. For example, a person may drink alcohol, but gradually decide that it is unhealthy. The two cognitions, therefore – drinking and an appreciation of the health risks – bring about dissonance, which is reduced if the person stops drinking. Alternatively, the individual might change his or her attitude concerning health risks and so continue to drink.

An experiment which demonstrates the reduction of dissonance by a change in attitude was carried out by Festinger and Carlsmith in 1959. The first stage involved subjects performing a dull, boring task (turning pegs on a board), following which some of the subjects were asked to lie about the experiment by telling another person waiting outside that it was interesting and enjoyable. Some of the subjects were told that they would receive $1 for doing this, while others were told they would get $20. Finally, after having lied to the waiting person, the subjects were asked to rate the task.

The results indicated, as dissonance theory would predict, that subjects paid only $1 to lie rated the experimental task more favourably than those subjects who received $20. For subjects in the high-reward condition, the payment was sufficient to justify the behaviour (i.e., lying), and so no dissonance was felt. However, those paid only $1 would have experienced conflict, and they reduced this by changing their attitude towards the experiment, making it consistent with their behaviour. As they had already lied to the person waiting outside, this was the only strategy left open to them.

Dissonance may also be reduced by making the dissonant elements appear less important or less attractive. This often occurs in cases of decision-making. If, for instance, you purchase a jacket, and then shortly afterwards see what looks like an identical copy in another shop at a much lower price, you will probably reason that the cheaper coat is the wrong size, an imitation or inferior in some way compared with the one you bought.

Brehm (1966) asked passers-by to rate several items in terms of their attractiveness, and then allowed them to choose one item from two of those rated, to keep as a gift. After having made a choice, subjects were asked to rate the items once more, and Brehm observed that subjects now rated their choice as better and more attractive, whilst at the same time decreasing the attractiveness rating of the item they had not chosen.

Another method of reducing dissonance is simply to 'increase the number or importance of the consonant cognitions' (Deaux and Wrightsman, 1984). In other words, individuals justify their attitude or behaviour by emphasizing their positive perceptions of it. For instance, heavy smokers, knowing full well the dangers involved, may argue that it aids their concentration and helps them relax. Here, the evidence suggests that people like to maintain a positive image of themselves (Aronson, 1980), which is achieved in such circumstances by reducing dissonance.

It has often been demonstrated that people will selectively choose information in order to confirm their attitudes and decisions. In an extensive survey, Ehrlich *et al*. (1957) noticed that, following a decision, people sought reassurance that it was correct by actively selecting information which was bound to be supportive of their behaviour. In the case of heavy smokers, although negative messages and attitudes about the habit will impinge daily, individuals may gain reassurance and comfort by seeking information and opinions which support their view, and by concentrating on 'positive' elements of the issue while ignoring negative ones.

Critics of cognitive dissonance theory have questioned some aspects of the methodology used in studies, particularly those involving deception (asking subjects to lie).

Bernstein *et al.* (1988) point out that it is difficult to demonstrate the existence of a 'state of psychological tension' upon which the theory is based, let alone measure it in some quantifiable way. Nevertheless, the scope of the theory provides an interesting explanation of attitude changes in forms which consider how individuals make decisions in their lives.

Other explanations of attitude change include self-perception theory, social-judgement theory and functional theories. The first of these was put forward by Bem (1967) in an attempt to provide an alternative to the role of dissonance reduction in attitude change. According to this approach, people's beliefs and attitudes are influenced by an observation of their own behaviour. Thus, by perceiving how we behave in certain situations, we are able to infer something about our attitudes.

A similar approach, and one which offers a cognitive perspective, is social-judgement theory. Here, people are assumed to know where they stand on many issues, and through their experiences have a knowledge about how they would interpret and judge situations: that is, individuals are able to judge what attitudes they would accept and which ones they would dismiss. Such cognitive judgements precede attitude change, which suggests that a knowledge of other people's values and what they think would enable us to predict their likelihood of changing attitudes.

Finally, functional theory lays particular emphasis on how people differ as individuals. The basic assumptions of this approach are that people have attitudes that best fit their own needs, and in order to change attitudes it is necessary to know what the needs are. This theory is especially useful in explaining the reasons why some people will change their attitudes in given circumstances, while others will not. Simply put, the theory would argue that each of us has quite different needs and so how effective a message is in changing someone's attitude will depend on the individual's requirements.

4.8 Questions and Exercises

1. List some of your main beliefs, attitudes and opinions, and attempt to describe how you acquired them.
2. Design a questionnaire to investigate attitudes to smoking.
3. Discuss the extent to which attitudes can be successfully measured.
4. Collect advertisements from magazines and list the ways in which the message is effectively communicated to the audience.

Social perception

5.1 Introduction

As the term implies, social perception is concerned with our interpretation of behaviour in social settings and generally refers to how we perceive others, whether it be favourably or unfavourably. Of particular interest to psychologists are the processes by which individuals form opinions of other people or groups of people. These include the means by which initial impressions are formed, the reasons for prejudice and discrimination, and also the development of liking and relationships with specific individuals through interpersonal attraction. The aim of this chapter will be to consider some of these areas, together with how researchers have attempted to investigate the processes involved.

5.2 Impression Formation

Our interactions with others take several forms; we pass people without even taking notice of them, we have brief conversations with strangers about neutral topics of conversation, and we have more enduring relationships with people with whom we come into regular contact. Even long-term friendships begin with early judgements in which individuals attempt to assess what someone else is like.

Often people tend to make snap judgements about others and categorize them according to characteristics such as physical appearance, dress, accent, and so on. Indeed initially these features are usually all we have to go on and as such can serve as a basis for future interactions. One body of research on how we form impressions of others has looked at the importance which we assign to the early or first information we receive, in contrast with later or more recent information.

The primacy-recency effect

Imagine you are to interview someone for a job. A woman enters the room and is polite, friendly and of smart appearance. For approximately the first half of the interview she gives an impressive performance and appears highly suited for the job, but as the interview nears its end some less favourable qualities emerge. Do you employ the person? Studies of the primacy-recency effect suggest that you would, for in many cases the primacy effect (first information) prevails.

In an early demonstration of this, Asch (1946) presented subjects with a list of adjectives describing a hypothetical character (e.g., hard-working, friendly, stubborn, etc.). The lists each contained six adjectives, and in one condition subjects were given positive characteristics early in the list and negative traits in the latter half. Subjects in the other condition had negative traits first and positive last. In other words, the lists contained identical adjectives but the order was reversed. Both groups of subjects were then asked to rate the impression they had of the person, and the results showed that those presented with favourable qualities at the beginning of the list rated the character more positively.

Luchins (1957) also found evidence for the **primacy effect** in a study involving a hypothetical person called Jim. Subjects read two paragraphs about the character: one which presented Jim as an extroverted individual (sociable, outgoing) and another which portrayed him as being somewhat introverted (quiet, shy). In order to test the effects of presentation order, one group of subjects were given the extrovert description first followed by the introvert description, while a second group had the reverse of this. After having read the description both groups of subjects are marked to rate Jim on a series of personality dimensions. As the primacy effect would predict, subjects rated Jim as being more extroverted if they read the extrovert description first, but more introverted if they read the introvert description first.

It seems from these studies that first impressions certainly do count, and although these particular studies used hypothetical characters other experiments have confirmed the effect with real people. However, it has also been demonstrated that under certain conditions the primacy effect may be weakened, and instead the **recency effect** occurs. One way in which this happens is if subjects are given a different task to perform in between the two extracts of information.

The recency effect is also found to be stronger, according to Luchins, when concerning interactions with friends and other familiar people; we tend to be more likely to remember our last meeting with them and use this as the basis for our impression of them.

Central traits

This approach to impression formation comes from the work of Asch (1946) who proposed that, when assessing another person, certain types of information are more important in influencing our impressions than others. Asch considered that these central or salient characteristics greatly affected our perceptions of people.

To demonstrate this, Asch used the trait 'warm–cold' and gave two groups of subjects a list of adjectives describing an imaginary person which was identical except that one group's list included the word 'warm', while another group had 'cold' in its place. When asked to choose adjectives from a second list which best suited the character, it was found that subjects in the 'warm' group tended to opt for more favourable traits (friendly, popular, etc.), while the 'cold' group chose quite different words.

It may be argued (as with the previous studies) that asking people to rate a fictitious character is somewhat artificial, but the effect can be equally powerful in more realistic settings. For example, Kelley (1950) successfully demonstrated the ability to influence subjects' perceptions of another individual by assigning a central trait to that person. The setting was an American college in which students were told they were to have a new lecturer (whom none of them had met before). Prior to his arrival, students were given a brief summary of the teacher, and for some of the students this included the description 'rather warm', while for others this was substituted by 'rather cold'. Would this label influence students' perceptions, and later assessment of the teacher? In fact it did, and from an analysis of students' ratings, Kelley discovered that students given the 'warm' trait rated the teacher much more favourably than those given the 'cold' description.

Furthermore, the students' behaviour was noticeably affected, as those in the 'warm' condition interacted more with the teacher in a class discussion.

However, Wishner (1960) criticized the significance of central traits such as 'warm–cold', and argued that their importance is largely affected by the context of the situation: it depends on the kind of other information provided about a person, and also on the type of judgements which a subject is required to make. Under different circumstances, it is argued, central traits may not be as effective. However, as we have seen with the Asch and Kelley studies, even if we only limit their application to particular conditions central traits can be very influential regarding the process of impression formation.

SPOTLIGHT   Do first impressions count?

Think for a moment about a person who is quite well known to you, and cast your mind back (if you can) to when you first met that person. What impression did you first have? Has this been subsequently borne out, or has your view changed? If so, why? Each time we see or meet someone new we often form an immediate impression, even with only limited information, such as what they are wearing, their accent, etc.

Having read the account of factors influencing impression formation, you should now be familiar with some of the experiments which have been carried out to investigate it. Some of the studies cited tended to use descriptions of hypothetical characters which, although advantageous in some respects, do tend to lack realism.

- Imagine you are sitting in a room waiting to meet your new boss (or teacher). Make a list of the things which will influence your impression of them.

- Design an experiment to test the primacy effect which occurs in impression formation. For instance, you could make a tape-recording of a 'character' in which favourable and unfavourable information is given, and then ask subjects to rate the person heard. Better still, if you have access to a video camera, make a short film of an imaginary interview candidate, and then have subjects rate the candidate for his or her 'suitability'.

Other influences on impression formation

Once formed, first impressions may be very resistant to change, and so may serve as a basis for any subsequent judgements made. As a result, impressions may become distorted because assumptions are being made from limited data. One aspect of this concerns stereotyping, which will be considered in more detail later. The further elements which are worth mentioning in this respect are the **halo effect** and self-fulfilling prophecies.

The halo effect

This is the tendency to use one particular piece of information known about an individual and assume that other aspects of that person's behaviour will follow the same pattern. Conversely, a general impression of a person may form the basis of more specific judgements.

This form of bias can be applied positively or negatively. For example, if you form an impression that a person is kind, then you are likely to assume that person possesses other favourable qualities whereas, if you perceive a person as being rude, you might attribute other unfavourable aspects to that person's character.

Self-fulfilling prophecies

Often people perceive others to 'fit' into certain categories on the basis of certain attributes and consequently make expectations of their behaviour. In this way first impressions may help to shape a self-fulfilling prophecy, whereby an impression held of someone may result in that person's behaving in a way which confirms the original impression. Thus if a teacher forms an impression that a student is lazy, the teacher may interact with that student in ways which promote the student's laziness, thereby creating a self-fulfilling prophecy ('told you so!').

One experiment which demonstrated how expectations can influence behaviour was carried out by Snyder, Tanke and Berscheid (1977); in it, male students were asked to participate in telephone conversations with female students. Some of the males were led to believe that the female they were speaking to was physically attractive, while other males were given the impression that their partner in the conversation was unattractive (in fact there was no such difference between the two groups of women).

When the conversations were analysed, it was noted that males speaking to 'attractive' females were much friendlier, livelier and generally outgoing than their male counterparts with 'unattractive' partners. Furthermore, differences in female behaviour were observed; independent judges rated the 'attractive' women as more interesting, sociable and humorous. Apparently the males' expectations (of an attractive partner) had influenced how they interacted, which in turn had elicited more positive responses from the females they spoke to.

The tendency to categorize people and make certain assumptions about them can also operate on a larger scale. When this occurs, it may lead to the formation of prejudice and consequent discrimination against whole groups of people.

5.3 Prejudice and Discrimination

As we have seen, people are often prepared to go beyond what they actually know about individuals or groups in an effort to categorize them. Social psychologists have recognized this, and contributed substantial research that illustrates how we all (whether professionals or lay persons) make inferences about others from limited information (embodied in an area known as 'implicit personality theory').

Stereotypes often arise following an initial observation or interaction with an individual. For example, after a brief (and unfavourable) encounter with a traffic warden, you may infer all other traffic wardens share the same qualities. Furthermore, other processes such as the self-fulfilling prophecy may take effect because subsequent encounters with members of this group may lead you to interact with them in a way which is influenced by the initial interaction (i.e., you may expect them to be unpleasant and behave with the individual accordingly, which in turn will elicit a negative reaction from them). In this way the unfavourable stereotype is reinforced.

While there is a tendency to assume that stereotyping is always a negative process, positive inferences may also be made, again on limited information: that is, favourable informations leads to positive stereotypes.

[Another feature of stereotypes is that they are based upon false assumptions, which means that they may lead to the formation of prejudice. For example, if a person is assumed to have particular attributes, and if these attributes are negative ones, than there may be a tendency to perceive individuals belonging to this group unfavourably.]

The term prejudice is derived from the act of 'prejudging', and may be defined as an unfavourable, negative attitude towards a particular group of people, based on negative characteristics which are assumed to be common to all members of that group (Reber, 1985). Thus a person may stereotype members of ethnic minorities and infer particular traits about them, which in turn will lead to the same person becoming prejudiced against members of such groups.

As we discussed in the previous chapter, attitudes may have several components. Regarding prejudice, a related concept, is that of discrimination which may be interpreted as the behavioural component of a prejudice. Thus to discriminate against someone is to behave negatively towards them because of a prejudice which you hold against that person and others like them. For example, if a person is prevented from getting a job because of the ethnic group he or she belongs to, then this is called racial discrimination. In an attempt to illustrate the main features of prejudice and discrimination we will consider two issues of importance in society: racism and sexism.

Racism

This is said to occur when prejudice and discrimination is shown towards individuals or groups because of their ethnic or racial background. Unfortunately, this is still a common feature within many societies, and exists at many levels. In Britain, prejudiced attitudes may be found particularly against West Indians, Pakistanis and Indians, often based on ignorance concerning these ethnic groups. This may involve discrimination in terms of jobs or acts of violence against such groups. Partly as a result of racial violence in schools the largest teaching union, the National Union of Teachers, recently proposed a series of guidelines regarding policies in schools which sets out to oppose racism of any kind.

Racism is also displayed at a broader level in various countries around the world. In South Africa, for instance, the black majority are actively discriminated against by the ruling whites. This results in, for example, blacks inhabiting unsuitable and often overcrowded dwellings separate from the designated 'white' areas. Employment and other aspects of life are similarly poorer in quality. Furthermore, this policy of racial segregation, or apartheid, is maintained and enforced by the white government.

Such treatment of ethnic minorities often results from stereotyping. This has been demonstrated in a number of studies in which subjects are asked to choose adjectives most fitting particular groups of people. Blacks, for example, were attributed qualities of laziness and ignorance, while Jews were considered materialistic and grasping (in Radford and Govier, 1982).

Racial prejudice, like other attitudes, may be learnt from various sources. Greenberg (1972), for example, found that white children with little everyday contact of blacks formed most of their views on this group from how blacks were portrayed on television. This reminds us of the powerful influence television may have; negative or positive portrayals can lead to stereotyping, prejudice and discrimination.

Sexism

This may be defined as prejudice or discrimination towards individuals or groups because of their sex. Although technically this could apply to both males and females, it is predominantly towards females that sexist views operate.

As with racism, false assumptions and generalizations may form the basis for how the group (in this case women) are perceived and subsequently treated. If, for example, an employer holds the view that women are weak and submissive, that employer may discriminate against women applying for particular jobs. This situation is further reinforced by the fact that in the various professions the majority of senior management positions are held by men.

Several studies have demonstrated discrimination against women in terms of their suitability for employment. Fidell (1970), for instance, sent out a number of character descriptions to heads of psychology departments at American colleges. The heads were asked to select from the descriptions those people considered most suitable for the position of professor within the department. The descriptions were identical in terms of qualification, academic background, and so on, but some forms referred to the candidate as male, and others as female. Assessment of the results showed that male candidates were offered better positions.

Although this study was carried out in the 1970s the sexism which it clearly illustrates is still rife today, although the situation may be gradually improving. Before going on to look at ways in which prejudice and discrimination may be reduced, we shall briefly consider the causes.

5.4 Causes of Prejudice and Discrimination

Several attempts have been made to explain the presence of prejudice and discrimination in society. We shall examine three possible explanations which are by no means mutually exclusive: that is, they may operate individually for whatever reason, or simultaneously.

1. Economic and political factors: this view emphasizes that prejudice stems from economic and political conditions, so when resources are limited or conflict builds up (e.g., as a result of territorial behaviour) prejudice and discrimination tend to result and are directed at those groups considered responsible, or in some way involved.

These factors often have a historical emphasis, too. For example, negative attitudes towards blacks in America are thought to be linked with the existence of slavery in the eighteenth century.

As another illustration, Aronson (1980) cites the introduction of Chinese immigrants into America for railway construction. The economic climate at that time (mid-nineteenth century) was good because jobs were plentiful and so there was no ill-feeling between the two groups. However, when construction work ended, jobs were more scarce and attitudes towards the Chinese now changed, with a tendency to view them in terms of negative stereotypes.

Prejudice may also have a political basis when conflicts arise over territorial boundaries. For example, in the Middle East disputes between the Arabs and Jews have brought about negative feelings and frustrations between each group, while in Britain, the presence of the British army in Northern Ireland has produced feelings of deep resentment by those opposed to it.

2. Frustration and 'scapegoating': in an earlier chapter we considered some explanations for aggression, one of which was the presence of frustration. It has also been suggested that frustration is a contributing factor in prejudice and discrimination. Allport (1958) considered that the build-up of frustration produced negative and hostile tendencies which would find an outlet against ethnic minorities.

In terms of prejudice, this view emphasizes that individuals experience frustration (perhaps because they are unemployed) which results in hostile feelings. However, because the cause of their frustration is not easily identifiable, their aggression is then displaced on to less powerful individuals or groups: i.e., this group is made responsible for the individuals' predicament. This is known as 'scapegoating'. Historically, several ethnic minorities have been used as scapegoats, such as the lynching of blacks in the American South in the late nineteenth century, and the persecution of Jews in Nazi Germany.

An early empirical study which demonstrates the role of frustration in prejudice was conducted by Miller and Bugelski in 1948. In it, participants were asked to report their feelings about minority groups, following which some of them were subjected to mild frustration (given difficult tasks to do instead of watching a film). A control group was also asked to rate minority groups, but without any form of frustration afterwards. All subjects were then asked to give their views about minorities again, and those in the frustrated condition displayed a marked increase in prejudiced opinions compared with the control.

3. Personality and prejudice: this view places the cause of prejudice with the individual and postulates that some people have a predisposition to be prejudiced because of certain personality characteristics which they have. This idea is based upon the work of Adorno and his colleagues (1950), in which they identified what became known as the 'authoritarian personality'.

Originally the team began to look at anti-Semitism (prejudice and discrimination against Jewish people) in Nazi Germany but, after moving to America, they extended their work and interviewed over 1000 white, middle-class Americans using various tests to ascertain their views towards minority groups.

One concept of interest was that of ethnocentrism: the tendency to view one's own ethnic group as setting the standard (i.e., being superior) with which to compare the practices and principles of others. The ethnocentric individual shows a dislike towards all those members of 'out-groups', and indeed rejects everything outside his or her own ethnic group.

Here, then, was a basis for prejudice which Adorno sought to measure. One particular form which was devised determined the extent of authoritarianism in an individual: the F-scale. In response to items such as 'Obedience and respect for authority are the most important virtues children should learn', the researchers found that people with a high score on the scale had a negative view of all minority groups; that is, it appeared prejudice was not specific in that people were not specifically opposed to Jewish or black people, for example.

Following lengthy interviews with subjects, Adorno *et al*, were able to link such attitudes with childhood experiences and upbringing, which they concluded led to the formation of the 'authoritarian personality'. Such individuals are characterized by: a rigid system of beliefs and in tolerance of weakness (both in themselves and other people) and an unusually high degree of respect for authority. Furthermore they believe that status within society is of great importance, to the extent that they feel superior to those people of lower status and have the right to expect subservience from them.

How do people come to hold such views? Concerning childhood experiences, it was noticed (again through interviews) that the child-rearing practices adopted by parents had a significant influence. The use of primitive methods such as severe discipline and the conditional use of love and affection by parents in order to gain obedience from their children was implicated. All of this results in a child who is emotionally insecure, and to a large extent highly dependent on its parents, while at the same time harbouring an unconscious hostility towards them. These qualities make for an adult who has a respect for authority and power, but who also has 'bottled up' feelings of anger and fear, which find a release via displacement on to minority groups.

Aronson (1980) points out, however, that this research was based on correlational data, which means that while there appears to be a significant relationship between upbringing and authoritarianism, we cannot conclude that the one causes the other.

With this in mind, this perspective has still make a useful contribution towards discovering factors involved in prejudice and has received substantial support both inside and outside the laboratory (see Gross, 1987).

The three approaches mentioned cannot fully explain all forms of prejudice, and indeed a number of other views exist. A different perspective emphasizes sociocultural factors as being influential, including rising populations in cities and urban areas, increases in technology, and so on, which have led to fewer jobs. Thus shifts in the morphology of society are seen as bringing about prejudice against ethnic minorities in urban areas.

Conformity to **'social norms'** has also been attributed as a potential cause of prejudice. This view puts forward the notion that, depending on the prevailing norms, an individual may be inclined to 'follow suit' and conform to the majority view, whether this involves becoming more prejudiced or less prejudiced towards another group.

The phenomenon of prejudice is a complex one and, as we have seen, may operate both at the individual and societal level. Despite the diversity of potential explanations, knowledge of the causes of prejudice may guide us towards achieving its reduction. It is to this issue to which we turn next.

SPOTLIGHT   There's no need to shout

In our discussion of prejudice and discrimination, we looked at two particular aspects, those of racism and sexism, which tend to represent the more 'well known' issues in this area. However, a number of other such '-isms' are worthy of consideration about individuals who are unfairly treated because of characteristics which they possess (e.g. disabled persons).

The elderly also tend to suffer from negative attitudes and behaviour imposed upon them. Common misconceptions include poor hearing, retarded intellectual capacity and diminished sex drive. Whereas in many so-called 'primitive' cultures elderly individuals are accorded deep respect for their wisdom and experience, in our own society 'ageism' all too often predominates.

• List the reasons why people may hold such 'ageist' views.

• Suggest ways in which prejudice and discrimination towards the elderly could be reduced.

• Apart from racism, sexism and ageism, list any other characteristics (or groups of people) that are potential targets of negative attitudes.

5.5   Reducing Prejudice and Discrimination

As we have observed, individuals may form a prejudiced viewpoint against others for many reasons. Once formed this prejudice may be highly resistant to change, but under certain circumstances unfavourable attitudes to others can be reduced.

Interactions based on equality

It is obviously not enough simply to be in contact with people to bring about our liking of them. What is more important is the context in which the interaction takes place. If every time you meet a member of another ethnic group it is under unfavourable circumstances, which presents them negatively, then this may simply serve to confirm your expectations and ideas of that person (which as we have said, may generalize to their entire group or culture).

All too often in the past minority groups have been portrayed as subservient, lower-class citizens, employed in degrading and menial tasks of employment, such as servants (Aronson, 1980). One way to reduce prejudice, therefore, is to have contact between groups on a basis which serves to promote equality and respect. As mentioned in an earlier chapter, television may be influential in this respect; increasingly nowadays we are seeing minority group members in roles which present them favourably. This policy of equal representation needs to be continued.

Another factor regarding equality of contact concerns desegregation whereby previously separated groups are brought together. (The system which operates in present-day South Africa is maintained by policies of racial segregation.) However, while desegregation may seem like the perfect solution, in practice the results are often discouraging. Aronson (1980) claims that often desegregation under the wrong conditions may even be detrimental towards racial harmony because, in many cases (such as with school-children), the contact between white children and ethnic minority children is not on an equal footing. What results in these circumstances is often an increase in hostility between groups which, according to Aronson, is due to a loss of self-esteem by those in the minority.

It is hardly surprising that this occurs: schools tend to be institutions which promote white, middle-class values, which may be totally incongruous to an Asian or West Indian child. In a review of the area, Stephan (1978) was unable to find any studies that showed increases in self-esteem among black children following disegregation; some 25 per cent of the studies actually found a decrease in self-esteem in these children.

However, with many of these studies, it may have been that desegregation only commenced in the middle and later school years, a time when individuals (regardless of ethnic group) are particularly defensive and eager to gain self-esteem and approval in the eyes of others. Succesful removal of intergroup hostility often requires much more effort at this point. Thus, desegregation is best when it commences from the early school years onwards; peer interactions between very young children set a worthy example for all of us to follow.

Counter-stereotyping

In effect, this aspect is related to equality because it concerns the kinds of experience we have of others: that is, so long as we only come into contact with minority groups under unfavourable conditions, then our stereotypes are simply reinforced. This applies to both racist and sexist attitudes.

On the reduction of sexism, Bem (1983) argues that parents can influence their children's attitudes from an early age by socializing them in a manner which counter-acts sex-role stereotypes. Apart from teaching them differences in anatomy, Bem advocates that parents can also ensure children are informed of the misleading presentations of the sexes in the media, and so on. In this way young children learn that males and females are essentially similar, and ideally later will realize that a person's sex is not a basis for prejudice or discrimination.

Furthermore, there is no reason why the suggestions which Bem (1983) made concerning parental influence in non-sexist attitudes could not be extended to incorporate the wider issue of racial equality. For example, parents may serve as effective models when interacting with minority groups. By such means, when children enter school, they already possess a balanced attitude, and one which will influence their perceptions of others in our multi-racial society.

Fostering cooperation

Prejudice has been shown to decline in environments where cooperation between groups is encouraged. If two groups are set a task which requires contributions from both sides for its successful completion, then conflict may disappear. Aronson (1980) refers to this as mutual interdependence.

Several studies have attempted to create situations involving cooperation, mostly with children. Aronson *et al.* (1978) devised a classroom method, which they called the jigsaw technique. In it, groups of students cooperate and work together to provide an overall learning experience. This makes individuals dependent upon each other for the completion of information, because each child has only one section of the material. However, the researchers found that, initially, children tended to behave competitively (after all, much of the educational system encourages competition between students), and it was only after a while, when children realized this strategy was pointless, that cooperation was generated.

Such techniques, though, have been shown to work. Several researchers have confirmed the beneficial effects of the jigsaw method in promoting intergroup relationships. If helping and cooperation is emphasized and made part of the task, then favourable attitudes between different ethnic backgrounds result. In addition, the individual members taking part in the exercise tend to increase their own self-esteem as compared with children in classes adopting more traditional methods and practices. Teachers also gave favourable reports of the outcome and continued to use the technique in their work (Aronson *et. al.* 1978).

One of the most famous field experiments in this context was carried out by Sherif and his colleagues in 1961. Known as 'The Robber's Cave Experiment', it provides a clear illustration of the creation of intergroup conflict and cooperation. The subjects were 22 white, middle-class American boys (aged 11–12) who arrived individually at summer camp, each not knowing any of the others. The researchers then randomly assigned the boys to one of two groups, following which each group was given tasks to promote cooperation within that group, such as erecting tents. This in effect produced an in-group solidarity and cohesiveness, strengthened all the more when each group gave itself a name.

One group of boys called themselves the 'Rattlers', while the others became the 'Eagles'. The researchers observed how definite codes of behaviour emerged, with each having their own rules of conduct, leaders and so on. Up to this point in the experiment, neither group was aware of the other's existence (this had been manipulated by the researchers as part of the study).

The next stage changed this; the researchers sought to introduce elements of competitiveness between the two groups of boys. This was achieved by bringing the two groups together and arranging competitive tournaments between them with prizes for the winning team. From them on, each group resorted to name-calling of the others, fights broke out and raids were carried out on the 'enemy' huts.

For the third phase, the researchers attempted to resolve the intergroup conflict. At first they introduced activities such as going to see a film together, but contact between the groups only strengthened their hostility towards each other. Efforts to stress cooperation and respect went unheeded and meetings arranged with group leaders failed to achieve positive results.

Finally, Sherif *et al.* introduced 'superordinate goals': those which can only be solved by everyone taking part. For example, the researchers disrupted the camp's water supply, which necessitated the boys' combined efforts to restore it. The breakdown of hostility was not instantaneous, but gradually, after various similar 'joint tasks', intergroup conflict reduced. Through mutual cooperation and communication, the two groups came to appreciate each other. Friendships formed between previous rivals, and most of the boys elected to travel home together on the same bus. Sherif *et al.* (1961) concluded that working together on superordinate goals had effectively reduced conflict between the two groups.

Returning to the issue of prejudice reduction, while the studies discussed serve to illustrate possible strategies in its elimination, critics have questioned the extent to which generalization occurs. That is, although conflict and negative feelings may be reduced in specific settings and with particular individuals, this attitude change often does not go beyond the situation to minority groups in the wider sense. Clearly there is much to gain from these studies, but prejudice and discrimination will only be undermined in the long term by tackling it at the broader level.

In the next section we consider factors involved in liking and attraction. As we have seen, negative or unfavourable attitudes toward others can arise for various reasons, but what influences our attraction to other people?

5.6 Interpersonal Attraction

Consider for a moment your circle of friends and acquaintances. How did your friendships with these people arise? Why are they liked? Although most of us interact with people on a daily basis, there are obvious differences in the quality of these interactions. Some people may simply be work colleagues, not necessarily liked or disliked as such. We also form more enduring relationships with particular people, who may provide a source of comfort, advice or simply company. Whatever the gains from these relationships, people show a need to affiliate with others at some time in their lives. In addition to our circle of friends we may form more intimate bonds with specific individuals: our life partners.

Why be with others at all?

Human beings obviously get 'something' from spending time with others. Many animals too, live in groups because this arrangement provides advantages which would not be found if leading a solitary existence. True, many people value a few moments of privacy, when being alone allows them to collect their thoughts or simply do as they please. However, there is a difference between being alone and 'loneliness'; the latter implies a sense of unhappiness and lack of belonging. Being with others provides a welcome 'tonic' to this situation.

Several reasons for affiliation have been suggested. Amongst them, and related to loneliness, is the idea that associating with others reduces anxiety. In an effort to test this, Schachter (1959) told subjects they were to receive electric shocks as part of an experiment. Some subjects were told the shocks would be painful (thereby instilling in them high levels of anxiety) whereas others were told they would be painless.

In fact, the study was not concerned with electric shocks because subjects were then asked to wait whilst the apparatus was made ready. All of the subjects were given the choice of waiting alone or with others, and of those in the high-anxiety condition, 62 per cent preferred to sit with others, while only 33 per cent of those in the low-anxiety conditions gave this request.

Other explanations for affiliation include the notion that being with others provides us with an opportunity to evaluate ourselves; for instance, by comparing ourselves with other people. This is known as social comparison. A different perspective is offered by social-exchange theory, which suggests that people tend to enter relationships and interactions because they expect some sort of return that will be to their advantage.

With more intimate relationships, these factors may still operate, at least initially, but apart from the 'benefits' gained from contact with people, what is it that attracts us to others? A substantial amount of research has been gathered on interpersonal attraction in the last twenty or so years. Several important factors have been identified, some of which will now be examined.

Physical attractiveness

Physical attractiveness has been shown to be a major determinant in influencing our attraction to others. Indeed there exists in our society what may be called the 'beauty industry', which encourages people to create an attractive appearance by the use of clothing, cosmetics and other accessories. Such industries represent a multi-million pound concern, which further illustrates the importance that we attribute to 'looks'. With this, however, comes the underlying assumption that 'attractive' and 'good' are one and the same, as discussed earlier with reference to stereotyping and the halo effect. Images presented by the media reinforce these stereotypes.

A famous experiment investigating the role of physical attractiveness was carried out by Walster *et al.* (1966), in which they arranged a 'computer dance' for college students. Prior to the event students were asked to fill in a personality assessment, after which they were informed that a computer would select a partner for them, although in reality the pairing was done randomly. When the students arrived, independent judges rated the attractiveness of each person, and later, in order to find out what each student thought of their 'date' for the evening, they were asked to complete an anonymous questionnaire. When the results were analysed it became apparent that physical attractiveness was the most important factor governing how much one person liked another, as well as predicting the likelihood that couples would see each other in the future. Qualities such as intelligence and personality were found to be of little importance.

Attractiveness may be important for a number of reasons, one of which suggests that being in the presence of an attractive person gives prestige and status to the individual concerned: that is, a man creates a good impression on others if he is seen with an attractive female. Does this work for females? Apparently not. In one study, Bar-Tal and Saxe (1976) presented subjects with pictures of male and female couples who differed in terms of attractiveness. When asked to attribute characteristics to the supposed husbands and wives shown, subjects rated unattractive males more favourably (e.g. higher intelligence and income, etc.) if they were paired with attractive females. However, unattractive women with attractive men tended to be judged solely on their physical appearance.

Despite the benefits gained (at least for males), a phenomenon known as the *matching hypothesis* suggests that people are attracted to individuals who are approximately equal to themselves in terms of attractiveness, as opposed to individuals who are more or less attractive.

This hypothesis has been confirmed. Murstein (1972), for instance, looked at the relative attractiveness of the partners in married couples and found that on the whole they were equally physically attractive. To test this, look at pictures of married couples yourself. Consider the level of physical attractiveness, and whether or not they are a 'good match'.

We mentioned earlier that our society places great emphasis on beauty and attractiveness, a feature which is true of other cultures. However, cultural differences may be found regarding what is considered physically attractive. In some African tribes, the males paint their face and body in an elaborate manner, and display to the females of the tribe in order to attract one as a mate. The ritual consists of various kinds of facial gestures and 'face-pulling' which emphasizes the decoration, the idea being that the more eye-catching the display, the more successful will be the result.

Facial decoration was also a method practised by the Ainu people (once natives of Japan). In this culture, young girls would have ornate moustaches tattooed on their face, as without it they were considered less attractive to Ainu males seeking a wife.

Familiarity

There is a popular saying that 'familiarity breeds contempt', implying that the more contact you have with someone, the less you come to like them. In some cases this may be true, particularly if a dislike for someone already exists or if negative stereotypes are reinforced by repeated exposure to the individual or group concerned.

However, in contrast to this view is the notion that familiarity and physical proximity (known as propinquity) lead to liking. Physical proximity to others permits regular contact, which in turn makes it generally likely that friendship will result. Support for this was provided by Nahemow and Lawton (1975) who observed social interactions among residents of a tower block and found more evidence of friendships between those living on the same floor than between people on different floors. Presumably, their initial nearness helps form a common link which, once established, is easily maintained. By the same token, if a dislike is taken to someone, we tend to avoid them, thereby making a compromise unlikely.

Mutual liking

Mutual or reciprocal liking suggests that we like people who like us in return, and conversely that we dislike people who appear to dislike us. This idea may be closely associated with self-esteem, since it is comforting and satisfying to receive approval from others, whom we then respond to in similar ways. This seems particularly true when we are placed in a vulnerable or insecure position. For example, Walster (1965) arranged for female students to take a so-called personality test. Whilst waiting outside an office to receive the results each student was approached individually by an attractive young man (in fact, a confederate) who made polite conversation and then asked her for a date. Shortly afterwards the subject was called into the office to be given the test results. For half of the women this was designed to test their self-esteem by presenting a positive and favourable summary, whereas the other half were led to believe their results portrayed them in a negative manner, thus lowering their self-esteem. Before leaving the office, the experimenter asked each student to indicate their liking for various people, including the young man in the waiting room. The rating for this person was found to be higher in those students who received unfavourable test results, suggesting that the lowering of their self-esteem led them to need reassurance. As this was provided by the young man, they reciprocated by rating him more positively.

Interesting though such findings may be, we may criticize the way in which these and similar studies are carried out. For example, in this particular experiment some students are made to feel temporarily inferior, and are also 'emotionally deceived' to some extent by the confederate just for the purpose of the study.

Similarity

It is often the case that our friends share similar beliefs and attitudes to us. Indeed, this may have been one reason for becoming friends in the first place. For example, non-smokers tend, by and large, to have non-smoking friends, and supporters of the same football team may have this common feature as one basis for their liking of each other.

Research confirms this link. For example, Byrne and Nelson (1965) found a significant relationship between attraction and similar attitudes when subjects were asked to rate people whose attitudes on various issues were known to them.

In a large-scale study, Kandel (1978) analysed the views and attitudes expressed by nearly 2000 teenagers and observed a number of similarities in opinions between friends. Furthermore, 'best friends' appeared to be similar in particular ways such as age, ethnic group and class at school. A recent study by Piner and Berg (1988) found that couples use a knowledge of similarity gained early in the interaction as a sound basis for whether the relationship may develop further. Whereas it was thought that intimate relationships take time, Piner and Berg concluded that knowing the other person is available combined with evidence of similarity may be sufficient for intimacy and familiarity to develop very early in the relationship.

However, the effects of similarity need not always lead to liking. For instance, Aronson (1980) describes a study which he carried out where subjects indicated greater liking of others who had expressed liking of them in return, even though such people had *dissimilar* attitudes of their own. He suggests that, although we usually tend to like people who share our values, people who find us attractive despite differences of opinion are sometimes liked more because we assume that they like us as people, not just because of what we think.

Complementarity

Although as we have seen that there is ample evidence to suggest a link between similarity and attraction, another perspective concerns the attraction of opposites. Some people in relationships tend to have complementary qualities, so that when combined a harmonious relationship results. Most couples have differences in some way, whether it be their individual interests or general disposition. For example, one person might be assertive and bold, whereas the other is more humble and easy-going. Winch (1958) carried out detailed studies of people in long-term relationships, such as married couples, and found that in many instances a complementary set of characteristics was evident (e.g., one partner being dominant and the other more submissive).

However, a significant factor seems to be the length of relationship (i.e., how long the couple have been together) because when couples are first becoming acquainted the overwhelming evidence confirms the importance of similarity (Deaux and Wrightsman, 1984).

Perceived competence

People tend to be attracted to those who appear capable, knowledgeable and intelligent, as opposed to those who are not. This may be because we infer other qualities to be part of the person, too: for example, if we are told that someone is intelligent and witty, we might expect that person to be good looking as well.

In addition, we may gain some satisfaction from being with people who demonstrate competence in what they do, although there does appear to be a point at which this no longer applies. If we consider the idea of social comparison mentioned earlier, then continually being in the presence of individuals who are 'always right' may begin to make us feel inferior. Thus a competent person may become more endearing in our eyes if he or she occasionally shows signs of imperfection. Aronson (1980) cites a good example of this which took place in America in 1961. The then President, John Kennedy, was responsible for an unsuccessful attempt to invade Cuba but, following this event, opinion polls actually reported a rise in his popularity among Americans. Perhaps this display of incompetence made Kennedy more 'human' and consequently more likeable.

In an effort to test this notion, Aronson, Willerman and Floyd, (1966) conducted an experiment in which subjects listened to a tape recording of candidates for a college quiz show called 'College Bowl'. Altogether four tape conditions were devised on which a 'candidate' was interviewed for a prospective place on the show.

The tapes were designed in such a way that the student either sounded very superior and highly competent or just of average ability. Furthermore an 'accident' was created where the candidate was heard to knock over a cup of coffee. The conditions were arranged as shown in Table 5.1. Next, subjects were asked to rate the candidates in terms of the impression they created, and how likeable they seemed. The results were as follows:

> Condition 1: most highly rated
> Condition 2: rated in second place

Condition 3: least highly rated
Condition 4: rated third place

These findings support the view that, although competence is valued, people are frequently perceived as more likeable if they are competent but occasionally make an error. Aronson *et al.* (1966) termed this characteristic 'the pratfall effect'.

Table 5.1   *Variables in experiment by Aronson* et al. *(1966)*

Condition 1	Condition 2	Condition 3	Condition 4
Superior student	Superior student	Average student	Average student
having	without	having	without
accident	accident	accident	accident

As we have seen, interpersonal attraction is a highly complex process, and many of the factors discussed above may operate exclusively or together, depending on the context of the interaction. A knowledge of the factors ought to allow us to predict whether person A would like person B in any given situation, but often a diversity of other elements impinges which makes such a task extremely difficult. All we can say is that the characteristics examined make attraction more likely.

Human relationships present a fascinating topic worthy of extensive study. We are already in a position to understand and appreciate many of the reasons for affiliation and attraction. Current developments are beginning to shed light on areas which were once considered 'out of bounds' concerning the realms of scientific study, such as the concept of romantic love.

5.7   Questions and Exercises

1. Discuss the factors which influence impression formation.
2. List the stereotypes held for the following:
   (a) students;
   (b) bank managers;
   (c) traffic wardens;
   (d) vegetarians;
   (e) sports car drivers;
   (f) psychologists!

3. Design a poster to promote racial equality.
4. Identify examples of sexism from advertisements and suggest how they may be changed to reduce such an impression.
5. Why do people like other? Discuss with reference to empirical studies.
6. Design and carry out a questionnaire on interpersonal attraction (for example, you might compare the important factors for different age groups).

6 Perception

6.1 Introduction

A student called Steve whom we know always begins his psychology essays by stating the first principles. One of his favourite opening sentences begins: 'Ever since the dawning of the age of mankind . . .'. In fact Steve has a particular fondness for quoting the ancient Greeks in his essays and his position is that most of our current ideas about the world have their roots in those times. For instance, in 5 BC the philosopher Heraclitus proposed that knowledge comes to each of us 'through the door of our senses'. In other words, all that we can know about the world around us is what we can learn directly about it, using our bodily sensations. Such a view is also associated with the European philosophers of the 'empiricist' school, dating from the seventeenth century onwards. One of these, Thomas Hobbes, believed that all the concepts of the human mind 'cometh with the organs of sense'. Another philosopher called John Locke described the infant's mind as being a blank page (*tabula rasa*) on which life's experiences become written. The argument put forward by the **empiricists** is deceptively simple: it is that we can only understand of external reality what our senses can detect of it. Therefore, **sensation** becomes the primary source of all human knowledge.

The way in which a rudimentary sensation turns into more complex understanding was assumed to be simply a matter of prolonged and repeated experiences which the individual has with an object. Developing our knowledge of any stimulus object and its meanings was known to the philosophers as 'associationism'. For instance, having encountered a rose a number of times in your life this flower will have evoked many sensations in your mind associated with it. These associations will together form a more abstract concept of that flower whenever you bring it to mind. The smell of the rose becomes associated with its velvety touch, an evocation of summer months, verdant lawns, and so forth.

Considering the emphasis which is placed upon the act of sensation being basic to the growth of human knowledge it is hardly surprising that the early psychologists of the nineteenth century devoted so much time to investigating how the human senses work. One of these early pioneers was Wilhelm Wundt, who argued that sensations contained both a 'quantity' element, such as hardness, coldness or size, and a 'quality' element, such as dangerous, attractive or good. For instance, if you cut yourself on a knife you may think of all knives as being dangerous implements. The physical property of sharpness may therefore take on the psychological property of dangerousness. Wundt called this product a *vorstellung*, by which he meant the effect that our previous encounters with a stimulus has when it combines with the immediate impact it makes on our senses. The manner in which present and past experiences culminate in our perception of a stimulus object is the topic of this chapter.

We begin by describing the physical and physiological events which are collectively called 'sensation': that is, the ways in which the body responds to energy impinging upon it from the environment. This section of the chapter is necessarily technical and unless the reader is particularly concerned with the biological principles of perception it is possible to skip these pages without a loss of understanding of the section on the general issues of perception. In this case it is possible to pick up the story at section 6.6. We shall later examine perception as a purely psychological event: for instance, by considering the ways in which our state of mind may influence what we make of our immediate environment. Finally, we briefly consider the **Gestalt** theory of perception.

6.2   Classification of Sensory Receptor Systems

One way in which the senses can be classified is according to the source of the stimulus to which they normally respond. *Distance receptors* receive information from a distance: in the case of light, sound or smell, for example, energy travels from the stimulus itself through space before reaching our senses of vision, hearing and olfaction. *Skin receptors* lie on the surface of the body and respond to a stimulus which makes direct contact with us, such as the senses of touch, temperature and taste. *Deep receptors* lie buried inside the structure of the body and they respond to changes in our internal 'environment' such as body posture ('proprioceptors'), or other biological states such as body temperature, levels of blood sugar, and so on (the so-called 'entroceptors').

Sensory receptors may be gathered together forming a sensory organ (such as the eye, ear or tongue) or else remain scattered over the body surface (such as the receptors for temperature and touch). When receptors are gathered into a sense organ they may influence each other as occurs in the instance of 'lateral inhibition', which will be discussed later in relation to the visual system. Briefly, this is where one receptor inhibits the activity of its neighbours whenever a stimulus is detected. The outcome of this interaction between neighbouring receptors in a sensory organ is more complex than that which occurs in other sensory systems. Sensory organs are, therefore, highly complex systems and they do not make a straightforward response to each stimulus encountered. In simple organisms the senses often play a part in controlling automatic behaviour patterns – such as reflex movements to or from strong light, or away from loud noise – but in humans and other complex animals sensation is only a small part of much more complicated information processing systems.

6.3   Principles Common to Sensory Systems

Receptor potential

A sensory receptor produces a response to a stimulus which is proportional to the amount of energy it receives. The larger the amount of energy received (e.g., the brighter the light) then the greater will be the response or output of that receptor. Therefore sensory receptors tend to produce what is termed an 'analogue' response to a stimulus, such that the size of their output signal depends upon the size of the input energy.

Generator potential

Sensory receptors do not have direct connections to the brain. They relay their responses via sensory neurones (see Chapter 15 for description of a **neurone**, or nerve cell). A sensory neurone carries information from the receptor itself to the spinal cord and from there upwards to enter the brain. Usually many sensory receptors converge on, or share, each sensory neurone. Sensory neurones themselves do not behave like the receptors in that their response to input is not an analogue one. Rather, and in common with most other neurones in the nervous system, the sensory neurone makes a 'digital' response. You can think of an ordinary electric light switch as making a response of this type. If you do not apply sufficient strength to the switch then the light does not come on. It is as though your inadequate input to the switch is being ignored altogether. However, provided that you apply sufficient strength at the second attempt, the light will come on. Furthermore, it makes no difference how much force you apply to the light switch over and above that needed to make it work; striking it hard does not make the light come on brighter! In the same way, if the overall output of the various sensory receptors which connect to a sensory neurone is great enough, then it makes a digital response. Conversely, if the sensory receptors do not make a large enough aggregate input to their sensory neurone then it makes no response at all. When the response has been produced in the sensory neurone it is then termed the 'generator potential'.

Adapting and non-adapting sensory receptors

When a stimulus is applied constantly to a sensory receptor then the level at which that receptor responds may or may not decline. In adapting receptors a constant stimulus may eventually produce no response from them, even though its first appearance did. There are three possible types of sensory receptor depending upon how they respond to a constant stimulus.

1. *Slow-adapting sensory receptors*; with these, the response or output of the receptor gradually diminishes over a number of seconds after the constant stimulus first appears.
2. *Fast-adapting sensory receptors* cease to respond often within a second of the application of the constant stimulus.
3. *Non-adapting receptors* are those whose output continues for as long as the stimulus is present. Pain receptors seem to be of this type.

Range fractionation

Each sensory receptor, whether or not it forms a sensory organ, will only respond to a part of the total range of energy available in the environment. For instance, in the case of the eye some of the sensory receptors (in this case called 'cones') are sensitive to red, some to green and some to blue light. None of the cones respond to all three colours and this selective part of the sensory range is referred to as 'fractionation'. This principle is illustrated in Figure 6.1 in which one other important idea is shown. This idea is that even where we possess sensory receptors for dealing with a particular energy form such as light, humans are by no

84

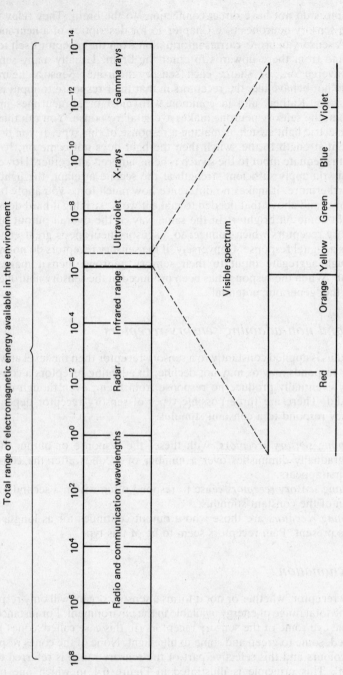

Figure 6.1 The visible spectrum

means able to detect the whole range of that energy modality. Indeed, even though humans have a relatively good sense of sight we are still only able to deal with a tiny amount of the potential energy available to us in the environment. Other animals are capable of detecting energy which it is beyond human capacity to sense, and that is why the high pitched dog-whistle is silent to us but not to dogs.

Of the entire range of light energy (i.e., electromagnetism) available in the environment, humans are only able to detect a tiny portion. Different animal species have different capabilities in this regard. For instance bees are able to 'see' ultraviolet light and this enables them to detect the sun's direction on a cloud-covered day. The human visual system is only able to respond to the range shown in Figure 6.1 because the individual receptors of the eye cover only this narrow energy span. Even within this small range each receptor is able to respond to only a fraction of the visible spectrum.

6.4   The Human Visual System

The retina of the mammalian eye receives light which has been focused on it by the lens (see Figure 6.2). The purpose of the retina is to transform the energy it receives into a form that can be used by the nervous system. This process is called

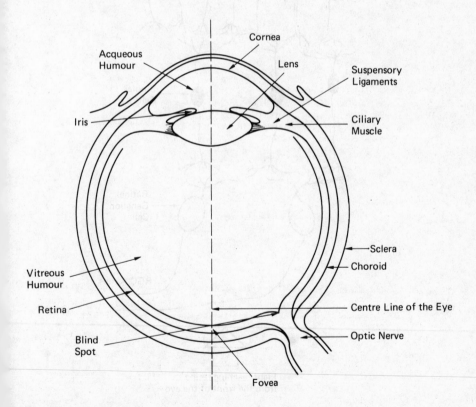

Figure 6.2 The human eye

energy **transduction** and it is achieved by the photoreceptors of the eye which are called the rods and cones. Rods and cones are situated beneath several layers of cells, as is shown in Figure 6.3. Light must therefore pass through these inner cell layers as well as through blood vessels and other components of the eye before it reaches the receptors. The pathways to the brain are shown in Figure 6.4.

The rods and cones possess substances which respond to light by undergoing chemical changes. The end result of these changes is an analogue response in the electrical property of the receptor. In other words, the greater the change in light intensity that occurs in the visual field then the greater the change in electrical

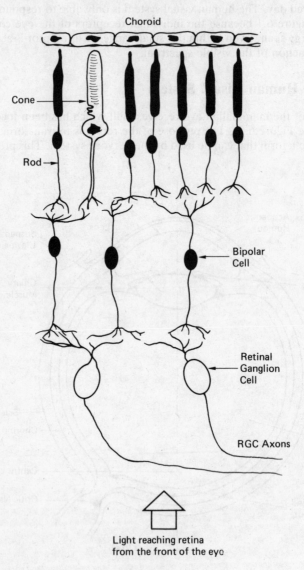

Figure 6.3 The structure of the human retina

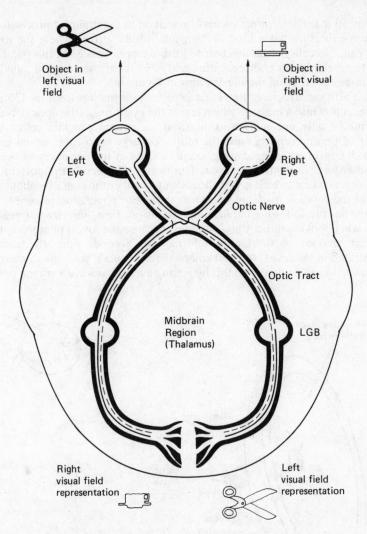

Figure 6.4 The visual pathways from the eyes to the brain

response will be in the photoreceptors. Rods respond to the scotopic property of light: that is, the range from black to white incorporating the intermediate shades of grey. Rods are especially valuable for vision in weak light intensity conditions, such as during nightfall, and this is why such vision is almost colourless. Cones respond to photopic properties of light, which in effect cover the three colours of red, green and blue.

The electrical response, which is generated in the photoreceptors in response to light, is transmitted to the subsequent cell layers; these are called bipolar and retinal ganglion cells. The structure of the retina means that information which has been transduced by the photoreceptors must pass *inwards* towards the centre of the eye and this creates a small problem. Having directed the transmission pathway to the inner surface of the retina, it now becomes necessary to find an exit point so that the information may be sent on to the brain for processing. The human eye threfore has a kind of 'plughole' on its surface where the axons of retinal ganglion cells collect together to form the optic nerve. At this point on the retina there can be no photoreceptors and so in theory you have a 'blind spot'. This can be tested using the illustrations in Figure 6.5.

With the basic structure the retina encodes information from its 130 million photoreceptors into a message which leaves the eye through the optic nerve, itself consisting of only one million axons from the retinal ganglion cells. A large number of photoreceptors must therefore converge onto each retinal ganglion cell. Such convergence, or sharing, occurs mostly at the periphery of the retina rather than near its centre, or fovea. This brings us to another important fact of retinal organization, which is that the rods outnumber the cones by about 25 to 1 and that the fovea is made up of almost the entire population of cones. So the structure has the following implications for vision. First, the clearest vision you have is when looking directly at a stimulus, because the foveal photoreceptors do the least amount of sharing of information. Second, since the cones are concentrated in the fovea, the best colour vision occurs if you look directly at the stimulus. You can demonstrate this by getting a friend to wave a crayon or felt-tip

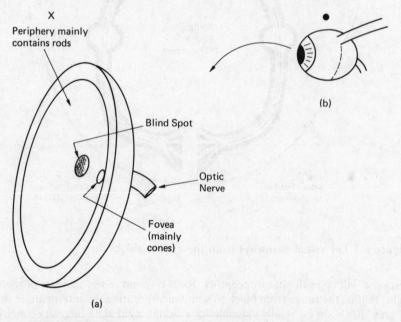

Figure 6.5 The blind spot
        a How to test your blind spot: close your left eye and gaze at the cross – you should still be aware that the circle is present, but by moving the book nearer or further from you there will come a point at which the circle will disappear; this is where it covers your blind spot
        b The location of the blind spot in the eye: the blind spot is located at the point where the optic nerve enters the eye; the small illustration at the top right shows how the eye has been cut to show this anatomy.

pen at the periphery of your vision so that you have to guess its colour. You will be surprised how difficult it is to identify colours in this region of view even though you will perceive movement easily. Third, because rods provide you with the best vision in low light conditions in a darkened room, you stand more chance of identifying objects by looking to one side of them rather than at them directly.

Other cell layers of the retina serve to transmit the electrical responsiveness of rods and cones in a lateral (or sideways) direction. These layers are the horizontal cell and amacrine cell layers. This lateral flow of information has several important effects, such as that of 'lateral inhibition'. Lateral inhibition is where the activity generated in one photoreceptor by the application of light will cause it to inhibit its neighbouring receptors. Provided these neighbouring photoreceptors are themselves also stimulated by the same light stimulus there will be mutual inhibition. However, where there is a border between light and dark zones it is possible that one photoreceptor will inhibit the activity of its neighbours without itself being affected. In such cases the stimulated receptors will have heightened responsiveness (further increasing their ability to inhibit neighbouring photore-ceptors laterally) and the neighbours may become completely inactivated for as long as the stimulus has its effect. The result of this process is that whenever we view a border between two contrasting intensities of light, the edge between them is actually made sharper by lateral inhibition than that contrast is in real terms. In effect we have an enhanced edge (or contour) detecting mechanism built into our eyes. Lateral inhibition is a feature of all sense organs where the basic receptor units gather together and interact in this way.

Kuffler (1953) recorded the electrical responses made by retinal ganglion cells (RGCs) when beams of light were shone on or nearby their retinal position. He found that RGCs have a characteristic 'receptive field' which is shown diagram-matically in Figure 6.6. When the light is shone in the peripheral region of the receptive field (i.e., on any of the points labelled A in the diagram) then the cell becomes inhibited. This means that all its activity may cease for as long as the stimulus lasts (forgetting for the moment that more usually a constant stimulus will lead to an adapted response, see above for a discussion of slow- and fast-adapting receptors). When the light is moved to points which are nearer to the centre of the cell's field (i.e., point B in the diagram) then the cell becomes excited. This means that its activity will increase for as long as the light stimulus remains on. Light falling on the boundary between these two antagonistic regions (point C) may produce no observable changes in the cell's output: that is, their effects cancel each other out. Kuffler called RGCs with this type of responsive-ness 'on-centre, off-surround' cells. He also discovered that some RGCs have the opposite response pattern to this, which he called 'off-centre, on-surround' cells. A yet further type of RGC he discovered would respond momentarily whenever the stimulus was turned on or off. These he called 'on–off' cells, which are examples of the process of adaptation referred to above. Subsequent research has shown that this shape of receptive field, with its circular and antagonistic components, is typical of RGCs as well as those which appear at the next stage of the visual system: the structure called the lateral geniculate body, or LGB.

The LGB acts as a form of relay station which simply receives input from RGC axons and then transmits this information directly to the visual-processing region of the brain called the occipital cortex. The LGB is part of a brain structure called the thalamus.

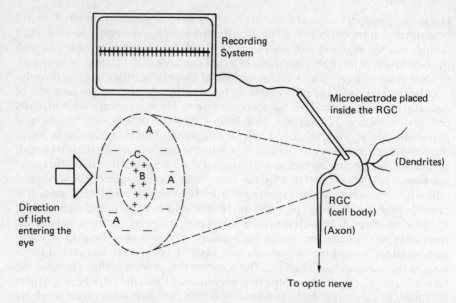

Figure 6.6 The 'receptive field' of one RGC: the 'receptive field' refers to the area of retina which, once stimulated by light, will cause a change in the activity of that RGC; Kuffler discovered the concentric organization of the RGC receptive fields, and this particular type is called an 'on-centre, off-surround' cell (see text)

6.5   Visual Processing by the Brain

Hubel and Wiesel (1962) recorded the electrical activity of neurones which are situated in the visual cortex of the cat. They identified two kinds of cells which have their own type of 'preferred stimulus' (i.e., a stimulus which has been found to produce the maximum response from the cell). Obviously, the stimulus itself does not directly affect the cells of the visual cortex, but it is applied via the retina and optic nerve pathways to where the cell is being recorded from, in the occipital cortex. One type of cell they found they called a 'simple cell', and it responds to lines of a particular orientation which happens to appear at a specific location within the visual receptive field of the cell. Figure 6.7(a) and (b) illustrates the basic response pattern made by one such cell. The second type of cell is known as the 'complex' type, and these cells also respond only to lines of one particular spatial orientation. However, complex cells will respond to their preferred stimulus wherever it appears in their visual field. Additionally, complex cells will respond when the stimulus moves around the visual field, provided that the same orientation is maintained. Hubel and Weisel found that both the simple and complex cells are organized in columns within the occipital cortex. Yet another designation was later added to this scheme, the so-called hypercomplex cell, which requires the same kind of line information as the complex cell but additionally has the criterion that the line must be of a particular length.

From what is known about the anatomy of the frog's visual system it has been suggested that the superior colliculus (a structure of the midbrain) in the

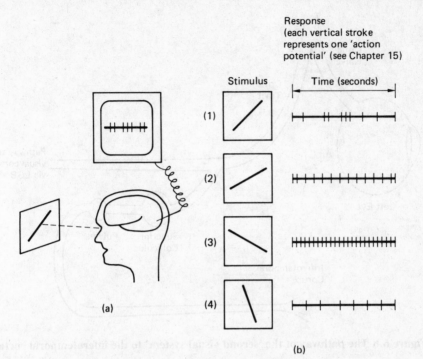

Response
(each vertical stroke
represents one 'action
potential' (see Chapter 15)

Figure 6.7 The single neurone
      a Recording from a single neurone in the visual cortex of a subject
      b Responses recorded from the single neurone as various line
      orientations are displayed (in this neurone, its 'preferred' orientation
      seems to be (3) because this line has produced the greatest response
      rate)

mammalian system (which includes humans) may also play a part in visual processing. This is possibly a secondary system of vision which may serve a separate function from the occipital one. It is shown diagrammatically in Figure 6.8. Kluver and Bucy (1939) had found that a region of the brain called the inferotemporal cortex (iftc), situated in the temporal lobe (the anatomy is described in Chapter 15), is involved in the perception of objects. Whereas the occipital system is involved mainly in analysing the fine details of the appearance of objects, it seems from the comparative studies that the second system is responsible for locating them in space. In other words the occipital system asks 'what' the object is, whereas the inferotemporal system asks 'where' it is. Kluver and Bucy syndrome results from damage to the iftc, and in monkeys it causes them to be unable to make sense of even familiar objects. For instance, a monkey with lesions of the iftc is unable to distinguish food from non-food objects, and tends to place most things it comes across in its mouth. Humans with similar damage may fail to recognize even members of their own family or close friends. This deficit is not real blindness because their vision is perfectly intact apart from this inability to recognize the familiar; Kluver and Bucy called this condition 'psychic blindness'.

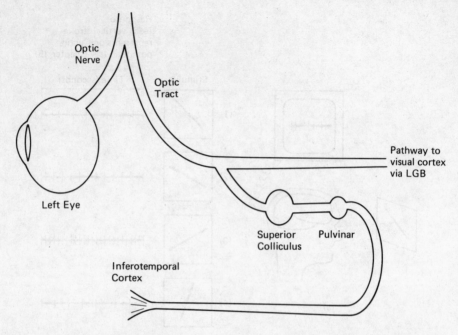

Figure 6.8 The pathway of the 'second visual system' to the inferotemporal cortex

The exact purpose and importance of this 'second' system of vision in humans is therefore controversial but it does seem to be essential for the analysis of complex stimuli and their recognition.

6.6   Sensation and Perception

Strictly speaking, sensation refers to the process of receiving information, whereas to perceive means to interpret and understand. Perceiving, and not seeing, is believing. As mentioned earlier in this chapter, the pioneer psychologists of the nineteenth century expected to achieve a deeper understanding of how the human mind works from their studies of the sensory systems. This initial optimism was soon dispelled since it soon became obvious that the process of perception is infinitely more complex than the mere collection of physical 'facts' from the environment. One of the first to recognize this was von Helmholtz in 1860. Von Helmholtz stated that perception contains experiences which are not in the stimulus. He referred to the 'unconscious inference' made when we perceive. By this he meant that we make assumptions and guesses about what each stimulus object or event means. For instance, the object in Figure 6.9 is probably instantly recognized by you despite the fact that it consists solely of nine ink lines on a page. You have inferred the existence of the garage and yet *nothing* about your sensation of it will have given you this information. Von Helmholtz proposed that unconscious interferences are of three types.

1. *Irresistible* (that is, beyond consciousness), so that even knowing that you are being tricked by an optical illusion will not cause you to see it differently; the process is unconscious.

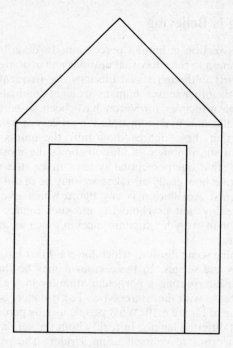

Figure 6.9 What do you perceive here?

2. *Learnt*. Illusions which are based upon cultural experiences such as a given mode of architecture (see the Müller–Lyer illusion in Figure 6.10) demonstrate that we have become accustomed to interpreting perspective because of our previous experiences.
3. *Inductive*. This means that our mental representations of a stimulus is not an exact copy of it but is merely an analogy of it.

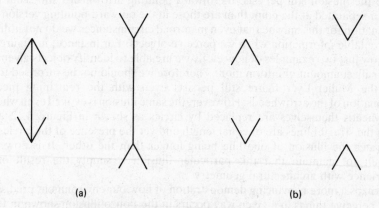

(a)   (b)

Figure 6.10 The Müller-Lyer illusion
          a If you measure the vertical lines, you will be surprised
          b Now measure the spaces between the two sets of arrowheads at their
            points

6.7   Perceiving is Believing

The subject of this section is human perception. In describing the process of perception it is common to refer to visual illusions and in doing so here two points are emphasized. First, although visual illusions are frequently used, the same principles apply to the other senses; humans are sight dominated and it is only for this reason that the principles for vision have been so carefully worked out. Second, the use of illusions to demonstrate the process of perception often leads students to think that these figures show only the quirks of our perceptual systems. This is not so: although an illusion shows the most dramatic form of distortion of 'truth' that our perceptual systems make, the whole point of the exercise is to illustrate how easily mistaken we may be in our general perception of objects and events. An illusion is any figure which gives rise to a bizarre interpretation of reality, but psychologists use such figures to understand the process of perception in everyday circumstances in which we may be less aware of how we bend reality.

Begin by examining some illusions which have a direct basis in our perception of ordinary objects and scenes. In these cases it may be that our senses have become so used to interpreting a particular stimulus in a given way that they cannot readily dispense with the 'stereotype'. For instance, consider the famous Müller–Lyer illusion of Figure 6.10. What people usually perceive here is that the vertical lines are of differing length. In reality both the vertical lines are equal in length, as you can prove to yourself using a ruler. The psychologist Richard Gregory proposes that this illusion arises because of the architectural perspective implied in these two arrangements of lines. And yet even when these figures are viewed from the horizontal plane, by turning the book sideways, you should find that the illusion persists. How can the architectural interpretation be sustained now (buildings do not lie down in this way)?

You must have answered that although buildings do not lie down, people will have gained experience of such views of them when they have tilted their heads or when lying down themselves and viewing the same arrangement. However, as Figure 6.10 shows, even when the vertical lines are themselves removed from the figure the illusion still persists: the inward-pointing arrowheads still seem to be further separated at the point than are those in the outward-pointing version. The explanation for this may be that even in normal circumstances we do not utilize all the available information when we perceive objects. For instance, in Figure 6.11 we show just two examples of how easily we are able to identify objects given even the smallest amount of information. Therefore we should not be surprised to find that the Müller–Lyer figure still persists even with the remaining piece of information of the arrowheads. However, the same illusion is evoked even when the arrowheads themselves are replaced by circles as shown in Figure 6.12. Once again the straight lines are of equal length and yet the presence of the circles now generates the illusion of one line being longer than the other. It is now more difficult to maintain that this particular illusion is simply the result of our experience with architectural geometry.

Perhaps a more convincing demonstration of how our environment predisposes us to perceive things in a given way occurs in the Ponzo illusion shown in Figure 6.13. Can you think of a scene which might include this particular arrangement of lines? (Refer to Figure 6.14 for an example.)

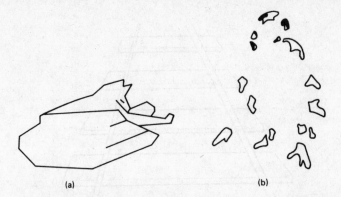

(a)   (b)

Figure 6.11 Identifying objects from the barest amount of information: a is a cat and b a sprinter at the blocks (or some may say a frog)

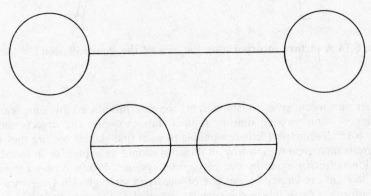

Figure 6.12 Which of the straight lines is longer?

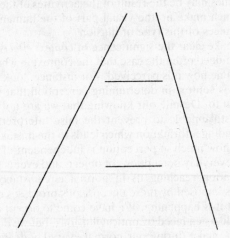

Figure 6.13 The Ponzo illusion

Figure 6.14 A picture incorporating the idea of the Ponzo illusion

Other instances arise to show how we are influenced by our real-world experience when viewing illusory figures. For example, the objects shown in Figure 6.15 all seem perfectly reasonable to us at first glance, but are they really?

There is no logical reason why all illusions should be explicable in terms of the same kind of error made by our perceptual systems. Whilst it may be true that some illusions are caused by our use of 'incorrect strategies' in Gregory's terms, there are other cases where the very structure of our visual system seems to be causing the difficulty. For instance, the illusions caused by the various conglomerations of straight lines may be the result of the activities of the so-called 'line' and 'edge' detectors which make up the visual part of the human brain. Figure 6.16 contains some instances of this type of illusion.

Other illusions make clear the significance of *context effects* during the process of perceiving. It is indeed often the case that the context in which a given stimulus appears will determine how it is perceived. For instance, look at Figures 6.17 and 6.18. So important is context in determining perception that we *cannot* ignore it even if we may wish to. Despite our knowing that we are not perceiving a figure accurately we are still unable to prevent the false interpretation from arising; somehow the misleading information which leads to the mistake still gets through. The illusion shows how much of perception is independent of our conscious will. It is likely that our everyday perceptions of objects and events proceeds in just the same way. Information reaching us in normal circumstances may frequently contain inaccuracies imposed by these unconscious processes even though we are not then aware that it is happening. We have come to accept and even enjoy the misperceptions made when faced by optical illusions, but we do not notice the less evident mistakes we make during our normal everyday dealings with the world around us.

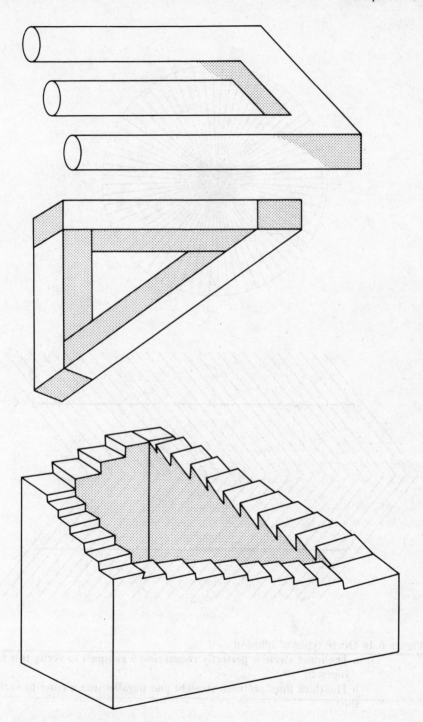

Figure 6.15 Impossible objects

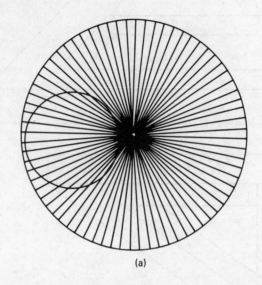

(a)

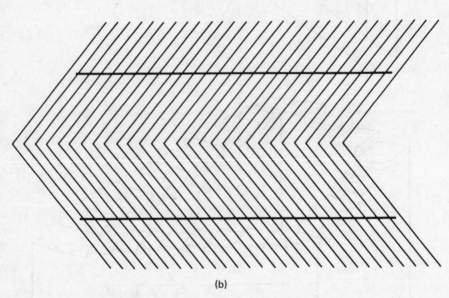

(b)

Figure 6.16 Other types of illlusion
  a The inner circle is perfectly round (use a compass to verify this for
    yourself)
  b The thick lines are both straight and parallel (use a ruler to verify
    this)

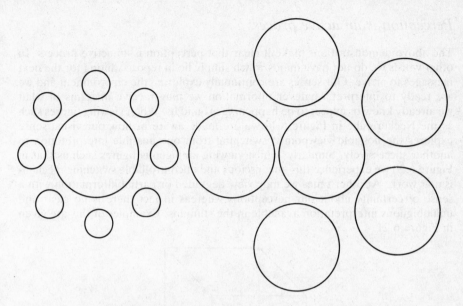

Figure 6.17 The context of the circles which surround the centre circles influence how we perceive them; both inner circles are equal in size (use a ruler or a coin to verify this)

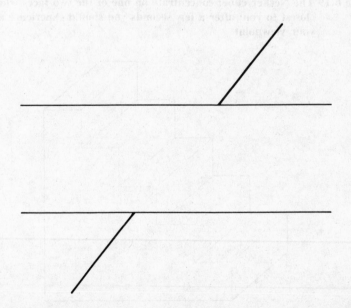

Figure 6.18 The thick lines are in reality continuous (place a ruler to join them together to verify this)

Perception is an active process

The above demonstrations make it clear that perception is an active process. In other words we do not have minds which simply lie in repose waiting for the next messages to arrive. Our senses are continually exploring the environment and we are ready to interpret whatever information we may receive in terms of what we already know or expect to be happening around us. When viewing figures such as the Necker cube in Figure 6.19 we are made aware of how our visual sense explores the possible viewpoints, switching from one possible interpretation to another successively. Similarly, whilst viewing ambiguous figures such as that in Figure 6.20 we experience this unconscious and uncontrollable switching mechanism at work. At other times we may view degraded or partial information with a sense of certainty about our perceptions whereas in fact there is no clear and unambiguous interpretation available in the stimulus. Examples of this are given in Figure 6.21.

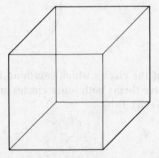

Figure 6.19 The Necker cube: concentrate on one of the two faces which appear closest to you; after a few seconds you should experience a switch in your viewpoint

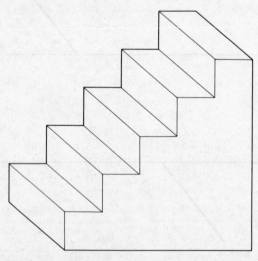

Figure 6.20 The Schröeder staircase: despite the common sight of this object you will be surprised to find the alternative viewpoint you gain by concentrating on it for a while

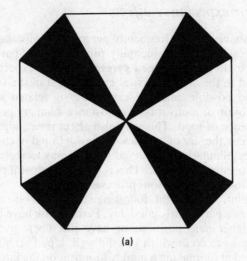

(a)

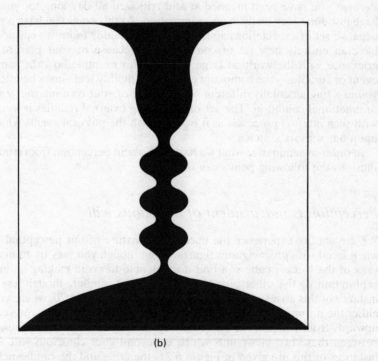

(b)

Figure 6.21 More optical illusions
          a Black or white? The cross will be seen to be either black or white,
             depending upon what you regard as the 'background'; after a while,
             you should observe a switching effect between the alternative views
          b Two faces or a candelabra? Again, in time, you will probably
             experience a switching effect

Perceptual set or expectancy effects

It was mentioned above that we frequently perceive (or mistakenly perceive) an event or object because we were mentally prepared for a particular object or event to arise. Such effects are termed **perceptual set** or expectancy effects and they may be related to the actual physical environment of the stimulus itself (its context). A second possible cause of expectancy is related to other internal factors, such as emotion or motivation. For instance a hungry person tends to see and smell the presence of food. This may also affect their judgements such that they may overestimate the size of, say, a well-known brand of chocolate bar when in a state of hunger. Similarly, a deprived smoker may exaggerate the size of a cigarette if asked to estimate its size. This is part of a general phenomenon that links perception into a 'whole-person' process.

To make this point, imagine the following scenario. You return home from work or college after a particularly good day. Perhaps you have heard about your promotion to a higher paid position, or have just been given a particularly interesting set of tasks to do in which you did well. Upon arriving home you are immediately shouted at for making a muddy footprint on the kitchen floor. In this situation you may just meekly apologize and shrug off the episode. However, now change the scenario to one where the event follows a particularly bad day. Perhaps you have been moaned at and criticized all day long for your work, or have just done very badly in an examination. At this point you have a particularly negative set of expectations about life and the muddy footprint episode may now have an entirely new set of consequences because of your present feeling of grievance with the world at large. Note in this example how the same external event or stimulus – the complaint about your muddy feet – may be interpreted by you in a fundamentally different way because of your own internal state of mind or emotional condition. The act of perceiving external realities is as much to do with such internal processes as it is to do with the physical events which impinge upon our sensory systems.

In order to summarize what we have said about perception from studying/visual illusions the following points can be made.

Perception is independent of conscious will

We are able to experience the unconscious nature of our perceptual processing when faced with unambiguous figures. Even though you may try to maintain one view of the Necker cube you find it impossible to avoid making an unconscious exploration of the other possible viewpoints. A similar, though less dramatic, instance of this arises with the Schröeder stairs in Figure 6.20, where you may see either the normal perspective or else an inverted version where you seem to look upwards from beneath the staircase. Again, a switching will be found to occur between these two viewpoints which is beyond your conscious will. Two other instances of this are given in Figure 6.21, the cross and the candlestick. Also, in Figure 6.22, the spacing of the dots may give rise to first one interpretation, such as seeing them as horizontally arranged, and then vertically or even diagonally as you continue to view them.

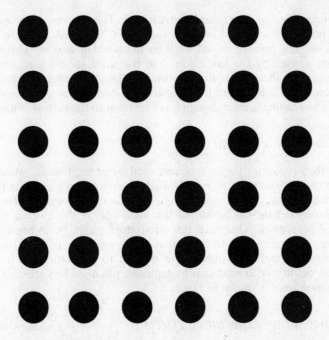

Figure 6.22 The way that you perceive these dots will vary as you view them, showing how active your perceptual system is in exploring the possible viewpoints of an ambiguous stimulus

Perception is an active process

We have considered a number of demonstrations of the active and selective nature of perception. More of these examples will be given in the subsequent discussion of perceptual set which has already been outlined above.

Perception is often creative

This is an essential part of interpreting any stimulus. For instance, when we see a building we are only ever aware of one, or at most two, sides of the structure at any one time. And yet we form much more than a two-dimensional image. We create for ourselves information concerning our past experiences with buildings having four walls, a roof, interior rooms, doors, a flight of stairs, and so on. The partial information received about any stimulus or event becomes embellished by the creative nature of our minds as we fill in the missing information.

Perception is influenced by context

The importance of context has already been emphasized and a number of demonstrations show this, the Stroop effect perhaps being the most dramatic of these. This is revealed by a series of colour naming words written in differing coloured inks (e.g. 'blue' written in green ink). The exercise involves getting a friend to point to each word in quick succession, your task being to name the colour of the ink pointed to rather than the word it makes. The conflicting information caused by the ink colour and the word should lead you to some confusion as you will no doubt find for yourself. This illustrates that the context of the ink colour (i.e., the word itself) is unavoidable in that you cannot prevent yourself from reading it even though it is irrelevant to the task of colour-naming.

Perception is rule-bound

Richard Gregory names the rule system used by perception as 'strategies'. An important issue concerning the rules is whether or not they are innate (present at birth) or whether they are learnt during growth and development. The so-called **nature–nurture debate** will be further discussed later in this chapter as it affects theories of perception. One such rule or strategy might be to regard anything resembling converging lines to imply that you are viewing perspective. The two sloping lines of the Ponzo illusion are enough to generate the experience of distance of 'depth' and similar cues to depth are often used by artists. One of the more common ones is shown in Figure 6.23.

Perceptual set or expectancy effects

There are many ways in which expectancy influences perception. To the *Gestalt* psychologists (described below) the world contains a number of natural shapes and configurations which humans are predisposed to seeing. The ancient Greeks believed there to be certain shapes, such as the circle, square and triangle, which were fundamental to our universe. This may explain why we so readily interpret Figure 6.23 as an overlying triangle rather than as three incompleted black dots.

Bruner and Mintern (1952) showed the importance of expectation when subjects were asked to draw what they saw in a series of stimuli presented to them. Some subjects were shown the figure

following a series of numbers whereas other subjects saw it following a series of letters. When asked to reproduce this particular figure, those who saw it in the number series separated the two parts to resemble the number thirteen:

whereas those seeing the letter series closed up the two parts to form the letter B.

Sanford (1936) gave a series of unfinished words to subjects to complete. He found that subjects who had been food-deprived prior to the task tended to invent words which related in some way to food: for example, the stimulus 'Me--' may have been completed as 'Meat'.

Perhaps the most important conclusion to be drawn from all of the above is that perception does not solely depend upon the physical relationship between the

Figure 6.23 The missing segments from the three black circles give the illusion of an overlaid white triangle

stimulus and our senses. Instead, the act of perceiving is connected to all other processes going on within the person at the time. When viewing familiar objects our memory and feelings about them may be involved. Even when we see an object for the very first time we are usually able to work out its probable use from our experience with other objects having the same general appearance. We would be able to associate the function of cutting with sharp edges, or smooth rounded shapes as having the purpose of a handle, and so on. Therefore, the information we use when perceiving does not all come from the object itself. The study of illusions and related figures has enabled psychologists to understand these processes more fully, and this has helped in relating them to the way in which humans perceive the world in everyday circumstances.

6.8 Is Perception Innate or Learnt?

The so-called nature–nurture debate in perception raises a number of issues, not the least of which is how precisely we define perception. For instance, research into this issue has primarily focused on vision. Second, within the study of visual perception there has been no clear aim in mind, with some investigations examining depth, others pattern recognition or constancy, and so forth. Third, research has chiefly involved animal studies despite their being proven species differences in many aspects of vision in particular. Fourth, the question of nature versus nurture assumes that perception exists as a result of only one or other of these processes (inheritance and learning), whereas other areas of psychological research have underlined the complexity of development which can involve sensitive learning periods as well as maturational changes in the formation of new knowledge or behaviour which is acquired by the individual. In short, the nature–nurture debate is simplistic in regard to modern psychological research and its treatment of human development which is now recognized to be a highly complex process involving many levels of interaction.

However, a brief consideration of the historical side of the issue may be helpful. First, perception must be given the broadest possible definition so as to encompass the many varying approaches which have been made. We may regard perception as the interpretation of the environment using prior assumptions about it. Perceiving often uses unconscious processing as well as contextual cues. And finally the internal state of the perceiver plays an important part in determining how and what is perceived. The two extreme views of the debate involve the empiricists and the nativists: the former argue that perception is a process which occurs through learning and may therefore be regarded as a skill. **Nativism**, on the other hand, holds that perception involves the use of innate predispositions. There have been five separate lines of investigation in this debate, as summarized below.

1. *Clinical evidence*, which involves the use of subjects with impaired perception. Most common subjects here are the congenitally-blind people who have their sight restored through surgery.
2. *Human **neonates** (newborns)*: the experimental opportunities are limited here for two reasons. One is that human infants are limited in their responsiveness and this makes it difficult to ascertain just what is being perceived by the neonate. A second reason is that the nervous system and the sensory and perceptual apparatus are not fully developed at birth.
3. *Animal neonates:* many non-human animals produce precocial young: that is, they are at a fairly late stage of development when born or hatched. Studies which have been done on such species have tended to show innate perceptual abilities. However, it is likely that there will be species differences between such neonates and those of humans which are said to be altricial (i.e., born at an early stage of physical development and developing fully much later on).
4. *Cross-cultural studies* involve the comparisons between humans brought up in widely contrasting environments, such as dense tropical forest versus essentially deforested tundra regions, and so on. Variations in the manner of perceiving the same stimulus shown by such peoples would indicate that perception is a learnt faculty.
5. *Distorting prism studies*: these employ some arrangement of eyepiece such that the visual world of the wearer becomes disarranged by inverting the image, for example, or by switching the left of the visual field to the right side and vice versa. Other studies have used displacements of the visual field to one or other side by varying degrees, or even employing some form of colour distortion. Such studies have concluded most often that the human adult has an immense capacity to adapt to such new forms of sensory input. However, this does not necessarily mean that the same is true for the infant; the adult may be in a much better position to use complex compensatory strategies for mentally coping with perceptual derangement.

6.9 *Gestalt* **Theory of Perception**

Gestalt psychology was an active area of research in visual perception in the period between the world wars. The three most prominent people of this movement were Wertheimer, Kohler and Koffka, who were also responsible for taking the *Gestalt* philosophy to America from their native Germany. Although there are over a hundred 'laws' of perception according to the *Gestalt*ist, most authors who have popularized this school have tended to select six of these as being representative of the approach.

The *Gestalt* theory began as an alternative to the nature–nurture debate which had tended to burden the theories of perception at that time. The central theoretical concern of the Gestaltists was the problem of how perceptual constancies are to be explained. A constancy literally means something unchanged. Hence, when we walk towards or away from an object we are looking at, its size on our retina changes as though the object itself either grows or shrinks. However, our perception of that object's size does not change; we perceive its size as constant and hence the term 'size constancy'. A similar effect occurs when the apparent shape of an object, such as a door, changes as it turns away from us. The fact of its apparent change in shape does not cause us to re-interpret it as a new stimulus because we perceive shape as a constancy.

The word *Gestalt* translates from the German for 'wholeness' of form. This means that humans seem to be programmed to identify objects by properties which are not concocted from a detailed description of each of their parts. Objects possess what are sometimes called 'emergent properties'. For example, when you hear an orchestra or a pop band playing a piece of music the effect it has on you is an overall sound and not simply a collection of different instruments. Likewise, in recalling the look of a familiar face you do not need to build up the image from knowing how each of the person's features looks in detail; you seem to have processed an overall picture of them without necessarily having all the features correct or clearly stored in your mind. Another famous example is that knowledge of the chemical structure of some compounds does not help you to predict how the compound itself will appear or behave. Water, for instance, is a compound of hydrogen and oxygen which are both gases. In the combination of two parts to one they form the peculiar substance which looks and behaves like neither of them.

According to the *Gestalt*ists the physical word around us is directly represented in the brains of humans in such a way that the image of the world is similar to reality as it exists for us. The word they use to describe this resemblance between the brain pattern and the stimulus itself is called 'isomorphism'. It was this particular idea which led to the decline in interest in *Gestalt* psychology as a whole since there was no physiological evidence to support such a notion. Therefore *Gestalt* approaches to perception have focused on explanations of how two-dimensional figures become interpreted by humans. The list of five 'rules' below illustrate the *Gestalt* explanation for visual perception.

1. *Preferred forms*: there are believed to be preferred configurations in the brain for certain shapes of stimulus and they are said to give the perceptual system a state of equilibrium. Any stimulus which, for one reason or another, does not fit these preferred forms will cause a state of disequilibrium. For example, a circle may be preferred to an ellipse and so in order to maintain equilibrium whilst we view an ellipse our perceptual system simply regards the ellipse as being a circle viewed end on. In the case of a more complex stimulus such as the Necker cube (Figure 6.10) the preferred form is the three-dimensional cube rather than its flat, two-dimensional pattern.

2. *Figure-ground*: in order for any object to be perceived it must be differentiated and set apart from its surroundings.
3. *Good and poor forms*: a 'good' form is one which is well differentiated from its surroundings and tends to impress itself upon the observer.
4. *Natural form*: scenes are often organized by the perceptual system according to certain natural assumptions it makes about form; for instance, the pattern

. . . .
. . . .

is perceived to be pairs of dots owing to their physical proximity to each other, and

000000
CCCCCC
000000

is perceived as three layers rather than six columns because of the similarity which exists in the items of each row.
5. *Symmetry of form*: forms possess in themselves a natural symmetry. Impossible figures are perceived to be natural forms even though there is an aberration incorporated into them by the artist.

Although the *Gestalt*ist approach has had a general influence in many areas of psychology, it no longer stands in its own right as a theory of perception. For one thing, it does not explain the complexities of the perception of objects in the real world. Also, the rules which the *Gestalt*ists use to explain perception are descriptive more than they are explanatory (i.e., they provide us with an account of what humans perceive but not *how* we perceive).

6.10   Questions and Exercises

1. Make up a table containing lists of the similarities and differences between the processes of sensation and perception.
2. Draw your own version of the cross and circle shown in Figure 6.5(a) but draw vertical lines around the circle so as to completely cover an area of about 5 cm square, with the circle in the centre. Now test again the position of your blind spot in each eye, but this time note what happens when the dot disappears: is there a 'hole' in the arrangement of lines you have drawn?

7 Attention

7.1 Introduction

SPOTLIGHT Attention and the infant

From the early hours of life a newborn infant must select from the thousands of sensations it experiences those to which it will attend. Sights, sounds, tastes, smells and even the jerky movements of its own limbs all seem to require attention. From time to time its own digestive pains and sounds come to mind, making the baby's world a flux of continuous experience.

Exercise

Try to imagine yourself to be a newborn baby meeting the world for the first time. What kind of things in your immediate environment would gain your attention? Write down the events which happen, such as sounds and movements, as they occur and make notes on which of those competing sensations a newborn would be most aware. In what ways would the newborn's experience of these stimuli be different from your own?

In Chapter 6 we found that perception is as much to do with internal mechanisms of the mind as it is to do with events and objects occurring in the environment. It was said that perception is a selective process. In other words, despite all the available information around us we construct meanings and interpretations by processing only certain aspects of what is 'out there'. Precisely what becomes processed in the act of perceiving is determined by the selective nature of our mental life. Selective perceiving may be partly a question of inherited predispositions; we may perceive only those aspects of the environment which are within our sensory capacity to detect. But we also select on the basis of learnt predispositions: for example, the environmental cues which we use to interpret depth ('cues to depth'). Perception is also selective on the basis of the immediate state of the individual and that individual's state of motivation, such as hunger. We conclude from all this that selective perception has the advantage of being economical in the sense that it reduces the processing of the potentially infinite amount of information available in the environment into a more readily 'digestible' form. When faced with a life-threatening situation we need to be economical in dealing with the information arriving at our senses. Even in normal circumstances our environment is a buzz of chaos, and we need to select from the many different events those to which we should attend at any given moment. Selective attention provides the means by which we reduce the workload on our mental systems. The restriction of mental processing to one event at a time is called 'selective attention'.

Although we seem to be conscious of a singular train of thought we are also able to switch attention between a number of simultaneous ongoing events, such as listening to the radio whilst watching the television whilst doing homework (a common combination of abilities shown by the modern teenager). Keeping track of several ongoing events has been aptly labelled the 'cocktail party problem' (Cherry, 1953). The issue is how are we able to 'tune in' to other peoples' conversations whilst keeping track of the one we may be currently engaged in. Furthermore, we are still able to respond immediately to hearing a familiar voice, or someone calling our names from across the other side of the room. Our ability to divide our attention will be discussed later in this chapter because here we focus on explaining how selective attention mechanisms may operate. In discussing research into this area it is necessary to know a little about a technique called 'dichotic listening' and 'shadowing' (see the Spotlight box below).

SPOTLIGHT   Studying attention

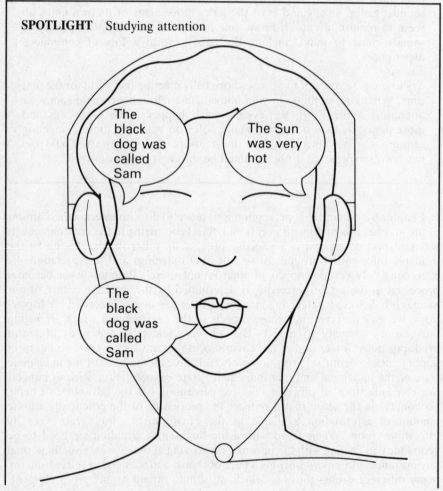

Figure 7.1 The dichotic listening task

The major technique used in conducting experiments on selective attention is the 'dichotic listening' procedure illustrated in Figure 7.1 above. The subject wears a set of stereo headphones through which two different 'messages' may be sent by the experimenter. The messages are most often two different sets of prose and the subject is usually given the task of 'shadowing' one of the messages. To shadow means to concentrate upon one of the messages by simply repeating everything heard in that channel. Subjects are therefore listening intently to one of the messages in order to repeat it aloud. The experimenter checks that the subject is performing this properly by listening to the original and echoed messages. The whole point of such exercises is to see what the subject is able to detect in the second channel (i.e., the message coming in through the unattended system); in the case of Figure 7.1 the message coming into the left ear is the secondary one.

7.2 Selective Attention

The chances are that whilst you are reading this a number of events are happening around you. Listen out for the sounds of traffic, people talking, music playing or weather noises. Unless you are alone there will be people moving around you and possibly other movements visible from the 'corner' of your eye. Yet despite all these potential distractions you are probably still able to focus your thoughts on the message conveyed here. Our ability to attend to one main event whilst being remotely conscious of others provides the psychologist with the paradox of how attention can be both a selective and a divided process simultaneously. We are probably never more aware of the dual nature of attention than when among a group of friends in an informal setting, sometimes concentrating on one conversation and sometimes with our thoughts 'spread' more thinly between a number of other events, such as who is with whom tonight, and so forth. For this reason Cherry labelled this selective aspect of attention the 'cocktail party' problem.

Cherry (1953) gave subjects a dichotic listening task to perform. This involved wearing a stereo headphone which enabled the experimenter to present one message to one ear and a second message to the other ear (see Figure 7.1 in the Spotlight box). However, what interested Cherry was how much of the unattended message the subjects were processing. He discovered that the information in the unattended channel was only analysed by the subject at a very primitive level. For instance, the subject was aware of the sex of the speaker but had no awareness of the contents of the message (i.e., what was said). Cherry concluded that the unattended channel was analysed for its physical properties, such as tone or pitch, but nothing deeper than that.

Moray (1959) confirmed this basic result by showing that the subject was unaware of the unattended message being in a foreign language, or even that is consisted of a short word-list being repeated over and over again. However, subjects were able to switch to this channel automatically when a familiar word was presented, such as the person's own name. This implies that the subject must somehow process the meanings of certain things in the unattended channel, otherwise their attention could not be diverted in this way towards certain selected events. You are probably familiar with this effect, for even when you are engrossed in conversation your attention is immediately snatched away as soon as you hear your name mentioned from across the room. But it has nonetheless proved difficult to analyse what and how we are able to analyse in the secondary channel.

Mowbray (1959) instructed subjects to attend to two channels simultaneously in a difficult task. They heard one story whilst silently reading a second, different story. Subjects were able to report one story only, the other showing no evidence of having been understood.

Broadbent (1958) devised a model to explain how he believed attention is controlled by a 'filter'. This model is illustrated by Figure 7.2. This simplified version of Broadbent's theory shows that information which becomes filtered out of the system (i.e., consciously unattended) will receive only a low level of analysis. This system explains much of the experimental findings of studies such as that of Cherry, Moray and Mowbray, yet it fails to explain how people respond to information such as their own name in the unattended channel. You may also be left wondering how we select what to select and on what criterion: in other words, what decides that the system should tune to one channel rather than another. This decision, however it is made, is evidently made very early in the processing of information and hence it is sometimes called an 'early selection' model. Selection is here based upon the physical properties of the stimulus and it is also referred to as 'sensory selection'.

Pavlov (1927) also discussed a process like selective attention in relation to his experiments on learning in animals. He described the process of 'overshadowing'. This occurs when an animal is trained to make a response to two equally relevant stimuli. A stimulus can be said to be relevant when it predicts an impending event in the animal's immediate environment. Whenever an animal is conditioned (see Chapter 12 for a detailed discussion of learning phenomena) to respond to the onset of two equal stimuli (e.g., a light and sound which always occur together in the experiment) one of them will act as the conditioned stimulus and will thereby 'overshadow' the second stimulus. Kamin (1968) observed that this is particularly likely to happen when one of the stimuli has been employed to train the animal prior to the introduction of the second one. In this case the first stimulus is said to 'block' the second. Both overshadowing and blocking show that our attention mechanism functions to select single events in the environment: the presentation of a compound stimulus will lead to one only being selected for attention. (Although these issues are more complex in relation to animal learning, they are used here only to establish this straightforward principle of attention.)

Sutherland and Holgate (1966) trained rats to approach one form of stimulus and to avoid another. The two stimuli were both rectangular but differed in two respects (see Figure 7.3): first, in orientation, one being horizontal, the other vertical, and second, in brightness, one being black, the other white. During a subsequent test the experimenters used either: (a) the same rectangles both placed horizontally, or (b) the white rectangle replaced with a black one, also in the horizontal position. Sutherland and Holgate found that those rats which had been attending to the orientation of the shapes during training now showed learning (i.e., a strong preference for one stimulus over the other) in condition (b). Similarly, those animals which had chosen to use brightness in learning to discriminate between the two stimuli showed such learning only in test (a). This implies that, having selected one feature of the stimulus (such as orientation) to attend to during training, the subjects have filtered out the other features (such as contrast) and show little or no learning of them.

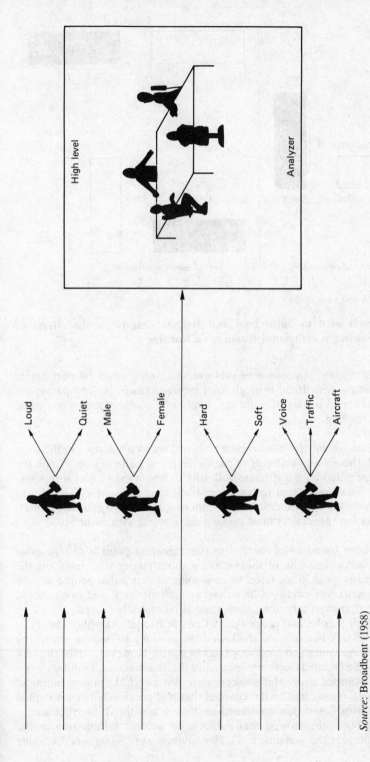

Figure 7.2 Broadbent's filter model of selective attention: the low level analyser examines only simple features of messages arriving, such as whether it is a voice or other sound, whether it is masculine or feminine, whether it is loud or quiet, hard or soft, and so on. Only the attended channel is analysed for meaning (high-level features)

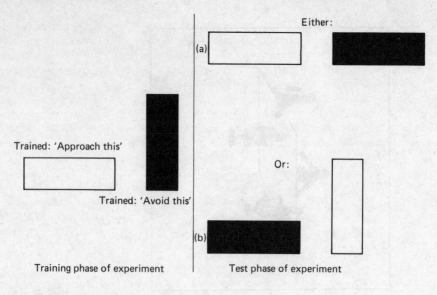

Source: Sutherland and Holgate (1966)

Figure 7.3 Stimuli used in Sutherland and Holgate's study on the effects of presenting a compound stimulus on learning

You can obtain some impression of this overshadowing effect by performing the following simple test. Read through the first five lines of the test paragraph below at normal speed but try to count the number of 'e's there are as you come across them in reading.

> During the experiment, for the teacher (subject) there is intense conflict. On the one hand, the obvious suffering of the victim presses him to stop, but on the other, the experimenter, a legitimate authority to whom the subject feels some commitment, encourages him to continue. Each time the subject hesitates to administer shock the experimenter orders him to continue. To extricate himself from the situation the subject must make a clear break with authority.

You should have found 61 of them. But the important point is to note your inability to do more than one of these tasks without taking your mind off the other. However, as we shall see later, there is some evidence that people may be able to be trained to perform two difficult tasks simultaneously, and so we should avoid assuming that this limitation of attention is biologically caused.

Treisman (1960) pointed out a number of flaws in Broadbent's filter theory of attention. In one task her subjects shadowed the message to one ear whilst the unattended message contained random strings of words. However, whilst the task was in progress the channels were reversed, and the shadowed and random-word channels were swapped over. Her subjects were not aware that the meaningful message had been transferred to the channel that had previously been occupied by the random words, and they continued to shadow it without interruption.

Treisman (1964) again showed that subjects do analyse information in the unattended channel at the semantic level. Her subjects were bilinguists (i.e., able to speak two languages fluently). They were given the task of shadowing a message in one channel whilst the unattended channel contained the identical message but in their second language. Treisman found that subjects were aware that the unattended channel was repeating the shadowed message and this must mean that they were making a semantic analysis of the non-shadowed channel. To explain this Treisman proposed a model in which the unattended message is 'attenuated' in much the same way that you would turn down the volume of the radio in order to concentrate on the message coming from the television. Her attenuator model is shown diagrammatically in Figure 7.4.

In Treisman's model, instead of blocking the meaning of the unattended channel the selection device simply attenuates them, causing less overall disturbance to the primary high-level analysis of information taking place in the attended channel. However, Treisman's model does not explain enough about the nature of the attenuator device: for instance, how the attenuator controls attention and how the things in the unattended channel are salient enough to be brought into primary attention. In other words, what is controlling the attenuator and what is the basis of its function? Is the attenuator control itself controlled by an attenuator control controller? Treisman's model therefore does not generate

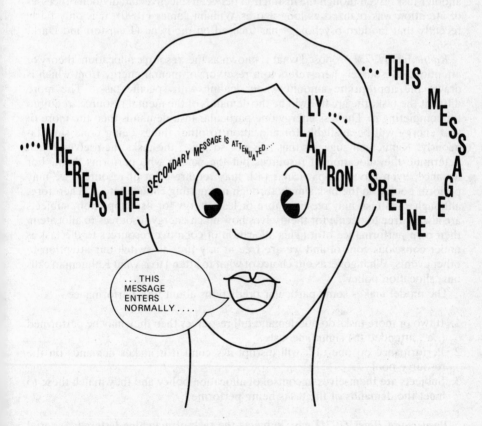

Source: Treisman (1964)

Figure 7.4 Treisman's attenuator model of selective attention

clear predictions owing to these and other issues relating to the complexity and ambiguity of its design. Another historical reason why Treisman's model was unpopular was that it did not fit into the two-process model (Atkinson and Shiffrin, 1970) of memory (this will be described in Chapter 8).

7.3   Divided Attention

The research into selective attention described above has produced models which for a time were productive in clarifying many theoretical issues. But of greater everyday interest is the problem of how we are able to divide our attention between two or more events or tasks, such as engaging in conversation whilst driving. Psychologists investigating the selective aspect of attention have always emphasized how limited our ability is for diverse attention. For instance, in the typical experiment of dichotic listening it was always found that subjects were unable to attend to more than one thing at a time. However, the tasks in which subjects were usually engaged, such as shadowing, were intellectually demanding and so it is not surprising that subjects had little mental power left for attending to another task. Even though the distinction between selective and divided processes of attention was realized as long ago as William James (1890), it is only fairly recently that modern psychology has focused on the issue (Johnston and Dark, 1986).

Kahneman (1973) proposed what is known as the 'resource allocation' theory of attention. 'Resources' here refers to a reservoir of mental energy from which is drawn the appropriate amount when dealing with specific tasks. The more difficult the task, the greater will be the demands of the mental resources required for completing it. The less energy one particular task demands then the more of that energy will be available for allocation to other things being done simultaneously. Kahneman suggests that it is not so much the tasks themselves which determine the allocation of resources but the person who performs them. For instance, even though a particular task may require a lot of resources we may perform poorly on the task simply through not putting enough into it. Therefore, although each task may require more or less energy for its completion, subjects are always free to decide for themselves how much energy resources to allocate in their own performance of it. This allocation of cognitive resources to the task is under conscious control and we are free at any time to switch our attention to other events. What governs our choice of what to attend to is what Kahneman calls our 'allocation policy'.

The model makes some particular predictions about task performance.

1. If two or more tasks do not demand full resources then they may be performed (i.e., attended to) simultaneously.
2. Performance on one task will disrupt a second if it makes demands on the resource pool.
3. Subjects are themselves in control of allocation policy and they match these to meet the demands of the tasks being performed.

Posner and Boies (1971) gave subjects the task of matching letters in a serial display. They were given a series of trials wherein a letter 'target' was followed briefly by a second letter 'probe'. The task was simply to respond as quickly as possible by pressing an appropriate button according to whether the probe matched the target or not: that is, whether they were the same letter or not. The second task was to tap a key with their left hand as soon as they heard a tone being played. The experimenters measured the speed of response to this second task and found that it varied depending upon exactly when in relation to the first task the tone occurred. Figure 7.5 shows the response time over the event sequence of task one.

At point A on the graph subjects were shown the fixation 'x' in the letter-matching task. This marker ensured two things: first, that subjects would look at the right spot in preparation for the appearance of the target letter and, second, that they would be prepared for the start of each trial since the fixation point always preceded the target by half a second. At point B the tone is faster responded to than at point A, presumably because the subject is in a state of readiness for the appearance of the target (i.e., they are becoming 'psyched up'). At C the target letter has now appeared on the screen and subjects are even quicker still at responding should the tone appear at this instant. At D the subjects produce the fastest reactions of all to the tone and this must reflect their state of heightened arousal in readiness to perform the letter-matching task. At points E and F subjects are slower at the tone task because they are in a late stage of preparation for the visual task. They are allocating most of their resources at this time to the letter task, which is for them the 'main event'. At G and H the second letter has arrived and so they are engaged at G in deciding on the question of whether the probe matches the target or not and also on what is the appropriate response to make. H indicates that the decision has been made and so resources are less tied up now; the response organization is already under way.

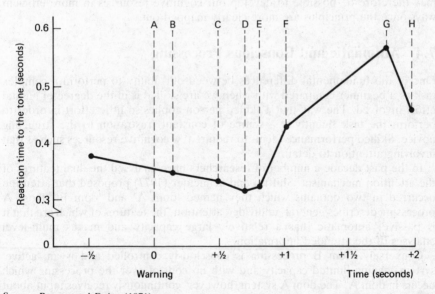

Source: Posner and Boies (1971)

Figure 7.5 Results of the study by Posner and Boies, illustrating their resource allocation model of attention

From this study it is possible to see many of the elements of Kahnman's resource allocation model at work. At the various stages of processing task one (the visual task of matching letters) there are differing cognitive demands being made on the subject's attentional capacity. In the early stages of each trial the subjects are not heavily committed to the letter-matching task and so will have more resources available for triggering a fast response to the tone. However, in the later stages of each letter-matching trial subjects focus their attention on the matching, decision-making and response organization, in particular from G onwards. The letter-matching task is at this point making maximal demands on the subject's attentional resources and so they are relatively slow in responding to the tone.

Norman and Bobrow (1974) criticized the earlier work on selective attention because the models had been based on tasks which made unusually high demands on the subject's attention. For instance, the task of shadowing is so difficult that there would be no cognitive resources left for performing any secondary task. Therefore, they argue, selective attention models imply misleadingly that humans have only a limited ability to divide their attention between tasks.

Furthermore, our capacity for dividing attention between tasks increases with practice on them (i.e., 'resources' may increase). A study by Hirst *et al.* (1980) illustrates this effect. They taught two subjects a task of reading whilst simultaneously dictating short sentences. They were tested on their ability to process the material with tests of recognition memory as well as comprehension. After 114 sessions one subject was able to read and dictate the sentences at a normal pace (i.e., at the speed of people engaged in dictation only). The second subject had similar ability with even less practice. This study suggests that our mental resources do not have limited capacity but may actually expand with practice. It may therefore be possible to develop our cognitive resources in more efficient ways once the principles are more clearly mapped out.

7.4   Automatic and Conscious Processing

One of the fundamental differences between our ability to perform a complex task as a beginner compared with when we are skilled is in the degree of mental effort involved. The way that a skilled person applies so little effort in order to perform the task fluently is a source of constant frustration to the struggling novice. Skilled performance seems to require few cognitive resources such as that involving attention to detail.

In the past decade a number of researchers have analysed the dual features of the attention mechanism. Shiffrin and Schneider (1977) proposed that attention occurred in two domains which they named 'dom A' and 'dom B'. Dom A processing describes general, undivided attention, the features of which are that it is passive, automatic, has a relatively large capacity and makes multi-level analyses of the attended information.

Conversely, dom B processing is consciously controlled and is an 'active' system, having limited capacity and with no control over the processing which occurs in dom A. The dom A system, however, continuously receives input about the environment which it processes unconsciously, although the system may be initiated by our conscious will. Tasks which are well-learnt have many of their elements stored in long-term memory so that they will be available during the automatic processing of events when such tasks are subsequently performed.

However, Broadbent (1982) has reiterated his proposal that the so-called dom B processing does influence dom A to the extent that whatever material dom A possesses is merely a by-product of the selective mechanism operating in dom B. To some extent Broadbent's views have persuaded researchers to revise the early model of unconscious processing described by Shiffrin and Schneider.

7.5   Questions and Exercises

1. Think of some everyday situations where the findings of research into selective attention may be of use (e.g., it would help in the design of offices, where people need to work closely together without causing too much interruption of what others are doing).
2. Describe briefly what the models of Broadbent, Treisman and Kahneman have to say about attention.

8 Memory

8.1 Introduction

The ability to process and retrieve information is known as memory. In a century of scientific research into this topic there is still no single dominant theory in psychology to explain human memory. This chapter, therefore, provides a brief overview of the models that are used to explain the many different facets of memory.

8.2 Sensory Memory

The sense organs themselves have a limited ability to store information about the environment. It is necessary that they should be able to 'freeze' information momentarily to enable the nervous system to 'read off' data at any given moment. Psychologists have studied two such sensory memory systems in greater depths than others – vision and hearing – and their respective systems are called 'iconic' and 'echoic' memory.

Iconic memory was investigated by Sperling (1960), who presented subjects with a very brief display (lasting just one-twentieth of a second) containing twelve random letters arranged in three rows. Subjects next heard a tone of high, medium or low pitch, which indicated to the subject which of the three rows they should verbally recall (top, middle or bottom). Sperling found that subjects were able to recall the majority of letters in any row *provided* that the tone was not delayed by more than a quarter of a second: that is, the 'icon' or sensory memory for the image lasts for approximately that length of time. When you view cinematic film you believe you are seeing the actors in continuous movement. However, as you probably already know, 'movies' are in reality made from a series of still photographs, each one in the sequence showing the subject in a slightly different position relative to the neighbouring frames. The fact that we do not notice the jumps between frames is because of the retina's ability to store the previous image for long enough to give the illusion of continuity.

Echoic memory refers to the ability of the ear to retain auditory information after it has been presented. Studies by Massaro (1970) and Crowder (1982) have shown that the 'echo' lasts approximately a quarter of a second: similar in time to iconic storage. It has been suggested that there may be two echoic processes, one of them being a short-term version as described by the above researchers, but another version being capable of processing information for several seconds following its presentation.

8.3 The Atkinson–Shiffrin Model of Memory

The most influential of the human memory system so far devised has been that of Atkinson and Shiffrin (1968), as illustrated in Figure 8.1. According to this theory the sensory memory (here called SIS, after 'sensory information store') has a relatively large capacity for storing information, even though it decays rapidly. The speed with which this information can be handled will determine to some extent how much of it is stored and how much lost through a process of decay (i.e., the critical $\frac{1}{4}$ second duration of the sensory memory mentioned above). Another means of losing information is caused by the limited capacity for storage which the next stage has: the so-called STM, or short-term memory store. This store has a capacity limited to about seven items only and so a 'queue' of information occurs between SIS and STM, making this the bottleneck of the system. This is intuitively true if you think of what is currently going on in your immediate environment. There is an infinity of events and objects surrounding you at all times and yet you are severely limited in your ability to keep more than a fraction of all this in mind at any one time.

The basis of STM is acoustic; this store operates by 'rehearsing' the information stored there using sub-vocal sounds. In some cases, such as when you are trying to memorize a phone number given to you by the operator, you may deliberately vocalize the information and this is similar to how STM rehearses information in its store. Given that sufficient **rehearsal** time (about 30 seconds) has occurred, the information in STM is transferred to the long-term store, called LTM, which has an infinite capacity and storage duration time. Whereas the *modus operandi* of STM is acoustic, LTM functions on the basis of the meaning of the material stored

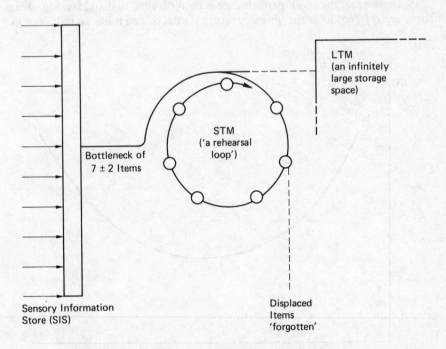

Source: Atkinson and Shiffrin (1968)

Figure 8.1 The Atkinson–Shiffrin model of memory: apart from the sensory information store (SIS) the system consists of two processes, a short-term store (STM) and a long-term store (LTM); the operation of the model is described in the text

there. In other words, meaningless items are incapable of being stored for long durations by LTM.

Testing someone's STM is simply a matter of timing. For instance, by reading to that person a list of words and then asking the person to recall the list immediately afterwards (at least within 30 seconds of their hearing the last word) you will be employing that person's STM. LTM may be similarly tested in this way but this time, instead of asking for immediate recall of the word-list, you now delay this request for a period of at least 30 seconds after they have been presented with the last word of the list.

8.4 Research Evidence

The serial position effect

When subjects are given a list of items to memorize, such as words, letters or numbers, their recall is usually better for the items which appeared early and late in the list than it is for the middle items. This is shown diagrammatically in Figure 8.2, which is based on a memory test using fifteen items. The Y-axis, labelled 'recall %', is derived from the performances of a number of subjects.

As you can see, the recall performance is better for the first and last four items. These are referred to as the 'primacy recency' effects, and it has an influence in a

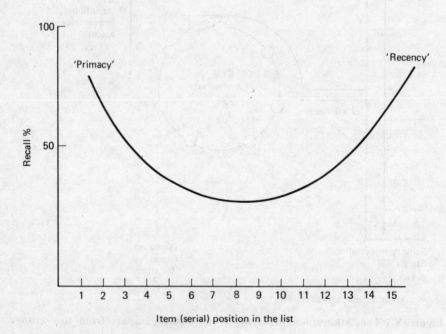

Figure 8.2 The serial position effect

number of other areas of psychology, such as in person perception (see Chapter 5). According to two-process theory the primacy effect is caused by the operation of LTM. Recall that LTM functions when items have been rehearsed in STM for more than 30 seconds. In theory, the earlier items of the list will have been processed for that amount of time when it comes to the subject being asked to recall the items. The recency effect is said to be a feature of the operation of STM because, after the presentation of the final item (assuming that recall is asked for immediately), less than 30 seconds will have elapsed since these later items were presented and hence STM will still be operating on these. However, recall will typically be poor on the middle items because they have been displaced following rehearsal in STM and yet they will not have been 'consolidated' or formed into LTM (at least not to the extent of the earlier items).

Hebb (1949) believed that STM works by a chemical process which is based upon the actions of the brain sending information round and round the same neuronal loops (for more on the chemical actions of neurones see Chapter 15). These loops Hebb referred to as 'reverberating circuits', and he believed that once this process had occurred for about 30 seconds then 'consolidation' would result. Consolidation refers to a structural change in the connections made between neurones: that is, new **synapses** being formed which result from the STM process. LTM is therefore a building process in the brain and this would explain how such memories can last over the lifetime of the individual because they are now part of the individual's neural anatomy.

Glanzer and Cunitz (1966) showed that rehearsal time in STM is proportional to recall performance. They presented their subjects with a fifteen-word list, serially. Three groups of subjects were formed to test the effects of three different rehearsal periods: (a) immediate recall (which permitted the full 30 seconds of rehearsal); (b) 20 seconds' rehearsal, and (c) no rehearsal.

Conditions (b) and (c) were controlled by giving subjects a difficult counting task to perform after they had seen the last of the items of the list. In condition (b) subjects performed this counting task for 10 seconds (thereby allowing 20 seconds for the processing in STM of the list). In condition (c) the counting task was continued for a full 30 seconds before they were asked to recall the word-list. This, in theory, left no rehearsal time at all for the word-list which meant that STM would be blocked for the later items in the list. However, LTM should remain unaffected because, until the counting task was given, LTM had been receiving items for storage from STM in the normal way. The results of the Glanzer and Cunitz study are shown in Figure 8.3.

As can be seen, group (a) subject showed the usual serial position curve (as illustrated by Figure 8.2). Group (b) had 10 seconds subtracted from their rehearsal time and subjects show a poorer recall performance in STM as a consequence of this. Group (c) subjects show virtually no recency effect, which implies that STM is ineffective for the last few items of the list.

Milner (1966) studied a patient referred to as 'HM' who had a defective LTM although his STM was normal. Conversely, a patient referred to as 'KF' studied by Shallice and Warrington (1970) had a normal LTM whereas his STM was defective, as plotted on the serial position curve.

Such studies as these supported the concept of memory consisting of two separate processes, a notion that is still favoured today even though the basic assumptions of the original model are in dispute.

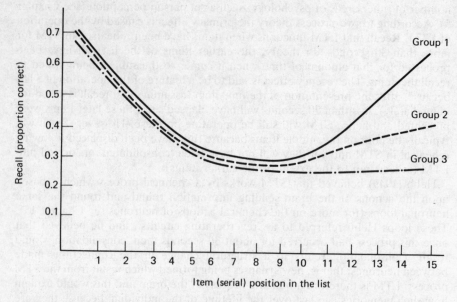

Source: Glanzer and Cunitz (1966)

Figure 8.3 The effects of rehearsal time on STM

8.5   Criticisms of Laboratory Studies of Memory

The laboratory findings which gave rise to the Atkinson–Shiffrin model were almost all based upon simple presentations of word lists which subjects had been instructed to memorize. Having memorized the items they would be given the task of recalling as many items as they were able. This experimental approach dates back to the pioneering work of Ebbinghaus (see Chapter 19) and is sometimes referred to as the 'bottom-up' approach; the theorists works from the basic stimulus materials and tries to discover how and why the subject makes sense of them. In more recent times such theories have given way to the so-called 'top-down' approach. This attempts to explain how memory works by investigating what the memory system takes for granted.

A pioneer of the top-down approach was Frederick Bartlett who described in his book *Remembering* (1932) the ways in which memory becomes altered after the event. This means that what we eventually come to recall of an event or episode we have experienced may bear little resemblance to the original 'facts'. According to Bartlett we construct a schematic representation of events which accords with what we think is likely to have occurred, rather than being able to use memory as though it were a video recorder. What we actually recall is our impression of things. This impression is formed from a mixture of reality and our own expectations, beliefs and interpretations of what happened. Thus, in a courtroom where eyewitnesses are sworn on oath to be truthful, they may each give entirely different accounts of the same event since they each have used their memories according to the ways that they schematized it. Bartlett introduced the term 'schema' to describe the ways in which people slot new information into their existing belief systems (see also the views of Piaget in Chapter 10 on the development of schemas).

8.6 Eyewitness Testimony

Research into the way that memory is influenced by a person's experiences subsequent to witnessing an event has been investigated by Elizabeth Loftus (1981). In a typical experiment subjects watch a visual sequence (on film or slides) depicting a crime or a road accident and they are then asked to recall these events. Depending upon which particular aspect of memory the experimenter is concerned with, a number of events may be interposed between subjects viewing the sequence and the act of recall. Loftus (1975) asked subjects to estimate the speed of a car that was seen to be involved in a road accident on film. The conditions manipulated by Loftus related to the use of a 'leading question'. In this instance, some of the subjects who saw the film were simply asked to guess the speed of the car as it 'passed the stop sign'. A second group of subjects were asked to guess its speed as it 'passed the barn'. In the original sequence a stop sign was indeed present at one point but no barn was present at any stage of the film, making this in effect a leading question. A week later all subjects were given a test of their memory for the filmed accident. The result was that 17 per cent of those who has been asked the leading question previously claimed to have seen the barn, whereas only 3 per cent of the other subjects did so. Loftus argues that eyewitnesses' memory may be influenced by their being asked leading questions due to a process of integration between the actual facts they are able to recollect and the inferences they make in the courtroom; for example, 'There must have been a barn otherwise I wouldn't have been asked about it.' Loftus has also shown that the use of emotive words such as 'smashed into' in a leading question about speed can significantly alter an eyewitness's recollection compared with a more neutral expression such as 'ran into', as in the instance: 'How fast was the sports car going when it (smashed)(ran) into the bus?'.

8.7 Levels of Processing

One aspect of the criticism aimed at the Atkinson–Shiffrin model of memory is that the evidence which supports it is derived from studies where subjects were tested under highly artificial conditions. For instance, they would be instructed to expect a test of their memory for the materials they would be shown (i.e., the test was of subjects' 'intentional learning'). But in everyday use we more often have to recall some event or other without realizing at the time that we will need this information later. In other words, in most cases we use our memory under conditions of **incidental learning**. For instance, if I ask you to recall the colour of the clothing worn by your best friend the last time you met this would be a test of your incidental learning. You are probably aware, as you try to recall this information, that you do know the answer even though retrieving this information may take some time and effort. You may need to ask yourself about that last occasion, what you were both doing, where you were, what happened that was unusual, and so on before you are able to recall it.

Craik and Lockhart (1972) described a new approach to the study of memory and at the same time introduced the new theory called 'levels of processing'. First, their technique involved giving subjects tasks to perform on (usually) a list of verbal materials, such as counting the number of letters, making up rhyming words for them, and so on. Next, and unbeknown to the subjects, they would be tested for their memory for the materials they had been working with. Comparisons are possible with this technique between the incidental learning of those engaged in the various tasks. Craik and Lockhart found that subjects who performed what seems to be 'deeper level' processing in the tasks had better memories for the materials compared with those 'shallow' tasks, such as merely counting vowels. Figure 8.4 illustrates the results of a hypothetical experiment involving three such tasks:

(a) checking letters for capital or small case (physical features only);
(b) making up rhyming words for each in the list (employing both physical and sound features of the words);
(c) fitting each word in the list into a sentence of their own making (involving not only knowledge of the words but also meanings).

It is evident that the 'deeper' the task then the better the recall performance becomes. In Figure 8.5 an analogy is drawn between the decision-making structure of a hypothetical 'Organization for Dealing with Linguistic Tasks' and the operation of the levels of processing model. In the illustration a new message is about to enter the system: the word 'LOP', with its messenger at the head of the elevator. The Alphabet Department will be able to affirm that these are valid

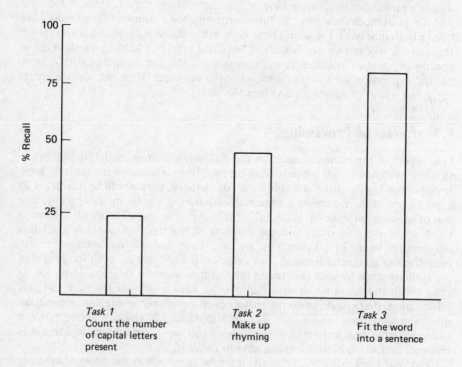

Figure 8.4 Task 'depth' and recall ability in a hypothetical experiment

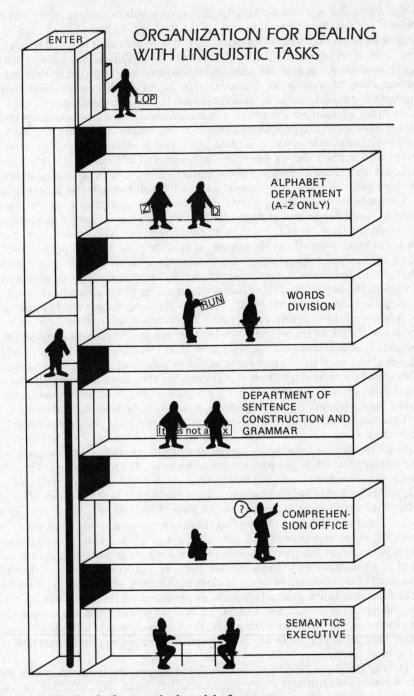

Figure 8.5 The 'level of processing' model of memory

English letters and if that is all the Organization is able to achieve then it will have been a very shallow task. However, if the message is then handed over to the Words Division they will affirm that the word 'lop' does exist and that it means 'to cut from trees; to trim'. But the Comprehension Office may object that the message remains ambiguous since capital letters may also imply that it is an abbreviation of some kind. The deep thinkers of the Executive office may be brought in to crack the code; this represents levels of processing.

In order to maintain information in the system Craik and Lockhart proposed that it must receive 'type I' or 'maintenance' processing. This is in effect the same process of rehearsal as was described in the two-process model of Atkinson and Shiffrin (described above). However, in contrast to that model, the levels theory predicts that rehearsal merely maintains the memory for as long as it is continued, with no guarantee that long-term storage will result through this process alone.

On the other hand, they propose that 'type II' or 'elaboration' processing will lead to more permanent storage. In the Organization analogy it is possible to maintain the message in the system at a shallow level (type I processing) but, in order to make its mark on the system, it must be passed to the deeper levels of semantic analysis (type II processing) where the greater 'depth' will ensure that the system maintains a more durable record of the message. Elaboration is therefore the key to improving memory, according to the levels model.

Rogers, Kuiper and Kirker (1977) showed that a yet deeper level of processing occurs, called the 'self-reference effect'. This is a task wherein subjects are asked to decide if each of the words in the list they are presented with applies to them personally. For instance, if the word is 'trouble', then the subject has to decide if this could be used to describe some aspect of their lives. Of course, commercial advertising executives try to use this effect when they employ models to advertise their products with whom 'ordinary' people can associate themselves, so as to make their particular brand of product more likely to 'stick' in our minds.

Craik and Watkins (1973) showed that rehearsal time does not 'deepen' the memory for material, as would be predicted by the two-process model. They gave subjects the task of listening to a series of words but only having to keep in mind the last word which began with a given letter (say, 'D', for instance). Therefore, in the sequence bold ... day ... fish ... track ... dirt subjects would hold day until the word dirt was heard some seconds later. Dirt would in turn become discarded when the next D-word appeared, and so forth. Using this elegant technique it is possible to vary the length of time that subjects spend rehearsing given words. For instance, in the sequence dog ... baby ... drain ... gold ... risk ... deed the word drain is rehearsed for approximately twice as long as the word dog (words being read at a constant rate to the subjects). If the two-process theory is correct then the recall of drain should be twice as likely as the recall of dog because it has been rehearsed that much more. However, as predicted by the levels model, type I (maintenance) rehearsal does not influence recall probability; only deeper forms of processing can do so. In other words, the results show that subjects are equally likely to recall any of the D-words irrespective of the length of rehearsal time they have been given.

Despite the many elegant studies which have supported the levels model there are a number of criticisms which other researchers have made of it. For instance, the notion of 'depth' is only an intuitive one and cannot be measured in any scientific sense. To say that one task requires 'deeper' processing than another is only descriptive, and yet this is a fundamental concept of the theory. Second, it has been shown by Morris, Bransford and Franks (1977) that the typical results of the levels type of experiment only occurs if the memory test is of the 'free recall' type (i.e., where subjects are free to recall the words of the list in any order they choose). Morris, Bransford and Franks proposed that free recall tests tend to help 'deeper' tasks more than they do 'shallow' tasks. Furthermore, when subjects are given 'cued recall' tests – that is, where they are given a hint as to the word required from the list – so-called 'shallow' tasks sometimes produce better recall performance.

8.8 Semantic Memory

The term semantic memory refers to how we store our knowledge of the world around us. This means how we encode meanings in our life and not simply the hard 'facts', such as the capital city of France. Theories of how such knowledge is represented in the human memory system are still in their infancy, there being comparatively few models of how this may occur, and little concordance exists between them.

Hierarchical network theory dates from the late 1960s when Collins and Quillian (1969) proposed that knowledge is stored in a network which contains nodal points, as shown diagrammatically in Figure 8.6. Before the theory is explained it may be worthwhile examining the technique upon which much of the work depends in order to support the model's assumptions. This is the so-called 'sentence verification' method, in which statements are presented to the subject which may be either true or false. Sometimes the subject is initially given the 'facts' and then asked to verify whether or not given statements, based upon these facts, are valid. Subjects are timed in their speed of response to the test statements and from this measurement of reaction time assumptions may be drawn concerning the act of information processing. Collins and Quillian utilized this technique in order to investigate how people seem to have organized their existing knowledge structures. In other words, the questions would be based upon the general knowledge of subjects and not upon material presented to them in the study. For instance, the question 'Do canaries have lungs?' is a question which is designed to test how knowledge structures about these animals are represented. It is unlikely that the person has ever been told explicitly that canaries do possess lungs and yet, from what they know concerning the attributes of the animal world, it is a fair assumption that they would be capable of answering this question. For the moment, examine your own thought processes as you try to answer the question yourself: 'Do canaries have lungs?'

It is likely that your answer, if you formed one, went along these lines. First, canaries are birds and birds are animals. Animals breathe and so it is virtually certain that they have lungs (your not being aware of gill-bearing birds may confirm this judgement). Collins and Quillian argued from their results (represented schematically in Figure 8.7) that the more nodes which the answer search crosses when processing such a question, then the longer will be the response time. In the case of a question such as 'Does a frog eat?' the response time should be quicker than a question which asked 'Can a frog swim?' because fewer nodes are crossed in retrieving the answer. The hierarchical network model seemed able to explain these findings and became an influential starting point for semantic memory research.

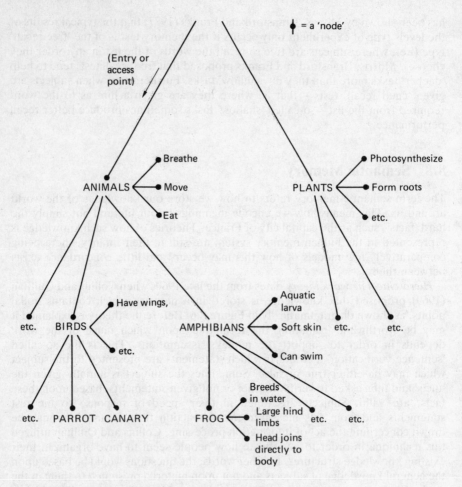

♦ = a 'node'

(Entry or
access
point)

ANIMALS
• Breathe
• Move
• Eat

PLANTS
• Photosynthesize
• Form roots
• etc.

etc.   BIRDS
• Have wings,
• etc.

AMPHIBIANS
• Aquatic larva
• Soft skin   etc.   etc.
• Can swim

etc.   PARROT   CANARY   FROG
Breeds in water
Large hind limbs   etc.   etc.
Head joins directly to body

Source: Collins and Quillian (1969)

**Figure 8.6 Schematic diagram of Collins's and Quillian's hierarchical network
model**

Since the original statement of the hierarchical network model by Collins and
Quillian it has become evident that it is inadequate as it stands. For instance,
Rips, Shoben and Smith (1973) found instances which prove the model incorrect.
In the case of a question such as 'Is a bear an animal?', subjects take less time to
verify this affirmatively than they do when replying to the question 'Is a bear a
mammal?' In the network there are fewer modes separating the second case
(between bear and mammal) than the first (between bear and animal), and so an
important prediction of the model fails.

Spreading activation theory was first formulated by Collins and Loftus (1975),
who propose that instead of knowledge being represented in a hierarchical
structure it is stored according to the degree of relatedness. For instance, your
memory for the word 'tree' would be stored in association with words such as leaf,
green, furniture, wood, sap, and so forth. The closer the relatedness of the words

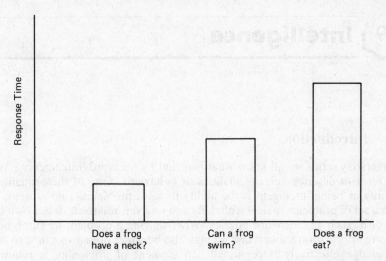

Figure 8.7 Typical finding of a sentence verification task (based on the network model in Figure 8.6)

then the closer they will be in the semantic store. The links which connect words (concepts) in the representation are crossed in the same way as nodes are traversed in the hierarchical model, and so many of the same predictions for the previous model hold. However, since it is not activated via a single pathway (i.e., from the highest search point downwards in the case of the hierarchical model), response times do not necessarily reflect rigid knowledge structures. Once 'activated', a concept which you may be requested to gain access to may spread via its connecting links to neighbouring concepts; hence associations such as 'spoon' may elicit the responses 'fork', 'knife' and 'stir' since these are directly connected in the network to the sought word. In the case of a question such as 'Is a table a piece of furniture?', the concepts 'table' and 'furniture' may simultaneously become activated and would spread from both directions until their paths intersected.

The problem of how human knowledge becomes represented in memory has continued to be an active area of research and it is likely that this will lead into models of greater and greater complexity as information technology progresses into the next decade. Although the issue is almost insoluble in the foreseeable future the reason for its popularity lies in the application of these concepts to work in artificial intelligence, and specifically in the field of *expert systems*.

8.9 Questions and Exercises

1. Write down a list of fifteen words and test a group of your friends for primacy and recency effects in STM (refer to the section on the Atkinson–Shiffrin model for details). To plot the graph you simply need to take the average (mean) recall scores for each of the fifteen words.
2. Think of three tasks which seem to you to be 'shallow', 'deep' and 'medium' in terms of the levels of processing model of memory. Try to justify why you have graded them in this way.

9 Intelligence

9.1 Introduction

In everyday terms we all know what is meant by the word 'intelligence'. We use the term to describe certain qualities of behaviour. One of these qualities we identify as being intelligent is the ability to solve problems. Life presents us all with a set of problems to deal with daily and we even add some of our own for the fun of it, such as crossword puzzles. When solving a problem we often need to acquire information about it and we may also be under pressure of time to use our knowledge effectively. Occasionally an element of originality is required in everyday problem-solving and we need to develop ideas of our own even in these mundane situations. People who seem best able to cope in these circumstances seem to possess superior speed of thought, originality and mental alertness which all seem to add up to the term 'intelligent'. Such descriptions are most often used by people when asked to say what intelligence means to them. To say that someone is intelligent usually means that we have seen some of these qualities in their behaviour or in their general attitude to life. Such people have an everyday approach to things which has a feel of 'good sense-ness' about it. Yet despite this apparently obvious characteristic about people it has become clear to psychologists who have attempted to define the term 'intelligent' that we do not all agree on what is implied by the word.

For instance, suppose someone learns things only slowly and yet they are able to use their knowledge both effectively and originally once it has been acquired. Are they intelligent? Is it possible to be intelligent in one situation but not in another? It is not uncommon, for example, for a person to be regarded by their workmates as bright and competent and yet to be considered as dull by friends or relatives. Are there different kinds of intelligence? It seems that some people are intelligent at solving problems which enable their lives to run smoothly. They tackle their finances and everyday life with both skill and good sense, whereas many of life's geniuses have been known to lead themselves and their loved ones into a life of rack and ruin because of their one-tracked minds.

Detectives, mathematicians and scientists all tend to deal with problems in which they must converge their thinking upon a single correct solution. Economists, politicians and businessmen, on the other hand, need to be divergent and flexible in their approach to the problems which confront them and they are often faced with having to devise and choose between a number of equally plausible solutions to the same problem. Which of these two types of thinker is more intelligent? Is intelligence something that may be taught to people? Just what is the very nature of the concept of 'intelligence'? Even after a century or more of research psychologists have not been able to get close to answering these questions. It is not surprising to find that most of the work on this topic has been concerned more with the practical applications than with attempting to establish a firm theoretical base. Therefore the pragmatic definition is one which defines intelligence as being the thing which is measured by an **IQ** test. In order to proceed with this definition it becomes necessary to start with an explanation of what IQ tests are attempting to measure or else we shall end in the circular argument that IQ tests are things for measuring intelligence! Before proceeding to examine the current notions of human intelligence in psychology we shall therefore start by outlining the historical development of the IQ testing movement.

9.2   The Development of IQ Testing

Alfred Binet

In 1904 Alfred Binet was appointed as member of a commission set up by the Ministry of Public Instruction in Paris which was to study the problems associated with subnormal children in schools. Binet was assigned to the task, in collaboration with other specialists, of devising an objective means for assessing intellectual performance. In his quest of measuring intelligence Binet relied upon no particular theory of intelligence and cared not whether it was an innate or a learnt ability. Rather than approach the problem with preconceived ideas he simply treated the concept from first principles. To him, a subnormal child was simply one who was not performing as well as the rest of that age group. With this in mind a test was constructed in which problems in a mental test are referred to as test 'items' and Binet screened items for his first test on the grounds so that:

(a) they would discriminate between the performances of children in different age groups;
(b) they would not depend upon the use of ordinary knowledge which the child may or may not have acquired in school lessons (i.e., children who do not attend in class are not necessarily dull);
(c) they would interest and motivate the child irrespective of age (in other words problems should be neither too difficult nor too easy and be of a practical nature wherever possible);
(d) they should appear in a scale of ascending difficulty such that all children from a given age group should be capable of answering the early items of the test with relative ease whilst only a very few should be capable of answering the final items correctly. Furthermore, given a time-constraint, few if any children should be able to complete the test in the time given.

The items in Binet's test were varied and they ranged, for instance, from asking the child to distinguish between a piece of chocolate and a lump of wood, to tasks which required them to repeat sentences or actions shown to them. Test scores were obtained by noting how many correct solutions in the test the child achieved. Examiners were presented with average or 'normative' scores (norms) for the different age groups to enable comparisons to be made for each given child with what is expected for their given age group. Incidentally, this age-related normative group approach was so successful that it formed the basis of intelligence testing over the following half a century and is still used in some tests even today.

In 1911 Binet and Simon published their 'Metric Scale of Intelligence'. Three years later the number of items in the test was increased and they were re-grouped according to the age at which between 50 and 75 per cent of children were capable of solving them. Figure 9.1 illustrates this procedure for one such item. In this revision of the test many items were added and some of the unsuccessful ones were omitted, which further shows how pragmatic an approach the mental testers were employing.

In 1911 there was a still further revision which extended the useful age range of children who could be tested to between 3 and 15 years. This revision also introduced the concept of the **mental age**. The child's mental age was determined by their level of error-less performance on the test compared with the age-related norm. For example, if the child is 7 years old and yet succeeds without error to the level achieved by the average 8 year old then the child's mental age is taken to be eight. For any correct answers they could achieve above this errorless position an allowance in months was made on top of their basal score. Using this principle it became possible to use a sophisticated way of expressing results which is called the 'mental ratio'. The mental ratio (or MR) is calculated in the following way:

$$MR = \frac{\text{mental age}}{\text{actual age}}$$

For instance, a child of 10 who scores a mental age of 8 in the test would have the MR of:

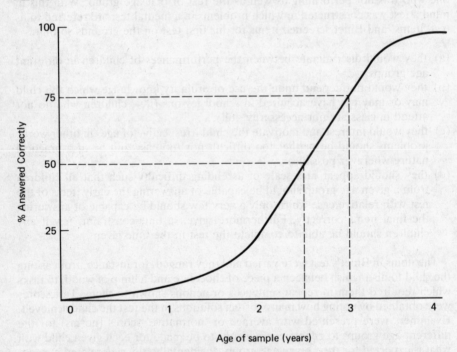

Figure 9.1 A test item 'Make a bridge from three blocks' is shown in the figure to be suited to $2\frac{1}{2}$–3-year-olds, according to the criterion adopted by Binet where between 50 and 75 per cent of the age group should be capable of answering that item

$$\frac{8}{10} = 0.8$$

Similarly, a 10 year old who has a mental age of 12 would have the MR of

$$\frac{12}{10} = 1.2$$

The important point to remember here is that a simple glance at the MR is enough to establish the child's position relative to the rest of the age group. An MR above one means that the child is above average whereas below one implies that the child is subnormal by a measured amount.

In a revision of the Binet and Simon test at Stanford University, Stern improved upon the MR index by converting it into an 'intelligence quotient', or IQ. This was achieved so as to remove the difficulty of working with numerical fractions. IQ is simply calculated from the basic mental ratio in the following way:

$$IQ = MR \times 100$$

Returning to the case of the child with a mental age of 12 and an actual age of 10 the IQ becomes:

$$\frac{12}{10} \times 100 = 120$$

Thus, if your mental and actual ages are equal then your IQ score is 100. Such an IQ suggests that you are of average intelligence for your particular age group.

With the publication of the Binet–Simon scale intelligence tests became established as practical instruments for assessing certain aspects of intellectual development and they could be used to facilitate predictions of future scholastic performance. These were the aims for which IQ tests were originally developed and in this respect they were successful. However, in the original form these tests were unmanageable because of the number of practical items included in the test. This fact limited the test to a one-to-one procedure of examiner to child. In terms of their original usage this was not a serious problem, but in cases where large-scale testing was required it became desirable to change the test items towards written and more abstract forms to which only one identifiable solution exists.

Such a modification was necessary for the purpose of developing the usefulness of IQ testing beyond the classroom where it had proved to be so successful. This sort of modification received an impetus when America entered the First World War and large numbers of people were recruited for army service, coming from a wide range of educational and cultural backgrounds. It was necessary at short notice to select those men who were able and suited to military service from those who were not, either because of intellectual or other shortcomings. In addition, from these large numbers of recruits IQ tests were used to select those who could best serve as officers and leaders. In order to achieve this two pencil-and-paper tests were used. The majority of recruits were tested on the so-called 'Alpha' test which was verbal. However, the problem with using only a verbal test was that many of the recruits came from educationally underprivileged areas of the country and some had inadequate reading or writing ability. To solve this difficulty a sister test called the 'Beta' was used, which was a non-verbal and **culture-fair** test.

The development of large-scale testing by the Americans proved to be successful as a selection device and so it was inevitable that after the war IQ tests would be used in a wide range of civilian activities such as education, government service and in employee selection throughout industry. In Britain IQ tests formed the basis of the 11-plus examination in many parts of the country in the decades which followed. Such *ad hoc* applications of mental testing as this led to widespread dissatisfaction in psychology since it often produced a bias against deprived social, economic or racial groups within a given society.

9.3   Construction of Modern IQ Tests

Despite an increase in statistical sophistication in measuring IQ since Binet's time there are fundamentally similar principles involved in the construction of the modern IQ test. The basic concepts of test standardization, reliability and validity have become essential words in the vocabulary of **psychometrics** (see Spotlight box).

Test standardization

In order to make any test fair to everyone who takes it, it is essential that all who take it do so under identical conditions. Testees must be given similarly comfortable surroundings, quietness and freedom from distraction, and be instructed in the test proceedings in the same manner. Failure to standardize testing conditions can impair the ability of the test to produce an accurate and reliable measurement of the person's ability. Even racial differences between the test administrator and the candidates may influence the performance of the testee (Katz *et al.* 1965).

Standardization of intelligence tests also involves ensuring that their measurement scales are, as far as possible, equivalent. For instance, if one test were to have an average score of 100 and another test a score of 50 then it would not be convenient since the same person's scores on both tests would not be directly comparable. Consequently, the scale of measurement of IQ tests has been given a standard form on which the 'average' performance produces a value of 100. In this respect the IQ scale has not altered since the work of Stern referred to above, in which average performances were derived from age-norms. However, instead of utilizing age-related norms the modern method of testing adult intelligence is to select some other criterion, such as occupational or educational group, as the norm. Hence a candidate applying for a place as trainee in the field of industrial management could be tested against the appropriate normative group by extracting scores from successful managers in the same field of employment. Similarly, recruits for the armed forces could be tested against the appropriate norms for the military using previously-derived standards. In principle this is no different from the method employed by Binet at the outset of his work: that is, in order to establish the position of any individual relative to his or her group (in Binet's case, their age-group), the standard performance for that group is first established by extracting large numbers of scores from the 'population' in question.

SPOTLIGHT Forms of reliability and validity used when referring to psychological testing

Reliability means the consistency with which a test is able to reproduce the same scores from the same individuals. There are a number of ways of measuring a test's reliability, some of which are described below.

1. *Test-retest*: the same test is re-taken by the same people. With IQ tests this should not affect scores very much provided that the solutions to the first test are not discussed. However, there will inevitably be some improvement when sitting the same test for the second time.
2. *Equivalent forms test:* this is used when the test manufacturer has produced two different forms of the same test. This used to be a popular method and some tests, such as the 1937 revision of the Stanford–Binet IQ test, could be obtained in equivalent forms L and M.
3. *Split-half test*: this is where one-half of the test items are correlated with the other half. The split is most often achieved by dividing odd and even question-numbers, and this enables the degree of internal consistency of the test to be evaluated.

Validity means the extent to which a psychological test is measuring what it is designed to measure. Again, there are a number of ways of ascertaining the validity of any test.

1. *Predictive validity*: this examines how accurately a person's score on the test will predict their academic (in the case of IQ tests) performance.
2. *Concurrent validity*: this measures a person's performance on the given test and compares that again his or her performance on other tests which are regarded as measuring the same ability or faculty. For instance, in the case of a new IQ test its concurrent validity may be checked by correlating scores with existing IQ tests.
3. *Face validity*: this means literally to check the 'face value' of the test to see whether each item really is testing what the manufacturer claims it is. Another aspect of face validity regarding IQ tests is whether or not the level of difficulty of the items is appropriate.

In addition to knowing the average or 'mean' performance for the normative group, it is also necessary to have some measurement of the spread of scores in the population in order that something can be known about the deviation of any individual's score from the group's average. For instance, it is not very helpful just to know that a person is 'below average' in relation to a particular normative group because that does not tell us whether that person is mentally deficient or just below average! The technical term for this measurement of spread from which deviations are calculated is called the *standard deviation*, and it is further described in Chapter 17. Suffice it to say, by way of example, that to be one standard deviation below the mean indicates that the person has a lower IQ than

84 per cent of the normative group they have been tested against. The illustration of Figure 9.2 shows the standard normal distribution as applied to intelligence tests, and it is an essential part of modern test construction.

9.4 Theories of Intelligence

In the introduction to this chapter it was made clear that psychologists do not agree on a definition of what intelligence is, even though the practice of intelligence testing has become a major industry in its own right. Part of this problem of defining the substance of intelligence stems from that fact that the word was in colloquial use long before psychologists began to research the subject. As with many such concepts handed over to science in this way, it often proves difficult to describe them in a way which makes them amenable for research. For instance, imagine yourself trying to investigate a concept such as 'being happy'. It is evident enough to you when the feeling itself is present, but not everyone experiences happiness in the same way and it does not become expressed in the same way in everyone's behaviour. Can you imagine trying to devise a scale for measuring 'happiness'? However, so as not to dodge the issue altogether, a selection of ideas from theorists over the past century is included here in order to give a flavour of the kind of thinking which has guided research in the subject.

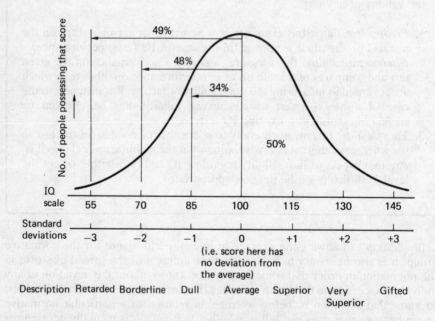

Figure 9.2 The standard normal distribution for IQ: scores below average would be less than 100 and they would have a negative standard deviation; likewise above average scores are over 100 and they have a positive standard deviation.

Francis Galton

In 1869 Galton published the book called *Hereditary Genius*, in which he reported studies of the families of famous men. He claimed that individuals obtain their intellect by means of descent. His own family provided him with some evidence for this viewpoint because he was related to several eminent figures of his day, including Charles Darwin and the Wedgwood family. Galton reasoned that people inherit much of their physiological make-up from their parents and this would therefore include the qualities with which their sensory and nervous systems function. For instance, if we are lucky enough to have inherited a good set of sensory systems such as eyes and ears, we will be more likely than others less well endowed to have the ability to perceive and understand the complexities of the world buzzing around us. Conversely, anyone having sensory defects would not be able to deal with the world on the same level as normal people. Galton drew attention to the possible value of studying identical twins in order to investigate just how important inheritance is to intellectual performance.

Cyril Burt

Burt was influenced by the ideas of Galton and he defined intelligence as being an innate all-round cognitive ability. In his studies Burt showed there to be a high *correlation* between intelligence and the degree of relatedness between two people. In other words. the closer the familial relationship between two people then the more similar will be their IQs. However, in more recent years some of Burt's data has been discredited and so psychologists have therefore become suspicious of his conclusions about the inheritance of intelligence.

Charles Spearman

In 1904 Spearman defined the term intelligence as being a 'general ability'. He had been studying and testing school-children and had paid particular attention to correlations of ability which occur between specific subjects. He found that some children performed well in the entire range of tests they had been given, whereas others performed at a below-average level all round. From such results he concluded that a child's performance on any test will depend upon that child's broad level of general ability, which he referred to as 'g' (general intelligence), as well as upon any specific abilities the child may possess which are relevant to the task in hand. The specific abilities he referred to as 's' factors. For instance, people's musical ability will depend upon their possessing sufficient general intelligence to learn the technical aspects of the skill as well as their possessing what we may call the 'natural gift' for music, which in Spearman's terms is the relevant 's' factor. The way in which general and specific factors make up a person's ability in any particular task may be conceptualized using Figure 9.3, which shows the theoretical connection between g and s ability.

Later, Spearman suggested that 'g' is determined by the inheritance of some form of mental power which is derived from the nervous system. In this respect Spearman's views echo those of Galton before him. Spearman's concept of intelligence as being a general ability which underpins everything we do has been influential in guiding theories in Britain, whereas in America the tendency has

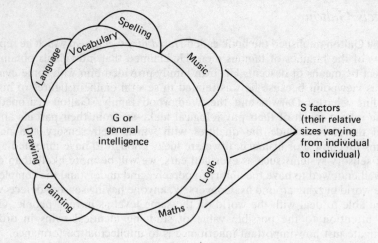

Source: Spearman (1904)

Figure 9.3 Spearman's model of intelligence structures

been to regard intelligence as being the sum total of a collection of a number of separate faculties or independent abilities.

Thorndike

Thorndike (1903) exemplifies this approach with his definition of intelligence as constituting 'a host of highly particularized and independent faculties'. As a consequence of his studies of numerous test performances Thorndike suggested that four groups of abilities exist, within each of which specific skills may be required. The four groups were sentence completion, vocabulary, arithmetic and direction following. This segregation of skills underlying intelligence was influential in determining the course of intelligence theories in America, notably in the work of Thurstone and Guilford.

Thurstone

Thurstone (1931) developed the new technique of factor analysis for investigating personality traits. In 1938 he employed his method in the analysis of 240 college students who had completed a battery of 56 tests. Thurstone argued that his analysis showed no evidence for the existence of any general form of intelligence, but that in fact eight grouped factors seemed to be present. These he later reduced to six: numeracy, comprehension, spatial ability, word fluency, reasoning and memory. These fundamental skills Thurstone labelled the 'primary mental abilities'.

Guilford

Guilford represents the extreme view of intelligence as being a collection of segregated abilities and in 1967 he identified 120 factors as making up the structure of human intelligence!

Hebb

Hebb (1949) argued that intelligence is an inseparable compound of both inherited and learnt characteristics. We may inherit a given potential which may be called 'A', but the extent to which this endowment becomes nurtured into the adult form will depend upon both circumstantial and personal factors. For instance, being born with potential giftedness does not mean that the person becomes inevitably superior since it is as much a question of how, and to what extent, environmental influences operate on the person during development. The product of this personal development of the intellect Hebb referred to as intelligence B, and it has indivisible properties regarding inheritance and learning.

Vernon

Vernon (1960) added a hybrid structure of intelligence which goes some way towards conciliating the British and American views. His model is called hierarchical in that he views the overall intelligence to be unified as 'g', according to Spearman's views. However, beyond that, Vernon proposed that there are both practical and academic facets to this structure. For each of these two components he goes on to itemize a number of factors which underlie them, such as numeracy, literacy and reasoning (A, B and C) skills under the academic branch. Going beyond this level he describes specific factors which further underlie concepts such as comprehension, as illustrated in Figure 9.4. A second contribution by Vernon to the intelligence debate is his observation that if Hebb is correct in his analysis of intelligence types A and B, then all that we can hope to know about an individual's intelligence is that which they have developed. In fact only a tiny portion of this product can ever be measured in any realistic test of intelligence, given the restrictions placed upon written tests to include only convergent problems (containing one correct identifiable solution) and to be of a theoretical rather than a practical nature. As a consequence of this Vernon proposes that the fraction of intelligence B which IQ tests measure should be referred to as intelligence C, which is merely the ability to do the particular test in question. Any IQ test is only able to sample a tiny amount of a person's intelligence in the broad sense of that term.

9.5 Determinants of IQ Test Performance

Racial factor

There is no doubt that different racial groups perform at different levels on IQ tests which were designed by and for people from European and American cultures. The early studies of immigrant recruits into the American army during the First World War originally showed this to be so. American negroes performed at around one standard deviation below whites on the contemporary tests. Therefore the debate which concerns psychologists in this area is to what extent this finding of racial differences shows real, as opposed to simply measured, differences in intellectual functioning.

There are many logical fallacies attached to the view of racial superiority, in intelligence as in other areas of ability. There are two categories of fallacy to

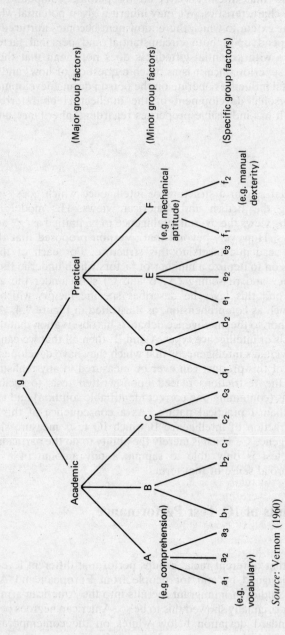

(Major group factors)

(Minor group factors)

(Specific group factors)

g

Academic   Practical

A   B   C   D   E   F

(e.g. comprehension)   (e.g. mechanical aptitude)

a_1 a_2 a_3 b_1 b_2 c_1 c_2 c_3 d_1 d_2 e_1 e_2 e_3 f_1 f_2

(e.g. vocabulary)   (e.g. manual dexterity)

Source: Vernon (1960)

Figure 9.4 Vernon's hierarchical model of the structure of human abilities

consider. First, the differences between national groups should not be called 'racial' even when large superficial differences such as colour are involved. A precise account of the ancestry of any one group of individuals which stretches back many tens of generations is practically impossible to obtain. The second fallacy is that, because different racial groups are sharing the same geographical locality, they must necessarily be experiencing similar cultural influences. The effects of inter- and intra-cultural attitudes, socioeconomic circumstances and the cultural biases of testing make it impossible to make clear statements about intellectual differences or otherwise between racial groupings.

Social and educational background

In an early study, Gordon (1923) made an extensive survey of canal boat children and found that the mean level of measured intelligence decreased with age. Similar studies have been carried out in the United States on the mountain children of Georgia and Kentucky. These results could be explained in part by the lack of educational opportunity in isolated communities such as these, as well as their inability to develop sociolinguistic skills to a sufficient degree. As they get older the rudimentary skills that were developed initially may diminish through lack of practice. Another likely explanation for this effect is the means by which the studies themselves were done. It has been suggested that tests of verbal intelligence favour white middle-class children over those from more impoverished (materially speaking) homes. These points were made by Bernstein (1965) relating to the use of language codes which emphasized the disadvantage of working-class children entering the education system. Help and encouragement given to children by teachers is known to be influenced by the value judgements made in the classroom, an effect known as 'Pygmalion in the classroom' (Rosenthal and Jacobsen, 1968).

Teachers' expectations

In a study by Rosenthal and Jacobsen in 1964 in San Francisco (Oak School), they told teachers at the outset that they were interested in testing the validity of a method they had developed for predicting academic achievement in school-children. The test they actually gave to the children was a straightforward IQ test, although the teachers were unaware of the true nature of the study. Teachers were informed that on several future occasions these pupils would be re-tested to monitor their progress. Next, twenty of these children were chosen at random and given the label 'spurters'. A casual remark was made to teachers at a staff meeting which 'leaked' the information about who the 'spurters' were. When these same children were tested again some months later it was found that in the younger age groups those who had been labelled (randomly by the researchers) as 'spurters' did actually show increased IQ levels. When describing the children's behaviour teachers rated the spurters as having a better chance of success in later life, and as being generally happier, more curious and more interesting children than the others. There are two possible explanations for this effect: either teachers spent more time and effort in coaching those children they expected to do well, or/and the more positive self-esteem gained by these children when gaining more teacher-attention raised their own expectations and performance levels. When questioned on this matter the teachers did not believe they had spent more time with the spurters.

Rubovits and Maehr (1973) conducted a study of student teachers in America who were given micro-teaching sessions with both black and white students. From each of their groups they were told (spuriously) of 'gifted' students in their classes. It was found that when a white student had the 'gifted' label then teachers (all white and female) gave that student more overall encouragement and praise than others in the group. However, when the so-called gifted person was a negro then teachers gave *less* attention and encouragement to that person than to the others. This again illustrates the importance of teachers in the intellectual development of the students in their trust, since cultural mismatches evidently lead to both inadvertent changes in levels of expectation of performance as well as in the actual educational interactions which occur in the classroom.

Maturation and ageing

Between the ages of 5 and 11 the rate of development of individuals tends to be fairly uniform, and so tests which are administered to children on entry to the primary school remain useful predictors. However, as we have already seen from the 'Pygmalion' effect, teachers may influence the course of events in the classroom if this information is to hand. Furthermore, in adolescence test scores become much less reliable as indicators of how well an individual will succeed in the coming years. This is probably because at this stage of life many personal and social changes arise which may guide the individual in a number of different directions. Personality and motivation levels may influence performance in school examinations and other forms of intellectual assessment. Many tests fail to show increases in performance after the age of 15 years, and only those who proceed into higher education tend to show increases in IQ beyond the age of 20 years. Brighter individuals tend to sustain their increasing level of *measured* intelligence longer and also show a slower decline, on average, at the other end of the age range. This implies that intelligence is related to some extent to the degree of mental stimulation gained through employment, since higher educational performance generally leads individuals into more stimulating varieties of work. Another important factor in determining IQ scores is the attitude of the person being tested and this will change with age. Whereas a younger person may strive to achieve his or her best performance, an elderly person may treat such tests as trivial and meaningless compared with his or her own life. But even when IQ seems to be declining in the elderly it is not clear which aspects of the complex skills involved are deteriorating. For instance, it may be 'mental agility', or speed of working, memory faculty or even the ability to comprehend instructions; in other words, a decline in general intellectual efficiency does not necessarily follow from a fall in measured intelligence (IQ).

Physical determinants

It is a common fallacy to think of intellectually bright people as being physically frail in stature or health. It has been found that exceptionally bright children are above average in health and physique. It is likely that the converse effect is also important: someone suffering from ill-health is less likely to perform well in mental tests as well as being at a disadvantage relative to classmates in the everyday affairs of the classroom.

Gender differences

It is widely accepted that girls generally perform better at tasks involving verbal skills than do boys. This difference begins at an early age, although the difference becomes only slight by teenage years. Boys, on the other hand, usually do better at spatial and mathematical tasks than do girls, but again the differences decline as they get older. As regards general scores of IQ, no difference is found between males and females.

Speed of working

IQ tests are often criticized on the grounds that they favour the quicker worker at the expense of the careful one. There is some justification for the argument that tests are by their nature not able to measure certain ways of thinking. However, some psychologists have argued that speed of thinking is one of the important criteria by which we judge a person's intelligence.

Practice effects

For most people their first IQ test proves to be a novel experience and so it is not surprising to find that on taking a similar test later they may improve their scores by as much as five points. But on the whole there is no evidence to suggest that coaching does greatly influence performance, and in any case strict controls apply on the supply and use of IQ tests beyond what are regarded as their legitimate places.

Birth order

It has been found that first-born children (i.e., the eldest child of each family) tend to have higher IQs than later-born children. Evidently if a genetic explanation were true this would not be so and it seems to imply that the additional care and attention given to the first-born provides them with an advantage over their siblings.

9.6 Artificial Intelligence

During the Second World War some psychologists became involved in the design of controls for complex operating systems such as occur in aircraft cockpits. This involved them in working alongside specialists in ergonomics (the study of the human–machine interface) and cybernetics (automatic control systems for machines), which later led to the development of the fields of cogntive psychology and artificial intelligence (AI). These two fields have, in more recent years, formed part of the same enterprise in trying to understand human mental processes in terms of an 'information processing' approach. AI is specifically concerned with modelling the human mind using computer programs. The word 'artificial' emphasizes the modelling aspect, whereas 'intelligence' refers to the main aim of replicating mental faculties in the area of problem-solving in particular, which in humans is regarded as requiring intelligent behaviour.

The argument put forward by Turing (1950) was that if a computer could make responses to a human in such a way that the human could mistake the computer for another human, then the machine may be said to 'think' as humans think. This simple and yet useful principle has guided AI research for two generations, although it has recently come under severe attack on logical grounds (see Frosh, 1989, for a review of the arguments). The later version of the Turing test is known as that the Church–Turing hypothesis, which proposes that whatever is human-computable is also machine-computable.

Newell and Simon (1956, 1961) developed the General Problem Solver (GPS), which pioneered the problem-solving approach in AI with a program which was able to solve highly sophisticated mathematical problems developed from formal logic. Representations of game-playing computers followed, and today it is possible to buy chess computers quite cheaply which will beat all but the finest players.

AI has not been restricted to simulating thought processes but has also been working in a number of different areas such as in modelling human vision (Marr, 1982), although 'seeing machines' are a long way from possessing the visual abilities of human beings. However, they do make a reasonable job of emulating the frog!

Human memory research has also been modelled using the AI approach; in particular the work of Shank and Abelson on 'scripts' has been a productive contribution. Programs use a 'script' as a means of interpreting and 'conceptualizing' events. For instance, a visit to the hairdressers involves you in a series of social transactions which are scripted almost as though they were scenes from a play. The appointment is booked, there is a comfortable waiting area, the staff treat the customers with politeness and hospitality, the hair 'operation' is carried out, you pay the operator, you are bidden goodbye, and so on; most of this behaviour will conform to the 'visit to the hairdresser' script. Given that we utilize such a pre-scripted model in our social lives such behaviour forms the basis for the way we interpret and store information from our experiences in daily life. We 'hang' our experiences on such convenient coathangers set out for us in our memory systems. Shank and Abelson (1977) utilize this concept in SAM (script applier mechanism), which was developed by them to process information about a visit to a restaurant.

One of the most important, through least successful, areas of AI has been in the development of processors for human speech. Computers deal with keyboard communication by translating the 'high-level' language used by the operator into a 'low-level' code that is ultimately transcribed into electrical impulses which are then stored magnetically within the system's 'hardware'. Human spoken language is not a logical system, and therefore representing our use of spoken – or, for that matter, written – language is not proving to be a very practical enterprise, even though immense strides towards our understanding of language have been made using this approach.

In the future AI knowledge may be used to improve human thought by training us how to think more clearly. There is some irony here since it is entirely feasible that our slaves may ultimately become the masters in a way foreseen by science fiction writers for two generations!

9.7   Current Intelligence Research

Apart from practical applications, the traditional 'psychometric' concept of intelligence made little theoretical advance throughout its long history. The idea of intelligence as being a 'thing' in the human brain was never unanimously accepted in psychology and it seems likely that cognitive psychologists may inherit the term for a 'new look'. Although researchers are still trying to establish biological correlates of intelligence, such as localized functioning in the brain, 'evoked' potentials and response times, there has been a more analytical viewpoint which has begun to reassess the meaning of the term 'intelligence' from a rational perspective.

Howe (1988) has argued that the traditional concept of intelligence was never more than a descriptive one; it provides an account of the apparent facts (just as do words such as 'happiness') but without providing an analytical and scientific framework for debate. For instance, knowing that a person scores consistently poorly in an IQ test does not provide any insight into the person's ability or their potential, since a myriad of social factors may be responsible for consistently low performance scores. In the treatment of some abnormal states of mind such as depression, for instance, it has been discovered that it is possible to re-direct a person's thinking patterns away from the negative and towards the positive facets of their lives. Such fluidity in cognitive processing implies that thinking is an aspect of mental life which has an immense capacity for change in a suitable training environment.

To many cognitive psychologists the term intelligence is largely redundant, since it forms merely an 'emergent property' of systems which are involved in thinking. Such theorists as Johnson-Laird (1983) focus more on the dynamic processes of thought and the way in which individuals represent their world mentally than they do upon a spurious IQ score which is said to be a measure of overall mental capacity for that individual. Arguably, the complexity of the human mind deserves to be treated with more regard and respect than it has received from the psychometricians.

9.8   Questions and Exercises

1. Using Binet's concept of the 'mental ratio', calculate the MR of a child who is 12 years old but has a measured (mental) age of 14 years.
2. Give a brief account of Binet's criteria for test construction.
3. Using the standard normal distribution of IQ in Figure 9.2 estimate the proportion of people with IQ scores greater than 85.

10 Cognitive Development

10.1 Introduction

What exactly goes on in children's minds? How do they represent the world, arrive at decisions or work problems out?

It was once thought that children were merely miniature versions of adults but this view, as we shall see, was a completely naive one. On the contrary, children have quite different and characteristic ways of thinking when compared with adults.

The term 'cognition' is used to cover a broad range of abilities, all of which involve internal, mental activities. These include processes such as reasoning, interpreting, assessing and representing. The approach now favoured by cognitive psychologists focuses upon how the individual represents information mentally, with one aim being to explain behaviour at the level of the reasons, judgements and rationale used.

For instance, if a young child is able to solve a task involving mental reasoning, then the cognitive psychologist would ask how it was achieved and what strategies the child adopted. One way of doing this is to simply ask the child to explain his or her actions, and note the explanation offered. Indeed this 'clinical method', where the subject responds freely to questions and problems, was (and still is) widely used as a technique for gathering information, especially about mental events.

In this chapter we will discuss the cognitive-developmental theory of Jean Piaget, the eminent Swiss psychologist who made a significant contribution to the study of child development. We will also briefly consider Piaget's research into moral development, itself an important facet in a child's life.

10.2 The Work of Jean Piaget

As a student, Jean Piaget (1896–1980) originally trained in the discipline of zoology although he also had a profound interest in philosophy, especially a branch called epistemology (the nature and limits of human knowledge). Some time after graduating he developed an interest in psychology, and became involved for a while in testing children's intelligence. After working in this field, Piaget moved toward combining elements from his various interests, a direction which was to lay the foundations of the theory for which he is now best known: that is, he became engrossed in using scientific principles to understand the acquisition and development of knowledge.

We shall look at Piaget's theory of intellectual development in a moment, but first it is necessary to consider some of the underlying assumptions on which it is based. One of the main features is the emphasis upon interaction between the child and the environment: that is, intellectual abilities develop as a result of the maturing child's efforts to make sense of their experiences with the world. This further entails the notion that the young child is an active participant in the process, and very much responsible for subsequent development. This, of course, completely opposes the views held by learning theorists, who (as you may recall) stress the importance of reward and punishment, shaping and imitation. However, Jean Piaget's stance here is quite clear; it is not fair to think of his theory as being one which supports the nature (or innate) argument. Rather than the child being 'born' with particular modes of thought, instead the child's interactions and experiences with objects and events lead to the development of new ways of thinking and organizing information.

The concept of intelligence for Piaget involves (successful) 'adaptation to the environment', and indeed the gaining of knowledge is of primary importance in facilitating this adaptation. In other words, the accumulation of knowledge (which comes with experience) helps the child and, for that matter, the adult, adjust to the environment. Ultimately, our very survival depends upon it.

10.3   The Development of the Intellect

Infants are thought capable of representing their world from the earliest moments. Such representations are referred to as *schemata* (a single representation is a schema). These are essentially mental plans which serve to guide actions, provide the basis for interpreting incoming information, and serve as an aid in problem-solving. In a neonate, schemata involve relatively simple actions such as sucking, grasping and looking, which at this stage are mainly reflexes. These gradually become combined with others as coordination and thinking develops. (Piaget calls the inborn tendency to coordinate existing schemata and combine them together to form more complex ones 'organization'.)

With increased experience, schemata become more elaborate, and new ones are formed as the child deals with objects and events. As adults, our schemata enable us to execute complex sequences of events and integrate ideas. Furthermore, we are able to employ operations (technically more complicated mental structures), which Piaget saw as representing logical thought.

Operations (operational structures, operatory thought) are not present in the newborn child, and are generally only acquired in middle/late childhood (7/8 years onwards). Although, like schemata, operations are modes of representing information mentally, they are more advanced in that they have the additional characteristic of being *reversible*.

For example, when planning a series of moves during a game of draughts, it is possible to imagine how the board will look after the moves, and then to mentally reverse the sequence and so return to the original position. Mathematical calculations also share these properties; $7 \times 2 = 14$, but the sequence may also be reversed by using division: $14 \div 2 = 7$. Whereas a young child is capable of grasping the initial steps, they do not appreciate the characteristic of reversibility. Piaget considered mental operations to be an integral part of thought and, as we shall see, incorporated the term into three of his stages of development.

We have already spoken of the importance which Piaget placed on adaptation, but *how* does the child adapt to the environment? According to Piaget, adaptation is brought about by a continual striving (on the part of the child) to achieve balance or harmony with his or her surroundings. This comes about through the complementary processes of **assimilation** and **accommodation**.

Assimilation usually means to take in or incorporate, and in Piaget's theory refers to the individual's efforts to deal with new objects or events in the environment using already existing schemata. Thus new events or objects present no problem as such, because they are interpreted using ideas which are familiar. For example, if a young child learns (perhaps through parental labelling) that objects moving in the sky are called birds, then the next time a bird is seen this will be *assimilated*, as it fits the schema for such objects. However, imagine one occasion when the young child looks up to see an aeroplane which, because of its different features, cannot be assimilated. Instead, the existing schema is modified to cope with the new situation, a process referred to as accommodation. The next time an aeroplane is seen the child is able to assimilate it, since the schema for objects in the sky has been elaborated to include such objects. (What would happen if the child later saw a helicopter?)

Piaget claims that adaptation results in a state of harmony or balance (known as equilibrium) which arises following the assimilation or accommodation of a new object or event (the process of achieving equilibrium is called equilibration). However, because young children are constantly meeting new situations, this state of harmony is likely to be only temporary: if a child comes across something new, then disharmony (or disequilibrium) results, and continues until the balance is restored either by assimilation or accommodation.

The process continues in this way indefinitely (one can never 'know' everything), but with each successful negotiation of a new situation cognitive progress is gained; the child is 'better equipped' to deal with information than previously.

10.4   Piaget's Stage Theory

For Piaget, cognitive development takes place over a series of four, qualitatively distinct, periods or stages, each characterized by certain accomplishments. As a developmental theory it aims to encompass the life span, and for this purpose Piaget assigned approximate ages to each stage; these span the period from infancy through to adolescence and adulthood.

An important feature governing progression through the stages is the principle of *invariant sequencing* (or invariant order). This means that, although individual children may pass through the stages at different rates, the order in which they proceed is unchangeable.

For example, a child of 6 years may be at one stage for one set of tasks, but at a more advanced stage for another task, and so may in effect progress through the various stages faster than a peer. However, the order is the same for all children regardless of their ability; that is, the stages cannot be missed out or skipped. Piaget arrived at his conclusions from detailed observations of children, and from 'clinical' interviews in which their responses to questions were recorded.

As the theory was largely concerned with logical reasoning and problem-solving, in many cases simple experiments were devised in order to permit young children to demonstrate what they could (or could not) do. As we shall see, more significance was usually placed on the *explanations* which children provide for their actions, rather than the researchers just noting whether a correct or incorrect response was given.

Table 10.1   *Piaget's stage theory of cognitive development*

Name of stage	Approximate ages
Sensori-motor	Birth to 2 years
Pre-operational	2–7 years
Concrete operational	7–12 years
Formal operational	12 years onwards

The sensori-motor stage

As the name suggests this stage (or at least the early part of it: in fact Piaget detailed six sub-stages) involves the infant interpreting information through the main senses, and coordinating motor activities (i.e., muscular movements) such as reaching and grasping. Behaviour largely consists of reflexes at first, and the infant may enter into a repetition of self-centred movements and actions known as primary circular reactions, such as shaking arms and legs. Gradually, though, interest is directed towards objects which are deliberately acted upon: striking a hanging toy rattle, for example. These are secondary circular reactions. Schemata are still relatively simple, and centred largely around physical rather than mental events.

A major achievement during the sensori-motor stage is the acquisition of the *object concept:* the appreciation that objects are permanent and continue to exist even when they are no longer visible. This ability, which represents a significant advancement in intelligent behaviour, is only gradually attained from around 8 to 12 months of age.

According to Piaget, younger infants do not have this understanding. For example, if a 4 month old is playing with a toy which is then hidden under a cloth, the child will lose interest, as if the toy had 'disappeared'. Only if the toy is partially visible will the child attempt to retrieve it.

In terms of cognitive development, once children have grasped the notion of object permanence they are demonstrating the beginning of intellectual behaviour. In effect, it signals the appearance of symbolic thought, and shows that they have the ability to represent objects and events mentally; this is something which becomes more effective from now onwards.

The pre-operational stage

Symbolic thinking is greatly enhanced in this stage of development, when children become able to manipulate ideas and perfect their language skills, thereby providing another dimension to their thought processes. One way in which children's use of symbolic thought is displayed occurs during play. Indeed Piaget refers to one period of play as 'symbolic' or 'pretend' play, when children will take on imaginary roles, such as pretending to be a pop-star or television character. In addition, they will imitate behaviour they have seen on a previous occasion. It is also quite common for children to make objects stand for something else (i.e., symbolize). For instance, an empty shoe box may become a space-ship. Together with their increasing confidence in language, all these features provide evidence that children are thinking in symbolic terms, a move which takes them out of the present, so to speak, and creates a basis for further cognitive progress.

Despite these advances, the child's thinking is still restricted in many ways. These are best considered by using the two sub-stages which Piaget intended for pre-operational thought.

The first phase is referred to as the pre-conceptual period (approximately 2–4 years). Bernstein *et al.* (1988) defined a concept as a category of objects, events or ideas which share common properties. Thus we may regard this period as a time when young children experience difficulties because they *cannot* properly understand the relationship between things. For instance, children will often assign feelings to objects and events which they come across, believing that a chair is tired because it has been continually sat upon, or that the sun can see them when it shines. This tendency is known as *animistic thought*.

A further limitation upon the child's thinking at this stage is called **egocentrism**, whereby the child sees things only from his or her own point of view, and is unable to appreciate things from another perspective. This can be demonstrated in the following dialogue between a 4-year-old girl and an adult:

> ADULT: Do you have any brothers and sisters?
> CHILD: Yes.
> ADULT: What are their names?
> CHILD: Janet and Alan.
> ADULT: Does Janet have any sisters?
> CHILD: No.

In this example the young girl concerned is unable to see her sister Janet's perspective, and therefore answers the last question incorrectly.

Piaget and a colleague, Inhelder, used a simple model of three mountains in an attempt to demonstrate the egocentric qualities of children (see Figure 10.1).

Typically the child (subjects tested ranged from 4 to 12 years of age) was asked to give the view of the scene from the doll's perspective, picking out the photograph of the appropriate display. Piaget found that in such test situations young children (i.e., pre-conceptual) tended to give their own view rather than the doll's, from which he concluded they were egocentric.

Similar conclusions may be made from children's drawings and paintings at this age. For example, if a 4 or 5 year old is asked to paint a pilot's-eye view of a scene, often they will represent houses and cars from a frontal position (i.e., as they would see them at ground level), and they are not, until older, able to use an aerial view consistently.

The latter half of the pre-operational stage (the intuitive period, 4–7 years of age) is marked by an improvement of sorts in the child's mental capabilities, although often when questioned children give what is, in their view, a satisfactory explanation for their actions, such as 'that one goes there because it is long.' In this period, Piaget was interested in children's abilities at tasks such as seriation, classification and conservation, which (as we shall see) are not fully grasped until the next stage.

Seriation tasks are those which involve placing a list of items in order, such as shortest to longest. If a 5 year old is presented with a number of sticks of varying lengths, and asked to arrange them 'to make a staircase', the youngster will usually place the sticks in a haphazard fashion and, while demonstrating some

Source: Piaget and Inhelder (1956)

Figure 10.1 Child and the 'Three Mountains' model

attempt at consecutive order, will very rarely use any kind of systematic comparison (such as holding one stick against another). A similar test is that of the falling sticks problem, which is shown in Figure 10.2. Here the child is asked to arrange the cards (which are placed in a random order in front of him or her) to show what happens when a stick falls to the ground. Not only are the children at the pre-operational stage unable to perform this task correctly, but they often have difficulty in appreciating the correct sequence when it is arranged for them by someone else.

Some of Piaget's most famous experiments concern conservation: the ability to understand that features of a substance (e.g., volume, area, number, weight, etc.) stay the same despite alterations in their appearance. For instance, if you are shown two identical pieces of card, one of which is then cut into smaller pieces, it is simple for you to deduce that the amount of the card in the original pieces has remained unchanged. However, this is not so with pre-operational children (see Figure 10.3).

In Piaget's experiments (see Figure 10.4), a child is presented with two identical containers which are then filled with the same amount of water. Having agreed that there is the same amount in each, the child then sees the liquid from one vessel transferred to one of a tall thin shape (or to several smaller containers). The child is then asked if the amount of water is the same in each, or whether there is more in one container than the other(s). Pre-operational children generally report that there is now *more* in the tall container. This lack of understanding is partly a result of *centration* by the child, which means that they focus attention on one particular aspect of an object or situation at the expense of others. In the liquid example, the visual appearance (of the water levels) is centred upon, while less regard is given to the original set-up when the quantity was seen to be identical. Furthermore, the child is not yet able to use mental

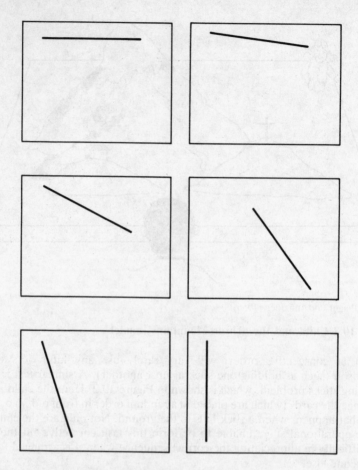

Figure 10.2 The falling sticks problem: arrange the cards above to show a stick gradually falling to the ground

operations, which in this case means that they cannot reverse the procedure and imagine the two containers as they were before.

This way of thinking, which is characteristic of pre-operational children, is referred to by Piaget as transductive reasoning, because children's judgements and decisions at this stage are largely arrived at without any form of logical deduction. However, the emergence of operational thought and logical reasoning signifies the end of this stage; the child now progresses to a higher cognitive level, one which brings with it a greater flexibility in thinking and problem-solving.

The concrete operational stage

Many of the previous limitations are no longer apparent when the child enters this stage. From 7 years of age onwards, children are much less egocentric and as such are now capable of appreciating perspectives other than their own (i.e., they are able to *decentre*).

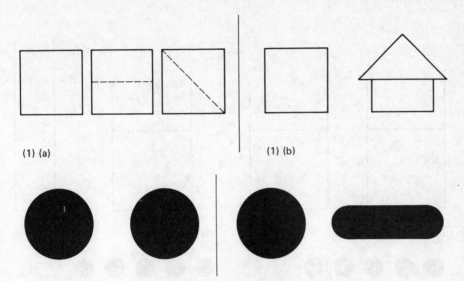

(1) (a)   (1) (b)

(2) (a)   (2) (b)

Figure 10.3 Conservation tasks used by Piaget
    (1) Conservation of area
    a (Pre-operational) child agrees amount of card is same in each piece
    b Card is rearranged by experimenter; child, when asked, now says there is more card in the 'house'
    (2) Conservation of substance
    a Child agrees amount of plasticene is the same in each ball
    b One ball is rearranged by experimenter; child, when asked, says there is now more in 'sausage' shape

Conservation tasks also become easier to understand. According to Piaget, this is due mainly to the appearance of mental operations, which (as we mentioned earlier) allow the child mentally to reverse changes which have taken place, and so comprehend that the substance before them is exactly the same quantity as before. This appreciation also makes basic mathematical operations such as multiplication and division simpler to follow. As well as applying the reversibility of operations, the fact that children are able to decentre means that their attention is no longer restricted to specific aspects of a situation, which also helps in solving conservation problems. Conservation comprises several abilities, and in order for the child to use them fully a wide range of different experiences may be required. Indeed, Piaget recognized the importance of the opportunity to use and experience different materials in order to facilitate cognitive development. Thus a child with little experience of area or volume may be slower grasping those aspects of conservation.

Although it is during the concrete operational stage that conservation problems are largely mastered, the sequence in which individual aspects are acquired is uneven. Generally, number conservation is gained before that of length, with weight and volume emerging later (why do you think this is?), a phenomenon known as *horizontal décalage*.

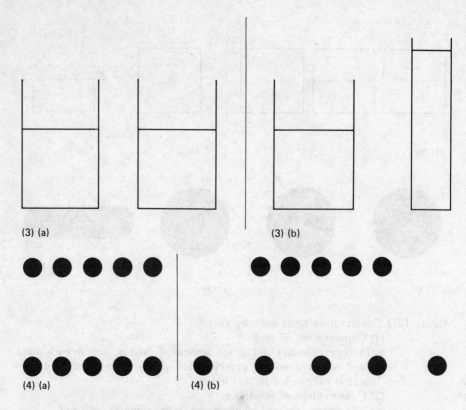

(3) (a)   (3) (b)

(4) (a)   (4) (b)

Figure 10.4 Conservation tasks used by Piaget
(3) Conservation of liquid
a Child agrees that the amount of liquid is the same in each beaker
b One amount is transferred to a different-shaped beaker; child, when asked, says there is now more liquid in the taller beaker
(4) Conservation of number
a Child agrees that the number of counters is the same in each row
b One row is rearranged by the experimenter; child, when asked, says there are now more counters in the lower row

The child's increasing ability to represent and order information means that they are also able to perform tasks such as classification: they can group items into hierarchies and categories, and explain why certain things belong together. This demonstrates that children can 'apply rules' about objects and events in their environment, as well as showing their increasing grasp of important concepts.

SPOTLIGHT   Testing Piaget's claims

Piaget's findings were largely based around detailed observations of his own and other children but, as well as observation, he and his colleagues devised a number of problems and tasks for children in order to discover the way they think.

- For this exercise, first compile a list of Piagetian tasks which appear in this chapter, and consider ways in which you could test them. For example, as a variation on the three-mountains task, you could use three different objects (an assortment of toys, dolls, etc.), and, with a little imagination and improvisation, you should be able to vary the other problems, too.

- If you have access to children of the appropriate ages you could try the tasks on them but, better still, arrange to visit a local primary school. Record your findings carefully (a tape recorder would be useful) and comment on what they show.

Further evidence of cognitive progress is shown in the task of seriation, of which children are now capable. For example, a 9 year old can place a series of objects in order on the basis of size or weight. This ability is important, since it shows that children recognize that certain relationships exist between objects, particularly regarding the principle of *transitive inference*. Simply put, this refers to an underlying logical 'rule' governing such relationships. If, for example, we are told that x is bigger than y, and y is bigger than z, the logical conclusion that x is bigger than z can also be deduced. In a more practical application, the same can be said concerning the relationships between numbers. Failure or difficulty with this principle, therefore, may mean that children struggle with fundamental concepts when learning mathematics in school. Experience with numbers in a variety of practical settings is vital for young children's progress.

By middle childhood, then, significant gains are evident in the child's ability to 'handle' and manipulate information, essentially stemming from the use of (mental) operations. However, there are limitations, because the child's thinking is largely restricted to real or solid objects (hence the term 'concrete operations'). If the seriation problem above were represented in the form: x is bigger than y, y is bigger than z, a concrete operational child would have difficulty determining the relationship, between x and z because they are not 'real' things as such, and furthermore are difficult to imagine. However, if children are given dolls named 'Mr X', 'Mr Y' and 'Mr Z' to place in order, then the hypothetical aspect of the problem is removed and they can successfully carry out the task.

In the technologically advanced world of the 1990s children, and adults for that matter, have little need to rely on mental arithmetic when electronic calculators can provide the answer effortlessly. Nevertheless, when such instruments are not readily available, even adults take comfort in concrete-thinking by counting on their fingers!

The formal operational stage

Around the age of 11 or 12 children become capable of thinking in purely abstract terms: that is, without the need to rely completely on real objects and events as such.

In a sense, they are no longer 'tied' to concrete aspects as they have a more flexible array of cognitive strategies at their disposal. For instance, Piaget argued that the individual can now reason about hypothetical problems, make logical

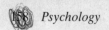
deductions from given information, and furthermore will approach possible solutions systematically, rather than tackle them in a haphazard fashion.

An item such as $x > y > z$ should no longer present difficulties, since the young person is now capable of dealing with the information in its abstract form. Further evidence of this increased flexibility in thinking can also be seen in logical reasoning problems such as:

> All vampires have purple teeth.
> This monster has green teeth.
> Is it a vampire?

When faced with a problem like this one, a concrete operational child would be likely to dismiss the statements with a comment of 'There's no such thing as a vampire', which confirms the view that real or probable events still dominate their thinking. On the other hand, a young person in the formal operational stage will consider the information as a hypothetical proposition, and arrive at a logical deduction based on the information as it is presented.

In the pursuance of their studies, Piaget and his colleague, Inhelder, devised and presented a range of tasks in order to investigate formal operational thinking. Some of these involved providing children with various items and then asking them to find out how things worked, together with supplying detailed proof.

In one such task, the child is given several metal rods (of different lengths which may be attached together), and asked to state what factors govern differences in their flexibility. When faced with this problem 9 and 10 year olds carried out random tests and were far from systematic in their approach, whereas children of 11 and 12 onwards worked from a series of **hypotheses** and subsequently proceeded to test each of them one by one.

Similarly, in the 'pendulum experiment', children are asked to find out what factors influence the rate at which a pendulum swings. Subjects are provided with various weights and are allowed to alter the length of string, the height from which the attached weight is dropped, or the initial push to start the swinging motion. As with the rod problem, children still at the stage of concrete operations attempt to vary all the factors together, without working to any kind of formulated plan. In contrast, the older child considers all the possibilities separately, carefully testing each in turn, until the correct solution is obtained.

This final stage was considered by Piaget to represent the peak of intellectual ability, a point when the cognitive strategies and operations are maximized. In developmental terms it is also significant since it comprises the remaining life span, beginning as it does in pre-adolescence and extending into adulthood.

10.5 Piaget on Moral Development

Although Piaget is largely associated with the development of the intellect, an early part of his research focused upon 'the moral judgement of the child' (Piaget, 1932). Morality concerns the process whereby individuals gain a sense of what is right and wrong, and for Piaget an important issue was that of the child's moral thoughts, and how these changed with age.

In order to study the development of moral judgements, Piaget and his colleagues questioned a large number of Swiss children using much the same methods as they had used to investigate logical and deductive thinking. They were interested primarily in three main aspects: children's respect for rules, their thoughts on lying and stealing, and finally children's regard for each other in various situations, particularly concerning the notion of justice.

Children's views of rules were established largely by watching them play games, such as marbles, and observing their attitudes towards cheating and other aspects of the 'rules' of the game.

In assessing views on lying and stealing, Piaget presented pairs of stories to children which portrayed children in different situations. For instance, they involved a child stealing for a selfish reason (e.g., stealing a toy from another child because of envy) contrasted with theft that had altruistic motives (e.g., stealing for a hungry friend). In the same way stories in which characters lied compared improbable but harmless lies with those in which the lie was 'minor' but potentially harmful.

On the issue of justice, and again using stories, Piaget was interested in children's opinions of punishments for wrongful acts, whether or not collective punishment was acceptable, and also their views on immanent justice (i.e., that the punishment comes from the thing itself). In one example, he presented a story about a child who damaged a toy belonging to someone else, and asked subjects which of several punishments was appropriate (i.e., fair).

Similarly, to test collective justice, children were asked if it was permissible to punish a whole group when only one of them had committed an offence. Concerning immanent justice, a story was related of two children stealing from an orchard in which one of them was caught while the other managed to get away, only to have an accident later.

From their conversations with children and the information they collected, Piaget and his colleagues defined two periods of development for moral judgements and reasoning. In the first of these stages (approximately 5 years to 11/12 years) the child is seen as a *moral realist*. This is characterized by a view of rules as being absolute, unchangeable and much respected, laid down by authority figures such as parents. In such a system (sometimes known as external morality) children tend to perceive adults as always being 'right', and regard a lie told to an adult as being worse than a lie told to another child. Furthermore, young children tend to pay more attention to the scale of the wrong-doing, which may be interpreted as another form of centration (just as in the conservation tasks). Moral judgements are thus based on the consequences which the 'action' has, with little or no regard for the intentions behind the deed. One story which illustrates this concerns two boys, one of whom (Johnny) is trying to help his mother in the kitchen when he accidentally knocks over a tray and breaks fifteen glasses. Another boy, Billy, breaks one glass when he is trying to take a biscuit from a kitchen cupboard. In this instance, young children tend to judge the first boy as being 'naughtier' simply because he broke more glasses.

Concerning the notion of justice, Piaget found that moral realists were very definite in their views on punishment. They believed in both collective and immanent justice, and based their judgements on external constraints rather than attempting to relate the punishment to the severity of the crime for themselves.

At around 11 years of age children's views of moral issues change noticeably as they begin to base their judgements more on fairness and reciprocity (e.g., taking turns in a game). This shift, to a system of *internal morality*, occurs as children gain knowledge that rules may be changed as long as fairness is maintained. This represents an important step in cognitive terms since it shows that the child is able to decentre, and thus appreciate the view of the game from another perspective.

Children at this stage (moral relativism) are also more willing to take intentions for actions into account; in the story of the two boys the second would be considered the greater offender, since he intended to steal the biscuit. Furthermore, older children do not dismiss lying as being totally unacceptable as they are more likely to consider the circumstances involved, recognizing that under certain conditions lying may be defensible. In addition, moral relativists are more fair in their opinions of justice, which is reflected in a concern that the punishment fit the crime, a rejection of collective punishment and a view that immanent justice is less acceptable.

Piaget considered that moral development was firmly linked with cognitive development, and that it was important for a child to attain the appropriate cognitive level before certain moral judgements could be made. Indeed, this view was also shared by another cognitive development theorist, Lawrence Kohlberg, who extended and refined the ideas of Piaget. Kohlberg presented children with hypothetical moral dilemmas such as the 'Heinz dilemma', in which a character steals a drug in order to cure his sick wife. Subjects are asked whether Heinz was right or wrong to do so, although more importance is placed upon the *reasons* given. From children's answers to such dilemmas Kohlberg formulated a stage theory of moral development, in which children's judgements of moral issues change with age over three broad levels, each of which reflect certain changes in cognitive development.

Critics of this approach, however, have argued that the development of morality cannot simply be a result of improvements in cognitive abilities. Furthermore, they point out that responses to hypothetical dilemmas do not represent a true picture of how the subject would really behave in given circumstances.

10.6   Piaget's Theory: a Critical Evaluation

Piaget's impact upon child psychology has been enormous. Largely as a result of his work, a vast body of research arose to test his ideas and confirm or refute his claims. For many years educationalists and teachers revised their approach to young children, and applied Piagetian principles in the classroom, seeking actively to involve children in their learning (see Spotlight box).

SPOTLIGHT   Piaget's theory and education.

Many of the principles which Piaget outlined in his theory have been applied to the classroom. For instance, you will remember that Piaget saw children as being actively involved in their own learning, and he proposed that letting children discover things for themselves ('discovery learning') was a much better way to progress than learning of a passive kind (i.e., children having facts talked at them, or learning by rote). Indeed, current strategies in teaching practice are much more in favour of student-centred learning, a method which represents the very antithesis of the more traditional styles.

- Compare traditional teaching with that of discovery learning, and outline the advantages and disadvantages of each method.

- Consider the implications of each of the following in the teaching of children: (a) stages of development (particularly concrete and formal); (b) invariant order of stage progression; (c) assimilation and accommodation.

In this final section we will examine a number of criticisms which have been levelled against the theory, together with a look at some of the empirical studies which have cast doubt on Piaget's claims.

First, let us consider Piaget's assertion that cognitive development takes place over a series of qualitatively distinct stages, which has been disputed by some workers. Rather than conceiving of development as changing in line with specific periods, they argue that progression occurs in a continuous manner over time, without abrupt stop–start mechanisms. Another problem in this respect is the existence of *décalage* (as mentioned earlier); some abilities are accomplished in a way which is not smooth and orderly and this presents a problem that as yet has not been satisfactorily explained.

Still on the theme of stages, critics have pointed out that Piaget does not provide a precise account of how children 'move' through the stages, other than to acknowledge the role of individual experience as being of importance in attaining different capabilities. Terms such as 'assimilation' and 'equilibration' are vague and difficult to test, even though much of the theory rests upon their existence.

A general criticism of the theory lies in the methodology used. Piaget and Kohlberg relied heavily on the **clinical interview**, which is more or less a 'formal conversation'. There is a danger (which Piaget himself acknowledged) that the child may be misled in such situations into giving the experimenter precisely the answers which he or she is seeking.

Second, during the sensori-motor stage (0–2 years) a major accomplishment concerns the development of object permanence, a feat which Piaget claimed occurred from around 8–12 months of age. However, a number of studies by Tom Bower in the 1970s have revealed this figure to be a considerable underestimation of infants' abilities. In a series of experiments evidence of the object concept was apparent in infants aged 4–6 months, and in some cases in infants as young as 8 weeks; this is much earlier than Piaget anticipated.

Third, perhaps the most thoroughly researched area of development, both by Piaget and subsequent investigation, is that of pre-operational abilities. According to Piaget, pre-school children are egocentric, a view which he claimed to have supported with his colleague, Inhelder, in the three-mountains task (Piaget and Inhelder, 1956).

Recent findings, however, have demonstrated that the context in which the experiment takes place is of great importance. Borke (1975), for example, adapted Piaget's idea and presented 3 and 4 year olds with various three-dimensional displays. These comprised:

(a) a set-up of three mountains similar to the one used in the original experiment;

(b) a simple layout of a house, a cow, and a horse alongside each other, and a boat on a small lake;

(c) a farmyard/ranch display, complete with buildings, figures, trees and animals (see Figure 10.5).

A fourth display featuring a fire-engine was used for practice trials, a factor lacking in Piaget's study, and which Borke felt could be important.

A doll named Grover was then introduced into the procedure, and the experimenter explained that a game was to be played in which Grover would drive around each display, occasionally stopping to look at the scenery. When this

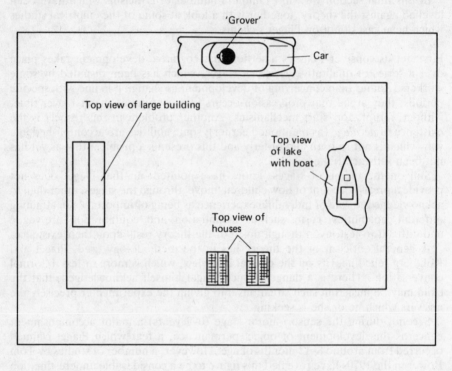

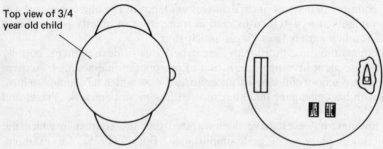

Source: Borke (1975)

Figure 10.5 Display used by Borke to demonstrate decentration in 3–4-year olds

happened the child was asked to rotate a turntable on which was a duplicate of the main display until they were looking at it in the same way as Grover was. Once the child was thoroughly familiar with the task (which was demonstrated using the fire-engine display), they were tested individually on each of the three displays, and their ability to replicate Grover's viewpoint assessed on several occasions. The results showed that both 3 and 4 year olds performed well on all the displays apart from the one showing the three mountains. Two important conclusions may be reached from this experiment: first, it suggests that the nature of the task which pre-school children are expected to do is a decisive factor. When faced with the three-mountains model – in spatial terms a more complicated display – young children tend to make more errors. This may have been because the scene was difficult for 3 or 4 year olds to relate to, whereas the other displays had more meaning and relevance for them. Second, it provides evidence that Piaget had underestimated the decentering abilities of young children. In this study the subjects are still at the beginning of the pre-operational stage, yet they are clearly not egocentric.

Margaret Donaldson, in *Children's Minds* (Donaldson, 1978), refers to several other studies which contradict specific aspects of Piaget's theory. For example, another investigation of egocentrism was that carried out by Hughes in 1975. Children aged between $3\frac{1}{2}$ and 5 years were given the task of hiding a doll first from one policeman doll, and then from two policeman dolls (see Figure 10.6). Even in this latter condition, which requires the child to take two different perspectives into account, approximately 90 per cent of the subjects were successful. Once again, this study illustrates that pre-school children are more competent than Piaget had claimed, whilst also providing additional evidence in favour of tasks which make more sense to youngsters.

Piaget's studies show that egocentrism may be demonstrated under certain experimental conditions when, for example, children misunderstand what is expected of them, or the task has little meaning for them. However, given proper

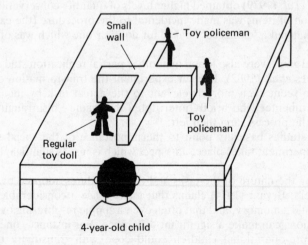

Source: Hughes (1975)

Figure 10.6 Hughes's policeman doll study

consideration, pre-schoolers show a high degree of competence. Ironically, the failure of children to decentre in the earlier experiments may have been due at least in part to egocentrism in the researchers and their inability to appreciate the view of the world through a young child's eyes!

Context appears important in conservation tasks, too. McGarrigle and Donaldson (1974) gave pre-operational children (aged 4–6 years) tasks of number conservation, first of all using Piaget's standard procedure whereby an adult disarranges one row of counters. Under these conditions of 'intentional transformation' only about 16 per cent of the children seemed able to conserve the number.

However, in the second test a procedure of 'accidental transformation' was incorporated, involving a character called 'Naughty Teddy' who appeared from a cupboard and disarranged a line of counters. Subsequently, when the child was asked the number of items in each row, performance improved significantly: 63 per cent stated that the number had not changed.

The researchers concluded that the revised setting in which the counters were accidentally moved by 'Naughty Teddy' made it easier for children to understand that nothing has changed, whereas when an adult experimenter intentionally intervenes there is an implied notion that 'something' must have altered. Furthermore, as Smith and Cowie (1988) pointed out, 'traditional experiments in number conservation seem to make the child think that the experimenter is asking about the length of the row of counters rather than the number' (p. 308). By introducing a character which alters the setting to the level of a 4 year old, basic logical operations are relatively easy to comprehend, and misinterpretations made less likely.

However, some recent studies have criticized the procedure used in the 'Naughty Teddy' experiment, and questioned the extent to which the 'accidental transformation' is effective, suggesting that the child will link the introduction of Naughty Teddy as being a deliberate and therefore important aspect of the experiment. In a partial replication of the McGarrigle and Donaldson experiment, Light *et al.* (1979) obtained higher levels of quantity conservation when the transformation of items was made incidental to the procedure (the experimenter casually exchanged a 'damaged' beaker for another one which was of a different shape).

Substantial gains were also found in another partial replication study conducted by Hargreaves *et al.* (1982). In their experiment the transformation of materials was made to seem even more irrelevant to the actual task by incorporating a second experimenter who briefly interrupted the 'game', disarranging a row of counters in the process, and then left.

All these studies basically point to the importance of the social situation in which the experiment takes place, an aspect which is just as significant as the task itself.

Concerning the nature of the tasks and the procedures adopted by Piaget and his co-workers, Bryant (1974) claims that many place a considerable load upon the young child's memory, and that often even a simple re-phrasing or re-wording of key questions can make a significant difference. For instance, one researcher found that pre-operational children could cope with transitivity tasks if the problem was repeated several times, thereby giving them a greater opportunity to memorize it. (You will remember that according to Piaget such tasks are normally accomplished in the stage of concrete operations, and only then when 'real' items are used with which to make the comparison.)

Fourth, Piaget's assertion that formal operational thought is attained by all normal individuals (from approximately 12 years onwards) has also been subject to criticism: when presented with problems involving logical-deductive reasoning many adults experience difficulty unless they are familiar with similar tasks and the strategies required to solve them. In fact, a number of researchers argue that Piaget's theory placed too much emphasis on abstract, scientific modes of thinking which have little relevance to most people in their everyday lives.

Finally, another serious flaw centres around the conclusions reached by Piaget. As Bryant (1982) remarks, much of his work illustrates situations in which young children fail or lack certain abilities, and he then wrongly deduces why this failure occurs. However, as we have seen, a host of other variables can account for these differences, including the nature of the test situation. Child psychologists, such as Bower, are quick to point out that just because a child fails to demonstrate a particular task does not mean that they are unable to do it.

In the light of these criticisms, it is clear that other explanations for cognitive development need to be considered. Jerome Bruner (1964), for example, felt that Piaget neglected the underlying processes of growth, and so his perspective attempts to offer a further explanation of the ways in which the child represents the world.

A different view is that offered by the learning theorists, who maintain that behaviours involving cognitive processes develop as a result of their consequences (whether they are rewarded or not).

Another possibility is the information-processing approach, which concentrates on how the child acquires and uses information, together with how this information changes as a consequence of mental capacity. Psychologists here look at a range of abilities such as attention, memory and perception, all of which have an important influence upon how incoming information is processed.

Finally, in contrast to fundamental processes such as thinking, memory and language, the relatively new field of social cognition focuses upon the role which social factors play in the individual's interpretation of information.

Whilst a single explanation for cognitive development will not suffice, Piaget has made a substantial contribution to our understanding and appreciation of the complex mind of the child. His work has presented challenging and original ideas which have provided researchers with the impetus to extend and modify his observations.

10.7 Questions and Exercises

1. 'Child psychology would have been a meagre thing without Piaget' (Bryant, 1982). On the basis of this statement critically evaluate Piaget's theory of intellectual development.
2. Design an experiment to investigate egocentrism in young children.
3. (a) Make notes to show you understand the following terms: (i) assimilation, (ii) accommodation, (iii) operations.
   (b) Give your own examples of each.

4. (a) Outline and describe Piaget's approach to moral development.
   (b) Devise some moral dilemmas which would be appropriate and then present them to relevant age-groups in order to test Piaget's claims.

⟨11⟩ Language and communication

11.1 Introduction

Language may well be the most indispensable tool at our disposal. The potential for human language is infinite. Infants are able to communicate with those around them even before they are able to produce 'words', and by 4 or 5 years of age children are competent in their native tongue. By using this system of symbols and rules we are able to communicate our feelings, intentions and ideas to the outside world. In fact, the 'drive' to do so is often so overwhelming that mute children have been known to create their own system of communicating to others. Studies of deaf people confirm that the sign language used by such individuals is a rich and versatile one, with many of the subtleties and capabilities of speech.

Examples of communication also abound in the animal kingdom. By means of visual displays, calls, odours and so on, animals are able to convey information to others. In a famous study, Karl von Frisch (1967) demonstrated that bees are able to inform other members of the hive about the distance and direction of food sources using an elaborate display which takes the form of a dance. However, in most cases the methods employed by animals in the communication process are limited. For instance, diverse though such displays are, an animal is only able to indicate its present state of intention: to attract a mate, ward off a rival, inform others of danger, and so on.

Human language, in contrast, is characterized by the principles of *productivity* and *creativity*, which means that the speaker can combine words and phrases to generate a verbally limitless number of messages. It is this flexibility (amongst other things) which is considered to set people apart from animals in linguistic ability.

In this chapter we will consider some of the processes involved in language acquisition, together with two of the major theories in this area. We will also look at the sequence in which young children grasp the features of the language spoken around them, as well as instances where the process does not run smoothly. Finally, although some psychologists have disputed the existence of 'true' language in animals, extensive research with apes has produced intriguing findings, and an examination of these studies is included.

11.2 The Structure of Language

Every language may be broken down into individual speech sounds which are produced by movements of the mouth (lips, tongue) and vocal chords. These individual sounds are called phonemes, and within each language there are 'rules' permitting how they may be combined. Even within one language the sound of one phoneme may alter depending on these adjacent: for example, in English, /a/ is pronounced one way in 'take' and another in 'tack'.

Indeed, one reason for the difficulty experienced when learning a new language is that of being unable accurately to produce the individual sounds which it comprises. Furthermore, phonemes tend not to transfer across languages: for instance, the sounds of /r/ and /l/ are treated differently in English, but in Korean and Japanese they are regarded as variations of the same phoneme.

While phonemes themselves have no bearing on the meaning of a word, morphemes do. They are the smallest linguistic unit that conveys meaning. Some morphemes are referred to as 'free' in that they may stand alone. The majority of words are of this kind (e.g., cat, cook). Others are called 'bound' because they cannot be used unless they are tagged on to another morpheme (e.g., '–ed', and '–s'). Such additions, together with various other suffixes (letters added to the end of a word) and prefixes (letters added to the beginning of a word) function to modify word meaning. Many of the larger words in a language are in fact simple ones to which suffixes and prefixes have been added (e.g., 'mal-nourish-ed'). The way a sentence can be built up is shown in Figure 11.1.

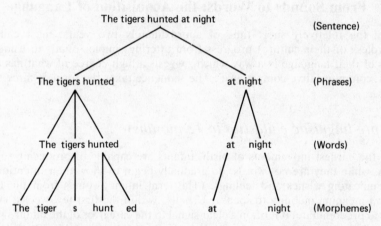

Figure 11.1 The 'parts' of a sentence
NB: the morphemes in turn may then be distinguished in terms of constituent phonemes.

While the use of a single word can often be effective in the communication process, it is restrictive. Thus words may be grouped into larger units, such as phrases and sentences, allowing a much wider range of expression. However, the way in which words are arranged must follow certain rules. This involves syntax and semantics.

Every language has a definite structure, together with in-built rules concerning how words may be arranged to form linguistically appropriate information. Collectively this is known as grammar, and one aspect deals particularly with rules governing how morphemes and words may be combined together to construct sentences. This is syntax.

Semantics, on the other hand, refers to the study of meaning, which within language concerns the meaning of words, phrases and sentences. This may be appreciated by considering the following three sentences:

> The student picked up the book
> The book picked up the student
> Student up the picked book the

What is wrong with the last two?

Apart from learning the syntax and semantics of a language there are also those elements concerned with the appropriate use of language in different social contexts, an aspect known as pragmatics. For example, when children alter what they say depending on their audience, they are demonstrating an appreciation of this principle.

From our discussion so far it might appear that language acquisition would be a daunting task for the young child. Yet this is not so for, as we shall see, children follow an orderly sequence (without being directly taught) in which they rapidly become familiar with understanding and producing their native tongue.

11.3   From Sounds to Words: the Acquisition of Language

Within the relatively short time of approximately two years, most children (regardless of their culture) progress from uttering simple sounds to using the words of their language in a way which suggests a high degree of what has been called 'communicative competence'. The sequence takes the form of three basic stages.

The pre-linguistic child (up to 12 months)

From the earliest movements of birth, infants are capable of producing sounds which, while they are not words, do gradually begin to show their intentions of communicating wishes and feelings. (The term infancy comes from the Latin *infantia* meaning inability to speak.) Usually, within the first few weeks, crying tends to predominate; it is often a clear signal to the caregiver of the infant's state. Research suggests that parents are able to distinguish between different cries and the meanings they convey. For example, three basic patterns of crying can usually be identified: a hunger cry, an anger cry and a pain cry, each characterized by different sounds and rhythms.

Around 4–6 weeks, babies begin to produce 'ooo' vowel sounds. This is referred to as cooing, and usually indicates a state of contentment and pleasure, as it frequently stems from activities involving parent–child interactions. These early vocalizations are regarded by some workers (e.g. Trevarthen, 1974) as representing the beginnings of conversation: for instance, observations of video recordings of mother–infant interactions demonstrate 'turn-taking' during the dialogue, which is accompanied by variations in facial expression, sounds and gestures whereby each person responds to the other just as in adult conversation (see Figure 11.2).

At approximately 6–9 months of age the infant's linguistic abilities are increased with the onset of babbling, when infants begin to combine vowels and consonants into strings such as 'baba', 'dada', 'gaga'. Often these are repeated several times (e.g., 'dadadadad'), a feature known as echolalia. The emergence of babbling is determined by maturation rather than learning since it appears in all infants around the same time, regardless of culture, and the onset period is the

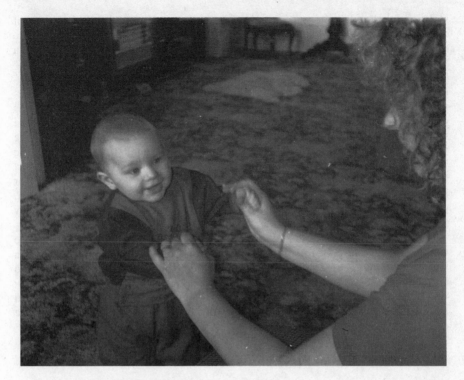

Figure 11.2 Mother and infant in 'conversation'

same for deaf infants (although in them a gradual difference in tone emerges, suggesting the importance of feedback from one's own voice).

From around 9 months of age onwards infants begin to show clear intentions of communicating to those around them. Apart from a general increase in babbling, this is achieved by the use of gestures, including pointing and gazing (an infant will stretch out their arms and gesture towards the parent to signal a wish to be picked up or cuddled, for example).

Before infants are capable of uttering their first words it is apparent that they can comprehend what is said to them, and will respond appropriately to simple instructions and questions such as 'Put it down', 'Give it to me', and so on. Towards the end of the first year the sounds which infants make begin more and more to resemble those of the language spoken in their environment.

One-word utterances (12–18 months)

As might be expected, children's first words refer to things of importance in their world, and their observations of it. Frequently, the first 'words' spoken are not even words in the true sense. For instance, a 1 year old was heard to say 'dit' for all objects in the air (such as aeroplanes, clouds, birds, leaves, etc.) and 'gok' for solid objects on the ground (car, dog, stone, etc.).

A child's vocabulary initially covers important people, objects and actions (e.g., 'daddy', 'milk', 'more', 'no'). At this point in language development, words serve as labels but, when accompanied by gestures and emphasis, a variety of meanings must be conveyed. Thus, if a child says the word 'ball', it can mean one of several things: 'I want the ball', 'There is the ball' or 'Look at the ball'. When a word is used in this way it is known as a *holophrase*.

In addition, young children may attribute different meanings to words compared with adults. The particular features of this are *overextensions* and *underextensions*, which often arise from children's usage of single words. Overtextensions occur when the child uses one word for many situations or objects (e.g., using the word 'daddy' for all men). It has been suggested that this characteristic arises due to similarities in shape, size and other perceptual similarities between the intended object – in this case the child's father ('daddy') – and other men. Apart from objects, children may overextend words for actions, such as using 'up' for movement in any direction. Children may also underextend words to begin with, so that a word is restricted in its use by, for instance, using the word 'doggie' only for the family pet and not for other dogs.

How does children's understanding of word meaning develop? According to Clark (1979), children form a hypothesis about a word's meaning, and test it in a variety of situations. By this method, and presumably through feedback and correction from those around them, children arrive at the same meaning for a word that adults use. However, this is just one process in developing word meaning; adult correction alone cannot suffice because often children will create *original* words and utterances.

Two-word utterances (around 18 months)

By about 18 months, children have a vocabulary of approximately 20–50 words and around this age they begin to produce simple two-word combinations. These may be considered as shortened versions of adult sentences, and tend to comprise mainly nouns and verbs. The information often resembles the concise format of a telegram, and for this reason two-word utterances are sometimes referred to as *telegraphic speech* (e.g., 'more drink', 'all gone', 'mummy shoe'). Like a telegram, such messages contain only the essential content words, with *functors* (e.g., 'to', 'are', 'is') and other connective words omitted initially. Although this basic sequence was once considered to be a universal feature of language acquisition it has recently been questioned. Rice (1989), for example, in an extensive review of the area points out that the sequence may vary depending on the language to be acquired. Furthermore, she maintains that although a regular pattern is noticeable to a large extent, there are individual differences between children in specific aspects; some toddlers may show preferences mainly for nouns, while others do not. However, these simple sentences widen the child's communication power, enabling a greater variety of expression and meaning.

Also of significance is the rapid growth in the size of the child's vocabulary, an aspect which occurs at a disproportionate rate over the following months. For example, where a child may use around 15–20 words at 18 months of age, it is common to find a vocabulary of several hundreds words early in the second year, which increases further in the subsequent pre-school period. Such a dramatic progression could not be due to individual word acquisition, but instead is thought to involve a process referred to as 'fast-mapping', whereby children quickly absorb and learn new word meanings as they are used in interactions around them.

According to Rice (1989), children are able to do this with considerable proficiency even if they have only perhaps heard the new word used appropriately once or twice. Exactly how young children carry out this process is not fully understood, although Rice suggests that children quickly 'latch on' to probable word meanings, whilst also applying their knowledge of syntax and other aspects of grammar.

SPOTLIGHT   Studying language development

Language development takes place over an orderly and relatively rapid sequence, with the transition from pre-linguistic utterances to simple sentences occurring in a matter of months.

A simple method of studying language in children is by tape-recording their interactions with adults and other children. In the latter case you may notice, for instance, that young children enter into a special dialogue with each other.

- Tape record a 'conversation' between a 1, 2 and 3 year old with an adult.
  Write the discourse down in full (this is known as a transcript), and compare the content of each. For example, the words used by the youngest children may not be true words as such, but merely their simplified attempts at them.
  Also note the way in which the adult speaks to the child. Do they use **motherese**?
  Are the adult sentences short or long? (In studying language, some psychologists measure what is known as the 'mean length of utterance' or MLU.)

- Finally, consider some of the disadvantages of the method you have used.

11.4   Beyond Simple Sentences

Between the ages of 2 and 3 years, children's utterances begin to lengthen, and previously omitted words (such as functors) begin to appear. However, although utterances are longer and more complex (comprising three and four words) certain limitations in understanding and usage are evident.

Children may demonstrate what is referred to as 'overregularization' (or overgeneralization: Mussen *et al.*, 1984) in which, for instance, English-speaking children may avoid irregular characteristics of the language and continue to apply only regular forms. Thus, a 3 year old might say 'The gooses runned away', which at first glance appears ludicrous but only if compared with adult speech. In fact, such utterances demonstrate an important appreciation of syntax, and in particular here those rules concerned with the use of plurals and verb tenses. Linguistic advancement continues in the remaining pre-school years (3–4), characterized by further increases in complexity and length of utterances as sentences are expanded. Often this may come about by linking two shorter sentences with a connective word (e.g., 'I'll use this and you use that'). The speech of children at this stage becomes increasingly like that of adults, and the productive vocabulary (of the child) by now is often well over 1000 words.

One particular area in which children show a gradual but steady improvement around this time is in their use of questions. Although children are able to respond appropriately to questions before they are capable of producing them themselves, usually from about the age of 3 onwards they demonstrate further grammatical competence by their phrasing of questions.

Asking a question involves a number of complex linguistic operations. For example, 'Where are you going?' requires the insertion of the question word ('where') and the rearrangement of the verb and subject (are, you) in addition to a rising pitch in the speaker's voice. Initially, young children's questions comprise only the rising pitch without the other variations (e.g., 'Baby's toy?'). With increases in vocabulary and utterances, though, children begin to string questions together using appropriate question words; to begin with, however, 'wh' words are merely added to the start of the sentence without altering the word order.

Pre-school children will often convey an interest in language for its own sake. The young child may be heard, for instance, 'experimenting' with language, particularly during play when language itself becomes a source of pleasure. Thus children may chatter to imaginary play friends and display a certain inventiveness and creativity with songs and rhymes, and somewhat later show an appreciation of humour and jokes.

Upon entering school, children's linguistic abilities are in many ways comparable to those of adults. In addition, many of the skills which they have acquired by this stage provide an important base upon which to develop the complex process of learning to read.

11.5 Impaired Language Development

The discussion of language acquisition so far has centred around normal development, but several cases have been documented where children have been subjected to conditions of extreme deprivation, resulting in detrimental effects upon their linguistic, social and emotional development. 'The Wild Boy of Aveyron' was a young boy found living wild in forests around Aveyron, France, in the late eighteenth century. Presumed to have been abandoned at an early age, he was discovered when about 7 and taken to Paris, where he was studied by the physician, J. Itard.

On his return to 'civilization' the boy (who was named Victor) was observed to crawl on all fours, liked to eat raw meat and would behave aggressively if anyone moved towards him. Despite several years of intense work and 'training', Victor's behaviour altered very little and, apart from a few sounds, he never learnt to speak. Although accounts of such 'feral children' are rare they do vividly portray the effects of early experience and the consequences of social isolation on an extreme scale. Other cases of deprivation have shown similar effects and are perhaps all the more distressing because many involve human cruelty.

One particular example involved a young girl, Genie, whose father had kept her locked in a small room for almost 12 years because he thought she was retarded. Her contact with people was limited, consisting of brief visits by her mother (who was virtually blind) who came to feed her, and her brutal father who discouraged her from talking by beating her if she made any sounds. When found, at $13\frac{1}{2}$, she was taken into care and initially her language development was rapid; within months she was producing two-word utterances and, gradually, longer sentences. However, some five years later, following detailed training and therapy, her speech was still like that of a toddler: she experienced difficulty in wording questions appropriately, forming tenses, using auxiliary verbs, and stringing ideas together into one sentence (Curtiss, 1977).

In this instance, although Genie managed to accomplish base language skills, her failure to make further progression without any real success highlights the importance of the early, formative years, particularly opportunities for social and linguistic interaction (speaking and being spoken to), regarding normal development. Studies such as these also support the existence of a 'critical period' in language acquisition: namely, if appropriate responses that are not acquired within a given time, then they never will be.

In contrast to these vivid examples, equally perplexing are language disabilities which largely involve children who, for various reasons, experience difficulty in becoming competent language users. The consequences of failing to grasp even the rudimentary concepts of language can have a profound influence on the development of later skills, such as reading and other aspects of intellectual attainment. Furthermore, an inability to communicate verbally and express oneself properly, even at pre-school level, will impede the child's progress in many ways, not least because they cannot make their feelings and wishes known. In our society, where much importance is laid upon these abilities, such difficulties represent a serious handicap.

The literature refers to such children in various ways, including language-impaired, delayed or disabled when a general problem is identified, and specific language-disabled when a particular disorder is thought to be involved. This diverse range of labels, whilst not providing much reassurance for parents of such children, does however show that the 'syndrome' is recognized and being addressed.

What makes these disabilities intriguing is that in many cases the child's only handicap is with language: that is, they perform perfectly well on other non-linguistic tests, and general measures of ability. Undoubtedly this is an area which requires further investigation. At the moment no single cause has been identified, although some writers suggest that the problem stems from difficulties experienced by certain children with cognitive representation and processing (Rice, 1989).

11.6 Theories of Language Acquisition

Language acquisition takes place within a social context; children normally, as we have seen, rapidly come to master the language which is spoken around them. Having objects, people and actions labelled by others is certainly one way in which children's vocabularies and understanding of word meaning increases, but the underlying mechanisms by which they come to grasp the principles of syntax and grammar have not been thoroughly established. Several explanations have been offered, of which two opposing perspectives will now be briefly outlined.

Learning theory

Supporters of this view claim that language is learnt, just like any other behaviour, through the processes of observation, imitation and reinforcement. Skinner (1957), for example, argues that the principles of conditioning (i.e., rewarding, punishing, shaping, etc.) are important in moulding the young child's behaviour. Thus, from the outset, infants are rewarded for producing sounds because they gain attention from the parents. These early vocalizations are shaped by means of differential rewards (e.g., parent shows approval) and punishments (e.g., parent ignores or disapproves). Gradually the sounds lead to 'words' which are themselves reinforced, and so on, until the child produces speech which is equivalent to that of an adult's.

The role of observation (modelling) and imitation is also regarded as influential in language acquisition by learning theorists such as Bandura. Young children often 'pick up' what they hear spoken around them and repeat it (sometimes embarrassing their parents!) and the accents which people have are further evidence of the role of imitation.

Furthermore, it can be demonstrated that reinforcement techniques increase the frequency of vocalizations, but often such studies are carried out under experimental conditions (i.e., deliberately manipulated variables) and so tell us little of processes at work in real life.

Essentially, although conditioning and imitation do contribute towards language acquisition, they cannot offer a complete explanation. For one thing, children are creative in their language production, and will often say phrases and sentences which they could not have heard before thus ruling out the possibility of imitation. Another flaw in this explanation of language learning concerns the extent to which young children make errors (e.g., underextensions, overgeneralizations, etc.) and later spontaneously correct them in their own speech. This phenomenon would seem to imply that the young child is actively thinking about language rather than simply being moulded by others.

A further example which demonstrates this concerns the notion of language correction. It was once thought that one way children learnt language was by having parents (and others) correct mistakes they made, the intention being to 'put them on the right track'. Thus, once corrected, the child would avoid making such errors again. However, in reality this is not the case. Consider the following statements:

Child 1: Mummy, I've got chocolate on my new coat.
Child 2: I wuv you.

Although the first statement is grammatically correct, the parents' response is hardly likely to be one of approval, whereas in the second example the child is likely to be rewarded (hugged, cuddled). The point is that parents are, on the whole, not concerned with shaping their children's speech into grammatically appropriate forms. If the notion of correction applied, we would expect the parent in the second example to be more interested in the grammatical structure of the utterance rather than its assumed meaning. Empirical studies confirm this; findings by McNeill (1966) and Brown *et al.* (1969) show that such parental influences cannot account for the child's gradual appreciation of syntax, and furthermore there was little evidence to suggest that explicit shaping or correction were directly responsible for the child's mastery of grammar.

The question, then, is whether or not direct parental intervention is of any help in the child's language learning. In this respect studies have looked at the effects of motherese, and training methods such as recasting. (According to Smith and Cowie (1988) some psychologists prefer the term 'Baby Talk Register' as this does not have sexist connotations.) Motherese is the simplified version of speech used by parents and older children when speaking to young children. Typically, this consists of modified speech, adapted so that the recipient is better able to understand. Vocabulary is kept simple, sentences shortened and words delivered at a slower rate, with important content words frequently being repeated. Does the use of motherese facilitate the infant's language acquisition? Findings from empirical studies tend to differ. For example, Furrow *et al.* (1979), in a naturalistic observation study, tape-recorded the dialogues between mothers and their 18-month-old children, and found that babies whose mothers used simplified speech were more competent in their use of language when assessed several months later than a comparison group in which the mothers' speech was not adjusted.

However, Gleitman *et al.* (1982) were unable to detect any beneficial effects of motherese in their study in which mothers and infants (of a similar age group to those in the study by Furrow *et al.*) were observed. This discrepancy in findings may lie with how the studies were conducted. For instance, both examples involved observation in natural settings, which means that rigorous control of variables is not possible, and so other factors may have influenced the results especially as the studies took place over a period of time (by definition an essential element when looking at language *development*).

Regarding specific training, a number of studies have investigated the effects of adults expanding or enlarging a child's utterances, together with the concept of recasting sentences (i.e., rephrasing what the child says in some meaningful way), for example:

Child:	Juice gone
Parent:	Yes, your juice has gone (*expands*)
Child:	All gone
Parent:	Would you like more juice? (*recasts*)

Nelson (1973) demonstrated that recasting children's utterances could improve their linguistic competence in specific ways. The subjects, 2 year olds, were 'trained' in the use either of questions or of complex verbs (e.g., future tenses), and marked differences were noticed between the two groups. The grammatical aspects they were trained in were enhanced, but only for these specific elements; recasting did help, but the children's improvements were limited: that is, those trained in certain kinds of questions showed no gains in the phrasing of complex verbs and vice versa.

From studies involving motherese and specific training it is apparent that such methods can be effective, but although these techniques may facilitate development they are not essential for language acquisition. At best we can say that certain types of 'environmental input' are more appropriate than others. For example, Nelson (1973) has found a relationship between an 'authoritative' adult style, characterized by frequent use of instructions and commands, and a slower rate of acquisition of naming words by the child. This would suggest that the child needs to be actively involved in exchanges, rather than the discourse being one-way and adult-dominated. To this end, Rice (1989) recommends 'social interactive routines' such as book-reading, where the child and parent go through a book together, as being a beneficial exercise for the child's language development skills.

The biological approach

An alternative viewpoint of language acquisition is presented by nativists who argue that humans are biologically predisposed to acquire language. Thus, whereas the learning perspective discussed above stresses the contribution of the environment (nurture), with the emphasis being upon *performance*, the biological model is concerned with innate properties, with an emphasis on *competence* and underlying comprehension.

Chomsky (1957) has suggested that humans are equipped with an inborn *language acquisition device* (LAD) which enables them to quickly grasp the fundamental principles of a language. This would certainly help to explain how very young children soon develop a mastery of language without explicit teaching. Indeed, evidence in favour of this approach comes from the relatively orderly sequence in which language is acquired (i.e., pre-linguistic, one-word, two-words, etc.) and that this is by and large considered universal. (As was stated earlier, though, recent findings have cast doubt on this assertion of universality suggesting that culture *does* matter; see Rice, 1989.) Humans also possess a unique vocal apparatus allowing speech production, together with specialized brain areas such as Broca's area and Wernicke's area for language production and comprehension.

According to Chomsky, the LAD allows children to grasp rules of grammar and put them into use in their speech, even though they are not aware of doing so. Once a child has mastered the basics, this presents them with the potential for limitless combinations; the ability, for instance, to create and understand an infinitive number of utterances.

The notion of a 'predisposition' for language is also held by other theorists. Lenneberg (1967) argued that the brain is particularly 'sensitive' to acquiring language within a defined period. This so-called critical or sensitive period was considered to be from birth to the onset of puberty: the optimal time for gaining mastery of a language. Support for this position is provided by observations that adults learning a second language almost invariably speak it with an accent, unlike native speakers. Studies of feral children (such as Victor) also add weight to the notion that children require a period of exposure to language in their early years if acquisition is to proceed normally.

However, criticism of the nativist view is also plentiful. For instance, how does this theory account for language-impaired children. If language acquisition is a resilient, pre-programmed and innate sequence, then the presence of children who experience specific difficulty must challenge such a model.

The concept of a critical period has also been refuted. While cases such as those of Genie are thankfully rare, the evidence, at least in this particular instance, clearly shows that some development in language is possible beyond puberty, albeit at a cursory and basic level. Therefore environmental influences, such as specific training, may be capable of modifying the critical period to some extent.

Our discussion of theories, then, has been limited to two contrasting approaches, although in this complex field a number of others have been proposed. Another perspective, the interactionist view, stresses the importance of interaction between children and their experience in the environment, and argues that infants are already competent communicators before they begin to use words as such. Language is not considered to be a process which stems from conditioning, shaping or imitation, and neither is it viewed in the context of an innate brain mechanism. Instead, language in general, and grammatical rules in particular, develop as a result of the child's emerging cognitive abilities and knowledge, very much in accord with Piaget's ideas on intellectual development (see Chapter 10).

Still on the cognitive theme, a recent model was proposed by Nelson (1989), who argues that language acquisition takes place over a series of phases via what he calls the 'rare event learning mechanism' (RELM). By means of this mechanism, which incorporates many important cognitive processes (such as attention and memory), learners extract information from what they hear such that they are able to glean much of the rule system involved in the language spoken around them.

Despite the abundance of theories mentioned, each has its faults, and as yet no one model can satisfactorily account for the ways in which young children accomplish what is, after all, a remarkable feat.

SPOTLIGHT   Inventing a language

Essentially, language is about communicating information and ideas. Every spoken language in the world enables users to express themselves in an infinite variety of ways. However, even a language system as rich and diverse as English may sometimes convey ambiguity or lead to misinterpretation, depending both on *what* is said and, perhaps more importantly, *how* it is said. An appreciation of the immense value of our language, together with the frequency with which difficulties in interpretation may arise, should become apparent after trying the following exercise.

- Devise an alternative method of communication, using whatever system of symbols you consider appropriate, e.g., pictures, words or non-verbal means.
    In order to test your new language, use it to represent a simple sentence such as 'The man waved his hand'.

- How well does your language system communicate messages?
  Does it have a basic set of rules?
  What are its limitations (i.e., is it time-consuming to use)?
  Would it take long to learn, and begin to be used effectively?

11.7   Language in Other Animals

As we have seen, human beings appear unique in terms of producing speech, and indeed for centuries many people maintained that language was an ability of which only humans were capable. Certainly it is true that humans are anatomically specialized for speech, but whether or not language is unique to us really depends on how the term 'language' is defined.

Since the 1950a a number of studies have been conducted which have attempted to teach language to non-human primates (usually chimpanzees and gorillas, as they are highly sociable and their intelligence level at maturity is thought to be comparable with that of 2–3-year-old children); many of these have met with success, depending on the criteria for 'language' used.

An early attempt by Hayes and Hayes (1951) aimed to teach a baby chimpanzee called Vicki to talk by rearing her as if she were human. However, after about six years, and despite the possibility of subjective interpretations by the researchers, Vicki only managed four sounds which could be described as 'words'.

It soon became apparent that chimps were incapable of producing human utterances, and subsequent research concentrated instead on teaching sign languages, a move which capitalized on chimps' dextrous abilities. A now-famous experiment began in 1966 and was conducted by R. and B. Gardner (1978) of the University of Nevada, USA. They set out to teach a female chimp, Washoe, the system of American Sign Language (ASL). The Gardners acquired Washoe when she was about 12 months old and, from the start of the study, they signed to each other using ASL when in her presence. New objects and activities were frequently introduced to the chimp, whenever possible accompanied by the appropriate sign (with the hope that Washoe would associate the two). The main teaching methods employed were instrumental conditioning (i.e., Washoe was rewarded for using correct signs), and imitation (the Gardners would correct Washoe's errors, and one would then imitate the modified version).

Around four years later, Washoe had a vocabulary of approximately 160 signs, which included everyday objects and some others, such as 'apple', 'toothbrush' and 'tickle'. Furthermore, she demonstrated appropriate generalization (i.e., having learnt the sign for an action, such as 'more', she was able to apply it to several activities such as 'more food' and 'more tickle'; young chimps have a great fondness for tickling and being tickled). In addition, and perhaps more significantly, Washoe began after a time to combine signs to form simple phrases and sentences (just as would a young child): for example 'open food drink' would be signed to request that the refrigerator be opened. From instances such as these it could be inferred that this young chimpanzee was using a set of rules (i.e., grammar) to combine words because the basic word order was appropriate. Other attempts to teach language to chimps have been carried out, using different methods. Utilizing instrumental conditioning, Premack (1971) taught a chimp, Sarah, to use plastic shapes which represented words. These could be fixed on to a magnetic board by Sarah, and arranged to make simple sentences. When the correct symbol was chosen she was given a food reward, and in the course of the study developed a relatively extensive vocabulary. However, although Sarah demonstrated a basic competence resulting from her training (e.g., she produced messages such as: 'If Sarah good, then apple'), it appeared to be a simple case of association, as she rarely initiated conversations or devised original messages.

In another variation, Rumbaugh (1977) trained Lana to communicate via a computer keyboard which was adapted so that symbols on each key represented 'words'. The symbols were presented on a screen and gradually Lana came to recognize them and use them appropriately. Furthermore, the computer was able to respond to her use of the keys, and provide reinforcement when deserved. By this method Lana was able to interact with her human observers who used the same 'language' to communicate with her.

However, many critics dispute the notion that these studies truly demonstrate 'language'. Terrace *et al.* (1979), for instance, report that from observations of another chimp, Nim Chimpsky, it became apparent that much of the 'spontaneous signing' was little more than rote learning and imitation. This conclusion, they claimed, also applied to the findings from previous studies. After making detailed studies of videotapes it was argued that, in some cases, the chimps may have merely been responding to subtle cues given by their observers. Furthermore, the combinations produced by chimps did not really qualify as language since young children are capable of creating messages they have never heard before, whereas the chimps only communicated their present needs.

The debate will obviously continue. Perhaps the main problem lies in wrongly attempting to apply human criteria to the apes, as any comparison will inevitably be based upon human standards. In expecting (or hoping) that apes will learn language as we define it, it is possible that we are imposing limits on their full potential. That chimps are able to display even a rudimentary grasp of our method of communication surely indicates something of their intelligence.

In contrast to this work, other researchers are in favour of observing the ways in which such intelligent being communicate among their own kind. Menzel (1975), for example, points out from his observations of chimps in their natural habitat that they possess a highly elaborate system of communicative gestures, and one which is perfectly tuned to their way of life. Indeed, systems of communication in all species function to enable individuals and groups to thrive in their own particular environment.

Whatever the perspective argued, though, this area holds for us an intrinsic fascination. The possibility that we may 'converse' with other species and discover something of their perceptions and thoughts is a concept which truly captures the imagination. An intriguing example, finally, is provided by Jane Goodall (cited in Blakemore, 1988), who made the study of apes her life. One story recalls a chimpanzee, Lucy, who was taught sign language, and reared virtually like a human child. Some years later, she was placed among a colony of wild chimps, an experience which she obviously found distressing, as indicated by the message she conveyed one day to a visitor at the reserve where she was captive. Despite the restrictions of her previously acquired sign language, Lucy's feelings were all too clear: 'Please help. Out.'

11.8   Questions and Exercises

1. Using a tape recorder, compare and contrast the language of a 2 year old with that of a 5 year old.
2. Discuss the contention that language is unique to humans.
3. Write down ONE example of (a) a sentence that is syntactically and semantically correct, (b) a sentence that is syntactically correct but semantically incorrect, and (c) a sentence that is syntactically and semantically incorrect.
4. Critically discuss two theories of language acquisition.
5. Make a list of the ways in which people communicate with others that *do not* involve speech.

(12) Animal learning

12.1 Introduction

In its everyday usage the word 'learning' usually refers to understanding and storing information, ideas and facts that are regarded as important in our society. However, with such a wide and abstract concept it would be impossible to investigate how learning occurs or to find out what steps could be taken to improve learning in schools and at places of work, so psychologists have chosen to use the very simplest examples of learning in order to make this task easier. For instance, instead of attempting to find out how people could best learn about atomic physics it is easier to analyse tasks such as learning to walk, or to grasp objects. Obviously these simple skills involve the study of infants as the main subjects. But an even easier starting point chosen by the early psychologists was that of learning in animals.

12.2 Ivan Pavlov and Classical Conditioning

Pavlov was a Russian physiologist who studied reflexes in the digestive system of dogs. A reflex is an automatic bodily response to a stimulus. Reflexes are common to all animals and they serve as fast reactions in cases of emergency, such as removing your foot from a sharp stone. Pavlov observed that although most reflexes are built into nervous systems, there are some which appear to be learnt. In the chief example Pavlov studied, a dog will salivate as a reflex whenever the smell or taste of food is sensed. This is a natural reflex observed in many animals, including humans, and it prepares the mouth for the initial digestion of food as it enters the system. But some of Pavlov's dogs would also salivate to other stimuli besides food. For instance, some of his dogs salivated at the sight of an empty food pail. Such a reflex must have been learnt by the dog associating the pail with the food it normally contained. And, since salivation is not a conscious behaviour, it showed Pavlov that a reflex can be a learnt as well as an inborn behaviour. He described the type of reflex which has been learnt as a 'conditioned' reflex or response.

In a classical conditioning study the experimenter begins by choosing one of the naturally-occurring reflexes of the animal and then presents two stimuli to it. One of these stimuli is called the **unconditioned stimulus** (or UCS) and this is the 'natural' one which produces the reflex. The second stimulus is called the *conditioning stimulus* (or CS), which may be anything which the animal is able to perceive, such as the ring of a bell, the sight of a flag, or any other event the experimenter chooses. This CS is presented either just before or simultaneously with the UCS. This pairing together of the CS and UCS is done repeatedly for tens or even hundreds of times ('trials'). The purpose of this is as follows. Presenting the UCS alone will evoke the reflex itself (by definition, the UCS is the natural stimulus for doing so). But when the UCS appears together with a new stimulus on a number of occasions then the CS itself can evoke the reflex. When the CS can do this the reflex it produces becomes known as a 'conditioned response', or CR. Having shown that a natural reflex can become conditioned Pavlov then went on to investigate other aspects of this learning.

An interesting issue was for how long this CR would last once it had been conditioned. To test this Pavlov presented the CS alone for a number of trials (i.e., without following it with the UCS). With this procedure the animal soon loses its CR. In other words, the conditioned reflexes will die out, or become 'extinct', if not consistently supported by the UCS. Pavlov found that extinction is not like 'forgetting' the CR, because various events may cause a CR to reappear. For instance, a sudden event which startles the animal during the extinction trials may reinstate the CR, if only briefly. 'Spontaneous recovery' may also occur; this is shown when the animal has been removed from the experiment for a period of time and then re-tested with the CS. It is found that this causes an immediate recovery of the CR. Pavlov believed from this that extinction is caused by some kind of inhibition in the animal's nervous system which prevents the CR from occurring. A final demonstration of the unusual nature of extinction was shown to Pavlov when he tried to re-train a CR after extinction. It was found that re-learning a CR after extinction may be more rapid than the original learning.

Pavlov also investigated the phenomenon of 'generalization'. This is what happens when a stimulus that is similar to the CS (but not identical to it) is presented to the animal. For example, if a dog has been conditioned to salivate in response to a bell which has a pitch of middle C then a bell of another pitch will also cause the dog to salivate. The nearer in pitch the new bell is to the original (CS) then the more salivation will occur. Sounds of less similarity to a bell may also cause salivation, but to a much lesser extent. This relationship is called the generalization gradient, and is shown in Figure 12.1.

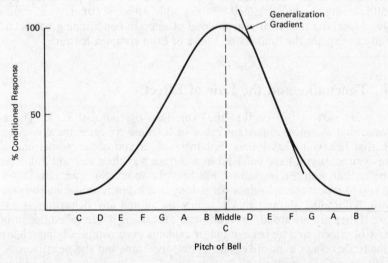

Figure 12.1 Generalization curve showing the gradient (slope of the curve) for an experiment involving conditioning a response (such as salivation) to the sound of a bell of pitch middle C

An effect related to generalization is one called 'discrimination'. This is the process where the animal learns not to generalize. In other words, the animal can be trained to respond to no other stimulus than the original CS on which it was trained. This occurs when the animal has been presented with a range of stimuli which are similar to the CS during training. However, when these other stimuli are presented the UCS is never paired with them. Only the CS will therefore have ever occurred with the UCS. For instance, if the CS has been a bell of pitch middle C then the animal will be presented with a range of other bell sounds including other pitches. None of these other bells will have been paired with the UCS. Gradually the animal's generalized responses to these other bells will become extinct. Discrimination is where the CR has become specific to the CS and only to that stimulus.

Pavlov reasons that although this form of conditioning was shown through simple experiments on animals, it could explain much of animal and human behaviour. He believed that reflexes, once conditioned, may act as the stimulus for another response, and so on, until chains of reflexes build up into complicated patterns of behaviour. Although his optimism for this theory was ill-founded there have been a number of valuable applications of classical conditioning theory which are commonplace today, some of which are discussed in a later section.

12.3   Instrumental or Operant Conditioning

According to Pavlov's theory of classical conditioning, even when we are learning something as complex as mathematics we are merely conditioning our reflexes into 'chains' of actions and reactions. Eventually these reflex chains will form into complete and complicated sequences of behaviour. As we shall see later, there has been a successful application of this work in understanding and treating simple behaviour disorders, such as phobias. But not many psychologists agree that all learning can be explained by the simple principles of classical conditioning. However, the theory of instrumental or operant conditioning has been held by many to explain the fundamental laws of even complex learning.

12.4   Thorndike and the Law of Effect

In the early part of this century the American psychologist E. L. Thorndike proposed that the most important cause of learning concerns the consequences which that behaviour has for us. For instance, if you obtain something which pleases you after you have behaved in a certain way then you will link together that behaviour with the pleasure it has brought about. Such an association will cause you to repeat the behaviour for as long as it keeps reproducing the pleasure for you. Thorndike showed that teaching an animal any behaviour is easy to achieve if they are rewarded, or 'reinforced', for doing it. He called this principle the 'law of effect', and he believe that it explains even complex human learning. Originally there was a 'positive' and a 'negative' law, but the negative one was soon disproved. Thorndike's ideas were based upon very simple experiments in which an animal was rewarded for solving some kind of problem. The most famous was the puzzle box from which cats could escape by operating a catch with their noses or paws.

12.5 Skinner and Reinforcement

B. F. Skinner was influenced by Thorndike's explanation of learning, and he investigated the law of effect and how reinforcement controls learning. Skinner used the word 'reinforcement' to refer to the consequences of a behaviour (i.e., the pleasant or unpleasant experience it leads to). For instance, if a child is taught to say 'please' by its parents giving sweets each time this word is used then the sweet acts as a 'reinforcer' of that behaviour. It is in this case a pleasant or satisfying consequence for the child and so s/he learns to say 'please'. In order to investigate the exact relationship between reinforcement and learning Skinner invented a special apparatus called the Skinner Box (see Figure 12.2).

Skinner placed a hungry animal, usually a rat or pigeon, into the box and observed its behaviour. The animal first explored the novel environment but eventually it stumbled upon the food-producing mechanism. For rats a press of the lever caused food to drop into the tray. The mechanism for a pigeon was to peck at the coloured disc. The appearance of the food pellet in the tray was therefore dependent upon the animal producing the correct response. The animal ate the reinforcer and experienced the pleasure of reducing its hunger. Next, according to prediction, the animal repeated this behaviour because it had become associated with the reinforcement. Very soon the pecking or lever pressing was about all the animal did in the box (apart from eating, of course)!

12.6 Positive and Negative Reinforcement

Positive reinforcement

When an organism is hungry or thirsty then eating or drinking is satisfying to it. Satisfaction is the concept which Thorndike used to explain how the law of effect

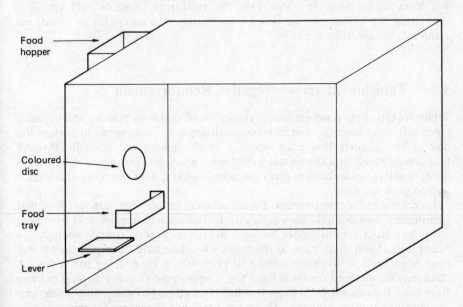

Figure 12.2 The Skinner box

causes learning. Pleasure is felt when the animal's need is satisfied. Obtaining food will reward an animal for its food search, and the particular behaviours which led up to the discovery of food will be reinforced. Consequently, the next time that the animal is hungry (assuming it is in the same vicinity), it will repeat those behaviours again. Such reinforcement is called 'positive' because it causes the animal to repeat its actions in the anticipation of obtaining something it wants. Positive reinforcement happens in the presence of something the animal wants and therefore causes it to approach.

Negative reinforcement

The most important principle of all reinforcement is that it 'energizes' or activates behaviour. In other words, reinforcement makes the organism active rather than inactive. Positive reinforcement makes the animal active in its attempt to obtain what it wants. **Negative reinforcement** also makes the animal active, but this time because it wants to avoid or to escape from something unpleasant. For instance, a person who fears spiders will avoid situations where they expect to find them, such as attics. Such fear energizes a strong and unpleasant feeling of repulsion. Avoidance – or escape-seeking – behaviour is caused when organisms are faced with something they dislike or fear. If they succeed in their avoidance then this will reinforce that particular avoiding behaviour. People are said to have 'escaped' if they remove themselves from the situation they dislike or fear. If people behave in such a way that they do not experience being near the object of the fear, then they are 'avoiding' it. The exact means by which they escape or avoid is the negative reinforcement. For instance, if the lever in a Skinner Box has to be pressed in order to stop cold water from being sprayed, then the animal will learn this behaviour. Remember that it is not receiving positive reinforcement; the lever is pressed so as to avoid negative reinforcement (i.e., something it does not want to happen). In either case the reinforcer (food or cold spray) is energizing the animal. In the case of energizing it to escape or to avoid, the reinforcer is said to be negative.

12.7   Punishment versus Negative Reinforcement

Whilst investigating reinforcement Skinner found that both positive and negative types will cause learning. For instance, in order to teach a pigeon to peck at the disc in the Skinner Box both types of reinforcement are possible. Positive reinforcement will give the animal something it wants for pecking the disc, such as food; negative reinforcement gives the animal what it does not want whenever it *fails* to peck the disc.

In contrast to the effectiveness of reinforcement for learning Skinner found that punishment does not have such clear effects. Punishment is a different treatment altogether from reinforcement because its aim is to stop, or 'de-energize', a behaviour. If you think back to the times when you have been punished it will have been because someone wanted to prevent you from doing something. A child may be smacked for breaking a toy. The purpose of this is to stop her/him from breaking other toys. Skinner concluded that trying to stamp out a behaviour by punishing it does not work. There are a number of reasons for this.

1. The results of punishment are unpredictable: sometimes it works, sometimes not.
2. Even when an unwanted behaviour has been stopped, other behaviours the parents might find undesirable may start in its place: for instance, a child smacked for picking its nose may then start to bite its nails.
3. Punishment usually stops a behaviour only for as long as the punisher is present. When the punisher is absent the behaviour may become more frequent than ever. This is called a 'suppression' effect, and it makes punishment difficult to administer.
4. It is always more difficult to de-energize an unwanted behaviour than it is to energize a wanted one. This is probably because humans are naturally active creatures.

12.8   Primary and Secondary Reinforcement

The above discussion has all involved 'primary' reinforcement. Primary reinforcement is the direct consequence of the organism's behaviour which precedes it.

Secondary reinforcement is the term given to objects or events which occur in the environment whilst the primary reinforcer is given. Secondary reinforcers may be objects in the immediate environment, such as chairs or other artefacts, and they are always present at the arrival of the primary reinforcer. Secondary reinforcers can themselves influence learning. For instance, if the lever is removed from the Skinner Box after a rat has been trained to press it for food, then the animal will spend its time near to the food tray. The food tray itself has been reinforcing for the rat because previously the animal has experienced pleasure from eating whilst close to the tray. Similarly, a young child may enjoy sitting in its high chair to play because it has received secondary reinforcement by being placed there at mealtime (i.e., food is again the primary reinforcer). Secondary reinforcement may also be an event, such as the click of the food dispenser as food drops. Anything that is consistently present when the primary reinforcement occurs can act as a secondary reinforcer.

12.9   Partial and Continuous Reinforcement

Another of Skinner's major discoveries was that reinforcement given in different ways has differing effects on learning. Recall that in classical conditioning reinforcement must be given *continuously*. For instance, if a dog is being trained to salivate at the sound of a bell then each and every time the bell is heard food must accompany it. Failure to do this weakens the association the animal has learnt and extinction commences. But Skinner discovered that this is not the case with **instrumental conditioning**. In fact continuous reinforcement is less effective in this form of conditioning than non-continuous or 'partial' reinforcement.

12.10   Schedules of Reinforcement

There are two basic ways in which reinforcement may be partial. First, instead of reinforcement being given for each lever pressed in the Skinner Box, sometimes food is withheld. This would be a *ratio schedule*. For instance, a ratio of 1:2 would mean that one pellet of food would be given for every two presses of the lever.

A second way of arranging partial reinforcement is to give the food reinforcer after a particular interval of time *so long as at least one lever press response occurs in that interval.* For instance, in an interval schedule of ten seconds, provided the lever was pressed during each ten-second period then a pellet of food is delivered every tenth second. Failure to press the lever at all in any interval will mean no food is presented that time. This type of schedule is called an *interval schedule* because it is based upon time intervals. Skinner observed that a subject's behaviour will change in predictable ways depending upon the type of reinforcement schedule that is used.

Fixed ratio (FR) schedule

Where a ratio schedule is said to be 'fixed' it means that after a definite number of times that the response (e.g. lever pressing) occurs a reinforcer is given. In an FR5 schedule, every fifth lever press will be reinforced by food.

Variable ratio (VR) schedule

As the name implies, with a 'variable' ratio schedule there is no definite frequency of responses for producing a reinforcer. Where VR schedules are controlled by the experimenter they are usually arranged around some average number. For instance, a VR5 would mean that in the long run the animal receives one reinforcement for every fifth response. However, on any single trial that number may vary. Consider the example in Table 12.1: you will see that on trial 3 the subject had to press the lever six times before reinforcement was given, compared with only twice on trial 2.

Table 12.1 *Example of a VR5 schedule*

Trial no.	Number of lever presses before reinforcement given
1	5
2	2
3	6
4	3
5	3
6	2
7	5
8	9
9	7
10	8
	Total = 50
Average rate of reinforcement per trial	$= 50 \div 10 = 5$

Fixed interval (FI) schedule

Interval schedules give reinforcement at the end of each time period *provided that at least one response was made*. When this interval is 'fixed' it means that the experimenter keeps the interval unchanged. For instance, an FI20 in the Skinner Box means that at least one lever press must be made within each interval for the subject to be reinforced every 20 seconds.

Variable interval (VI) schedule

Unlike the FI schedule a variable schedule does not have fixed time periods per trial. The experimenter decides only upon the actual sequence of interval; durations will vary around this average. For instance, in a VI10 the sequence of intervals might appear as illustrated in Table 12.2.

Table 12.2   *Example of a VI10 schedule*

Trial no.	Interval length (in seconds)
1	10
2	15
3	5
4	2
5	18
6	15
7	5
8	15
9	3
10	12
	Total = 100

Average interval = 100 ÷ 10 = 10 secs.

On the first trial the interval was ten seconds and, provided a lever press occurred in that time, reinforcement would be given. On the second trial the subject had to wait for 15 seconds before receiving reinforcement (assuming the lever was pressed).

12.11   Comparison Between the Different Schedules

Knowing how reinforcement affects an organism's behaviour is important because each schedule does this in a different way. Using continuous reinforcement a subject's learning is usually slower overall compared to any of the four partial schedules: FR, VR, FI and VI. But the speed at which learning occurs is not the only way to judge how effective the teaching method has been. Another important consideration is how long the subject will retain what they have learnt.

Skinner investigated this using extinction. All that is required to cause extinction in the Skinner Box is to disconnect the food dispenser from the lever mechanism. A rat which has learnt to operate the lever for food reinforcement will gradually stop pressing if reinforcement is not given. This is a process called extinction. Skinner found that an animal trained using partial reinforcement will continue to operate the lever long after one that was trained using continuous reinforcement. He called this the 'partial reinforcement extinction effect', or PREE.

Extinction is a convenient guide to how well learnt a behaviour has become. If the rat continues to operate the lever long after reinforcement is stopped then the learning is said to be 'resistant to extinction'. The different schedules of reinforcement each have unique effects on the speed of learning, the manner of responding and its resistance to extinction.

Continuous reinforcement

Learning is initially very rapid but gradually begins to slow down. The most wide use of this form of reinforcement is to start off conditioning before transferring the subject to one of the partial schedules.

FR schedule

With a low ratio, such as FR2, the subject receives reinforcement after a small number of responses (in this case after every second one). This makes the schedule similar to continuous reinforcement because with low FRs learning is initially rapid before decelerating. With higher FRs the rate of learning is less likely to decline. For instance, a rat which has been trained to make 500 lever presses for each food reinforcer will maintain a relatively high rate of response. Of course, it would be necessary to have built up the ratio of 1:500 because this could not be trained from the start. During extinction the animal will seem to be resistant because at least 500 responses will occur. However, in contrast to the variable schedules there will be few unreinforced 'units' of 500 responses before complete extinction happens. On FR schedules it is essential not to omit reinforcement if responding is to be maintained.

FI schedule

The rate of initial learning with FI schedules is usually slow compared with continuous reinforcement or FR schedules. Also, once a behaviour such as lever pressing has been learnt, the responses will usually be concentrated in the last few moments of each interval. Although the subject is only required to make a single response in each interval in order to gain the reinforcer, this is not what usually happens. Typically the subject will start late and accelerate their responses towards the end of the fixed interval. There are individual differences between animals in this behaviour.

VR schedule

As with the FR schedule, just how fast the behaviour is learnt and how long it is retained depends upon the ratio (average) itself. A VR of 200 would never be learnt from scratch. A VR of 2 would be rapidly learnt but also rapidly become extinct. However, generally speaking, VR schedules produce slow responding but learning that is very resistant to extinction. In other words, the subject is slow to learn but retains the behaviour for long periods. The most obvious use of such a schedule would be to maintain a behaviour which was initially taught using a ratio schedule.

VI schedule

Recall that with FI schedules the subject's behaviour eventually settles down to a point where they will commence and accelerate their responses late in each interval. However, with VI schedules such responding would not work because the length of the interval on each trial differs. Responding in the last few seconds of a VI schedule of one minute would as often as not fail to be reinforced because the interval is sometimes longer and sometimes shorter than this time. Subjects tend to spread their responses throughout the interval more with VI than with FI schedules and will therefore produce more of them in each trial. VI schedules also produce learning which is very resistant to extinction.

12.12   Applications of Learning Theory

Both classical and operant (instrumental) conditioning techniques have been applied to human behaviour and such demonstrations suggest how simple reflex responses might originate. Several studies have also highlighted how the basic principles might be used to change behaivour.

Applications of classical conditioning

The association which takes place in conditioning may offer an explanation as to the development of behaviours such as phobias. A phobia is an irrational and intense fear of some object, event or situation, such as snakes, spiders or open spaces.

Watson and Rayner (1920) demonstrated the classical conditioning of fear in a young boy. 'Little Albert' was an 11-month-old boy who was allowed to play with a white rat and initially showed no fear towards the rat, but as he played a metal bar was struck behind him causing a fear response (an **unconditioned response** or UCR). After several presentations of the noise together with the rat the boy displayed the fear response to the rat alone. This may be shown as follows:

Rat ————————————————→	no fear
Noise (UCS) ————————————————→	fear (UCR)
Rat (CS) + Noise (UCS) ————————————————→	fear (UCR)
Rat (CS) ————————————————→	fear (CR)

It was also noticed that generalization occurred because Little Albert showed fear towards similar objects, such as cotton wool.

Treatment (of phobias) using classical conditioning techniques

The principles of classical conditioning not only explain how phobias develop, but also offer a means of treating them.

Extinction of the response may be brought about by presenting the CS alone a number of times. In a case such as the above the rat could have been presented several times without being accompanied by the noise (although this was not done with Little Albert).

Another approach involves '*stimulus substitution*' whereby the unpleasant stimulus (noise) is substituted for something pleasant, such as a toy or a sweet. Here, the aim is to replace the fear response directly by associating pleasure with the CS, and since we cannot experience more than one opposing emotion at a time the feelings of pleasure should displace those of fear. This method, involving two competing responses, is known as *reciprocal inhibition*.

Wolpe (1958) developed and refined this procedure, which has been adapted as a way of treating phobias whereby patients are taught to relax in order to inhibit the fear response. Together with muscular relaxation the patient is gradually, over a number of steps, encouraged to imagine the fearful situation or object, usually based on a hierarchy of steps. For example, if a person has a fear of snakes, then – while relaxing – they are asked to imagine situations with snakes varying from their least fearful to most fearful. Over a gradual process each step is dealt with until the patient reports having no anxiety to their most fearful situation. This technique is termed *systematic desensitization*, and has been found very useful in the treatment of specific phobias. Some critics argue, however, that patients may experience difficulty in transferring from imaginary to real situations.

Two types of therapy which represent a difficult approach to that of systematic desensitization are *implosion* and *flooding*. Here the patient is subjected to their most fear-evoking stimulus at the beginning, without a gradual build-up of steps. The intention is to reduce anxiety by making patients confront their fear all at once, with the result being extinction of the fear response.

Implosion makes use of imagery in that the patient is encouraged to imagine (with help from the therapist) their most fearful situation.

Flooding works by exposing the patient to 'the real thing' (e.g., a fear of snakes would be treated by using a real snake).

Such therapies have yielded successful results and flooding is considered by many to be the more effective of the two. However, because of their highly stressful nature they are not suitable treatments for the old, young or infirm, and the possibility exists that, instead of extinguishing the patient's fear, they might intensify it.

Aversion therapy involves a pairing of the 'unwanted' behaviour with an unpleasant event as in the basic classical conditioning procedure. For example, when treating alcoholics, an emetic substance (one which causes nausea and vomiting) is paired with alcohol so that, after a number of presentations, alcohol alone brings about the vomiting reflex. This can be shown as follows:

Alcohol (CS) + Emetic (UCS) $\longrightarrow$ nausea and vomiting (UCR)

Alcoholic (CS) $\longrightarrow$ nausea and vomiting (CR)

The main criticism of aversion therapy is that it has a high relapse rate – that is, the improvement by patients may be short-lived – and they soon return to their old behaviours. There is evidence, however, which suggests that patients have been 'cured' for up to a year, and some would argue that this is better than nothing at all.

Treatments using operant conditioning techniques

These techniques apply the principles of reinforcement in that the desired behaviour is rewarded immediately it occurs.

Programmed learning

This stems from the work of Skinner and is essentially a teaching or instructional method in which information is presented to students step by step in units known as frames. In this way the students' behaviour is conditioned by having their correct responses immediately rewarded. (This may simply take the form of satisfaction at having given the correct responses.) Programmes can be of two kinds: linear, or branching.

Linear programmes present and reinforce one unit of information at a time, and the student must give the correct response before moving on to the next unit. Frames are presented in an ordered sequence, and when the student has completed one s/he moves on to the next. An extract from a linear programme is shown below in Figure 12.3.

Branching programmes tend to consist of larger frames but also allow flexibility of response. Rather than presenting information in a linear format they provide several other possible answers to a question, only one of which is correct. Such programmes also allow for incorrect responses to be made and, when this happens, the student is presented with a remedial frame which points out the error and then retests the information. If all the test questions are answered correctly then the student is allowed to skip these remedial frames.

Programmed learning offers several advantages over conventional teaching methods. It allows students to work at their own pace, and provides immediate feedback in the form of knowledge of results. However, the teaching machines are expensive and this method of learning may not suit everyone, as some students may find it boring and monotonous (see Figure 12.4). Other methods which are based on programmed learning involve the use of computers to facilitate teaching. Computer-assisted instruction (CAI) and computer-assisted learning (CAL) represent recent advances in this area. For example, Joyce (1988) reports on the use of computers as counselling tools in which patients use a technique known as the Therapeutic Learning Program (TLP) to identify their problems and eventually resolve conflicts via interactive sessions with a computer.

Several workers have shown that programmed learning may be an effective teaching method, but it is best used in conjunction with conventional techniques, complementing them rather than replacing them.

Behaviour therapy (behaviour modification)

This represents an attempt to apply the principles of conditioning in order to treat a range of behavioural disorders, such as schizophrenia and autism. The emphasis is on the behaviour itself rather than any underlying cause but its supporters argue that behavioural disorders are acquired in much the same way as other (learnt) behaviour patterns.

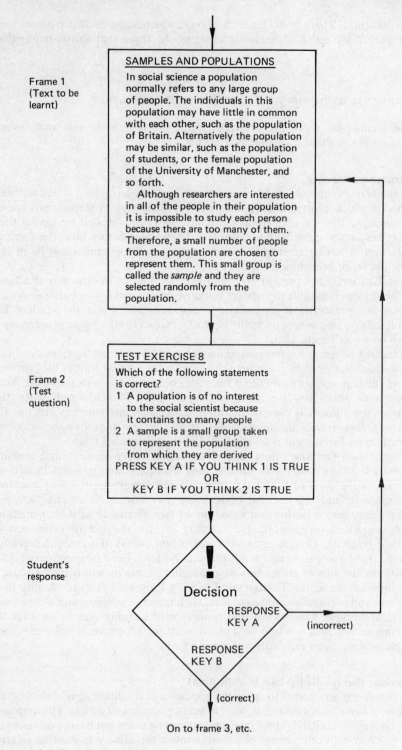

SAMPLES AND POPULATIONS

Frame 1
(Text to be
learnt)

In social science a population
normally refers to any large group
of people. The individuals in this
population may have little in common
with each other, such as the population
of Britain. Alternatively the population
may be similar, such as the population
of students, or the female population
of the University of Manchester, and
so forth.
   Although researchers are interested
in all of the people in their population
it is impossible to study each person
because there are too many of them.
Therefore, a small number of people
from the population are chosen to
represent them. This small group is
called the *sample* and they are
selected randomly from the
population.

TEST EXERCISE 8

Frame 2
(Test
question)

Which of the following statements
is correct?
1 A population is of no interest
   to the social scientist because
   it contains too many people
2 A sample is a small group taken
   to represent the population
   from which they are derived
PRESS KEY A IF YOU THINK 1 IS TRUE
        OR
KEY B IF YOU THINK 2 IS TRUE

Student's
response

Decision

RESPONSE
KEY A

(incorrect)

RESPONSE
KEY B

(correct)

On to frame 3, etc.

Figure 12.3 Extract from a linear program

Figure 12.4 Learning with computers

One application has been in the development of the *token economy system* in which desired behaviours are rewarded by means of tokens. It is based on the principles underlying primary and secondary reinforcement whereby behaviour such as tidying one's room entitles the patient to tokens which are collected and later exchanged for valued rewards such as a coach trip or visit to the shops.

This type of programme has been introduced in mental institutions, prisons and educational establishments and is very effective in modifying the behaviour of those with even severe behavioural problems (Walker, 1984). However, difficulties may arise in that the individual could become dependent on the token system and experience problems when placed in a real-life setting outside the institution.

Behaviour 'shaping' has been used with the mentally handicapped in attempts to develop speech in autistic children, for example (the symptoms of autism include total unresponsiveness to the environment and a marked lack of interaction with others). The shaping procedure works by reinforcing successive approximation to the desired response. With autistic children any existing vocalizations (noises, moans) are given positive reinforcement, such as attention and praise. Building upon this the child may make spontaneous sounds or imitate the therapist, and this would be rewarded. Gradually utterances might be shaped into words and phrases. Such techniques are time-consuming and require considerable skill in order to achieve results. It is also important that parents be trained to use shaping techniques in order to provide continuity and, ideally, lasting gains.

The main criticism levelled against behaviour modification techniques is that they work by treating the overt behaviour and symptoms rather than the underlying cause, although this debate really involves the very foundations upon which behaviourism is built: namely, that the only aspect worthy of psychological study is observable (and thus measurable) behaviour.

Biofeedback

Biofeedback ia a technique which employs operant conditioning as a means of modifying bodily functions such as heart rate and blood pressure (normally under involuntary control). It works by providing information (i.e., feedback) regarding physiological changes which the patient is then trained to control.

Developments in this area stemmed from the experiments by Miller and DiCara (1969), who demonstrated the possibilities of controlling what were previously considered to be involuntary behaviours. Basically, rats were given a paralysing drug (to prevent muscular contraction) and then trained to alter various autonomic responses for the reward of brain stimulation (a highly pleasurable experience, referred to as EBS or electrical brain shock).

Since such studies research has investigated the applications for human behaviour and several claims of success have been made, although many workers express doubts about the effectiveness of this technique and question the results which have been claimed for it.

12.13   The Competence–Performance Issue

Just because a person being observed seems to be unskilled or incompetent in what they are doing does not mean that they are so. For instance, the person at work who does a poor job in front of the supervisor may be doing so deliberately in order to avoid being given extra work! Similarly, students who lack confidence or who are shy may not raise their hands when a teacher poses a question to the class. Such behaviour would be a poor guide to what students know. The term 'competence' refers to the person's real knowledge or ability, but all the teacher knows of the students' ability and knowledge comes from observing their 'performance' either in class or in exams. The teacher assumes that the student who obtains a score, of say, 5 per cent in a test knows very little. The 5 per cent is a performance score and the teacher assumes it is a good measurement of the student's competence. Of course, often it may be. But there may be occasions when a test performance does not reflect the student's competence. There is always room to doubt whether any test score is accurately reflecting the person's competence. This is made more clear by research into **latent learning**.

12.14 Latent Learning

The psychologist Tolman demonstrated that behaviour does not necessarily reflect what the subject has learnt. His experiment involved two groups of rats which were placed in a maze. In one group each rat was placed at the entry to a maze and, when they reached the goal box at the far end, they were rewarded (reinforced) with food. These animals were tested repeatedly using this same procedure. Rats in the second group were placed in the same maze but they received no reinforcement upon reaching the goal box. Tolman showed that the reinforced group learnt to run the maze faster on each successive trial, whereas the non-reinforced group made no real improvement during this first phase of the study. Judging from the performances of the two groups up to trial 10 in Figure 12.5, the non-reinforced group (NR) have not learnt the maze. Conversely, the reinforced group (R) have shown from their performance substantial learning of the maze. This difference between the groups is what we would predict from the theory of operant conditioning. Remember the operant (or instrumental) conditioning proposes that what governs learning is the reinforcement that the subject experiences. Subjects in the NR group have not been reinforced and so, according to the theory, they will not have learnt the maze.

However, from trial 11 Tolman changed the conditions for the NR group. They were from then on reinforced by food in the goal box, just as the R group had

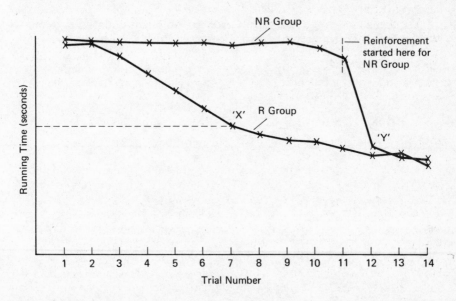

Source: Tolman (1948)

Figure 12.5 Tolman's study illustrating latent learning by rats in a maze-running problem

been from the start. In theory the NR group should take as long to learn the maze from trial 11 onwards as the R group did from trial 1. But as you can see from Figure 12.5 that is not what happens. Whereas it took the R group seven trials to reach the running speed 'x', the NR group achieved this speed after a single trial after reinforcement commenced (point 'y'). In other words the NR group had learnt the maze ('competence') but this was not evident in their behaviour ('performance'). The learning that does occur but which is not evident in behaviour is referred to as 'latent learning'. This issue is also raised as part of the competence–performance debate in the development of language and intelligence (IQ testing).

12.15   Questions and Exercises

1. Explain, using appropriate terms, how someone might develop a fear of going to the dentist, and outline how generalization and discrimination might occur in this situation.
2. Compare and contrast the effectiveness of three classical conditioning techniques which have been used to treat behavioural problems.
3. Design a linear programme to test a topic of your choice. For the same topic consider how your programme could be adapted into the branching format.
4. Construct a token economy system to train a hyperaggressive child to adopt a more socially-acceptable behaviour. Outline the sequence involved and give details of the reinforcements used, together with the desired responses.
5. Assess the contribution which operant conditioning techniques have made towards the treatment of human behaviour disorders.

13 Animal behaviour

13.1 Ethology

Ethology is the scientific study of animal behaviour. Ethologists study behaviour in an evolutionary context and look for universal principles governing its inheritance (phylogeny) and development within the individual (ontogeny). Since Darwin's work on the origin and evolution of species it has become generally accepted that the same laws and principles which apply in natural selection have also operated to bring about human evolution. The structure and behaviour of our species have evolved as products of natural forces which have acted upon our lineage. During the adverse conditions which arise from time to time in the ecosystem survival will occur only in those individual animals best adapted to overcome them. These natural forces include climatical changes, such as an ice age, droughts, floods, competition for food, the ability to avoid predation, seeking a mate, protecting the offspring, and so forth.

Although all species have evolved in response to similar natural pressures there have been a variety of means arising during evolution for dealing with these conditions. For instance, structural advantages have enabled the giraffe to exploit the vegetation which is beyond the reach of other ground-dwellers. Conversely, it has been behavioural adaptation which has enabled the lion to evolve through its tendency to use cooperative hunting strategies. Consequently the human species can be said to have evolved by similar means of structural and behavioural 'fitness'.

In the past twenty years there has been an assimilation of ideas into ethology which extends our interpretation of even complex social behaviour through evolutionary principles. These ideas stem from the new discipline of sociobiology, which is outlined later in this chapter. But first some explanation is needed to justify studying animals at all, given that psychology is aimed exclusively at reaching an understanding of human behaviour (see the Spotlight box).

SPOTLIGHT Animal studies and human behaviour

Darwin's evolutionary theory proposes that humans possess an 'animal' nature: we have evolved, as have other species, through ecological pressures which have shaped both our physiology and our behaviour. Studying animal behaviour in natural settings may help in clarifying the effects of ecological forces and thereby help us to explain this side of human nature. Animals also produce simplified versions of behaviours exhibited by humans and this is of itself helpful. But even though the behaviour observed in another species may not occur in humans it is often useful to study differences as well as similarities of behaviour between species. This helps our understanding and appreciation of the diversity and perhaps the origins of particular behaviour patterns in the natural world. Sometimes there are ethical reasons why an area of study in human behaviour may be problematical and in such cases animal 'models' may be necessary. Examples of this may be in studying sexual or aggressive behaviour where systematic studies on humans would be difficult to perform. It is also the case that in studying animal behaviour a greater degree of objectivity is possible than when the observer is studying his or her own species. Finally, in studies which require the subjects to spend long periods of time in controlled laboratory conditions, it is usually simpler and cheaper to use non-human species.

Which species? Ethologists do not confine themselves to the study of a limited range of species and in fact deliberately aim to diversify their knowledge of behaviour in the animal kingdom. However, the branch of psychology which investigates animal behaviour (**comparative psychology**) has brought only a limited number of animal species into the laboratory. These have been mainly the rat, mouse, pigeon, monkey and hamster. The albino rat has been a particular favourite and it has even been bred in psychology laboratories for its tameness and docility, which makes it quite unlike its 'natural' cousin. The areas of psychology which have been advanced by the study of animal behaviour are numerous, and include: sexuality, .aggression, attachment, territoriality, navigation, maternal behaviour, learning, psychopathology, social organization, communication and brain-behaviour influences.

13.2   Basic Ethological Concepts

This section provides a brief description of the basic concepts used in ethology. Ethologists, in common with social scientists, have established their own set of core ideas and lingo which constitute a particular paradigm for studying behaviour.

Sign stimuli and social releasers

Although an animal's sense organs are capable of responding to a range of energy in the environment, there are usually certain features which evoke instinctive responses. These automatic responses are triggered off, or 'released', by the occurrence of any stimulus which contains the appropriate features. Such a stimulus is referred to as a 'sign stimulus'. When the releasing features of a sign stimulus form part of the structure or the behaviour of another animal which has evolved a signalling function, then it is called a 'social releaser' (Lorenz, 1935). For instance, in the three-spined stickleback the male responds to another male aggressively if this second animal has red underparts. In the mating season adult male sticklebacks develop a red belly area which acts as a releaser for aggression in other males and for courtship in females. Whereas males will tolerate the presence of non-reddened males, their immediate reaction to the red belly is one of aggression. During the mating season male sticklebacks prepare nests within a territory which they defend against other males. They will, however, attempt to entice females into this territory and will respond to another social releaser which is usually evident in the female at this time: a belly swollen with eggs. This stimulus releases courtship behaviour in the male which takes the form of a zig-zag dance, the aim of which is to attract the female towards the prepared nest where she may lay the eggs to be fertilized by him.

Tinbergen (1948) used different models possessing either red or swollen underparts and he was able to elicit the appropriate response of either aggression or courtship behaviour depending upon which model he used. A study by Lack (1943) showed that the red breast of the robin similarly acts as a social releaser for aggressive behaviour among males. Tinbergen used simple models in a variety of other studies. Herring gull chicks peck at the parent's bill. This action causes the parent to regurgitate food on to the ground which it then feeds to the young. Using models Tinbergen discovered that the chicks aim their pecking at a red spot on the parent's bill. A similar behaviour occurs in cliff-nesting gulls such as the kittiwake but, rather than causing regurgitation, the bill-pecking makes the parent itself gape so as to enable the young to feed directly from its throat. Regurgitating food on a ledge would probably mean that some of it would be lost. In both cases, however, the bill acts as a social releaser for the chick's behaviour.

The gaping response of the young chaffinch can be elicited both by shaking the nest and by imitating the call of the parent. Tinbergen and Kuenen (1939) showed that nestling thrushes respond to the sight of the parent's head by gaping. This in turn leads the parent to feed them. This mechanism is present in a number of bird species and is used to advantage by the cuckoo, which not only competes by destroying nest mates but also produces a vast gape that elicits all of the feeding attentions of the foster parents. The sign stimulus of the gape is the brightly coloured lining of the throat of the nestling.

Sometimes a stimulus can be made to be 'supernormal': that is, it will trigger off a response even more effectively than the natural sign stimulus. For instance, Tinbergen (1948) showed that an oystercatcher will attempt to incubate a model egg of supernormal size in preference to one of her own. The huge gape of the cuckoo acts as a **supernormal stimulus** which elicits preferential feeding from the foster parents.

Ethogram

Ethologists usually begin their study of an animal species by describing, classifying and cataloguing the range of behaviour patterns observed. Such an approach reflects the biological training which most ethologists have had. Biology and zoology utilize taxonomic systems in classifications such as that describing animal and plant life. A taxonomy which classifies the behaviour repertoire of species is called an ethogram.

Modal or fixed action patterns (MAPs or FAPs)?

An ethogram contains a breakdown of the behaviours which are both unique to a given species ('species–specific') as well as those which are common to other species. Behaviour patterns which are species–specific are often of the kind known as 'fixed action patterns' (Lorenz, 1937). A FAP is a stereotyped series of actions which is automatic in appearance – almost robot-like – and once these actions are triggered off by an appropriate stimulus they run through as an entire sequence to completion.

No human parallel exists with which to illustrate this form of behaviour. However, in some animal species the ethogram may consist almost solely of such automatic behavioural sequences. An instance of a FAP occurs in the greylag goose in her action of retrieving eggs from the nest. In this FAP she begins by extending her head and neck over the egg and then makes rhythmic dipping movements of the neck to and fro at alternate ends of the egg. Such motion gradually draws the egg towards her breast and she continues with it until the egg is retrieved to the nest. It is a FAP because it consists of an entire sequence of behaviour which, once started, she continues through to completion even if the egg is removed by hand. This same behaviour will occur if the egg is replaced by a cylinder. In such a case the to-and-fro neck motion is unnecessary because of the object's natural stability, and yet the full FAP is observed to occur.

Barlow (1977) has recommended replacing the term 'fixed' by 'modal' to take account of his discovery that when many FAPs are timed in detail and with some accuracy it is found that a great deal of variation exists in the relative speeds of the units of behaviour involved. Not only do different members of the species vary in the manner in which FAPs are performed but there is also variation in the way they are reproduced by the same individual over a number of occasions. The term modal action pattern, or MAP, is intended to convey that there is a rough equivalence in these sequences but they are not as 'fixed' as was previously believed to be the case.

13.3 Evolution and Behaviour

Describing how behaviour evolves is a perplexing matter because, unlike with structural evidence, there is no historical record to dig up. Inferences may be drawn from palaeontology and archaeology about the ways our human ancestors have probably behaved. For instance, the residues of animal bones and stone axes at a human encampment from some two million years ago implies that early humans were organized hunters. However, there is continuing controversy among palaeontologists even concerning the scant evidence that has been uncovered to date. In any case this approach has not attracted the attention of psychologists who are not, in general, convinced that firm scientific evidence can accrue from such an approach. Yet the question concerning evolution of behaviour in animal species has been addressed by Lorenz. For instance, Lorenz (1941) made a detailed analysis of evolutionary developments among the Anatinae (duck and geese species). He classified 47 behaviour patterns and made a taxonomy according to which of the twenty species displayed each of the listed behaviours. This approach enabled Lorenz to identify which FAPs were common amongst these species and which ones were rare. The implication of this is that a FAP which is shared by all the species in the taxonomy must, logically-speaking, have had an ancient evolutionary origin. Conversely, behaviour patterns which occur in only a small number of species would have evolved more recently. For example, the piping sound made by lost fledgelings is common to all Anatinae, whereas the ritualistic head-shake occurs exclusively among ducks. This implies that the head-shake evolved following the phylogenetic division between duck and geese species.

Lorenz (1958) applied his method to a study of the ritual display found in various species of duck (see Spotlight box below for a discussion of behaviour rituals). On the basis of this study Lorenz concluded that the mallard is the most primitive of the duck species because it shows all the rudimentary patterns of behaviour common to most of these species, the majority of which have become elaborated in the other species during their evolution.

SPOTLIGHT Behaviour rituals

A behaviour ritual has no obvious function other than communication. Usually a ritualized behaviour pattern is a variation of a sequence of actions which still have a functional use for that species. Sometimes the ritualized form is more exaggerated than the functional one; for example, during courtship the male zebra finch makes an elaborate wiping motion of its beak on the branch next to a female. At other times a ritual may be less obvious and briefer than the functional version (the ritual preening of the wing performed by mallard ducks is barely noticeable, being just a touch of its feathers with the beak). Rituals are very stereotyped sequences which makes them unambiguous as social 'messages', such as the 'head-throw' of the goldeneye duck (a ritualized drinking gesture) which shows a variation of less than 20 movie frames (less than a second) between individuals, and is much less variable even than this in the case of one individual (Dane and van der Kloot, 1964). According to Hinde (1982) ritualized behaviour may have one of three origins.

1. *Intention movements* are where uncompleted functional movement occurs because the animal becomes either distracted or else is insufficiently motivated to complete them (e.g., the wing flapping observed in many water birds which does not lead to flight).
2. *Displacement*, which is derived from the work of Lorenz. He employed what is termed a 'hydraulic model' to explain motivation. Briefly, this proposes that behaviour is driven by an energy force from within the animal, and if the normal outlet for a given behaviour is blocked then some form of displaced activity occurs serving to release this pent-up energy. A displacement activity may evolve into a ritual. For instance, an animal which has the aggressive urge for attacking another but which is prevented from doing so through a fear of retaliation may have this energy displaced by engaging in another action, such as preening.
3. *Automatic responses*. The autonomic nervous system controls the involuntary activities of the body such as urination, feather erection, skin coloration, etc., and these responses may arise whenever the animal enters a state of emotional arousal.

One of the most detailed and thorough investigations of behaviour ritualization was made by Huxley (1914), concerning the courtship behaviour of the great crested grebe. Huxley identified a number of ritual behaviours such as that of appeasement, head-shaking, the 'penguin dance', the 'cat position', and so forth, all of which involve the courting couple in a symbolic language of gesture. He concluded that the purpose of the elaborate ritualized behaviour which he observed in the grebe served to reinforce their pair-bond.

Lorenz regarded his work on behavioural evolution as his finest. He distinguished between the processes of 'homology' and 'analogy' when describing behavioural adaptation. A homology is a similarity in the behaviour (or physiology) of two or more species which has arisen because they share the ancestral line at some stage in their evolution. Hence the inciting behaviour which occurs in females of most Anatinae is a homology even though there is a wide variation in the precise form it takes and with regard to the situation which evokes it. In geese the female lowers her head and makes a sweeping movement towards an intruder which has the effect of inciting the gander to attack. However, the same sequence of behaviour in goldeneye ducks serves as a ritual during courtship. Despite this functional difference it is possible to identify the basic pattern and to say that it is homologous to these species.

An analogy, in Lorenz's terms, is where a similar behaviour pattern occurs in two or more species but it is a common adaptation to similar ecological pressures and circumstances, there being no reason to suppose that an identical evolutionary origin exists for it.

Lorenz (1974) extrapolated from his basic argument concerning evolutionary processes in behaviour to explain the possible cultural homologies which may have arisen in human societies. However, Klopfer (1975) has argued that in practice it is never possible to distinguish between what may be a homology and what is an analogy even in terms of physiological structures. A second difficulty is that at one level of explanation a given structure has the properties of a homology, whilst at another it more resembles an analogy. For instance, the 'eye' of the earthworm is an analogy to the human eye in that both are light-sensitive organs, but at the biochemical level they are both homologies. However, Lorenz's approach uses what is at present the only means of writing a systematic and structures account of behavioural evolution: informed guesswork!

13.4 Evolution and Predator–Prey Relationships

Animals do not feed at random. Some herbivores (e.g., the giant panda) have a diet which is restricted to a single species of plant. Even carnivorous animals have a limited range of prey. The reason for this specialism of diet in all species is adaptation. We say that adaptation occurs when the behaviour and physiology of a species is suited to its survival in a particular ecological niche. For instance, when a predator's sensory systems are attuned to the stimuli present in its most common prey then it will be physiologically adapted for hunting this species. Conversely, a prey is often unusually sensitive to the kinds of stimulus (e.g., visual, auditory and olfactory) which are predominant in the predators to which they are most at risk. Parasitic species are likewise highly specialized for living on the host which supports them. Such relationships may be symbiotic (when there is mutual advantage to parasite and host) or purely parasitic, in which case the host suffers by its presence.

Some examples of predator–prey relationships can be given from a range of species. Moths are popular prey for many bird species which are usually able to catch them in flight because of their excellent vision. Some moth species use visual mimicry to avoid capture: the clearwing moth, for instance, deceives its feathered enemies by having the appearance of a stinging hornet. Birds meticulously avoid it as a consequence. Similarly, night-flying moths have evolved a sensitivity to the high-pitched sounds emitted by bats and they will evade capture by suddenly free-falling as the bat approaches. However, some species of bat have subsequently evolved with a flight trajectory which allows for this falling motion and so are able to capture even these evasive moths.

Hinde (1954) describes the mobbing response of chaffinches towards any large-headed, short-necked silhouette. Since owls and cats feature largely among their predators, these small birds have evolved a simple and effective strategy to foil them whenever the flock is present. The mobbing behaviour creates a hazardous and confusing situation for the would-be predator and even small dogs have been known to evoke this response from them. The fact that even hand-reared magpies will also show mobbing towards a predator suggests that this is not a socially learnt behaviour but an innate tendency. Tinbergen (1948) used a range of model bird silhouettes to show the importance of visual stimuli for eliciting defensive behaviour in a number of bird species.

Many mammalian predators rely on social organization to hunt and kill their prey, which is often both larger and faster than themselves. A panicking herd of antelope or zebra may fall easy victim to the ambush of a pride of lionesses. Wolves also hunt in well-organized packs. Conversely, the Canadian musk ox defends itself against organized attacks, by forming an organized defence. The adult oxen will form a circle around the young and point their fearsome horns outwards against an attacker. Hall and deVore (1965) found that baboons also protect their young in a similar circular formation when in convoy. Their enemy is the leopard, and the strongest male baboons will usually combine against one to ward off any attack.

Predator–prey relationships always form a delicate balance between the optimal strategy of one species against another. Predators which become so efficient as to cause extinction of their main prey would have a poor evolutionary strategy.

13.5 Genetics and Behaviour

Evolution depends upon the genetic transmission of information. This is true for both behavioural and structural characteristics of species. Even before Mendel's discovery of genetic principles, humans had selectively bred for specific behavioural and structural traits in a number of animal species. Domesticated animals such as cats, dogs, cattle and horses have all been systematically mated so as to produce desired characteristics to the point of exaggeration. Horses required for strength or for speed were obtained by deliberately selecting them from the stock of mares and stallions which possessed these traits. Current livestock are products of centuries of selective breeding by agriculturalists. In psychology laboratories the albino rat and the Syrian hamster have been selectively bred to produce strains having unnaturally mild temperaments.

Behaviour geneticists select species to study which have a relatively short natural lifespan. This enables the study to include often in excess of twenty generations in order to follow the inheritance of specific behaviour patterns. For this reason the fruitfly *Drosophila melanogaster* has been a popular choice of animal species amongst geneticists. However, the very limitation of genetical studies to such species has meant that psychologists in general show little interest in this work owing to the dissimilarity between the behaviour of these animals and humans.

Animal behaviour is always a complex interaction between genetic and environmental influences. Even where a physiological trait is controlled by a relatively small number of genes, their effects on the development, or on the expression of that trait, can be surprisingly complex. In the case of behavioural studies we are usually dealing with complex polygenic systems, where perhaps thousands of genes are involved even in the simplest behaviours.

Manning (1961) selectively bred *Drosophila* for either slow- or fast-mating speeds. Many hundreds of mutant genes have been identified in this species and the position of the genes alone each chromosome has even been mapped out. Some of these mutations have primary (i.e., direct) effects, such as the wing mutations called 'vestigial' and 'dumpy' which influence the ability of the male to stimulate the female during courtship. The sequence of events in normal courtship is as follows: the female becomes receptive three days after emerging from the pupa, and reaches a peak on the fourth day. Around this time a male will approach her and tap her body with his forelimbs. He then begins to stimulate the female by a sequence of rapid wing beats, first with both and then with one wing. This creates an airstream which passes over the antennae of the female and makes her responsive to his subsequent attempts to mount her. If the male does not provide the correct information with these vibrations (as happens in the case of the wing mutations) then it takes longer to make the female receptive and she may even become aggressive to the male. In the case of mutations of the female's antennae she will not receive normal stimulation from the male's wingbeats and will then also be unresponsive to his courtship routine. In Manning's study he showed that selective breeding led to a situation after eighteen generations whereby 80 per cent of the fast-breeding group completed their mating before the slow-breeding group had even started. After 25 generations the fast group were completing the sequence within three minutes whereas the slow group took over 40 minutes. During the natural course of evolution it could happen that ecological pressure might favour those individuals able to complete the mating act in the quickest time. For instance, the appearance of a particularly voracious predator would have such an effect. In this case such an adaptation in mating speed would soon emerge through natural selection.

Apart from the primary mutations, there are others which have secondary or 'pleiotropic' (i.e., indirect) effects. For example, males which have various eye mutations have lower mating success rates than normals. Bastock (1956) observed the effects of physical mutations on courtship and mating in paired *Drosophila*. He found that a white-eyed mutant (having only a small amount of pigmentation) responded inappropriately to the female. Similarly the bar-eye mutant has a visual deficit. The yellow-bodied mutant male produces normal wing vibrations and yet also fails to mate normally. In these cases it appears that a visual abnormality or signal interferes with communication during courtship. This finding is difficult to explain because *Drosophila* are known to mate in light or dark conditions equally well.

Connolly selectively bred *Drosophila* for high- and low-activity levels and found that distinctly different general activity levels existed between the two groups after several generations. Southwick (1970) has studied the relative importance of inheritance in aggressive behaviour in two strains of laboratory-bred mice. He defined aggression according to three separate tendencies: (a) chase and fight; (b) the latency (i.e., time delay) before attack; and (c) the percentage of injuries inflicted.

Southwick deliberately selected two strains which were most unlike on all three tendencies. The CFW strain is highly aggressive, with short attack latencies. The A/J strain is generally non-aggressive and requires considerable latency and provocation before an attack can be elicited. He reared the CFW pups from one litter with A/J strain parents. As a control condition he followed the 'cross-fostering' method (i.e., A/J pups were also reared with CFW parents). Southwick found that the cross-fostered CFW pups grew into adulthood no less aggressive in their behaviour than those reared with parents of their own strain. This implies that aggression in the CFW strain is genetically determined. The cross-fostered A/J pups grew to be slightly more aggressive than others but they were reported to be nothing like as aggressive as any of the CFW animals. The overall conclusion from this study is that aggression in mice has a strongly genetic basis. However, it is of course true that aggression in mice is a much simpler pattern of response than the equivalent human behaviour and so no extrapolation or a relevant parallel is available from such studies.

Broadhurst and Levine (1963) selectively bred rats for two different levels of 'emotionality'. They defined emotion as reactivity to stress measured by rates of defecation in a so-called 'open-field' test (in fact this is a circular arena with grid lines on the floor). In three generations there were significant differences between the two strains in terms of their defecation scores.

Tryon (1940) produced similar results in a study where he selectively bred rats for maze-solving skills. Rats were initially selected from a stock of 142 animals and then mated according to their error rates when running a complex maze. After eighteen generations the 'maze-bright' group ran the maze with an average of 24 errors, whereas the 'maze-dull' group were making 130 errors on average.

13.6   Maturation and Behaviour

In addition to the classification of behaviour into the categories of learning and instinct (or, more correctly, 'species–specific') there is a third way in which behaviour patterns may emerge. Maturation is the development of new behaviour patterns as the organism grows older. Such developments seem to be part of a predetermined sequence of changes within the organism because they are only slightly affected by the environment. Such behaviour is not 'instinctive' in the classical sense because it does not emerge until the individual has reached a certain age. To illustrate the basic principle of the process of maturation, consider the physical development occurring in the human female at the time of puberty. At this time girls commence menarche (i.e., the onset of the menstrual cycle), and soon afterwards they begin to ovulate. Apart from extreme circumstances, such as chronic fasting (e.g., in famine or anorexic conditions), the occurrence of menarche at this point in the development of the female is inevitable. The awakening in the female of sexual interest in males at this time leads to a set of behaviours which are triggered by these underlying physiological developments. Maturation is therefore a process of physiological and psychological changes which are dependent primarily upon age. Some illustrations of this process follow which are taken from the substantial ethological literature on this subject.

Spalding (1873) kept a number of young swallows in cages which restricted their wing movements. When they were at the age when flight normally begins in this species he released them and found that they flew as readily as feral swallows do at that age.

Grohmann (1938) reared pigeons in cardboard tubes that restricted all wing movements. A control group of animals were allowed normal wing-flapping movements in the nest. The experimental birds were then released from their tubes and their ability to fly was compared with the ability shown in the maiden flights of the control group. Grohmann could detect no difference between the two groups in the development of flight.

Carmichael (1926) maintained half of a batch of newly-hatched salamander tadpoles in a mild anaesthetic and the rest in normal water for the first five days of life (i.e., the period during which swimming activity normally develops). The anaesthetized group respired and grew at normal rates but their swimming movements were eliminated for the period of the experiment. On the fifth day both groups were observed in fresh water and when the anaesthetic had worn off (after approximately 30 minutes) there was no observable difference between the swimming ability of the two groups.

Schjelderup-Ebbe (1923) reared domestic chicks in an incubator where they were kept isolated from the sounds of their own species. When they had matured it was found that they could crow as normally-reared animals do.

Gesell and Thompson (1929) gave one of each of a number of pairs of identical twins two weeks' practice in climbing stairs when they were 46 weeks old. The second twin of each pair was given no such experience. When the second twins were allowed to climb stairs in their 50th week they took only two days to reach the ability level of the first twins who had already had a fortnight's practice.

Although maturational processes in behaviour have been studied for a long time by ethologists, their impact on the study of human development is fairly recent (with the notable exception of the work of Piaget, discussed in Chapter 10). The debate concerning the development of 'attachment' in humans (Chapter 1) illustrates the resistance put up by psychologists to ideas that behaviour may be genetically determined. The process of the bonding of the infant to its parent was first observed in ethological studies by Lorenz, as is described in the next section. The important point to remember about maturation is that the way in which the environment influences the individual depends more upon chronological age than upon the existence of specific environmental events. The maturational changes caused by the phenomenon called **imprinting** will illustrate this point further.

13.7 Imprinting

Lorenz (1935) investigated a phenomenon which had first been observed by Spalding in the nineteenth century: at a certain period after hatching, the young of many bird species will commence following the parent. The knowledge of what to follow, however, is not genetically determined. In fact, at this critical stage in their development, Lorenz found that goslings of the greylag species are liable to follow anything that happens to be moving close to them at the time. Of course, in nature the most likely large moving object would be the parent, but Lorenz showed that during this critical period they can be made to follow virtually anything in motion, be it animate or inanimate. Furthermore, having commenced following, the young bird forms an 'imprint' of the object it has followed and this causes two apparently irreversible effects: first, in the short term during which the young need protection they will persist in this following response to any further movement made by the imprinted object. This is known as 'filial' imprinting. Second, when the animal matures into the adult, its social and sexual interest is directed towards objects which have the physical characteristics of the imprint. This is called 'sexual' imprinting.

This second effect implies that what has been learnt during this early experience is that the animal now regards itself as belonging to the class of objects it has imprinted. After this relatively brief exposure to the stimulus during the critical period the animal's future responsiveness becomes limited. Lorenz found it relatively easy to cause greylag goslings to form an imprint of humans and he himself became the object for a number of studies. In greylags the critical period was found to be between 12 and 17 hours after hatching. Lorenz came to regard this period as immutable for any given species and he also claimed that once imprinting has occurred to one object it was then irreversible. Furthermore, after the imprint has formed the young animal begins to show heightened fear of other moving objects in the proximity, an effect which is called 'stranger fear'. Since Lorenz's pioneering investigations of imprinting it has become evident that a number of modifications are needed to his original formulation. These relate to the process as he described it and also to the fact that certain differences exist between species which have since come to light. Although Lorenz's work was confined to the social development in avian species (birds), similar early learning seems to produce parent–offspring bonds in other species, notably the formation of 'attachment' in mammalian species, including humans (Chapter 1). But the rest of this section deals only with the concept of imprinting as it applies to non-human species.

Immelman (1967) cross-fostered zebra finches, Bengalese finches and African silver bills with the young being raised until maturity with the fostering species. When they had matured it was found that members of each species would select their mates not from their own but from their fostering species.

In a study conducted in the natural habitat Harris (1963) interchanged eggs from the nests of the lesser black-backed and herring gull species. On his return to the site in 1969 he found 29 mixed pairs nesting: that is, they had adopted the fostering species as their own.

These studies illustrate how important the imprinting process is to the future development of the individual. Studies by Hess (1959) in an experimental laboratory setting have helped to clarify the early view of imprinting (see Spotlight box).

SPOTLIGHT   The double concentric runway

This arrangement is useful for testing imprinting under controlled conditions. Objects may be suspended from the rotor arms A and B and tested either in pairs or singly for their capacity to cause imprinting (hence innate 'preferences' for a range of different sizes, shapes and colours may be tested). Each object can also be made to emit different sounds so that auditory as well as visual cues may be presented. Finally, it is possible to lay obstacles in the path of the young bird to test the 'strength' of imprinting (i.e., its determination to follow the imprinted object given differing degrees of difficulty, see figure 13.1).

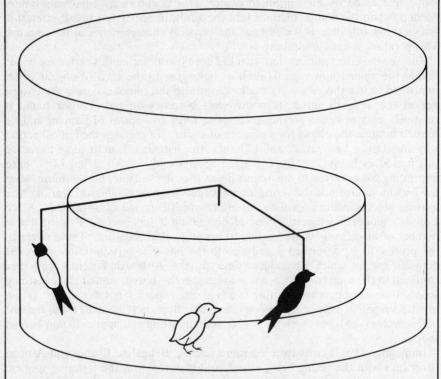

Figure 13.1 The double concentric runway used by Hess and others to investigate imprinting phenomena

Hess used the concentric double runway apparatus shown in Figure 13.1. He kept newly hatched ducklings in isolation and darkness until they approached the 'critical period'. They were then released individually into the runway and a model of either a duck or drake was moved around so as to cause imprinting. Each model made an artificial sound during their exposure to it. In a subsequent test the drake and duck models were used in a number of different conditions, being either still or moving, silent or sound-emitting, and all combinations of these. Hess observed that silent objects had less imprinting power than those emitting sounds, and that an intermittent sound was the most effective. Hess also found that some of the birds he tested had imprinted outside the so-called 'critical' period which Lorenz had described. When obstacles were used to hinder the ducklings' progress when following the model this strengthened imprinting. In a later study Hess (1964) showed a similar strengthening effect when the bird was given mild electric shocks during its following of the imprinted object.

Lorenz's description of the critical period as being a maturational stage of development has been criticized by a number of researchers. Although there is a heightened sensitivity of the animal to form an imprint at a certain stage in its development this process is more affected by the environment than a strict definition of 'maturation' would allow a young bird. For instance, rearing a young in isolation extends the critical period and this has brought about the modified term 'sensitive' period to account for this (Guiton, 1959). Furthermore, although filial imprinting seems to be an irreversible event, it has been found in a number of studies that the longer-term sexual imprint can change with experiences subsequent to the sensitive period. This is particularly likely to occur if the original exposure to the imprinted object was brief and if the individual is then socially-reared among its own species, in which case normal conspecific mating is likely.

However, the importance of the sensitive period for early learning goes beyond the study of imprinting. For instance, Klopfer, Adams and Klopfer (1964) found that the goat has a heightened sensitivity for the odour of her neonate within the first hour following birth. If they are separated for this first hour she will no longer recognize the offspring as her own.

Human neonates and lambs also seem to have heightened sensitivity for the smell or taste of milk soon after birth because, once suckled by bottle, they will often no longer take the mother's nipple. Another example of a sensitive period for learning is to be found in the dog since, if pups are isolated from human contact between the third and tenth week, they will not be tameable thereafter. Further instances to be found in primate species are given in Chapter 1 in the section on attachment, which is where the study of imprinting in animals forms finds a human parallel.

13.8 Sociobiology

Animals sometimes draws a predator's attention to themselves to divert it from their mate, nest or offspring. This may involve alarm calling (by finches and thrushes), feigning injury (by the crane), conspicuous escape bids (by rabbits) or by prominent changes in colouration (by cuttlefish). These examples, together with the suicidal defence behaviour in many insect societies, provide a problem for Darwin's evolutionary theory (which he himself recognized) because they each would lessen the survival chances of the individual behaving like this. The result would be that such individuals would on average produce fewer offspring than those who behaved selfishly, who would in turn leave offspring who behave selfishly, and so on. Therefore, **altruism** would diminish still further with each successive generation because all individuals displaying this behaviour are selected against.

However, since Hamilton's work (1964), sociobiological ideas have emerged to explain how altruism would have a selective advantage under certain circumstances. For instance, if we assume that the basic unit in evolution is not the individual animal but rather its complement of genes, then it is possible that closely-related animals (i.e., those who share many of the genes in common with that individual) would be the most likely to benefit by such acts as alarm calling. The reason is because the relatives of the alarm caller would tend to be physically close to the caller at the time. Therefore, having social groups based upon kinship would mean that each member would tend to show apparently altruistic behaviour but in reality altruism is here having a protective function only for those particular genetically-related individuals which form the kinship group.

SPOTLIGHT   Sociobiology for beginners

Sociobiologist E. O Wilson developed many of his ideas on the innateness of social organization from studying insect societies.

In your local woodland look for a rotting tree and pull away part of the bark. You are almost sure to uncover some insect groups and so can watch their social behaviour. Ants are particularly socialized animals but you may also see something of interest in many beetle species too. You will probably see what appears to be a complex social structure of individuals, each of whom have their own job to carry out, almost as if they were working in cooperation with each other to achieve the task. It may seem as though their behaviour, or 'work', for the day has been determined by a leader or a committee, but the sociobiologists argue that such complex interactions are merely preprogrammed in their genetic structure.

This simple principle used to explain altruism has led to the development of a new science of behaviour called sociobiology. Sociobiology has sprung from a branch of biology called behavioural ecology, its aim being the 'scientific study of the biological basis of all social behaviour' (Wilson, 1975). The full impact of sociobiological views of human behaviour has yet to be felt in psychology but it has already merged with ethological theory, giving new insights into animal social behaviour. The limited space restricts discussion here to the briefest of outlines. The best introduction to sociobiological theory is through the work of writers such as Dawkins (1986) or Barash (1977). Many other authors do not give this subject a fair and objective coverage.

13.9   Kinship

An individual organism behaves socially because it provides the means of reproduction as well as being adaptive to those species which are social: that is, its advantages outweigh the disadvantages of solitarism. Survival is not simply gauged by the longevity of individuals because, unless animals reproduce, they become extinct at whatever age they live to! Kinship forms the basis for social living and therefore survival refers to the fecundity of those who are genetically related to one another. On average, the closer the relationship in kin terms between two individuals then the more similar will be their genetic structures.

13.10 Inclusive Fitness

In Darwinian terms an organism's 'fitness' refers to its chances of surviving long enough to reproduce itself. Sociobiological theory proposes that individuals not only behave so as to optimize their own procreation but they also cooperate with and protect close kin so as to enhance the survival of their shared genetic infrastructure. Inclusive fitness refers to the survivorship of all genetically-related individuals, since it is their combined 'fitness' which determines longevity in terms of their particular genetic constitution. Altruism is therefore more likely to occur between related individuals and to an extent which depends upon the closeness of their relationship.

13.11 Questions and Exercises

1. Discuss the contribution which the study of animal behaviour can make to the understanding of human psychology.
2. What are 'modal action patterns'? Give an example to illustrate your description.
3. Study any pet that you or your friends may have and try to identify behaviour rituals which that pet may show.
4. Using the cat and mouse as an example, try to describe which adaptations each of these species seem to have made in order to gain an advantage in their predator–prey relationship.
5. How does the term 'maturation' differ from the concept of an 'instinct' in terms of animal behaviour?
6. Make notes of the similarities or differences you may observe between the processes of imprinting (described in this chapter) and attachment (described in Chapter 1).
7. A complex animal society is often assumed to bear the hallmark of intelligent behaviour in its individual numbers. Is this necessarily so? Give examples to support your view.

14 Abnormal behaviour

14.1 Introduction

At the outset of their study of psychology students often expect the subject to be mainly concerned with abnormal states of behaviour. 'Madness' is the ubiquitous colloquial expression which appears in people's definitions of what psychology is about. However, the study and treatment of abnormal states is the central concern of **psychiatry** and not of psychology. Psychologists define abnormality as a deviation from the normal state, whereas psychiatrists use the term 'illness' to describe a categorically different condition from 'health'. Indeed, the notion of mental illness derives from the fact that psychiatry is a branch of medical science which is founded on the study of physical illnesses and disease states.

14.2 The Medical Model of Abnormal Behaviour

The development of psychiatry in the nineteenth century marked the end of an age of cruelty towards mentally disturbed people. Labelled as either 'possessed' by evil spirits or by the devil himself, these individuals were either tortured to death or else spent their lives in extraordinarily inhumane asylums. Some states of mental deterioration were known to be caused by physical illness and this led to speculation that mental and physical ill-health were of the same origin. Consequently the earliest scientific studies of mental abnormality were medical in terms of their description, classification and treatment.

To define all cases of disease there are two sets of criteria: first, an *aetiology* (i.e., a cause for the malady), and second, a *syndrome* (i.e., each medical condition is diagnosed by matching it against sets of known symptoms for specified disease states). Diseases themselves are believed to be of three types:

(a) *infections*, where a micro-organism (bacteria or virus) has invaded a body system or an organ (e.g., hepatitis);
(b) *systemic disorders*, where an organ malfunctions without prior infection (e.g., coronary thrombosis);
(c) *traumas*, which are caused by an external agent to the body (e.g., injury or poisoning).

The aetiology of mental 'illness' is viewed by psychiatrists as following a similar pathological pattern. The psychiatric perspective therefore classifies mental disorders according to disease criteria, and the most influential of the early diagnostic systems was that of Kraepelin (1896). His classification has had a lasting impact in Britain and formed the basis of the 1959 Mental Health Act. The system he devised is based on the syndrome approach; each disease is identifiable by a cluster of symptoms which associate with it. He introduced the view that biochemical disorder produces the condition we now call schizophrenia, which he called *dementia praecox* (pre-senile madness). He proposed that some metabolic failure was responsible for the other major psychosis called manic depression.

Bleuler (1911) introduced the term 'schizophrenia' into the medical dictionary, identifying it as a fragmentation of personality (i.e., the individual loses the recognizable unity of identity found in normal people). The continuing controversy over whether or not there is one single condition of schizophrenia will be discussed later, together with one other major form of psychological disturbance: depression. For the rest of this preliminary overview more will be said about the classification of mental abnormality.

British psychiatrists use the system called the International Classification of Disorders (ICD) published by the World Health Organization (WHO). The only other major scheme in use is the American standard called the Diagnostic and Statistical Manual of Mental Disorders (DSM) which, in its latest revision, deviates from previous versions as well as from the ICD system in some notable ways. However, the ICD system will be used here to illustrate the fundamental principles of the nosological approach.

14.3   Neuroses and Psychoses

The first major division of the ICD system is the distinction between two types of mental disorder known as neuroses and psychoses. A neurosis is a condition in which people interpret most events realistically (i.e., they do not show abnormal thought or emotional responses in most everyday situations). The neurotic is usually in tune with the 'normal' world, whereas the psychotic individual shows evidence of two major disturbances: first, disconnected emotional behaviour (i.e., either showing strong, shifting expressions of emotion or else being unusually placid in view of the events which may be taking place round about). A second feature of psychotic conditions is thought disturbance, such as responding to voices which only they can hear, or showing paranoia (i.e., behaving as though they are being persecuted, watched, followed or 'controlled' by other people).

14.4   Psychological Perspectives on Mental Disorders

The branch of psychology which deals with the treatment of mental disorder is known as 'clinical psychology'. The majority of these professionals working in Britain are employed by the local health authorities and usually work alongside psychiatrists. Therefore there is less conflict between this applied area of psychology and the medical specialists than might be supposed. However, there is no single perspective on mental abnormality in psychology apart from the general unease that is felt towards the long-standing 'disease' model which is used to diagnose and treat people who exhibit problematic forms of behaviour. There are two main counter-arguments here.

First of all, if someone is labelled as being 'mentally ill', then what are the criteria for the mental 'health' towards which the convalescing patient should be heading? The pathway to normal health of the mentally sick is therefore obstructed by the fact that no one has defined what 'normal' is like. In Rosenhan's words, 'the normal are not detectably sane' (an issue discussed later in this section). Often it is those individuals who are 'out of step' with the particular sets of attitudes and beliefs of their culture who come to be treated and labelled as deranged, and so definitions of good health are often couched in quasi-political terms, such as showing the appropriate 'adjustment' to life. The obliteration of all such signs and symptoms of maladjustment is therefore both the definition and the aim of the therapy. Psychologists and sociologists alike have questioned this process and have created the concept of 'deviancy' to explain it. Here, abnormality is regarded as meaning simply an extreme form of behaviour on the dimension of normality, and is not treated as being a discretely different condition or 'illness'.

Second, medical diagnoses also fail by looking solely at the individual's behaviour for evidence of illness. This emphasis on disease criteria overlooks the influence of environmental factors, such as family and social relationships or physical deprivations of poverty or unemployment, as being potential causes of mental breakdown. Abnormal behaviour may indeed be a 'normal' response to abnormal circumstances. The work of Laing and Cooper in particular has illustrated the importance of the home and social environment for predisposing psychotic disturbance. For instance, Laing's view holds that when psychosis develops there is often a transitional period where the person impersonates a caricature they create of themselves so as to please a person who has acted tyrannically in their lives. Although the main thrust of these arguments has been largely discredited in recent years, the DSM III system has at least required psychiatrists to take account of the home background when making their diagnoses (Robins and Helzer, 1986).

Rosenhan (1973) enlisted the help of eight 'pseudopatients', volunteers who would attempt to become voluntary admissions in mental hospitals in America by presenting to unwitting psychiatrists with a typical psychotic symptom: that of hearing voices in their heads. If they were successful in gaining admission then no further signs of 'illness' were shown. The intention of the study was to discover if, having been diagnosed as 'ill', the psychiatrists would be able to recognize normal mental health when they saw it and thereby release them. Twelve different hospitals were tested in this way by the team. On several occasions the pseudopatients were diagnosed as 'schizophrenic in remission'. The patients stayed for periods of between 7 and 52 days without there being a change in the diagnosis. Given the original presentation of the schizophrenic symptom, perhaps this course of action is not entirely unjustified. However, as Rosenhan himself points out, this label carries with it a destructive power in that person's life since it is indelibly etched on medical papers. In contrast to the oblivion of the psychiatrists to the trick, the fellow-patients would remark that there was nothing wrong with the (pseudo-) patients. Rosenhan's conclusions was that psychiatrists tend to err on the side of caution when making diagnoses and will therefore treat virtually any unusual or inexplicable behaviour as being symptomatic of the illness they have themselves labelled. For instance, to continue with demands that you are not mentally ill may itself become regarded as symptomatic that you are indeed unwell! In Rosenhan's study the pseudopatients openly took notes of their daily experiences and this was in one instance recorded by a member of staff as 'patient engages in writing behaviour'.

Goffman (1961) has claimed that institutionalization is a process which itself induces stress and behaviour change in patients which may become symptoms of maladjustment. The inmate may respond to such trauma by playing up the role of 'mad person' and Goffman argues that institutions encourage this response. In effect the pressures caused by the institution form a hindrance, rather than a remedy, in terms of the curing process, he argues.

Szasz has made the most sustained opposition to psychiatric classifications of mental disorders. In an early paper entitled 'The Myth of Mental Illness' he argued that: 'The notion of mental illness provides . . . an explanation for problems in living. We may recall in this connection that not so long ago it was devils and witches who were held responsible for men's problems in social living.' The 'problems in living' Szasz refers to become intensified by the treatment they receive on being identified as mentally ill. Where a condition has a clear neuropathological cause, such as epilepsy, Szasz's view is that the patient has a valid expectation that medical science can treat the malady. But psychiatry should not impose a sickness terminology on disorders which have no known medical substrate. This same terminology, Szasz argues, misleads because it fails to distinguish between the small minority of cases which have putative organic origins (and which should therefore properly be treated by neurological specialists), and the majority of psychiatric conditions which are not truly illnesses but merely people suffering from the multiplicity of 'life problems'. Table 14.1 summarizes the case for and against the medical model of classification and treatment of the mental disorders, and Table 14.2 provides a breakdown of the major drug treatments employed in treating the various conditions or 'illnesses'.

14.5   Schizophrenia

Schizophrenia is perhaps the most dramatized and discussed of all the mental disorders. It is recognized by a cluster of primary and secondary symptoms. The primary symptoms are those which are directly related to the condition itself, such as thought disorder (the patient may have bizarre notions about being the world's leading expert in brain disease, or more typically their thoughts may be simply vague and wandering). A second primary symptom is emotional disturbance, which can show itself as sudden, inexplicable switches of mood, sometimes from one extreme to another. In other cases this symptom shows itself as an unusually flat and unresponsive demeanour.

The secondary symptoms are so named because they are regarded as being dependent upon the primary states. For instance, the hearing of strange voices in the head or from someone in the sky is treated as a manifestation of the primary symptom of thought disorder.

Kraepelin made four subdivisions of schizophrenia into the catatonic, paranoid, Hebephrenic and simple types. The basis of his classification still holds today, although the DSM system has recently dropped the 'simple' category.

1. *Catatonia* is where patients occasionally adopt odd statuesque poses which they will hold for long periods of time. Wild mood swings are also typical of this condition.
2. In *paranoia* patients usually have grandiose delusions of their own status in life (e.g., regarding themselves as rulers or famous people). A second delusion is that of persecution experiences, such as feeling they are being watched or followed.

Table 14.1   *Medical model of mental disorders*

Pro-model	Anti-model
Many disease symptoms are known to respond to physical intervention, e.g., depression and ECT, PKU and diet, Parkinsonism and LDOPA, schizophrenia and the major tranquillizers, anxiety and minor tranquillizers, etc.	Removing or suppressing the symptoms of the condition is not necessarily 'curing' it. For instance, using a sedative may prevent the psychotic from pacing manically up and down but this is merely eliminating the symptom and leaving the true condition untouched. Similarly, ECT may temporarily lift deep depression but it may be doing so indirectly by its effect on memory (i.e., since the patient has reduced memory then he/she is no longer able to dwell on negative things).
Fewer and fewer patients are being incarcerated for long terms since effective chemotherapy was introduced in the 1950s. Many people are being released into their own communities who would otherwise be detained were it not for pharmacological treatment.	Community-based patients are restrained by a 'chemical straitjacket'; without drugs they are still as disturbed as ever. No genuine care is given by this treatment since as long as they are drugged they cause no one any problems. Recidivism is an almost inevitable result of failure to take the medication.
Chemotherapy is cheap, easy and convenient and most patients accept it gladly. Society itself needs protection from some of the anti-social behaviours we would all experience without drug use. Drugs are effective at this level and they can help to ameliorate the problem until more satisfactory treatments are found.	Drugs can lead to physical and psychological dependency: for example, tranquillizer ('tranx') addiction is common in chronic treatments. Society should face up to the problems of its own shortcomings and not be satisfied with hiding its victims. Drugs merely defer the reforms which are necessary in our institutional treatments of the underprivileged.
The medical classification of mental disorders has helped not only scientific research but also in the humane treatments given to these people. In any case the current situation is not in any way a finished product; better treatments may be developed once these conditions are understood more fully.	The diagnosis of mental disorders is not as straightforward as psychiatry professes it to be. By maintaining the 'illness' perspective psychiatrists are diverting attention away from other potential causes which relate to the general social and economic background of the person. Diagnostic standards are not consistent between different psychiatrists, let alone between different nations.

Pro-model	Anti-model
Symptoms not only assist in identifying the pathology, but the removal of the symptoms is tantamount to treating the illness.	'Symptoms' may be a set of perfectly normal responses developed in this person as a consequence of abnormal experiences (i.e., any normal person would form these symptoms if they were placed in such circumstances).

3. *Hebephrenia* is characterized by disorganized delusions, an unkempt appearance and the use of verbal neologisms. For instance, the patient may dwell on one syllable, saying, 'Day-away-asay-agay-afay-ajay' and so on.
4. *Simple* schizophrenia usually has an early onset in life and shows a gradual progression as the sufferer grows older. Wild delusions do not usually occur but the patient may show autism (i.e., complete withdrawal).

Causes of schizophrenia

Psychologists and psychiatrists have tested a number of hypotheses which have linked schizophrenia with all kinds of supposed causes, from biochemical to social, from neurological to personality or genetics. No possibility seems to have been overlooked. Some have even claimed that the condition does not exist (Laing: Scheff). It has been linked with faulty learning processes (Ullman and Krasner; Bannister and Fransella); a 'pink spot' in the urine (van Winkle); a rejection by the ego of external reality (Freud); genetic abnormality (Bender).

The influence of inheritance is suggested by the fact that 40 per cent of schizophrenic children were shown to have at least one schizophrenic parent and 11 per cent had both parents affected. Of course, these figures do not rule out early learning (Bender, 1955). Zubin and Spring (1977) suggest that what is inherited is not the disease itself but a propensity for developing it.

Some researchers have proposed a link between social–educational disadvantage and schizophrenia since it is more common amongst such groups. Of course, the condition may be either the cause or the effect of such circumstances. Ullman and Krasner (1969) propose that the schizophrenic person has suffered inappropriate patterns of attentiveness from their parent(s). The child has therefore come to act 'crazy' because this gains the attention they desire from others (i.e., this is the pattern of behaviour which the parents have unwittingly reinforced). Institutionalization of such people therefore increases their odd behaviour because greater and greater exaggerations are demanded of the symptoms in order to evoke the original responsiveness.

It has been found that the chronic (long-term) user of amphetamines sometimes enters a state resembling schizophrenia (called 'amphetamine psychosis'), and amphetamines are known to act upon specific pathways in the brain which carry the **neurotransmitter** called dopamine (DA). Amphetamine increases dopamine levels in the brain and it is perhaps the case that schizophrenics are suffering from unnaturally high levels of this neurotransmitter. In addition the neuroleptics (drugs used to treat schizophrenia) inhibit dopamine production and so this further connects DA and schizophrenia.

Table 14.2 *Drug treatments of mental disorders*

1 DEPRESSANTS	*Examples*
(a) *Major Tranquillizers ('neuroleptics')* These reduce the symptoms of psychotic disorders (e.g., schizophrenia). The particular symptoms involved are hyperactivity, stereotyped behaviour and social withdrawal. In their optimum dosage they induce Parkinsonian tremors which are then treated by another drug.	Chlorpromazine (largactyl) Phenothiazine (haloperidol)
(b) *Minor Tranquillizers* (unrelated to above) These act as anti-anxiety agents.	Diazepam (librium)
(c) *Sedatives* Used to induce sleep. Sleep disturbance and insomnia can itself lead to psychotic symptoms and so it is important that it is treated.	Barbiturates Fluorezepam

2 *ANTI-DEPRESSANTS*

(a) Monoamine Oxidase Inhibitors (MAOIs)	
Prevent the natural breakdown (catabolism) of some brain transmitters (e.g., dopamine and noradrenaline) and hence increase their presence in some brain areas. May cause a 'cheese reaction' (i.e., react with certain foodstuffs).	Imipramine
(b) *Tricylical antidepressants*	Dibenzazipines

NB: Other general problems with drug treatment are as outlined below.

1. They modify the person's behaviour in other ways besides that which is symptomatic of their disorder (i.e., they are non-specific in their action). These side effects can sometimes be distressing and may themselves require more drugs to remove or reduce them.
2. Most drugs are toxic to the body, especially the liver.
3. Many drugs lead to dependency.
4. Drugs can lead to tolerance (i.e., the dosage level must continually be increased because the body becomes 'tolerant', so more of the drug is needed in order to produce the same effect).
5. Some drugs may interact with the diet or with other drugs the patient is on. This can lead to serious side effects and even death.

Other studies have linked specific brain regions with the disorder. For instance, the corpus callosum, a large pathway which connects the two halves of the brain, has been found to have unusual electrical properties in schizophrenic patients.

In view of the many contradictions surrounding the definition, diagnoses and causes of schizophrenia a number of recent arguments have proposed a complete revision of the way this condition is conceptualized. For instance, Bental *et al.* (1988) question the reliability and validity of the term schizophrenia and urge researchers to take one of two steps: either re-evaluate the whole area of classification of abnormal behaviour, including schizophrenia; or specifically abandon the term schizophrenia and investigate the symptoms in isolation (i.e., disregard the traditional concept that this cluster of behaviour forms a unified condition).

14.6 Depression

Clinical depression has a number of identifying features or 'symptoms', such as feelings of hopelessness, anxiety, lack of interest or involvement with the surroundings, lethargy, hostility and indecision.

Psychiatrists diagnose the condition according to the extent of the cluster of symptoms. Additionally, if there is evident reason for the condition, such as a recent bereavement or loss of job, then it is likely to be classified as 'reactive' depression, which is an acquired form. This is even more likely to be so if the patient does not have previous bouts of depression in their 'premorbid' history. Should no cause be evident, and if the patient does have a history of depressive bouts, then, then their condition may be diagnosed as being 'endogenous' depression.

Clinical depression afflicts 1 per cent of the population. Approximately 11 per cent of all relatives, and 28 per cent of the siblings of a depressed person, are likely to be affected if the condition is endogenous. This suggests that inheritance is responsible to some extent but, of course, there may also be a learning explanation for these figures because such individuals tned to be sharing a similar environment. Depression affects females more than males (statistically) and common events which predispose reactive depression are bereavement, childbirth, menopause, illness (particularly where chronic pain is involved), unemployment, insecurity and loneliness.

Treatment of depression with ECT (electro-convulsive therapy) is successful, although it is not clear why. A course of 2–3 treatments a week for one month is normally given. ECT is known to affect the patient's memory and some have argued that this is the reason for its ability to ameliorate depression. Another technique which involves a major assault on the person is the induction of an insulin coma. Finally, drugs are used chronically and these have proved to be relatively successful, particularly in reducing suicical tendencies which are especially common in manic forms of depression. In manic depression rapid and irrational mood swings occur and the patient's thoughts may also be bizarre.

Drugs which *inhibit* the monoamine sites in the brain may also reduce the symptoms of depression. These drugs are called 'monamine oxidase inhibitors' (MOAIs), the first of which was iproniazid. This drug was initially being tested for its potential use in curing tuberculosis, but it was found to be more effective in producing euphoria in these patients, as well as reducing depression in those presenting both conditions. This illustrates a common situation in psychopharma-cological research; a drug treatment is as likely to be discovered by chance as by design. This also explains why some drugs have their effects understood only after they have been introduced as treatments.

Causes of depression

Explanations for clinical depression are as wide-ranging as those for schizophre-nia. However, in this instance a single approach will be discussed but at greater depth: the cognitive model. Beck (1967, and in various revisions since) proposes that depressed people have formed the habit of faulty thinking such that they regularly misinterpret events. For instance, if a car breaks down depressive people tend to personalize the situation by blaming themselves for not having it serviced recently, or for driving it incorrectly, and so on. Whereas normal people are more objective about the good and bad things that happen to them, depressed people selectively perceive negative events. Such habits of thought lower their self-esteem and this makes them even more likely to find fault with themselves. Beck claims that depression makes such people see failure or setbacks as typical of them. Negative events are also usually blown out of all proportion: for instance, finding a scratch on the car would be turned into a catastrophe.

Conversely, their judgement of their own successes or the good things that happen to them are either overlooked, minimized or attributed to chance. Their cognitive processing makes depressed people 'victims' of their own thoughts from which it is difficult for them to escape without help. Beck's therapy involves getting patients to restructure and re-evaluate themselves and the events that happen to them, making them more objective and rational in their thought processes.

14.7 Learned Helplessness

Seligman (1975) and Abramson and Martin (1981) developed a theory of depression which is based upon a simple animal model. The early studies involved giving a dog unavoidable shocks and then placing it in a second situation where a simple response was required (i.e., stepping over a low barrier to avoid shocks). Seligman found that such animals failed to learn how to avoid the electric shocks in this second situation whereas dogs tested without the unavoidable shocks first did. This, and further animal studies, became interpreted as the 'learned helplessness' theory. What the animal seems to learn in the first situation is that the shocks are an unpleasant but unavoidable part of life that must be endured; they learn that they have no control over negative events, and hence they experience feelings of helplessness.

Seligman extrapolated from the basic paradigm to explain how humans may become depressed. He reasoned that when people experience unavoidable stresses in their lives they learn that nothing can be done, and they must accept the misery of their condition. This belief leads to a decrease in their attempts to control or improve their lives because feelings of helplessness take away the incentive to act. Such negative attitudes and expectations make them into passive recipients of everyday problems which they fail to avoid, and hence a state of anxiety develops. Anxiety will predispose them to depression (as is known to be the case from clinical observations of patients who are chronically anxious).

Controversy arose over Seligman's original model: first, because it assumes that experience of uncontrollable negative events is sufficient to lead to feelings of helplessness, and second, because the model assumes that feelings of hopelessness cause clinical symptoms of depression. However, it is possible to explain the animal experiments much more simply than this. For instance, it is possible that what the animal learns during the first phase of the study, when it receives an unavoidable shock, is related to its mobility at that time (after all, it is unlikely that the dog is in a state of complete immobility when in this apparatus). The immediate response the dog will make when it is shocked will be to 'freeze' and, since the shock is only brief, it will learn this as an operant response to the situation (see Chapter 12 for an explanation of operant conditioning). The dog associates the removal of the shock with the response of freezing and has thus learnt not feelings of 'helplessness' but quite the opposite: control! The act of immobility under conditions of new stress (in phase two of the experiment, when avoidable shocks are delivered) is therefore a result of conditioning (Weiss, 1976).

Abramson and Martin (1981) reformulated Seligman's original theory by stating that only if people *attribute* the hopelessness of their situation to themselves (i.e., to a personal lack of control) will helplessness arise. For instance, if subjects are given a problem to solve which they know or suspect to be insoluble this does not impair their performance on a subsequent task. However, if they do not perceive it to be insoluble then this can be shown to impair their later performances on tasks (Buchwal *et al*, 1978). The concepts of 'stable' and 'global' attributions were introduced to explain individual differences in the development of helplessness. However, the theory was not generally adopted by clinicians working with the clinical syndrome because, for one thing, people with similar experiences of lack of control do not all develop depression; some do, most do not. Brown and Harris (1978) found that 90 per cent of clinically depressed people in their sample had indeed experienced stressful situations over which they could be said to have lacked control (e.g., bereavement, redundancy, delinquency in their children, etc.).

In a more recent formulation, however, Alloy *et al*. (1988) have renamed their model 'hopelessness' theory. Hopelessness depression is regarded by them as being a unique form of depression caused initially by a negative life event, such as family breakdown. Those who are vulnerable to feelings of hopelessness will habitually atribute their failure to get what they want from a situation to their own shortcomings. Thus perceiving themselves as responsible for the crisis may be an initiating factor for depression. In Seligman's original hypothesis depression was thought to arise from feelings of general lack of control over life events, but the uniqueness of hopelessness theory is that it emphasizes individuals' attitudes towards important events and their failure to work for or obtain the desired outcomes regarding these things.

In contrast to the learned helplessness model, the hopelessness theory accepts that the initiating life event may have been avoidable but that (a) it was not avoided, and therefore becomes open to negative retrospective evaluation in which the individual attributes some element of self-blame, and (b) this self-perception may have little or no basis in objective fact, but is rather a single interpretation. In other words, it does not matter whether or not other people confirm or agree that the event is significant or that the individual is responsible for its occurrence. For instance, suppose the person has been made redundant in common with other workmates: it may be that those others do not take the loss as seriously but this may not influence the way that a vulnerable individual regards his or her own situation. Vulnerable individuals may develop persistent negative thoughts and expectations and come to believe themselves incapable or unworthy of achieving the things they desire. The loss of a job may reinforce these feelings of incompetence, and failling to find work in the meantime may lead on to the negative expectation of ever finding work again. It is the general pattern of beliefs concerning the self and external reality which compounds itself in the development of the state of depression. Whereas the initial life event may trigger off the condition, some individuals are vulnerable owing to the manner in which they distort the facts of their situation and lead themselves to attend only to negativity and feelings of hopelessness. Thereafter, anything which serves to maintain their feelings of hopelessness may also maintain the depression.

Brewin (1985) argues that there is very little clinical evidence to support the idea that stress and vulnerability are sufficient ingredients for depression. The vulnerability of an individual, according to hopelessness theory, lies in the tendency either to construe events negatively or through self-censure when things go wrong. Brewin argues that this approach overlooks two points.

1. Depression itself (especially for one labelled as such) may invoke feelings of negativity. In other words, rather than negativity causing depression it could equally be that, having been labelled 'depressed', negative thoughts are instilled.
2. The impact of the life event as a trigger point for depression has not been properly measured or evaluated. For instance, in the clinical setting patients are urged to think up some starting point for their feelings which, from then on, form part of the aetiology as far as the clinician is concerned.

14.8 Community care

Since the 1959 Mental Health Act the intention of both politicians and professionals alike has been to move as many psychiatric patients as possible away from residential care into community-based operations. This policy is evident in the decline in the number of hospital beds in mental institutions since the 1950s (see Figure 14.1). Paradoxically, this decline corresponds with an increase in hospital admissions over the same period. This is explained by the fact that patients are nowadays spending less and less time in institutions. In most cases the length of stay is less than a month, although 16 000 patients are compulsorily admitted each year.

Funding for such a transition into community care has been made available by the various governments to the local authorities but much of this money has been re-directed to other uses and so little research or development has occurred into what forms of community care will best serve these patients. The impending mass exodus faces a vacuum in resources for the mentally disturbed because by 1991 not only are 60 hospitals to close, but in addition the government's target figure for hospital beds is 45 000, a reduction of one-third in just a five-year period. Astonishingly, this trend is accompanied by a cut in the budget for community

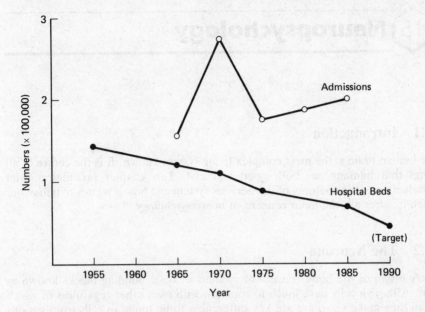

Figure 14.1 The number of hospital beds and admissions to mental health institutions in 1950–90

health care, £12 million having already been cut in 1988 alone. The implications for this policy on future mental health is spelt out by Cohen (1988), who puts the problem in a disturbing global context.

14.9 Questions and Exercises

1. Make a list of the differences between the way that psychiatrists view abnormal behaviour (the 'medical model') and the view(s) taken by psychologists over this issue.
2. Write a brief explanation of why the introduction of drug treatment in the area of mental disorders has led to such a massive fall in the number of long-stay patients in hospitals and institutions for the insane.

15 Neuropsychology

15.1 Introduction

The human brain is the most complex living system known. It is the centre of all things that humans do, both good and evil. This chapter provides a brief introduction to the anatomy of the nervous system and how it relates to behaviour which is, after all, the main concern of **neuropsychology**.

15.2 The Neurone

Every organ of the body consists of millions of basic building blocks known as cells. Although cells have much in common with each other regardless of which organ they make up, there are key differences to be found in cells from various body regions. For instance, cells making up the kidneys (the body's filtration system) take up the shape of tubes for carrying fluids. The function that cells have therefore determines their shape and how they work together as a system. In the case of the nervous system the basic cell is known as the neurone. The anatomy of the neurone itself will depend upon where it lies: the neurones which carry impulses to the muscles of the body are extremely large cells compared with those within the brain itself. This outline of how a neurone looks and works is therefore only concerned with general principles. Figure 15.1 shows a typical pyramidal neurone from the cerebral cortex, the largest structure of the human brain (see Figure 15.1).

The neurone may be described as having three basic parts: the dendrite region, the cell body and an axon. The general purpose of the neurone is to transmit a form of electrical energy from one point in the brain or body region to another. Sensory neurones send their information in an afferent direction (i.e., towards the brain), whereas motorneurones ('motor' meaning they serve to drive the muscles) send information in an efferent, or outwards, direction. The vast majority of neurones in the nervous system do neither of these things and are the so-called interneurones which connect together afferent and efferent pathways.

The dendrites of a neurone normally receive information from other neurones of the nervous system. The dendritic regions of some neurones have become specialized for transducing (converting from one form to another) energy from the environment, such as light, heat or sound, into the electrical energy which is used by the nervous system. These specialized neurones are known as receptors and they are discussed more fully in Chapter 6. For most neurones there may be over 2000 dendritic connections made with other neurones from which they receive their energy input or 'information'. The information received by neurones is in the form of an impulse, or **action potential**, about which more will be said later. Upon receipt of the impulse a dendrite simply transmits this information towards the cell body, which is a general receiving area for inputs from all the

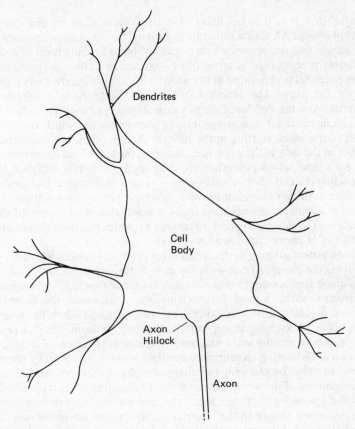

Figure 15.1 The neurone

dendrites which are connected to it. The cell body 'summates' the information which is received by it at any given moment: that is, its total energy account is determined by the sum of the total inputs which have arrived at that given instant of time. Dendrites do not transmit impulses (action potentials) but instead make an 'analogue' response to the energy they receive. An analogue response is one where the output is proportional to the input (i.e., the greater the amount of electrical input to the dendrite then the larger will be its energy output sent directly to the cell body).

The cell body of a neurone acts like a light switch (see section 6.3). This same principle applies to the action of the cell body in response to energy received from its many dendrites. Given that sufficient energy input is applied at any given amount of time then the cell body responds, whereas energy which is below this threshold is seemingly ignored. The response made by the cell body when the summated inputs from dendrites exceeds threshold is called the 'action potential'.

Action potential

Cell bodies generate a particular response whenever their input energy from dendrites exceeds the threshold level. This particular response is known as an 'impulse' or it is said to be 'firing', but the correct term for this response is the *action potential*. An action potential is a digital rather than an analogue response. That means that the energy which is transmitted is in some form of code, and it is not simply proportional in terms of its own energy to the energy it receives. The action potential is generated at the axon 'hillock' (see Figure 15.1) which is at the base of the axon. The function of the axon is therefore to transmit energy outwards from the cell body (in this case its energy being the action potential). The action potential is a momentary 'pulse' of energy which travels the entire length of the axon, starting at the hillock. Action potentials are identical to one another in the case of the same neurone (i.e., the size of the energy pulse does not vary each time action potentials are generated). The only variation in response made when the cell body receives energy greatly in excess of its threshold level is therefore in the number, not the size, of action potentials it will generate. In the case of a summated energy level many times higher than threshold the neurone will respond by generating and transmitting a series of action potentials until that input level of energy has been dissipated.

Action potentials may be recorded using electrical devices which are capable of displaying the change of energy in the axon as the impulse travels past. To use this technique it is necessary to implant a tiny electrode (named a microelectrode) into the axon, and this has enabled scientists to understand the complex electro-chemical events which occur when neurones operate. When the neurone is not 'firing' (i.e., delivering action potentials along its axon) there is an electrical difference between the inner and outer surfaces of the axon of 70 millivolts. This is known as its 'resting membrane potential', and it is achieved by the membrane, or skin, of the axon pumping out charged molecules of sodium, known as 'ions'. At the moment of the action potential the 'sodium pump', as it is named, ceases to eject sodium and as a result these charged molecules rush into the axon and thereby cause a change in the electrical charge across the membrane. The action potential is therefore partly electrical and partly chemical in nature. When this travelling pulse of energy reaches the axon terminal it can travel no further because there is a physical space separating one neurone from another, called the synapse (see Figure 15.2). Because electrical energy will not readily cross a gap another form of transmission occurs at a synapse.

15.3 The Synapse

Figure 15.2 shows a schematic representation of the synapse. In reality the space between one neurone and another is very much less than that shown in the diagram. The operation of the synapse is as follows. Upon the arrival of the action potential at the axon terminal the vesicles move towards the synapse where they may fuse with the membrane itself, as shown in the case of two vesicles which are in the process of expelling their contents in the diagram. The fusion of the vesicle wall with the axon membrane causes the neurotransmitter to be released. Neurotransmitters are chemicals which are manufactured and stored within the vesicles ready for release into the synapse. There are approximately 50 known different neurotransmitters in the nervous system, each found in certain specific regions and pathways. Once released into the synapse the neurotransmitter usually makes contact with the cell membrane of the neurone across the synapse. The region of neurone involved is usually its dendrite since, as we have already

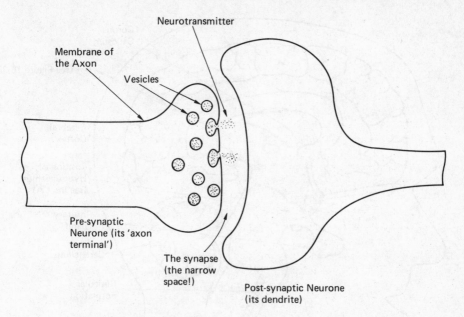

Figure 15.2 The synapse

seen, these most often serve as the collecting zones of information in neurones so far as inputs are concerned. The action of the neurotransmitter which does make contact with the dendritic surface of the next neurone is to cause the 'post-synaptic' neurone (as it is called in this case) to respond electrically. In other words, a chemical contact of the neurotransmitter will lead to an electrical change in the properties of the neighbouring cell. The combination of chemical and electrical processes is typical of the way in which the nervous system operates. In the case of the synapse the electrical action potential leads to the release of chemicals (the neurotransmitter) from the vesicles into the synapse which, in turn, induces electrical changes in the post-synaptic neurone. Any neuro-transmitter which does not find its way across the synapse is either denatured by other chemicals or is absorbed back into vesicles.

This simplified explanation of the events surrounding the action potential illustrates the way in which individual neurones work. But what of the brain as a whole? Despite the fact that neurones are the basic building blocks of the entire nervous system, the brain is not a homogenous organ. Different brain regions perform different tasks, both in the maintenance of body systems and in the control of behaviour. We shall take a brief overview of how this enormously complex organ functions. There is an element of 'Teach Yourself Brain Surgery' in every introductory chapter on brain functioning but, after all, it is necessary to begin with the most basic principles despite the difficulty of the subject matter.

15.4   The Human Nervous System

Figure 15.3 shows two diagrams of the main structures which made up the human nervous system. The 'central nervous system', or CNS, consists of the spinal cord

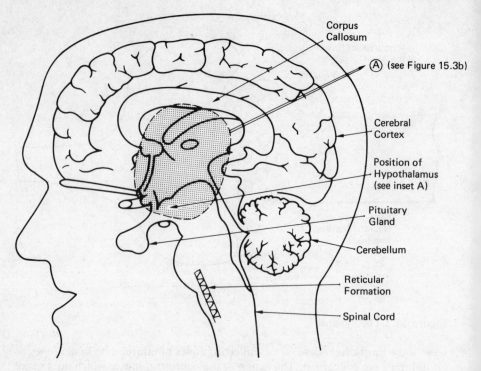

Figure 15.3a The structure of the brain (inset area Ⓐ shown below)

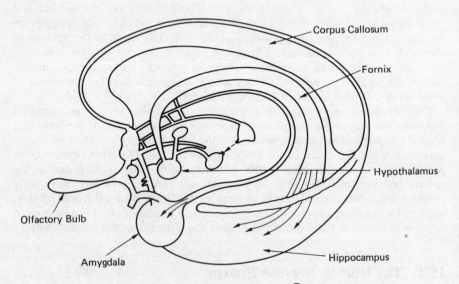

Figure 15.3b The structure of the brain: inset area Ⓐ

and brain. It develops as a tube of tissue in the embryonic stage of life. Eventually the long column or tube forms into the structure shown here; in other words the brain is no more than a huge swelling formed at one end of the neural tube itself.

The spinal cord

This has three major functions to perform:

(a) to receive information from sensory receptors (see Chapter 6 for a description of these) and to transmit this information from the various body regions to the brain structure which deals with it;
(b) to transmit information from various brain centres to the voluntary muscles of the body;
(c) to control a number of basic reflexes.

For the first two functions the spinal cord may be envisaged as a form of biological motorway because not only does it carry a heavy load of traffic in both directions (to and from the brain), but its structure is such that its rear (dorsal) half is exclusively for dealing with incoming traffic and the front (ventral) half deals with outward bound traffic heading for the muscles.

The function and arrangement of reflexes in the spinal cord is mainly biological (i.e., to ensure that in cases of potentially injurious situations the body will make a hyper-fast response by avoiding a dangerous stimulus). Hence, having picked up a hot plate, the spinal cord somehow makes its own decision concerning the danger that may be caused by this hot stimulus and then makes an avoiding response by causing the appropriate muscles of the hand to release the plate instantly. Only afterwards is the conscious recognition of the danger made possible and the pain felt! Reflexes are an indication of the healthiness of the nervous system and for this reason obstetricians use these responses as tests that all is well in the neonate.

The cerebellum

The cerebellum is involved in the coordination and production of complex body movement. Persons with damage to this part of their brains find any sequence of actions difficult. What are unconscious and simple movements to a normal person become strenuous and demanding of both mind and body to such a patient. Even the relatively straightforward action of walking – placing one foot before the other whilst maintaining a state of balance – is an exceedingly complex activity which requires careful thought and effort. The cerebellum is evidently involved in storing the 'how to' aspects of skilled movements; just as a computer is able to store within its memory knowledge of how to compile an account, or solve an arithmetic problem, so too does the cerebellum maintain a set of programs for solving the everyday problems encountered with the control of movement of the body through space. Animals with heightened movement and balance skills, such as cats and rats, have a relatively large cerebellum compared with other animals.

Reticular formation

The reticular formation is a column of neurones which exist in this region of the brainstem (i.e., the part of the spinal cord which enlarges as it enters into the brain). The system is composed of two parts, a descending one (DRAS, or descending reticular activating system, to give it its full name), and an ascending part, or ARAS. The main function of the reticular formation is in the control of arousal or wakefulness. There are two lines of evidence which illustrate this: surgery and drug experiments. Experimental operations on animals which have destroyed parts of the reticular system produce a comatose subject that never wakes again. Drugs which are known to produce states of alertness and heightened arousal increase the electrical activity in this brain region. Similarly, drugs which produce states of drowsiness seem to inhibit the electrical activity of the reticular formation. It has also been claimed that, by stimulating an electrode which has been embedded in the reticular formation, an animal performing a 'vigilance' task will improve in ability compared with the non-stimulated periods.

The hypothalamus

This region of the brain has an enormous range of tasks to perform, despite its relatively small size (only a few millimetres in diameter). It consists of a number of different regions designated by a complex system of labels which correspond to the anatomical location, such as 'ventro-medial', 'lateral', 'anterior', and so on. One function of the hypothalamus is in the control of 'homeostasis': that is, control over the internal environment of the body. This includes such things as glucose metabolism (including feeding), temperature regulation, thirst and drinking, sexuality and aggression. For most of these function the hypothalamus has a direct connection to the system of glands of the body known collectively as the 'endocrine system' (see the Spotlight box for an illustration of the endocrine system in the control of reproductive behaviour). The 'master gland' of the endocrine system is called the pituitary, so called because of its executive influence over the other glands of this system.

SPOTLIGHT   Hormones and reproductive behaviour

Hormones are chemicals which are manufactured by the endocrine glands and then released into the blood circulation. The blood transports hormones from their site of release (e.g., the adrenal glands) to the 'target' sites of the body, such as another gland, the heart or the brain. In the case of the sex hormones (oestrogen and progesterone in females, testosterone in males) there are both long-term developmental effects (such as sexual differentiation) and immediate influences on behaviour (such as sexual receptivity) to consider.

Most animals species have only brief periods of sexual activity per year ('seasons or 'oestrus') during which mating occurs. At one extreme there is the Palola worm which has a single night of the year. At the other are the primates (including humans) which have almost continuous sexual activity.

As a general rule, the more primitive the species the closer will be the link between hormonal condition and sexual behaviour. In addition to mating itself hormones influence the related behaviours of dominance, territoriality, courtship, nest-building and parental care. Brief examples of these various aspects of reproductive behaviours are given below.

In mammals such as the rat the importance of the sex hormones on the development of secondary sexual characteristics begins before birth. For instance, if testosterone is injected into the neonate female then oestrus will not occur when she matures. Testosterone or oestrogen injection into a pregnant female will lead to the development of hermaphrodite characteristics (i.e., mixed male and female features) in her offspring. These hormones therefore, have profound effects both on physiological and behavioural development. In arthropods hormones regulate metamorphosis as well as body growth. In insects hormones affect the production and release of pheromones which in turn may influence long-term changes in development (so-called 'priming' effects).

Regarding the immediate effects of the sex hormones many clear associations are understood. For instance, oestrogen production in female mammals is linked with the receptive (oestrus) cycle. Lordosis occurs in rodents only when oestrogen is present in their circulation. Progesterone maintains a pregnancy. Prolactin elicits nest-building in ring doves as well as maternal behaviour such as retrieving pups in female rats (even virgins). Testosterone increases both male and female aggression. Oestrogen acts as a pheromone to increase testosterone levels in a wide range of species. In red deer stages testosterone strengthens the antlers and stimulates seasonal growth of the testes as well as sperm production and aggression. In sticklebacks increased day-length stimulates the production of gonadal hormones which redden the belly and stimulates territorial and nest-building activity. Hinde and Steel (1966) found that increased day-length stimulates oestrogen in the female canary. Oestrogen itself leads to nest-building in this species. Zarrow *et al.* (1972) found that rabbits will build nests when given a combined injection of oestrogen and progesterone.

In primates the sexual skin of the female swells and reddens during oestrus. This acts as a visual sign of receptivity to males. But in the majority of mammalian species hormonal states combine with pheromonal communication to signal the reproductive status of the female. This is the case for primates (Michael and Keverne, 1968) and possibly also for humans (Comfort, 1971). In mice it has been found that virgin males do not discriminate between receptive and non-receptive females, whereas experienced males do. This indicates a role for learning in this otherwise highly biologically-determined behaviour.

The cerebral cortex

Undoubtedly the most important structure in terms of human psychology is the massive cerebral cortex. The word 'cortex' means crust, and it refers in this case to the outermost layer of the brain. The rest of this structure is called the 'cerebrum' or cerebral hemisphere (in the case of one half, for it is anatomically two distinct parts). The cerebrum has a number of areas, referred as as 'lobes' for convenience of description. These are the frontal, parietal, temporal and occipital lobes. In the case of humans there is a further sub-division referred to as the prefrontal lobe, as is illustrated in Figure 15.4. The cerebral cortex consists of a dense collection of cell bodies and it is this area which is stained grey by anatomists (hence the term 'grey matter'). The function of the various regions of the cerebral cortex is referred to as 'localization' (i.e., despite the fact that the brain normally works as a complete system, within that system the various parts perform specific tasks). Very briefly the cortex is concerned with tasks including vision (the occipital lobe), hearing (the temporal lobe), foresight (the frontal lobe) and language. Regarding functions like the processing of language the cerebral cortex is also said have what is called 'lateralization'. A function is lateralized if it exists in one of the cerebral hemispheres (brain halves) but not in the other. Language is a function controlled almost exclusively by the left cerebral cortex, and so this is a lateralized function.

The localization of functions is more apparent in some brain regions than others. The work of the brain surgeon Wilder Penfield has shown the fine degrees of localization that exists in two particular regions known as the sensory and

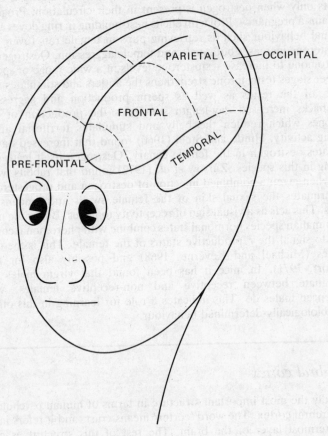

Figure 15.4 The lobes of the brain

motor strips of the frontal and parietal lobes. By stimulating small regions of these areas in the human patient Penfield was able to evoke either movements in individual muscles of the body, or else cause the patient to experience sensations in various body regions when the sensory strip of the cortex was stimulated. The technique simply involves passing a small electrical current along a micro-electrode placed upon the surface of the brain in the conscious patient (who just happened to be undergoing surgery for other, genuine, reasons at the time!).

15.5 Language and the Brain

The earliest studies of the language function and the brain were found in the case notes of surgeons who had observed the deterioration of speech or language comprehension in patients who had suffered similar brain injuries or diseases. It became apparent that damage to specific portions of the cerebral cortex in the left hemisphere led to particular disabilities with language.

The surgeon Broca (whose work is also described in Chapter 19) observed such a relationship between damage to a region of the left frontal lobe (i.e., the overlying cortex) and normal speaking ability. In a number of patients who had damage to this region (situated just above and in front of the left ear) the result was an inability to speak normally.

Broca's area is associated with the adjacent region of the brain known to be involved in control of the muscles of the facial and throat areas, and hence its involvement with the mechanics of, though not the understanding of, spoken language. Conversely, another region discovered by Wernicke in the nineteenth century has some function related to the comprehension of language but not its production. Damage to Wernicke's area leaves the patient capable of lucid and fluent speech but with no meaningful content! Such unfortunate people are able to echo language but their ability to communicate is obviously severely impaired.

Research in recent times has confirmed the division of labour of the language function in the left hemisphere and more has been discovered about the control of reading and writing skills. *Aphasia* is the term given to total loss of spoken language skill (dysphasia meaning the more common partial loss). *Alexia* is total lack of reading ability (and, similarly, dyslexia means partial lack). Finally, *agraphia* means the total inability to write. This division of function was advanced through the work of Desjerine in the 1890s and more recently by Geschwind (1965). Figure 15.5 shows the cortical areas known to be involved in a number of specific conditions relating to language loss. It is not uncommon for people to experience language deficits following a stroke, which often causes damage to the left hemisphere of the brain.

15.6 Split-Brain Studies

A remarkable series of studies involving surgically-modified patients has been conducted over many decades by researchers such as Sperry and Gazzaniga. The root of the trouble for the patients themselves was chronic and severe temporal lobe epilepsy, a condition which makes for an intolerable life in those people who are afflicted by it. One long-standing operation which ameliorates the severity of the condition is a 'split-brain' operation, which is almost literally accurate. The operation involves cutting the major nerve pathway which connects together the

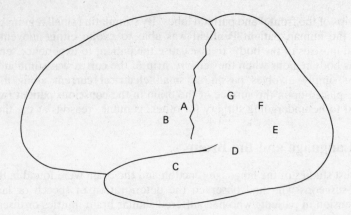

Figure 15.5 Language functions localized in the left hemisphere of the brain
        A motor strip region controlling vocal chords and tongue
        B Broca's Area
        C main area for auditory information processing
        D Wernicke's Area
        Injuries to area:
        E produce sensory aphasia
        F results in alexia with agraphia
        G results in conduction aphasia

two hemispheres in the normal brain (see Figure 15.3 for the location of this pathway, the corpus callosum). Surgeons were first called upon to conduct this operation as a result of observations that in this form of epilepsy there seemed to be a random barrage of electrical activity crossing the corpus callosum during a fit. It seemed worth considering the drastic act of severing this pathway so as to obliterate the apparent cause of the disorder. Indeed, not only was the condition greatly helped following the operation but there seemed to be no other complciations caused to the patient, surprisingly, considering such a major act of destruction to the brain. For many decades such patients were not systematically tested for changes in their behaviour. In the 1960s reports were made showing specific alterations in the way in which these split brains now dealt with information.

The visual system is so constructed that information appearing in the right visual field (everything to the right of centre whilst you are looking straight ahead) is sent to the brain on the left side (i.e., terminating in the occipital cortex of that side). Similarly, information from the left visual field crosses over in the visual pathway to enter the occipital lobe (cortex) on the right side. This crossing-over of information (or 'decussation', as it is called) is a general feature of the way that the brain is organized: for instance, the control of movement or sensation of your right hand is the responsibility of the left hemisphere of your brain, and so forth. It seems to be the task of structures such as the corpus callosum to ensure that information about the physical environment becomes shared by both halves of the brain (i.e., both hemispheres) by the process of connecting them and allowing for the transmission of such information between them. It seemed reasonable to expect that in the so-called split-brain patient this sharing of information would largely cease since there are relatively few other pathways by which this information could cross over.

Sperry, Gazzaniga and others employed a special apparatus for testing these patients in which a visual display containing words or pictures could be presented to either the left or right visual fields only. The information was presented at high speed so that only the appropriate hemisphere would be 'informed'. Using the procedure it was discovered that the two hemispheres of the brain are able to function as two independent systems in that what one half was conscious of, the other may be blithely unaware. This is most dramatic in the instance where a picture is 'shown' to the right hemisphere which, you will remember, has very little language ability since most of this skill is acquired by the left hemisphere during development. In such a situation, when patients are asked to report verbally what they have seen, they will say 'Nothing', the true case so far as the left hemisphere is concerned. Yet, when asked to point to one of a series of pictures they saw, patients are able to identify correctly the one shown to them, as long as they may use their left hand (controlled, you will recall, by the knowing right hemisphere!)

Such studies have led neuropsychologists to the conclusion that the brain has many lateralized capacities, with the tasks requiring a 'serial' mode of thought (i.e., tackling one thing at a time, such as solving an arithmetic sum via a series of stages) being typical of the abilities localized in the left hemisphere of the brain. Conversely, those tasks which require a form of thought called 'parallel processing' (i.e., involving the processing of several pieces of information simultaneously, such as appreciating a work of art, or listening to orchestral music) is typical of the manner in which the right hemisphere processes information.

These studies illustrate the complexity of the human nervous system. Not only does it behave with a degree of unity (what we might describe as producing the characteristic 'personality' of the individual), but it is also a highly coordinated assembly of different systems, each with their own immensely complex tasks to perform. As if that were not enough for one organ to perform, the human brain also has what is known as 'plasticity' of function. This refers to the way that a function which has been lost following a brain injury recovers. There is no actual recovery of function at the level of brain tissue; the central nervous system does not have the capacity to heal itself, and neurones that die as a result of injury cannot regenerate as do other tissues of the body. Therefore, the fact that an injury may leave someone paralysed in, say, one are a would apparently mean they will have a permanent disability. However, this is not the case because, although the injured area of the brain does not itself recover this function, it is evident that some other, uninjured brain region takes over this control function, and movement and sensation may eventually recover. The remarkable ability of the nervous system to recover function in this way is called 'plasticity'. As a general rule, the younger the person who suffers some form of brain injury then the greater are the chances of a complete recovery taking place. In others words, plasticity is particularly evident in the developing human, although this capacity is never completely lost.

15.7   Questions and Exercises

1. Give a brief account of how neurones process information in (a) dendrites, (b) the axon, and (c) at the synapse.
2. List as many differences as you are can between human and non-human reproductive behaviour.
3. Sketch the diagram shown in Figure 15.4 and write into each of the lobes in your drawing what brain functions reside there.

16 Personality theory

16.1 Introduction

There is no universal definition of personality. In everyday terms we treat personality as some kind of skill in relationships: for instance, someone may be regarded as having 'lots of personality'. At other times we may speak of people as in need of personality 'training', as though they have some deficiency which needs to be made good. Personality is regarded intuitively as the dominant impression that an individual makes on us, such as thinking of someone as being an 'aggressive' or an 'outgoing' type of person; the very essence of that person, as it were.

You may have already noticed inconsistency here. At one point we are treating personality as that which sets a particular person apart from other people, whilst at another we are using the term to classify or lump people together as being of similar types. This ambiguity is reflected in psychological theories of personality, because some concentrate on the uniqueness (or 'idiographic' features) whereas others try to identify similarities in personalities and to classify them into 'types' (the 'nomothetic' approach).

This chapter describes a number of different theories of personality. The selection of which theories to discuss is especially difficult in personality because of the size and scope of the area as well as the many conflicting views that it contains. As long ago as 1937 Gordon Allport could identify 50 different concepts that theorists were using when discussing personality. In the following pages no attempt is made to represent such a scope. Indeed, given the constraints of space, the only real consideration behind the choice becomes personal predilection.

16.2 Psychoanalytic Theory

Freud's contribution to personality provides the basis of most of the major psychoanalytical theories, including Alfred Adler, Carl Jung, Melanie Klein, Karen Horney, Henry Stack Sullivan, and others who are known collectively as 'neo-Freudians'. Adler has been chosen to represent this particular group.

Alfred Adler studied under Freud in Vienna. He developed his own theory which, like Freud's, regards biology as having the essential role governing mental processes. Adler was interested in the phenomenon of 'compensation' in biological systems. When a part of the body has a weakness or deficiency then some other part becomes stronger and more resilient in order to compensate for this frailty (if one kidney is damaged, for example, then the other develops the strength to do the job of two). If a person is left with a limp through injury to one leg then the other leg increases in strength to as to compensate for the additional load it is made to carry. Similarly, the other senses of blind or deaf people may become more responsive to the environment in order to compensate for the deficit.

It occurred to Adler that the mind also functions on the principle of compensation. For instance, someone with a weak physique may develop inferiority feelings about this which may in turn lead them to compensate by developing 'strong' mental power, such as becoming assertive or dictatorial. In striving to compensate for mental weakness a person may become concerned with body building in order to compensate. Such striving to eliminate feelings of inferiority may have one of three outcomes according to Adler.

1. *Successful compensation*: people make up for their weakness without imbalancing their lives by doing so.
2. *Sickness compensation*: people make a retreat into ill-health where they can gain sympathy from others for their misfortune. This condition provides an outlet for their inferiority feelings which they may exploit in another way (e.g., by appearing to be striving to overcome ill-health they seem to be mentally superior beings).
3. *Overcompensation*: a person who sets out to make up for a deficiency may become compulsive about the act of compensation itself. A physically weak person may end up as a domineering individual through shows of mental prowess: for example, becoming exceptional at mathematics or memory skills.

In contrast to Freud's description of the libido as being the essential life-force, Adler believed our mental life to be centred on one of two processes: either striving to avoid inferiority feelings, or else striving to feel superior to others.

J. A. C. Brown (1961) has argued that because the neo-Freudian group, including Adler, have not maintained the essential elements of Freudian theory, it is an error to regard them as 'neo-Freudians' at all.

16.3   Role Theory and Personality

William James (1890) described what amounts to an antithesis of personality theory. He proposed that what makes us into the people we are is the social role we adopt in life. 'Role' in this sense is a metaphor for a part in a theatrical production where the players' behaviour is scripted. In Shakespeare's words:

> All the world's a stage,
> And all the men and women merely players:
> They have their exits and their entrances;
> And one man in his time plays many parts

> (As You Like It: Act 2, Scene 7, l. 139)

Some roles, James believed, we choose for ourselves, such as the 'joker', 'athlete', 'expert', 'storyteller', and so on. Other roles are prescribed for us by virtue of our position in life, such as 'daughter', 'colleague', 'student' or 'neighbour'.

With socially-prescribed roles our behaviour is often associated with role expectations. For instance, a school-teacher is expected to be responsible, punctual, a good communicator, have knowledge, and so forth. These role expectations are made by the pupils, other members of staff, the parents and governors, and they determine both what the teacher may and may not do whilst in this role. The range of such prescribed behaviour is called a 'role set', and pressures are applied to individuals to make them accept and conform to this set.

Although some freedom of expression within the role set is tolerated (to varying degrees by different 'others'), the person is expected to remain within the boundary of the prescribed role set. For instance, a uniformed police officer who sits casually on the bonnet of a car in the centre of town would soon be made aware that this is 'out of role' behaviour!

George Mead (1934) proposed that we each have an 'I', which is the individual's core nature (approximating to the everyday concept of 'personality'), and 'social selves', which are regarded as 'Me' (i.e., representing the part of us which is put to use when we are dealing with external realities). Mead therefore combined two concepts of personality here. One regarded individuals as possessing an immutable core of being, and the other related to the social roles adopted when embarking upon social exchanges.

Talcott Parsons (1951) has described the differing ways in which people play the same prescribed role. For example, one person may identify with the job of solicitor as that of the social 'carer', whilst another may play the role as 'legal expert', or as 'the executive' and so on.

Goffman (1959) explains the differing behaviour people exhibit in the same role in terms of 'role distance'. This term refers to the extent to which people believe in the part they are playing. For instance, parents who are getting pleasure from a fairground ride may only show this enjoyment if their excuse for being there is to accompany a young child. When riding alone they may exhibit a look of nonchalance so as to distance themselves from the behaviour. Goffman also uses the term 'role conflict' to describe the difficulties we experience when facing contradicting role expectations. For instance, a child who is perhaps shy and withdrawn at school may have a boisterous 'personality' at home. Should the occasion arise when both the teachers and parents are present simultaneously, such as during the school's parents' evening, then the child will experience role conflict. Another example of role conflict would be that facing a shop steward who becomes involved in an industrial dispute. At such times of negotiation he/she faces the conflicting demands of behaving both as employee and antagonist. Role conflict causes stress because when two or more sets of expectations act simultaneously on the person then some form of resolution must be found. (This process is similar to the concept of 'cognitive dissonance' used by Festinger: see Chapter 4.)

Although role theory originated in the psychological writings of William James it has been developed mainly by sociologists such as Merton (1957), Mead (1934), Parsons (1951) and in the many works of Goffman. In many respects it is diametrically opposed to most psychological theories of personality. Whereas psychology treats personality as something enduring in a person's behaviour, role theory assumes that people will make multiple sets of social responses to fit their various social settings. Someone displaying such inconsistency in their behaviour to a psychologist may even be regarded as possessing the symptoms of multiple personality, a specific disorder which requires psychiatric treatment.

16.4   Humanism and Personality Theory

Humanists adopt an idiographic approach to personality: that is, they focus on explaining behaviour in terms of the uniqueness of individuals. One instance of this approach is that of personal construct theory by George Kelly. Kelly (1955) bases his approach to personality upon the ways in which people structure and classify their own social world. To Kelly it is the psychologist's job to utilize the individual's own world view as the raw material rather than to start by fitting people into the psychologist's own preconceived-scheme. Kelly argues that we can understand a person by examining how they have classified their own unique set of life experiences, which he refers to as their 'personal constructs'. A person uses constructs for the same reason that scientists devise hypotheses: that is, to test their predictions about the world. When formally testing a hypothesis the scientist conducts experiments and then interprets the results to assess whether or not the hypothesis made an accurate prediction. Experiments are therefore the means by which scientists confirm or refute their ideas, gradually building up an understanding of things as they see them. Kelly uses this scientific metaphor to explain the process by which each of us forms our own personality as we interact with the world. We formulate our own conglomerate of expectations or 'hypotheses' which we then proceed to test during everyday living. Our 'personality' is therefore determined by the way in which we anticipate events. This has the following implications for our behaviour:

(a) since no two persons have shared identical life experiences then no two construct systems can completely overlap each other (this means we are each unique personalities even though some people may resemble each other more than others);
(b) construct systems are 'teleological' (i.e. they orientate people towards the future rather than back to their historical selves).

Kelly devised the 'repertory grid test' as a means of examining a person's construct system. This test involves eliciting from the person descriptions of various others who are significant figures in their everyday lives, such as close relatives, neighbours, friends, and so on. The descriptions employed by the individuals concerned are then used as the basis for examining their constructs. This test has proved useful particularly in clinical settings. Some research has treated neurosis as being a state where the patient has formed a construct system which consistently fails to predict the events around that person. Where people form constructs which are so loose as to have no predictive capacity at all then this may predispose the individual to psychosis (Bannister and Fransella, 1980).

16.5   Type and Trait Approaches to Personality

A 'type' theory of personality regards people as fitting into discernible, discrete categories, each being qualitatively different from other types. An analogy would be the ways in which colours are classified. Given a sample of various colours we would find no difficulty in fitting each into one and one only category. An instance of such a theory is that of Sheldon, in which personality is regarded as dependent upon body 'type' (e.g., fat people are happy and extravert in their personality).

Conversely, a trait theory proposes that, although there may be differences between people, these are quantitative rather than qualitative differences. For instance, the dimension of extraversion–introversion is treated by Eysenck (1965) as a dimension and not a dichotomous state. Differences between people are therefore based on the extent to which they possess the specified traits. Some theorists describe personality as comprising a few traits whereas others may include many, but they are fundamentally agreeing about the constitution of personality. An analogy of the trait approach, again using the example of colour, is the way in which shades of the same colour may differ from one another. Although there may be a number of different shades of blue, say, their differences depend upon merely the amount of blue pigment which is present. Dark blue has a quantitatively larger amount of blue pigment in it than the lighter shades.

Personality tests

A test aims to quantify or measure personality. It may serve one or more of the following purposes:

(a) support the theory on which it is based;
(b) measure individual differences between people;
(c) classify people according to their common characteristics;
(d) be a clinical 'tool' for diagnosing abnormality of personality;
(e) be a research device.

Tests take a variety of forms, such as self-report questionnaires, behaviour check-sheets or inventories, as well as projective tests, such as the repertory grid test of Kelly. Some personality theorists regard personality as fundamentally unmeasurable (e.g., Freud).

16.6   Freud's Psychoanalytical Theory

Freud's theory of child development has had an impact on art, literature, film, medicine, philosophy and psychology, as well as in everyday aspects of our lives, such as through the media. Freud stands as a Colossus of twentieth-century thought despite having produced one of the most unscientific and unpsychological theories of all time!

Basic concepts

Freud imagined humans to be 'driven' by energy from within. This energy comes from the biological instincts we inherit, such as hunger, sex and aggression. If these instincts are ignored or repressed by the person then energy wells up inside them, causing a state of psychological tension. To maintain our mental health Freud believed that we need to find outlets for releasing the inner tension caused when the drive builds up. The part of personality which Freud claimed harboured the instincts is called the 'id'. The id is the energy reservoir which goes on filling up unless the instincts are satisfied. For instance, if you feel hungry but do not eat you get hungrier and hungrier until the desire to eat becomes unbearable. Freud believed humans have a life instinct he called 'libido', which aims for survival and procreation. He also referred to 'thanatos', which is the instinct for self-destruction.

The id (or 'it')

In Freud's theory this part of the personality is present from the moment of birth. During the first year of life the personality consists only of the id and this is why babies make so many demands. The id demands that the instincts and impulses be satisfied. If the instinct is not satisfied then energy builds up and the baby cries loud and long. The id is not a 'reasonable' part of the personality; it demands satisfaction whenever the energy levels have built up. Hence, once fed, the baby is only quiescent until hunger (or one of the other instincts) emerges again. The id knows nothing about reality and works selfishly to satisfy the body's needs, whatever the circumstances (and however inconvenient it is for the caretaker!). Since the id does not recognize 'reality' it is possible to release some of its energy by artificial means. For instance, if a hungry baby is given a dummy to suck on this will drain some of the id's energy for a short while. However, because the energy continues to build up this is only a temporary solution. Freud calls the object of an instinct its 'object-cathexis' (cathexis meaning to discharge, such as releasing steam from a pressure cooker).

Ego

At about the age of one year we all develop another side to our personality. Freud called this the ego. The ego is a vital development because it is part of the personality which recognizes reality (i.e., it distinguishes what is true and possible from what is impossible). For instance, once the ego has developed the infant no longer makes unreasonable demands on the caretaker, such as demanding food when they are out walking. That is not to say that the energy of the id no longer builds up. The ego is cunning in being able to divert this energy into some other area of behaviour so that it does not keep its tension on the child's conscious mind. One 'trick' used by the ego for releasing some of the id's energy is to 'discharge' it (cathexis) into some substitute object-cathexis. Remember that the id is unable to tell the difference between the real object of an instinct, such as food, and a substitute, such as dummy. The ego does not strive continuously to thwart or trick the id in this way. In fact the aim of the ego is to ensure that the instincts and impulses of the id are satisfied, but at the right time and place. The practical circumstances ('reality') is all that concerns the ego in this sense. For instance, without the development of the ego, toilet-training would not be possible.

Exercise
List some of the other 'civilized' behaviours which an infant has to learn so as to avoid social conflict. List these under (a) hunger and thirst, (b) expulsion of urine and faeces, (c) aggression, and (d) sexual curiosity (for instance, one activity under (a) might be learning to suck a thumb).

Superego

According to Freud, between the ages of three and five years the third and final part of the personality develops. The superego is the 'idealistic' part of us: that is, the part which strives to improve us, to make us 'good' in the sense of the community to which we belong. Usually at this age the direct cause of our 'moral' behaviour is what our parents prefer us to do and also what they punish and prevent us from doing. But these ideas nonetheless spring from society at large. The superego will often come into conflict with the id. This is because one part of us (the id) demands that we seek the pleasure of satisfying our bodily urges as soon as they arise (hedonism). The superego wishes to turn us into a 'good' person and this means that we try to develop moral attitudes rather than obey, for example, our sexual or aggressive instincts. The supergo strives to make us perfect and to make the ego behave accordingly.

Psychic energy

The id monopolizes all the psychic energy. This means that the ego and superego rely upon diverting the built-up instinctual energy for their own purposes. The id's sole intention for this reservoir of energy is to use it to gratify the instincts. The ego and superego 'tap into' this energy subversively and divert it for their own needs by a process called 'identification'. For instance, when an infant clutches a rattle to its mouth it is trying to satisfy its hunger need. The id cannot tell the difference between the rattle and an item of food and so, by using this energy outlet, the ego can delay the id's demands for food until a more realistic time (when food arrives at mealtimes!). But such tricks will only give the ego fragile control over the id because, if a need goes unsatisfied, the id reasserts itself and demands object-cathexis (i.e., real food in this case). The ego can continue to provide substitute objects for cathexis but the psychic energy may eventually overwhelm the ego. To defend against this the ego has various defence mechanisms such as 'displacement', as we shall see in a later section.

Sources of tension

Freud believed that there are four main causes of tension:

(a) physiological growth;
(b) frustration;
(c) conflict;
(d) threat.

Personality develops in response to these tensions because each individual finds his or her own way of dealing with them. Sometimes we observe other people coping better than us at reducing their tension levels and so we may 'identify' with them. Identification means adopting the personality of the other person by modelling ourselves on them. By this Freud does not mean we become exactly like them but only in those ways that help us to control anxiety. Identification can be with other people, animals, or even inanimate objects. We are also able to identify with an object or person who is lost to us through bereavement, for example. This serves to 'reincarnate' them. For young children the most likely models for identification will be their parents, as we shall see later.

Rewards and punishments

Parents reward their children for being 'good' and punish them for being 'bad'. This does not so much stamp morality into the child as cause changes in tension levels. Tension is the result of an excess of psychic energy. Rewards by the parent serve to reduce the tension because they give pleasure: an instinct. Conversely, punishment causes tension to increase and so the child obeys the parent not through moral reasoning but because by doing so this increase in tension is prevented.

Displacement

When the id demands object-cathexis the ego or superego may block the impulse and this may cause a 'dangerous' rise in energy levels (the psychic reservoir). Alternatively the ego may displace the impulse by using a substitute object. This is called displacement, and it may continue from one object substitute to another so as to prevent the energy levels from rising rapidly. However, a substitute object-cathexis is never as satisfying as the original and so there will never be a complete discharge of energy as long as this displacement continues to happen. Some substitutes are more effective than others at displacing the object-cathexis, and their effectiveness will depend on how closely the substitute resembles the original object-cathexis and also how 'acceptable' the substitute is to society at large (e.g., will it in turn have anxiety-invoking properties?). For instance, if a boy touches his genitals (sexual object-cathexis) and his mother punishes him he might begin to suck this thumb as displacement (i.e., a substitute). However, his mother may still not allow this behaviour and so she may decide to give him a lollipop to suck on.

Anxiety

The environment is a source of pleasure to the child because it is often there that the id's needs are satisfied. However, there are also dangers in the environment which threaten the individual, such as a punishing parent, an unfriendly dog, or a cat which scratches when its tail is pulled. The ego is always aware of reality and therefore usually perceives danger, whereas the id does not. The ego responds with fear to danger and if that danger is imminent then anxiety occurs. Freud identified three kinds of anxiety:

(a) reality anxiety, caused by a genuine danger in the environment, such as an angry dog;
(b) neurotic anxiety, which is the fear that punishment will occur if the id's impulses are not inhibited;
(c) moral anxiety, which is the fear that behaving immorally will cause a conscience to develop.

Anxiety causes a person to act so as to avoid or remove it. For instance, avoiding immoral behaviour will prevent moral anxiety. Diverting the id may also prevent neurotic anxiety. If an anxiety cannot be dealt with then it may become 'traumatic'. A traumatic anxiety causes the ego to respond by using one or more 'defence mechanisms'.

Ego defence mechanisms against anxiety

All defence mechanisms of the ego have two things in common: they distort or falsify reality, and they occur unconsciously. The main mechanisms used are: repression, projection, reaction formation, and fixation and regression.

Repression
Freud believed that most of our mind is unconscious. Our consciousness is therefore like the tip of an iceberg with the rest buried beneath the surface. By this he meant that we are only conscious of a small amount of what happens in our mind. Things in the unconscious mind are kept there by repression (like prisoners locked in jail). Anything that causes us alarm or anxiety in our consciousness may be suddenly ejected into the unconscious mind. For instance, we may fail to notice something which is right in front of us if by recognizing it we would become anxious. For instance, repressed anger may lead to arthritic pains in the arms (thus preventing someone from striking out), and repressed sexual urges may lead to impotence.

Projection
Of the three types of anxiety Freud mentions (see above) reality anxiety is the easiest with which to deal. Therefore, if a threat to the ego really comes from within (e.g., feelings of jealousy towards a friend may cause 'moral' anxiety), this can be 'projected' on to the outside world in one way or another. For example, the friend might be treated as though *they* are to blame by being a 'show-off'. This will allow the ego to reduce anxiety more easily. Projection therefore has two advantages:
(a) it reduces anxiety (e.g., the 'show-off' interpretation is easier to deal with than the 'jealousy' one);
(b) it allows the impulse to be expressed (e.g., if you admit to your own feelings of jealousy then aggression is turned inwards on yourself; however, if the friend is perceived to be a show-off then it is possible to vent aggressive feelings on them).

Reaction formation
This mechanism simply reverses the impulse. For instance, if the impulse is to hate or attack someone then the reaction formation will make them loved. Similarly, if a person feels deep shame at his or her own lustful feelings then he or she may become prudish and moralistic about sexual matters. However, reaction formation is only 'papering over cracks' because the impulse remains just beneath the surface. Therefore a moralistic attitude about violence may occur in someone who has a very short 'fuse' (they are quick to become aggressive). Of course, Freud was not saying that everyone who seems to love you really loathes you (or vice versa). He believed that when these feelings are caused during reaction

formation they are always in an exaggerated form compared with real feelings. For example, a child who is unloved by the parent may be 'smothered' with shows of love but without the real substance of the feeling itself.

Fixation and regression

Fixation refers to the stages of development (see later). A child who experiences a trauma in one of the stages may become fixated there. Although development from then on may appear to be normal it is found that any future trauma that person faces may cause their behaviour to 'regress' to the earlier stage where they fixated. This may explain some people's reactions, such as sobbing or temper trantrums. Freud did not believe regression usually happened completely but that the person would simply tend towards the behaviours which are typical of the stage where they became fixated.

Freud's stages of development

An outline of the stages of development is given in Table 16.1.

Oedipus complex

According to Freud the Oedipus complex applies to both boys and girls, although in different forms, during the phallic stage (between 3 and 5 years). During this period the child has an object-cathexis (i.e., a biological impulse) for sexual gratification using the parent of the opposite sex. This is shown in the child's general attitude to the parent as well as through their fantasizing about them during masturbation.

In boys the Oedipus complex means they become attracted to their mother and feel competition from their father. Feelings of hatred towards fathers may arise and they may interpret any punishment from their father as evidence that they are hated in return. Paradoxically, boys begin to identify with their father (i.e., act like him in terms of his personality: see section on identification above for more details). Identification at this time serves two purposes: first, to placate the father whom the boy hates and fears; and second, to supplant the father in the mother's affections. Part of the fear is based on the idea that the father may punish him by castration. Recall that at about the age of 5 years the superego develops. It is not coincidental that this happens at the same time as the Oedipus conflict. The first job of the superego in Freud's theory is to moralize and fight against the incestuous and violent desires happening during the Oedipus conflict.

In a girl the situation is different because she will already have formed a close and nurturant relationship with her mother and so the feelings are more difficult to transmute into hatred. According to Freud the girl also believes that since she has no penis that she must already have been castrated by her mother. However, she is attracted to the father because she experiences 'penis envy'.

The *castration complex* in girls shows itself as penis envy whereas in boys it is 'castration fear'. Freud does not think the same-sex parent is hated in the true sense such as felt by adults because he believes that people are sexually ambivalent (i.e., even in heterosexuals there is a 'latent' homosexuality whereby a hidden desire exists for the homosexual love).

Table 16.1 *Freud's stages of development and the appropriate ages at which they emerge*

Stage	Approximate age	Characteristics	Personality if fixation occurs
Oral	Birth–1 year	Swallowing, spitting out, biting, chewing, in the first year the child enjoys stimulating the mouth and lips	Hoarding, gullible, sarcastic, argumentative, dependent
Anal	1–3 years	Enjoyment of expelling faeces.	Mean, cruel, destructive, untidy, hot-tempered
Phallic	3–5 years	Masturbation and fantasy involving the opposite-sexed parent (leading to the Oedipus complex: see text)	Hysteric symptoms
Latency period	5–12 years	*Repression of the impulses occurs. Behaviour settles so that no evidence of the id is present*	
Genital	12 years onwards	The genitals become once again the focus of attention but now in relation to others (i.e., the first three stages were all to do with the person's own body: the so-called 'primary narcissism')	Fixation here normal

Freud's methods of investigation

Self-analysis

Freud saved the last hour of every day to analyse his own feelings and thoughts in terms of his theory. This method is called 'introspection' and was discarded by psychologists in the nineteenth century as being an unreliable approach.

Case studies

Freud made notes over hundreds of hours of interviews with each patient. During the session he did not take notes because he believed this would interfere with the concentration of both the patient and himself. The notes were therefore retrospective (i.e., based on what he could remember).

Free association

During each session the patient was encouraged to do all the talking with only occasional prompts from Freud. The patient was encouraged to say whatever came into his or her mind, however embarrassing it might seem. Freud found it easy to associate the things patients said, even though at first glance they seemed disconnected. These associations were, of course, Freud's own interpretations and chosen to fit in with his theory. Also, so as to respect the privacy of his patients, he did not discuss or publish his work with particular patients in detail.

Evaluation of Freud's theory

Freud's theory of development was moulded into a coherent structure only late in his life. During his long career he changed his ideas occasionally and this has led to some confusions about his meanings in particular areas of his writings (e.g., on identification and anxiety). He was also inconsistent about some aspects of his theory, such as the effects of the Electra complex on female development. His theory about neuroses is that they stem from childhood experiences, and yet Freud did not validate his ideas by studying children (apart from his own six, of course!). Freud did not use scientific methods even though he had been trained in these methods early in his career. The reason for this is that he did not think that it was possible to study the mind using a strictly scientific approach. Scientists, on the other hand, reply that theories which are not open to scientific analysis are worthless and have the status rather of being a religious faith.

16.7 Jung's Theory of Personality

Carl Gustav Jung became interested in psychoanalysis as an explanation for human behaviour after reading Freud's book on dreams. At the simplest level it could be said that what makes psychoanalysis different from other approaches to personality is its emphasis on the importance of unconscious forces acting on the person's thoughts, feelings and behaviour. The idea of an unconscious mind therefore implies that conscious action and thought is merely the outward expression of hidden areas of the mind. This inner self harbours all our intentions, motives and psychic energy. Since none of us has direct access even to our own unconsciousness (by definition) then merely questioning ourselves about these underlying forces is pointless.

To Jung the personality was a system. This meant that it operated as a conglomerate of separable components, each with their own function to perform. At the centre of the system was a structure called the ego. The ego is the only part of the human psyche of which we are consciously aware. It is that part of us which acts as our 'stream of consciousness'. The *personal unconscious* harbours thoughts and feelings which we have either failed to resolve or perceive consciously, or else those we have deliberately suppressed to prevent conscious awareness occurring. Freud emphasized the importance of subconsciousness as a means of avoiding anxiety states and Jung agreed with this part of Freud's theory and even accepted his explanations of the ego's defence mechanisms against anxiety (notably sublimation and repression).

Within the personal unconscious Jung believed there are a number of *complexes*. A complex is a collection of related thoughts, feelings and memories which correspond to specific experiences the individual has had. For instance, a visit to the dentist will have formed memories for the smell of the anaesthetic, for the touch of the crisp starched white gown, of the sharp, stabbing pain from the drill or for the sight of blood being washed down the sink. This constellation of experience usually remains submerged in the unconsciousness but at any time the complex may be brought into consciousness, such as when triggered off by handling starched linen sheets, or when smelling the familiar antiseptic aroma.

Collective unconscious

To Jung the collective unconscious is the store of our ancestral lives. In this store resides all the residue of our prehistorical life both in human and pre-human states. In much the same way as finger nails are vestigial remains of ancestral claws, Jung believed that so too are there ancestral remains in our psychological make-up. Every human alive therefore shares a number of predispositions which form the collective unconsciousness, such as fear of the dark, or of certain wild animals. The collective unconscious is a store of latent dispositions which, though they may not necessarily become expressed in every culture to the same extent, are nonetheless in a dormant form ready to be awakened should the occasion arise. Hence, what is a collective fear of snakes in humankind may not materialize into actual fear until it is triggered off by some evocative stimulus. Jung named these residual predispositions of the collective unconsciousness 'archetypes'. The archetype for the mother is already present in the infant at birth and the physical arrival of the actual mother will then trigger off the protogenic behaviour when she is recognized. The archetype for being followers of a strong leader may show itself as the polite respect and obedience common in everyday life but the complete submission of wills to a despot shows the full archetypal behaviour pattern at work.

The 'self' is Jung's name for the entirety of the individual's personality, including both conscious and unconscious minds. Although the ego is the conscious core of the personality, the self is more representative of the complete person. Jung regarded the self as the pivotal point of the personality which, in normal people, forms a point of balance between the conscious and unconscious minds.

Individual differences

In addition to the development of the personal unconsciousness, each of us differs in the way we organize our mental processes. According to Jung there are four such processes or 'functions': thought, emotion, sensation and intuition. We usually focus on one of the four and develop it as superior function. For instance, a scholar may develop thought as his or her dominant function which will, to a greater or lesser extent, lead to the neglect of the other three functions. Indeed, should one of these aspects remain repressed they may end up as *inferior* functions and be largely confined to an existence in the unconscious. Jung believed that such repression explains why the dreams of overly intellectual people are often florid and emotional (inferior functions may use such opportunities to release pent-up tension). He referred to this counter-action by one function as an act of *compensation*. Hence, an unconsciously cowardly person may compensate for this by showing overtly courageous behaviour as a trait of his or her personality. Likewise overtly 'machismo' traits shown in young men may be a compensation for a strongly feminine unconscious. An introverted unconscious becomes overtly expressed in extraversion, and so forth.

Personality development

Jung's theory of personality is unique in the way he emphasizes ancestral and racial forces in the mind, which come down to us as residues from our evolutionary past. But Jung also realized that humans are conscious of their personal future and they are driven by ambition and foresight. The teleological side of our nature seems to drive us towards the goals we set for ourselves; towards what Jung referred to as 'self-actualization'. In this sense each human life is itself a process of evolution, starting from simple origins and moving towards a more complex form of existence. Jung sees all development as stemming from the libido (life-force) which, in the early years of childhood and adolescence, is released in the vitality with which the person engages in energetic pursuits, passionate love affairs, forming a career, or just simply through impulsive and purposeless activity such as play. Adulthood brings with it a transition into more spiritual and intellectual activity which consumes the libido. Jung regards personality disorders as stemming from the individual's failure to find suitable outlets for the libido. The effect of this is that, instead of progressing onwards to the future, the person may begin to regress (i.e., turn inwards and develop an introverted ego). Jung considers this arises in everyone's life from time to time but we are normally able to resolve these periods of regression without help from others because the ego is thought to be a self-regulating system which will find its own balance. Therefore, far from being destructive, these occasional regressive bouts may assist individuals to form deeper insights into themselves as well as into the human conditions generally. Both knowledge and wisdom are acquired by the process of self-analysis and adjustments that people make during such times.

Jung's psychoanalytical method

In contrast to Freud's method of free association Jung developed a method called word association. Here, a list of words is read slowly to the subject who responds to each with a word of their own choice. Jung would monitor some aspect of the person's physiology during this procedure, such as their respiratory rate, heart rate, GSR (galvanic skin response), and so on, in order to determine whether any increase in anxiety occurs in response to the given word(s). Jung claimed that the individual's unconscious mind shows such signs of emotional disturbance when ideas relating to hidden anxieties are touched upon. People may also pause longer than usual when associating words with such ideas. For instance, the word 'hate' may evoke uncomfortable feelings which may indicate that they are involved in an ambiguous relationship (such as a failing marriage). Jung would utilize the results of each sessions as the basis for exploring their anxieties further. Jung also used dream analysis in his psychoanalysis because he agreed with Freud that dreams reflect the activity of the unconsciousness. Jung would also analyse artwork or doodles made by the patient because he considered these to be acts of the imagination which in turn reflect normally inaccessible thoughts and desires.

Evaluation

Although Jung's theory has influenced many thinkers, writers and artists he has, even more than Freud, been accused of creating concepts which are untestable and therefore fundamentally unscientific. Jung has been criticized for misunderstanding the principles of inheritance in his use of the term archetype as a hypothesis for racial and ancestral memories. J. A. C. Brown (1961) criticizes specific issues such as this and also articulates what many psychologists feel about psychoanalysis in general: 'psychoanalysts . . . go a long distance out of their way to complicate what is perfectly simple' (p. 106).

16.8 Questions and Exercises

1. Distinguish between the 'nomothetic' and 'idiographic' approaches to personality.
2. In everyday life we often speak of someone as having an 'inferiority complex'. In Adler's view such people may come to 'overcompensate' for this condition. What does he mean by overcompensation? Give some examples of how it may be seen in a person's behaviour.
3. List some of the behaviours which an infant must learn to inhibit during the early years of life in order to avoid conflict with its parents (e.g., in order to stop making unreasonable demands to be fed when in town with its parents a child may learn to suck its thumb in order to allay these hunger feelings).
4. Note down the sources of tension, described by Freud, which impinge on the growing personality. Give an instance of each of these and explain how 'identification' might operate in reducing them.
5. How does Jung's concept of the 'collective unconscious' explain the existence of a phobia in one person whereas others do not suffer?

17 Methods of research

17.1 Introduction

Psychology is the scientific investigation of human behaviour. In science, facts are not incontrovertible truths. An experimental result or a famous theory are mere interpretations of events. Like the detective at the scene of a crime the scientist can never be sure enough of the 'facts' since all there is to go on is the evidence that has been uncovered so far. But once sufficient data has been found the detective and the scientist may form a theory which brings together the 'facts' into a tentative explanation of events. Therefore, psychology does not give definitive answers or offer the ultimate explanation of human behaviour. Rather, it offers the best possible explanations of how human beings act, think and feel given the state of knowledge as it exists at the time.

The scales of measurement used in psychology vary in their ability to provide accurate and reliable information about behaviour, and the same is true for the methods used in the investigation. Before psychology was started as a science, philosophers used to make up their own explanations about what makes people behave as they do. These explanations were often 'armchair theories' based on 'introspection'. To introspect means to examine your own thoughts and behaviour and then try to explain everyone else's behaviour in terms of what you feel makes you 'tick'. From introspection it was hoped that the truth about human nature could be found. Unfortunately, whenever a controversy arose between philosophers, there was no way of settling the issue and little progress was made through the debates which occurred. Psychology therefore began as a scientific study of behaviour and tried to achieve two aims:

(a) to collect evidence and facts upon which to base psychological theory;
(b) to find ways of measuring and analysing behaviour.

This chapter is concerned with the first of these aims. A brief consideration is given to the main methods of investigating human behaviour, and these are set out in Figure 17.1.

Psychologists have a range of different methods with which to investigate human behaviour. These are: experiments, observations, cross-cultural studies, surveys, interviews, comparative studies, case studies, questionnaires and psychometric tests.

17.2 Experiments

All sciences are based on experimentation. An experiment is usually conducted in an environment such as a laboratory where background or extraneous variables can be controlled (lighting, temperature, noise levels, etc.). The experimenter

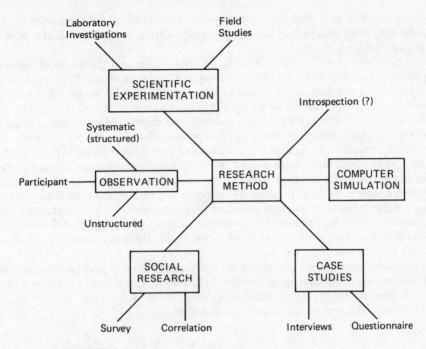

Figure 17.1 Methods of research in psychology

controls all such conditions which could alter the subject's behaviour during the investigation. For instance, a noisy environment may distract subjects having their intelligence tested. In addition to the background variables there are two variables which are unique to experiments.

The **independent variable** (IV) is that aspect of the experiment which the experimenter (E) manipulates (i.e., causes systematic changes to) so as to examine any effects this has on the **dependent variable**. For instance, in an investigation of the effects of a drug on memory the subjects would be administered with different levels of the drug prior to testing. The drug is therefore the IV.

The dependent variable (DV) is that aspect of the subject's behaviour which the experimenter measures whilst the IV is being manipulated. In the instance of testing memory after giving a drug them memory is the DV.

Subjects, samples and populations

Any person who volunteers to help in a psychological investigation is called a subject (abbreviated to S). In the experiment it is essential that subjects are selected *randomly*. Random sampling means that each person in the population has an equal chance of being selected. Subjects should also be selected *independently*. This means that the selection of one subject in no way influences the selection of another. For instance, if one person from a group of friends volunteers to assist then others from that particular group should not be included simply because they happen to be around. Such precautions are necessary to avoid *biased* samples such as including a group of friends who have similar views, age, gender, and so on.

Experimenters are conducted so as to discover general truths about human behaviour (see Figure 17.2): either relating to all humans, or specific groups such as pre-school children, adult females, college students, and so on. Obviously it would be impossible to test all the people in such a large *population* of individuals and so small numbers of these are randomly and independently selected to take part in the experiment. The small group of people selected in this way are referred to as the *sample*. If the sample is truly unbiased then what is found to occur in the experiment based upon these individuals should also be true of individuals in the population at large. In other words, experimental results are used to generalize from the sample to the population by *inference*. Measurement of the behaviour of the sample is used to infer or estimate that behaviour in the population. For instance, in the drug example, if we find that memory of the sample was improved after they have taken the drug then we estimate that this improvement is also true in the population.

Experiments are *inductive* in that they attempt to explain general principles of behaviour using evidence from specific observations. The scientific method is said to be *nomothetic* in that it generalizes from what is found in one group of individuals (the sample) to others (the population).

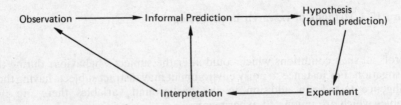

Figure 17.2 Experimental method

Experimental hypothesis

Scientific investigations always begin by devising a hypothesis or prediction of the outcome. For instance, in an investigation of sex differences in toy play in 3-year-old children, there may be reason to predict that one sex may participate more in object play than the other. In this case the hypothesis is said to be *directional* (i.e., not only is the investigator predicting that a sex difference exists in such play but also which of the sexes will show more of this play). Should no previous research have already examined the issue then the investigator may simply predict that a sex difference exists without specifying which sex will show more object play. This would be a *non-directional* hypothesis. The prediction which reflects the experimenter's belief prior to conducting the experiment is called the experimental hypothesis, or H1.

The hypothesis is a formal prediction. In this sense it must be a succinct and precise statement of what the experimenter expects to occur. For instance, the notion that 'boys play differently from girls' would not serve as a hypothesis because it does not specify the ages of the children concerned, the particular kind of play (e.g. pretend play, object play, etc), or the precise situation in which their play took place such as time of day and week, whether at home or school, and so forth. A hypothesis uses 'operational definitions'.

Operational definitions

Where a term or concept being investigated is vague then an operational definition will express the precise meaning which the experimenter tends to employ in his or her investigation. For instance, the term 'memory' might be operationally defined as the 'ability to recall a 20-word list after a two-minute interval from learning'. The term 'play' given in the example above might be operationally defined as 'the amount of time spent in manipulating a toy object'. Such definitions make the hypothesis more precise and therefore easier to test (i.e., prove either true or false). The notion that boys play in different ways from girls might now be written as the hypothesis: 'in a nursery setting, boys spend more time manipulating toy objects than do girls, at the age of 3 years'. (Can you state whether this is a 'directional' or a 'non-directional' hypothesis?)

Null hypothesis

The purpose of an experiment is to test whether or not a hypothesis is true. However, the hypothesis tested is not the experimental one. The null hypothesis is always what the experiment tests. The null hypothesis predicts that the experimental treatment (the IV) will have no influence on the performance (the DV) of subjects. For instance, the experimental hypothesis that: 'In the nursery, 3-year-old boys spend more time manipulating toy objects than do 3-year-old girls' would be turned into the null hypothesis that: 'In the nursery there is no sex difference in the time spent in manipulating toy objects'. There are many sound logical reasons why the null hypothesis is phrased in this way, but the primary purpose of the null hypothesis is to predict that the IV will *not* influence the DV. If no such effect is observed on the DV then the null hypothesis may be said to have been proved indisputably true. Conversely an experimental hypothesis, such as 'Eating sugar causes tooth decay' could never be proved true because it is always possible that some other variable (besides the IV) could have caused this effect on the DV (in this case, tooth decay). For instance, it may be that sugar itself causes some chemical change in saliva and that this periodical lack of protection from saliva is what leads to the decay of teeth.

The example just given (fictitious, by the way) illustrates that a statement predicting an effect of the IV on the DV (the 'experimental hypothesis') cannot be proved true with any certainty whereas the null hypothesis can be. Therefore, the null hypothesis provides the experimenter with a prediction that may be verified *without ambiguity*.

Interpreting experimental results

Although details of how to analyse experimental data are not given in this book, brief mention is needed here to emphasize an important principle of interpreting experimental results. Specifically, if the null hypothesis has been proved true then this does *not* mean that the experiment has been a failure. A result which informs the experimenter that the prediction made in the experimental hypothesis is untrue nonetheless adds to scientific knowledge. For instance, the finding that 3-year-old boys do not play more with object toys in the nursery (another fictitious example) is an important finding and needs to be reported as such. Despite its contradicting the experimenter's hypothesis it is still just as important to the advance of knowledge as if significant differences had been found. This is especially important when your result is at odds with the findings of other researchers. Of course, the experiment you conducted may have had its short-comings, but it is an error to describe an experiment (or any investigation) as having 'failed' because the hypothesis was not supported.

Experimental design

There are two main ways of designing an experiment so as to test a hypothesis. These are (a) the repeated-measures design, and (b) the independent-groups design.

Repeated-measures design

In this design each subject takes part in all conditions of the experiment. For instance, if we wanted to compare the effects of caffeine on people's reaction time then each of the subjects in our sample would be tested for their speed of reaction both with and without caffeine in their body. However, if we test the subjects first without caffeine and then give them each a cup of strong coffee we may find that they all become faster in the second test. But this decrease in reaction time may not have been caused by the caffeine at all: it could simply be due to the fact that all the subjects have become used to the reaction test and are better the second time because of their practice. To eliminate this problem of 'order effects' with repeated-measures designs a technique called 'counter-balancing' is used.

Counter-balancing   When an experimenter uses a repeated-measures design s/he must consider how to eliminate order effects, such as the practice which subjects will have had when taking part in the second condition. If the task involves a physical skill such as that involved in demonstrating reaction time then subjects will probably improve with practice. Alternatively, if the task is a boring one then they may get worse as it when tested more than once. This may be due to fatigue, boredom or just relaxation of effort. These are all order effects and counter-balancing is the means by which the experimenter cancels them out. Counter-balancing is achieved in the following way.

Rather than testing all the subjects in one condition followed by the next, counter-balancing means that the sample of subjects is arranged into groups. The number of groups involved will depend upon the number of conditions in the experiment. Let us take the simplest case of two groups. One of these groups will be tested on the first task, A, followed by the second task, B. The second group will be tested in reverse order (i.e., B followed by A). In the reaction time example, half the subjects tested will have been given no caffeine prior to their first test, whereas the other half will have drunk the strong coffee just before their first test. Prior to the second test there will need to be an interval of at least two hours for both groups. For the group taking the coffee test first they will need this time for the caffeine to be eliminated from their systems. The second group are also given the two-hour interval to ensure they are treated identically. To illustrate this general procedure see Table 17.1

Table 17.1   *Counter-balancing the subject order in a repeated-measures design*

Subject no	Condition	
	First task	Second task
1	with coffee	without coffee
2	without coffee	with coffee
3	with coffee	without coffee
4	without coffee	with coffee
5	... etc.	

Independent-groups design

In the independent-groups design each subject takes part in only one of the conditions of the experiment. For instance, if we wanted to find out if watching violent films increases the aggressive behaviour of children we could measure this behaviour in one group of children who had just watched such a film and compare it with another group who had seen a non-violent film of the same duration. Note that in this example the two groups are separate and independent (i.e., none of the children take part in more than one of the groups). In the case of this example the first group are referred to as the experimental group because they are given the experimental treatment (the violent film). The second group are referred to as a control condition because they are providing the basis of comparison against which the experimental group is tested. The problem of control groups does not arise in repeated-measures designs because the subjects are themselves acting as their own control condition in one of their contributions.

Matched-subjects design   The independent-groups design sometimes causes problems when one (or more) of the subjects in one group are simply more capable at the task than the others. Such superior performance in the experimental (or control) task can bias the overall performance of that group and thus cause the experimenter to draw false conclusions from the study. The repeated-measures design does eliminate this problem because the same group of subjects takes part in both the experimental and the control conditions. However, a third type of design is sometimes used in these circumstances, which is hybrid between the two previous designs and is called 'matched-subjects'.

In this design two groups of subjects are chosen, so it is similar to the independent-groups design. However, the second group of subjects are not simply selected at random from the population. Instead, each subject in the first group is paired with a partner who matches her/him in the charcteristic which is being tested in the experiment. For instance, suppose we are testing the effects of a drug on the ability of sprinters to improve their times. We could give the drug to a sample of athletes. Since we are going to assess the effects of the drug on the sample we need to compare them against a second sample of sprinters who, one-for-one, match the running ability of the first group. Suppose sprinter A from the drugged condition can run 100 metres in 10.5 seconds, then we need to match this athlete with another from the no-drug condition who runs at or near to this time over the same distance. Of course, in the case of drug trials we would also need to match them for body size and weight also. Next we need to find a suitable match for the second sprinter in the drugged condition, and so on.

The most frequently-used matched-subjects designs in psychological investigation have been twin studies, such as those involved in research into whether or not intelligence is inherited.

Table 17.2   *Summary of the advantages and disadvantages of using the two main experimental designs*

	Repeated measures	*Independent groups*
Advantages	Uses fewer subjects (i.e., half the number needed in the independent-groups design). No bias is caused to one group of the study due to the different starting levels of ability shown by some groups in the independent-groups design.	There are no delays between conditions for the subjects since each subject only takes part in one condition only. No order effects occur and so the design and its application are normally straightforward. It is possible to use this design on virtually any research problem.
Disadvantages	The design considerations, such as counter-balancing, sometimes make this a complex design to employ. Occasionally this design is impossible because of the nature of the study (e.g., in the case of a study of sex differences in ability it is not possible to use the same group (males, say) for the second condition as well).	The design is susceptible to being biased when subjects (or even one of them) in one group are superior or inferior in their general performance to those subjects in the other group. It is wasteful of subjects since they each perform only once in the study.

17.3   Observation Studies

Scientific investigations usually begin by a phase of observation. There are a number of ways in which **observational studies** can be done: unstructured, structured (systematic) or participant.

Unstructured observations are not commonly made since they provide no measurable data and take the form of descriptions of behaviour. The same criticisms which applied to introspection (where the person simply records their own thoughts, feelings and motives) also apply to unstructured observations of other people. In these cases the observer simply keeps some form of record of what they 'saw' at particular times during the study. Of course, from what psychologists already know about the role of subjectivity in both perception and memory, it is unlikely that any two observers in this unstructured situation will record the same account of an event they have both witnessed.

Participant observation is more a sociological method of research than a psychological one. The method simply involves the researcher in a close involvement with the day-to-day lives of the person(s) they are studying. This may mean that observers actually take part in the same activities in the workplace (or other environment which has been chosen for the investigation) as the persons under study. They literally observe events whilst participating in them as an insider. Of course, in order that the individuals being studied do not alter their behaviour as a consequence of being closely studied in this way (the so-called 'Hawthorne effect') then subterfuge is usually required. In this case the subjects themselves are not aware that the observer is in reality a social scientist conducting research. There is a definite matter of ethics involved in all investigations using participant observation, as you may well realize.

Structured, or systematic observation is often the starting point of scientific investigations under more controlled conditions. A systematic observational study is designed to limit the scientist to the recording of only a small number of events or behaviours. This enables much greater degrees of accuracy and reliability to be established because, by narrowing down the study to a manageable and predetermined phenomenon, the observer will be able to be more objective in what is recorded. In addition the observations are usually 'time sampled' (i.e., instead of sitting for long periods aimlessly noting down events the observer only records the event(s) of interest during certain intervals of time which have been systematically worked out in advance). For instance, the schedule of recording observations may require only the first ten minutes of every hour over one day to be 'sampled'. Even though the behaviour of interest may be occurring at other times in the day the focus of the study is only those intervals of the day which appear in the schedule. This prevents the errors which may arise from long periods of observation as well as providing a much more balanced view of the frequency or occurrence of the behaviour in question, because it is being recorded over a greater period of time (potentially) than would be achieved in a single sitting.

Figure 17.3 shows an example of what a systematic observation schedule may look like in an investigation of play behaviour in a group of children in a nursery school. Although the categories of behaviour being observed seem random they would usually form part of a codified system which could then be statistically analysed. In fact it is most often the case that data from systematic observations is in a form which may be treated with the usual scientific analysis, rather than being vague descriptions such as often occurs with other forms of observational study.

17.4 Case Studies

Although psychology aims to explain the general principles and laws which govern human behaviour, there are occasions when particular individuals are studied in depth. This is usually because of some specific unique trait or experience which they have had, such as brain injury or some form of social deprivation. For instance, if someone suffers an injury which damages part of the

---

OBSERVATION SCHEDULE FOR INVESTIGATION OF PLAY IN 3-YEAR OLDS

Date 27 Feb. 1990   Location St Mary's Nursery   Observer N.H.
                                    Playgroup

TIME	CHILDREN (code only)	MAIN ACTIVITY
9–9.10	A,B	Dolls in pushchair
10–10.10	C,D	Play fight with plastic swords. Ended with C in tears.
11–11.10	E,F	Playing with counters by stacking them on a board
12–12.10	G,H	Plasticine, then dolls.
1–1.10	A,B	Water fighting. Return to dolls at 1.07
2–2.10	C,D	Throwing ball to each other.
3–3.10	E,F	Looking at picture in a colouring book

Figure 17.3 Example of a schedule for a systematic observation study

brain then the psychologist would learn from what changes may occur in the behaviour or mental life of that person the relationship between the brain function of that area and behaviour in normal people. This is not simply a question of intruding into the person's life, because what has been learnt in such ways may help us to understand and to help people suffering similar traumas. Similarly, the study of people who have experienced unfortunate loss or deprivation in childhood (especially the attachment studies described in Chapter 1) has helped social scientists to suggest improvements in the institutional and community care programmes for them. However, the use of case study information has not been as valuable in the more general sense in psychology because of its concern with the uniqueness, rather than generality, of the subject(s) under study.

17.5 Large-Scale Social Research

There are occasions when a large sample of the population are studied rather than the usual small groups which psychologists use in scientific experiments. For instance, in the case of a study concerned with political attitudes there are so many shades of opinion that a small sample would not be representative of what is happening in the population at large. In such cases social scientists employ **survey methods** which are capable of reaching the large numbers of people required. Surveys often involve standard forms of questionnaire in which the respondent may either answer 'yes', 'no' or 'don't know' to each question, or else they may be more sophisticated and have a range of possible responses for each question, depending upon how strongly the respondent feels about the issue. One example of such a question might be:

> 'Do you believe that television should be censored in the way that it is?'

Strongly believe		Neutral		Strongly believe
YES	**YES**	**DON'T KNOW**	**NO**	**NO**

and the respondent simply ticks the place on the form which best represents their views. The advantage of this type of survey is that the data may be analysed in a more detailed way, so that not only may the percentages of people answering this way or that be known, but it is also possible to measure the strength of their beliefs simply by applying some form of scale to the responses, such as by counting the strong 'yes' response as '1' and the strong 'no' response as '5' (with the intermediate positions suitably labelled), and this would be amenable to more sophisticated statistical analysis.

17.6 Correlation

This is another technique which requires more subjects than usual in psychological investigations. The aim of correlation studies is to investigate whether or not two (or more) measured quantities seem to occur together in people. For instance, people who are tall tend to be heavier than those who are short; this is an example of a correlation between two physical characteristics. A scientist may wish to know if there is a relationship between intelligence and memory and so could employ a correlation study which measured the IQ and memory ability in a sample of people so that each of them contributed a score on both scales. The statistical technique of correlation then simply measures the extent (if at all) to which these two characteristics occur together in people. In other words, if a high correlation exists between memory and intelligence then it would mean that people who have good memories do well in IQ tests and, vice versa, that those having poor memory performance would have the lowest IQ scores, and so on. However, correlation is not a scientific technique in the true sense because it is not able to suggest a cause–effect relationship between the two characteristics.

Just because a correlation exists between the two characteristics this does not mean that one of them causes the presence of the other. In the example quoted, if the study did show that there was a high correlation between memory and IQ then this would not mean that being intelligent gives you a better memory than average, or that memory 'causes' you to be intelligent. No such relationship can be inferred from correlation studies, and this is their weakness.

17.7 Computer Simulation

This is related to the field of artificial intelligence and is concerned with modelling aspects of human mental life. Computers have been compared to humans in their ability to process information. The main area in which this has proved valuable is in cognitive psychology, where comparisons have been made regarding the way in which information is represented in memory. Other applications have examined the process of human problem-solving and attempts have been made to simulate this in playing games and in decision-making.

17.8 Questions and Exercises

1. Write yourself an observation schedule for use in studying the eye contact of a teacher with her or his students in the course of a lesson. Assume the lesson to be one hour long and that observations are to be recorded on the fifth minute throughout that time. Only one observation is to be recorded at each of those times: that is, whether or not the teacher is making eye contact with any student at that instant.
2. Having written out your schedule, perform the study! a word of caution: do not upset your teacher by failing to attend or follow the content of the lesson. If you think the teacher may be offended then ask permission to perform your study before the lesson starts (without necessarily giving full details). Analyse your results over the period of the hour and try to determine if any changes seem to have taken place over that time in the amount of eye contact observed.
3. Using Figure 17.1, make a list of the various methods of research used in psychology and put them into an order which you regard to be 'most scientific' to 'least scientific'. Try to justify your list when it is complete by writing the criteria down for what characterizes a 'good' scientific approach.
4. For a repeated-measures design which is going to investigate the effects of sleep loss on mental arithmetic, note down how you would go about counter-balancing the subjects in the two groups of 'sleep deprived' and 'normal'. Take as the criterion for sleep deprivation the loss of one night's sleep.

18 The work of the psychologist

18.1 Introduction

If psychology is broadly defined as the study of behaviour then it is not surprising that a wealth of career opportunities exist which involve the subject. Psychologists work in a variety of areas, many of which require a basic qualification in the subject often supplemented by higher qualifications and experience. Despite the diversity of occupations available, a common thread is that psychologists usually work with people (or with people in mind: for example, helping to design better working environments).

This chapter will outline the main specialist roles for psychologists, together with other careers in which a knowledge of psychology is useful.

18.2 The Clinical Psychologist

Clinical psychologists help people which behavioural and emotional problems. These may range from those associated with mental illness (such as schizophrenia or depression) to physical problems (such as assisting in the treatment of eating disorders). Most work in the National Health Service where they are involved in assessing, and subsequently treating, people of all ages.

The clinical psychologist seldom works alone, but instead is part of a highly trained team of other specialists such as doctors, nurses, psychiatrists and social workers. This enables the patients' problems to be diagnosed and treated from a number of perspectives, including a follow-up of their progress (after treatment).

A detailed knowledge of therapies and techniques allows the trained clinical psychologist to overcome problems such as the treatment of phobias by teaching patients how to relax in stressful situations (see Chapter 12). Similarly, they may provide teaching and training programmes for handicapped children and their parents, as well as teaching nurses how to implement behaviour therapies.

Apart from the various duties and roles described above, clinical psychologists may work in academic institutions carrying out research into, for example, the causes of psychotic depression, or they may lecture on various aspects of the subject at universities and colleges.

In order to become a clinical psychologist a first degree in psychology is required, followed by a higher degree or post-graduate training, possibly on and in-service (probationary) basis. Finally, on successful completion of The British Psychological Society's Diploma in Clinical Psychology (or its equivalent elsewhere), a person may take up a position with the health service, starting as a Basic Grade Clinical Psychologist and then moving up the scale as experience is gained.

18.3 The Occupational Psychologist

Occupational psychologists are concerned with the many issues arising from people in their work environment. They may be involved with the structure of organizations, productivity, job satisfaction, selection, personnel and training. Their general aim is to improve the quality of working life: for example, by indicating way to increase efficiency or combat stress, or by supervising staff-training schemes, so on.

Many work in industries and businesses where they may act as consultants in helping companies solve problems effectively. Occupational psychologists also work in universities and colleges, carrying out research into various aspects of employment and unemployment.

The job itself requires skill and expertise in all the many areas associated with people at work. On the one hand they must be familiar with the general processes that take place within an organization, whilst also showing an awareness of the individual's capabilities and limitations. They may operate alone or as part of a team with a number of other specialists such as personnel or training officers, senior managers and statisticians.

Entry into this field is gained usually by taking a first degree in psychology, after which a higher degree involving occupational psychology is carried out. From here suitable candidates may apply to individual organizations, perhaps starting off in personnel management. A number of larger companies have a clearly defined career structure with particular posts being dependent upon qualifications and experience.

18.4 The Educational Psychologist

Educational psychologists look at the ways in which people learn and so are concerned with the processes that take place both inside and outside the classroom. Much of their work may focus on children, where they may be responsible for diagnosing and treating problems associated with learning and education. In this respect they will often work alongside the child's parents and teachers and, in some cases, social workers. Educational psychologists may also work on devising learning programmes and as such develop new methods of instruction, including those involving computers (e.g, designing computer software for use by those with learning difficulties).

They may be given responsibility for children who are referred to them by other professionals and so act as special advisers where education is involved. If a child is referred to them, perhaps with behavioural problems, their work will entail observing the child in a variety of settings, including home and school. Apart from this observation they may often administer psychometric tests, the results of which are used to highlight particular problems and guide the psychologist in suggesting appropriate action or advice.

Educational psychologists tend mainly to be employed by education authorities where they may be responsible for schools within a particular area. However, they may also work within assessment centres and children's hospitals, as well as in further and higher education institutions where they are involved in teaching and training future teachers. Some may work in universities and colleges, where they conduct research into many aspects of the learning process.

The usual route to becoming an educational psychologist is first to obtain a degree in psychology, followed by a teaching qualification (such as the PGCE) in order to gain some teaching experience. Normally at least two years of experience are required before applying for a training course in educational psychology at a university of polytechnic, although this may vary. On completion of this course, a person starts work in the psychological section of an education authority.

18.5 The Criminological Psychologist

Criminology concerns itself with the study of crime, criminals and penology, and psychologists involved in this field may work in a variety of settings. Among these are positions in approved schools, remand centres and hospitals that deal with high security patients.

One of the main areas is within the prison service, working as a Prison Psychologist, with responsibilities that involve both prisoners and prison officers. The duties of a Prison Psychologist might include training staff in, for instance, interview techniques or how to cope with particularly dangerous situations that arise with inmates. They also deal with the assessment and treatment of prisoners from a psychological perspective, essentially concentrating on psychological problems which prisoners face (such as depression or institutionalization). Attempts are also made to understand why an individual is in prison, and the effects which imprisonment may be having upon them.

Criminological psychologists may also be found within branches of the Home Office working for government agencies, and in higher education where they lecture or carry out research on various aspects of criminology.

The normal route into criminological psychology involves post-graduate training within a chosen specialist field. Entry into the prison service as a Prison Psychologist involves first taking a degree in psychology followed by an application to the Home Office for the position of Trainee Prison Psychologist. Successful candidates are then posted to a prison where they work under the supervision of an experienced psychologist.

18.6 The Psychology Teacher

In recent years psychology has risen in popularity as a subject taught within schools and colleges, and as such there has been an increase in the demand for psychology teachers. A number of examining boards now provide at least one psychology syllabus as a guide for teachers, which outlines the course content and indicates the topic areas on which examinations are based. Typically these include a general introduction to the main theories and ideas of the subject together with an outline of experimental design and related concepts. Increasingly, with the introduction of new courses in education, psychology teachers may be called upon to service courses in which psychological aspects are found, such as nursing and management qualifications.

Normally, in order to become a psychology teacher a degree in psychology is preferred, after which a teaching qualifications is required. Several colleges of higher education run courses, usually a year in length, to train potential psychology teachers and, having gained a teaching qualification, a person may then apply directly to schools and colleges. The first year of employment as a teacher is often a probationary period, but upon satisfactory completion it then becomes a permanent post.

Psychology teachers also work in universities and polytechnics teaching undergraduates and post-graduate students, although for these posts a higher degree (such as a doctorate) is usually necessary. The majority of university and polytechnic lectures also tend to be actively involved with research.

SPOTLIGHT   What do psychologists do?

From reading this brief introduction to the work of psychologists, you may already be quite surprised at the scope and depth of their involvement in many walks of life. However, we have only given a fleeting glimpse, for in fact almost any job which involves people could at some time require or involve the services of a psychologist.

- List as many different jobs or careers that come to mind and consider whether a psychologist (or in fact a knowledge of psychology) could contribute to them.

18.7   Other Specialist and Non-specialist Careers

Apart from the careers outlined so far in this unit there are a number of other specialist and non-specialist fields within which a knowledge of psychology is useful, and in some cases a requirement. Some occupations allow for a combination of different fields, and one such example is psychiatric social work. As the name suggests, this is concerned with social work in a psychiatric setting. Often teaming up with other professionals (such as nurses, teachers and psychologists), psychiatric social workers are involved with children and adults who may be experiencing emotional difficulties and other problems. They might work in day centres for the mentally ill, assessing the patients' needs, providing support, and also helping in their adjustment to everyday life when they leave the centre. Other cases may involve working with emotionally disturbed children, giving guidance and support, and discussing problems with their families.

The normal entry requirement into this field is a relevant first degree and the Certificate of Qualification in Social Work (CQSW) which is offered by a number of colleges and universities.

Counselling is an area of psychology which involves helping people solve problems, make decisions and generally cope with the stresses encountered in everyday life. There are several areas within which counsellors may specialize. Some work in educational establishments where they provide a source of help for personal problems and vocational guidance, or offer advice and assistance with study skills. Counsellors also work in industrial and medical fields as well as in counselling agencies, which provide guidance on a whole range of relationship and marital problems, drug abuse, bereavement, depression, and so on.

Counsellors come from a variety of academic backgrounds and, whilst a degree in psychology is not essential, it may be useful in providing a framework for the methods and approaches found in the subject. Personal qualities and experience tend to be of greater importance than educational qualifications, although counselling skills can (to some extent) be learnt and several colleges run training courses for those interested in becoming counsellors.

Opportunities also exist in many areas and situations where research is important. Here psychologists may be involved in the application of psychological techniques and methods to people and their environment. Many government departments, agencies and universities have their own research units which employ psychologists. The nature of the research will depend largely upon the purpose which the agency or department serves but, as an example, applied psychologists and researchers might work within aviation designing surveys to investigate problems experienced by aircrew, such as the efects of long-distance flights and the factors which might be likely to induce stress.

Normally a higher degree together with relevant training is necessary for most research posts. Potential employers, such as government agencies, the armed forces and industrial institutions, will have their own clearly-defined career structure.

Although the careers outlined so far in this unit have required at least a first degree in psychology, a knowledge of the subject at pre-degree level is useful and in some cases a requirement for many occupations, particularly those which involve working with people. The following list is by no means complete but offers an idea of such careers: these include the nursing profession, personnel training, management, speech therapy, occupational therapy and market research. Finally, for further information regarding psychology and careers, contact: The British Psychological Society, St Andrews House, 48 Princess Road East, Leicester, LE1 7DR.

18.8 Questions and Exercises

1. Describe the similarities and differences in careers between any two specialist psychology positions.
2. Contact your local careers office and collect information for a project entitles 'Careers in Psychology'.
3. List the institutions in your area which might employ psychologists and contact them requesting information regarding job details, career structure, etc.
4. Devise and carry out a role-playing exercise based on an interview for a job as one of the specialist psychologists outlined in this chapter.

19 Historical issues in psychology

19.1 Introduction

This chapter has two aims: first, to provide examples of the major theoretical and philosophical questions which have run through the development of psychology; and second, to illustrate the importance of historical contributions to the development of psychological theories. Most students at the outset of their studies in psychology and the other social sciences shy away from historical readings. The reason for this is generally that they wish to acquire only contemporary knowledge (the state of the art, as it were). However, the discipline of psychology has perhaps just as many unresolved issues now as it did when it was a branch of philosophy in the early nineteenth century. The pages of current research journals still contain issues which have been approached from many angles for over a century or more, mostly without resolution. Indeed, a psychology textbook which included only the issues which have been resolved would be a very slim volume indeed. But it is also a useful task in this technologically-sophisticated era to return to the contributions made by the pioneers of the discipline who gave psychology both its direction as well many of its challenges. In this chapter a brief introduction is given to some of the issues which still lurk behind much of today's research. The second half of the chapter discusses some historical views of human behaviour which date mainly to the nineteenth century when, surprisingly, the reader will find echoes of views expressed in other chapters on current research issues.

19.2 The Nature–Nurture Debate

Philosophers ever since the time of the Ancient Greeks have discussed the relative contributions of instinct (nature) and learning (nurture) in forming human behaviour and personality. As we saw in Chapter 13, ethologists take for granted that across species there are varying degrees of how much both inheritance and learning may influence behaviour. Insects would illustrate one extreme of this scale, and primates the other. The origins of ethology date from Darwin's work on evolutionary theory, which expressed the idea that inheritance is a major cause of even complex behaviour patterns in many animal species. Ethologists such as Lorenz, Tinbergen and Huxley have described a number of instinctual behaviour patterns as well as giving accounts of why these have evolved.

Yet, despite all this, psychologists have tended to reject the term 'instinct' as a label for behaviour because, historically, it has been most often used to describe behaviours which a researcher could not otherwise explain. One such example which is often cited is that of William McDougall, who described a number of complex human social behaviours as instinctive, including the desire to acquire wealth!

Prior to the discovery of Mendel's work on genetics (1866) there was no biological foundation to explain inheritance and so this was one reason why contemporary psychologists rejected it so forcefully. Even though the scientists of that time understood that in order to breed winning racehorses the right pedigree was required, they did not recognize that inheritance operated in a similar fashion in humans, even playing a part in determining complex behaviour patterns such as personality, intelligence and emotionality.

Nowadays the nature–nurture debate still lies behind many psychological theories even though its ability to arouse fervent debate has diminished. The reason for the decline in interest in the issue is the discovery over the past century that much of human development occurs as an interaction between what is inherited and the environment which affects the growing offspring. In other words, behaviour is known to occur through other means besides purely nature–nurture ones. The pre-programming of changes in the lifespan which arise through the process of maturation makes most of the original debate redundant.

19.3 Reductionism in Psychology

Reductionism is the belief held by some scientists that in order to explain any natural event fully we must break it down into its smallest units. Only after explanations have been made of how the units themselves operate, followed by the discovery of how these units then function at their next highest level and so on, will we ever be in a position to understand the event in its true form.

However, the scientific approach to psychology has often been mistakenly assumed to mean that human behaviour must be analysed at the level of nerve cells before a theory can emerge. This is not the point of the scientific approach to the subject because no psychologist believes that behaviour must be reduced to the atomic level before it can be understood. The only issue concerning reductionism in psychology is to what level should we reduce our descriptions before we accept them as the 'best' explanations of behaviour?

Philosophers are once more the responsible agents for introducing the reductionist controversy into psychology. However, unlike the majority of such issues, reductionism is an implicit rather than an explicit debate. For instance, the level at which any given psychologist chooses to work will imply the things they are prepared to take for granted. Neuropsychologists assume that activity in the nervous system is causing the behaviour of the whole person (at least with regard in the specific research that they are conducting). Similarly, cognitive psychologists reduce the human mind into a number of operating systems such as the attentional system, the memory system, the perceptual one, and so on.

Social psychologists seek to explain behaviour by going beyond the individual processes. They look for explanations of behaviour in terms of how individuals relate to each other, and speak in terms such as 'social influence'. The level at which any theory of behaviour is aimed will indicate the point at which that theoriest assumes that ultimate explanations lie. In this sense the social psychologist who employs one set of jargon to describe interpersonal perception is working at a level incompatible with that of the neuropsychologist who studies perceptual processes in physical terms, despite their apparently similar concerns.

The philosopher J. S. Mill described the phenomenon using the term 'emergent properties'; by which he meant that, when an object is examined at a given level, it contains features or qualities which are irreducible. This means that things are fundamentally different in nature at each new level of study. For instance, sodium and chloride combine in certain proportions to give the white solid NaCl, or common salt. The texture, appearance and other qualities of salt are not predictable from any combination of sodium, which is a metal, and chloride (a gas), and so salt is said to have 'emergent properties'. Another, more psychological, example is the concept of beauty we see in a person's face. 'Looks' are not contained in the person's individual features but only in the way they come together to form the face. Similarly, in human behaviour there are levels beyond which it becomes meaningless to reduce a phenomenon in order to explain it.

However, most psychologists are content to take an 'eclectic' approach to their subject: that is, to accept, at least for the time being, that explanations must operate at different levels simultaneously. Sometimes the assumptions made by the different approaches seem to be in conflict to the student but this is an inevitable stage in the young science and, once accommodated to, can add to the excitement of its study.

19.4 Mind–Body Dualism

Is consciousness situated in the soul or in the brain? A surprising number of scientists, both past and present, take a religious view of the existence of the human soul. Dualism refers to the existence of a separate 'soul' which is not tied to any physical reality but is a separate and metaphysical entity. For behaviourists, such as John Watson, a concept such as consciousness is a meaningless one in psychology because it is beyond explanation, given that it has any credence as a term in its own right. The French philosopher Descartes believed that consciousness is situated with the soul in a gland buried deep inside the brain, known as the pineal. To Descartes, the unusual location of the pineal amongst all that brain tissue seemed to explain why consciousness seems to be a feeling 'above' the usual everyday activity of the brain.

In the second half of the twentieth century the debate over where consciousness is seated has re-emerged. This has been partly due to the discovery of the different brain waves associated with various states of consciousness (Aserinsky and Kleitman, 1953). It is also known that drugs alter consciousness by influencing specific brain structures.

Some writers, such as Griffin (1976), have claimed that it is plausible to study conscious awareness in animals. Others have relegated consciousness to being a function within a function as, for instance, in the models of Atkinson and Shiffrin or of Baddeley (1986), where consciousness is an executive in control of memory processes. Freud maintained that consciousness exists on more than one level and that there are essential relationships with unconscious processes which need investigation.

As this brief discussion illustrates, there is far from a general agreement about what the content or product of consciousness may be, or whether there may be some metaphysical force governing human thought, but the view of most psychologists is that these are issues best left in abeyance until more mundane knowledge has been established.

19.5   Historical Perspectives on Psychology

The rest of this chapter provides the student with a selection of ideas which were proposed by the pioneers of the subject. These are included in this textbook to illustrate how the roots of investigation in psychology were set by the nineteenth century philosophers and experimental physiologists. Most of the issues raised by the sample of historical figures still remain in current research effort. Some of their theories have been pirated by later psychologists and you should learn from this exercise that scientific ideas are rarely created anew from data; they are the products of many minds and over many generations.

Alexander Bain (1818–1903) believed that the philosophical method of introspection ought to be abandoned in favour of scientific observation. Bain believed that the brain was an essential area of study for psychology and that human beings are essentially active creatures, driven by the forces from within the nervous system. The energy for this driving force he thought came from habits, emotions and attitudes. Behaviour becomes 'shaped' from our earliest movements, which he thought occurred to begin with at random. This shaping of behaviour throughout life he believed to be the result of feelings of pleasure and pain which result from our activities, with those that bring us pleasure being repeated, but not those which bring pain. This line of reasoning was termed 'trial and error', which was later formulated in the hands of Thorndike into his 'law of effect'.

The German philosophers of the early nineteenth century linked psychology with the study of physics and began with empirical studies of the responses of sensory systems to stimulation. Hermann Lotze (1817–81) believed that the mind was reducible to physiology, specifically to the actions of the nervous system. He argued that only a few concepts were beyond scientific investigation, among these being such ideas as 'hope'.

Charles Bell (1774–1842) was a Scottish physicist who wrote about the 'specific energies of nerves' (1811). By this he meant that nerve pathways which mediate between the brain and our environment each deal with specific aspects or functions of that environment. The specific energy carried by a pathway will excite in the brain only one experience (e.g., sound energy does not produce hearing when applied to the skin, and light does not cause vision other than when applied to the visual pathways). When the same stimulus is applied to a number of different sense organs they will each deal with some different aspect of it: salt, for example has whiteness for vision, graininess for touch and flavour on the tongue. Whenever a sense organ is stimulated by energy other than its own only the one sensation occurs; when you press a finger against your closed eyelid it produces the sensation of lights flashing. These principles were later formulated by the German physiologist Müller, who is credited with having produced the more precise doctrine of the 'specific energies of nerves'.

Pierre Fluorens (1794–1867) was the first researcher to investigate the relationship between brain and behaviour in a scientific manner. Using animals he developed the technique known as 'ablation'. This method involves removing regions of the brain in the living animal so as to see what changes are caused to its behaviour. Such changes are then inferred to have been the result of the loss of functions suffered by the removal of that part of the brain. Fluorens' major discovery was that functions of the brain appear to be 'localized' (i.e., particular aspects of behaviour are controlled by particular brain regions). For instance, removing the cerebellum causes a loss of coordination in an animal's movements even though the ability to move the limbs is unaffected. He found that other ablations could cause perceptual blindness even though the pupils of the eyes still reacted to light. Despite these discoveries Fluorens wanted to emphasize the 'wholeness' of experience; although the brain may divide up its labour there is an essential unity of purpose to the whole system, which is the survival of the organism. Moreover, Fluorens found that when one area of the brain had been destroyed the resulting loss of function was often only temporary, showing the brain to be a self-regulating system. By this he meant that other regions must take over the functions which are lost when a part is destroyed. Fluorens discovered what neurophysiologists now refer to as 'plasticity' in the nervous system.

Pierre Paul Broca (1824–80) found that brain functions are not only localized in different regions but they may also be 'lateralized'. Lateralization is when one particular function is situated in one cerebral hemisphere only. Broca discovered that in the case of language there is an area in the left cerebral hemisphere which controls speech production. He called this area *circonvolution du language* (language area), but it was subsequently found to control only speech production.

Eduard Hitzig (1838–1907) and Gustav Fritsch (1838–1927) jointly discovered in 1864 that body movements are controlled by the brain on the opposite side: a region of the right cerebral cortex controls movements of the left side of the body, and vice versa for the left side of the brain. This is called decussation of function and is a general principle of both motor (muscle control) and sensory systems. The discovery that specific parts of the body can be caused to move independently by stimulating a brain region seemed to contradict Fluorens' hypothesis that the brain works as an integrated system. According to this new discovery the brain seems to comprise a multitude of separate control systems.

Ernst Weber (1795–1878) investigated tactile sensation (touch) and proposed that three different sensations are felt: pressure, temperature and location. Weber measured touch sensation by using two compass points pressing against the skin at different places of the body. He showed that with some body regions, such as the back, the points of the compasses need to be separated by a much larger distance than, say, on the back of the hand before the subject was able to report the presence of the second point (i.e., prior to this a single point only is perceived to be against the skin). Weber concluded from this that in some body regions there is a concentration of touch receptors and in other regions the receptors are more widely spaced. From this and other similar studies of sensory systems Weber proposed the idea of measuring the 'jnd', or just noticeable difference. A jnd is the least separation between one magnitude of the stimulus and another which the subject is able to perceive.

Johannes Müller (1801–58) conducted work on the 'specific energies of nerves' referred to above. Apart from this Müller discovered a number of important facts about human physiology which further advanced the theory of the mind as being a physiological entity. For instance, he discovered that, in addition to the purely reflex responsiveness found in the spinal cord, the brain is responsible for higher mental activities such as memory and thought.

Gustav Fechner (1807–87) believed strongly that mental events are mathematically related to the influx of energy from sense organs. He experimented in the field of psychophysics to show how sensory and mental experiences co-exist. His main work was published in 1860 and entitled *The Elements of Psychophysics*; in this book he outlined not only theoretical principles but also new ways of investigating mental responses to sensory events. Fechner's important theoretical contribution was his 'law' which relates stimulus intensity to sensation. This is described as:

$$S = k_{log}I$$

where S is sensation, k is a constant, and I is stimulus intensity. In words, the sensation caused by a stimulus increases logarithmically with its intensity. This means that a sensation increases tenfold in intensity each time the stimulus energy is doubled.

Hermann von Helmholtz (1821–94) made many discoveries in both physiology and psychology. For instance, in 1850 he succeeded in accurately measuring the speed of nerve impulses. He invented the myograph, which is a device for recording the *in vitro* contraction of muscle. In 1851 he invented the ophthalmoscope, which is a device for looking into the eye in the conscious patient. He developed a theory of colour vision which was initiated by an earlier physiologist called Thomas Young (the Young–Helmholtz theory). Helmholtz wrote a doctrine on the 'unconscious inference'. An unconscious inference is the set of assumptions we make whilst perceiving. It is the result of previous experiences with the stimulus (turn to section 6.12 for a discussion of this phenomenon). Modern psychology owes much to the work of von Helmholtz.

Wilhelm Wundt (1832–1920) is sometimes called the first experimental psychologist. This claim is mainly due to the fact that he established psychology as a science in its own right. His major contribution involved training the first generation of scientific psychologists in his purpose–built laboratory in Leipzig University from 1879 onwards. Although his greatest achievement was in teaching the experimental approach, Wundt did not himself believe that this was the only method psychologists should use in their investigations of human nature. Wundt, however, did stress the fundamental principle of using measurement and mathematical analysis as the essential part of psychological theorizing and this has remained so ever since.

Hermann Ebbinghaus (1850–1909) was the first psychologist to use experimental techniques for investigating one of the higher functions of the mind: that of memory. In 1885 he published a book describing the methods and results of hundreds of carefully-conducted experimental investigations into memory. Surprisingly for such a careful researcher, Ebbinghaus based most of his studies on testing his own memory for simple word-lists. In order to eliminate the effect of experience and prior learning, which would obviously influence memory performance involving everyday words, he invented hundreds of new words known as nonsense syllables or 'trigrams'. A trigram has three letters in the sequence of consonant–vowel–consonant (CVC) such as:

WUP   JOL   SAR   DAK   NEM

Using this approach Ebbinghaus formed a number of ideas which are still regarded as important contributions. For instance, he believed that a relationship existed between the amount of time spent in the original learning of the material and recall ability. He showed that *overlearning* is important to memory. He also described three processes of forgetting. Finally, Ebbinghaus described the effects of 'spaced' and 'massed' practice in learning which has implications for the learning of skills.

Georg Müller (1850–1934) is mainly remembered for his experimental work on memory. He made some major discoveries and inventions, such as the memory drum (a rotating device which automatically presents words to subjects during a memory test); the method of paired-associate learning; the serial position effect; and also the importance of parts- and whole-learning as a means of making learning more efficient.

Francis Galton (1822–1911) was the first 'psychometrician'. Psychometrics is the study of individual differences between people (the basis of the so-called idiographic approach in psychology). To do this Galton invented two important statistical methods which are commonly used today in psychology. The first of these is the use of the 'normal distribution' for describing how psychological characteristics may be dispersed in a population. Second, he devised a technique of measuring the degree of association between two variables, which is known as correlation (see Chapter 17). Galton also influenced the development of scientific psychology by always measuring behaviour. However, Galton's theories were sometimes (paradoxically) unscientific because he tended to draw unjustifiable conclusions from data. For instance, as discussed in Chapter 9, he concluded from a statistical analysis of the family relationships between famous people that intelligence must be inherited. He based this conclusion on the finding that eminent people occur more frequently in some families than in others. Since, he reasoned, the capacity to excel in any profession is linked with intellectual ability then intelligence must be an inherited phenomenon.

Although remembered for his contributions to psychology, Charles Darwin (1809–82) contributed an important perspective to behavioural science. Comparative psychology is the study of behaviour from an evolutionary perspective. Comparisons between human and animal behaviour allow us to discover the likely origins and functions of particular behaviour patterns. In his book, *The Expression of Emotions In Man and Animals* (1872), Darwin outlined his conviction that humans share many behaviours and even feelings with certain other species. He particularly drew attention to facial expressions which are common to humans, other primates, and even to more distant mammalian species. Darwin can therefore be said to be the originator of the scientific debate concerning the nature–nurture issue (i.e., how much of a given behaviour or mental experience has evolved and how much is the product of learning).

Douglas Spalding (1840–77) conducted experiments showing how behaviour may be inherited. He placed hoods on newly-hatched chicks so as to prevent them from gaining visual experience in the first three days of life. Within fifteen minutes of having removed the hoods the 3-day-old chicks were pecking at even very small objects with the same degree of accuracy shown by the normally-reared chicks. Spalding was also the first person to describe the process of imprinting which was later to be explored in detail by Konrad Lorenz (see Chapter 13).

C. Lloyd Morgan (1852–1936) wrote the famous 'canon' which states that 'in no case may we interpret an action as the outcome of a higher faculty if it can be interpreted as the . . . exercise of one . . . lower on the psychological scale'. Morgan was interested in discriminating between instinctive and learnt behaviour. He defined an instinct as behaviour which has the following features:

(a) it is common to all members of the species in question;
(b) it is uniform and repetitive in nature;

(c) it acts as a response to a specific stimulus;
(d) it is functional to that species (i.e., it aids survival).

Morgan described instinct as being an inherited response to a stimulus even though that response may itself become modified through learning, particularly becoming modified as a result of the good or bad outcomes it brings about for the animal. Such outcomes, he proposed, were 'reinforcement' for the given response: pleasure reinforces repetition of the response and pain reinforces its extinction. This terminology was adopted by the behaviourists in later years.

John B. Watson (1878–1958) developed **behaviourism** as a powerful theory in psychology. He argued that behaviour is the only subject matter of science because it is only the observable events which are capable of being analysed. In other words we cannot observe mental processes such as consciousness and so these are not terms which belong in the language of the psychologist. Watson also proposed that human behaviour arises through learning, with instinct playing only a very minor part. He argued that the basic event in all behaviour is the connection made by an organism between stimulus and response occurrences as it modifies its behaviour towards each stimulus that it encounters. An organism's behaviour is therefore reducible to the conglomerate of responses it makes and the units of this behaviour are the conditioned responses.

On the other hand, William McDougall (1871–1938) believed that instinct is essential to human behaviour. He used the word 'motive' to describe energy forces which are inherited. However, McDougall was not satisfied with the leading theories of motivation used by his contemporaries; for example, the so-called 'push' theories such as Freud's psychodynamic model, or the 'pull' theories, as described by the behaviourists like Skinner. McDougall conjured up metaphysical forces from within the human mind which he thought employed 'rational motives'. He described a number of social instincts such as 'gregariousness', 'self-assertion' and 'acquisitiveness'. These instincts were believed to be the inherited mechanisms responsible for maintaining the organism. However, McDougall's analysis was never popular amongst psychologists because it relied upon nativisim as the means of explanation. If anything, as a result of McDougall's theory psychologists became more convinced than ever that the word 'instinct' should be dropped from their dictionary of jargon.

19.6 Questions and Exercises

1. Describe two psychological topics which show how different levels of explanation may operate. An example of this might be as follows for the topic of gender:

    (a) someone's gender is a social phenomenon as illustrated by cultural differences in behaviour between the two sexes (level 1 – the sociocultural explanation);
    (b) gender is a biological phenomenon because sexual differentiation is maturational and involves hormonal events which are in turn controlled by the sex chromosomes (level 2 – the biological model).

Using this example, select another two topics and present them from at least two different levels.

2. Quote two physical studies from each side of the nature–nurture debate which seem to support these two explanations of behaviour.

3. Find one human behaviour which you think is not reducible to the actions of the nervous system (giving your reasons for why it could not be analysed in this way): for instance, you might select 'intelligence' or 'personality', since these are not fixed 'things' but change according to the person's experience.

Bibliography

* Recommended

Abramson, L. Y. and D. J. Martin (1981) Depression and the causal inference process, in J. H. Harvey, W. J. Ickes and R. F. Kidd (eds), *New directions in attitude research, vol 3*; Hillsdale, N. J: Lawrence Erlbaum.

Adorno, T. W., E. Frenkel-Brunswick, D. J. Levinson, and R. N. Sanford (1950) *The authoritarian personality*; New York: Harper & Row.

Ahrens, R. (1954) Beitrag zur Entwicklung des Physiognomie und Mini-kerkennes, *Zeitschrift für Experimentelle und Angewandte Psychologie*, 2, 412–54.

Aijen, J. and M. Fishbein (1977) Attitude–behaviour relations: a theoretical analysis and review of empirical research, *Psychological Bulletin*, 84, 888–918.

Ainsworth, M. D. S. (1989) Attachments beyond infancy, *American Psychologist*, vol. 44, 4, 709–16.

*Aitkenhead, A. M. and J. M. Slack (1985) *Issues in cognitive modeling*; New Jersey: Lawrence Erlbaum.

Alloy L. B., L. Y. Abramson, G. I. Metalsky and S. Hartlage (1988) The hopelessness theory of depression: attributional aspects, *British Journal of Clinical Psychology*, 27, 5–21.

Allport, G. W. (1935) Attitudes, in C. Murchison (ed), *Handbook of social psychology, vol 2*; Worcester, Mass: Clark University Press.

Allport, G. (1937) *Personality: a psychological interpretation*; New York: Holt, Rinehart & Winston.

Allport, G. W. (1958) *The nature of prejudice*; Garden City, New York: Doubleday Anchor

Anderson, J. R. (1985) *Cognitive psychology and its implications* (2nd edn); New York: W. H. Freeman.

*Andreasen, N. C. (1984) *The broken brain;* New York: Harper & Row.

Aronson, E. (1988) *The social animal* (5th edn); New York: W. H. Freeman.

Aronson, E. (1988) *The social animal* (5th edn); W. H. Freeman & Company: San Francisco.

Aronson, E., N. Blaney, C. Stephan, J. Sikes and M. Snapp (1978) *The jigsaw classroom*; California: Sage.

Asch, S. E. (1946) Forming impressions of personality, *Journal of Abnormal and Social Psychology* 41, 258–90.

Asch, S. E. (1955) Opinions and social pressure, *Scientific American*, 193, 31–5.

Asch S. E. (1956) Studies of independence and conformity: a minority of one against a unanimous majority, *Psychological Monographs*, 70 (9).

Asch, S. E. (1958) Effects of group pressure upon modification and distortion of judgements, in E. E. Maccoby, T. M. Newcomb and E. L. Hartley (eds), *Readings in social psychology* (3rd edn); New York: Holt, Rinehart & Winston.

Asch, S. E. (1955) Opinions and social pressure, *Scientific American*, 193, 31–5.
Aserinsky, E. and N. Kleitman (1953) Regularly occurring periods of eye mobility, and concomitant phenomena during sleep, *Science*, 118, 273–4.
Atkinson, R. C. and R. M. Shiffrin (1968) Human memory: A proposed system and its control processes, in K. W. Spence and J. T. Spence (eds) *The psychology of learning and motivation: advances in research and theory, vol 2*; New York: Academic Press.
Atkinson, R. C. and R. M. Shiffrin (1971) The control of short-term memory, *Scientific American*, 225 (2), 82–90.
Azrin, N. H., R. R. Hutchinson and D. F. Hake, (1966) Attack, avoidance, and escape reactions to aversive shock, *Journal of Experimental Analysis of Behaviour*, 9, 191–204.
*Baddeley, A. (1986) *Working memory*; Oxford: Clarendon.
Bandura, A., D. Ross and S. Ross (1961) Transmission of aggression through imitation of aggression models, *Journal of Abnormal and Social Psychology*, 63, 575–82.
Bandura, A., D. Ross and S. A. Ross (1963) Vicarious reinforcement and imitative learning, *Journal of Abnormal and Social Psychology*, 67, 601–7.
Bandura, A. (1969) Social-learning theory of identificatory processes, in D. A. Goslin (ed.), *Handbook of socialisation theory and research*; Chicago: Rand McNally.
Bandura, A. (1977) *Social learning theory*; Englewood Cliffs, NJ: Prentice-Hall.
Bannister, D. and F. Fransella (1980) *Inquiring man – the psychology of personal constructs*; Harmondsworth: Penguin.
Bar-Tal, D. and L. Saxe (1976) Perception of similarity and dissimilarity in attractive couples and individuals, *Journal of Personality and Social Psychology*, 33, 772–81.
Barash, D. P. (1977) *Sociobiology and behaviour*; New York: Elsevier.
Barlow, G. W. (1977) Modal action patterns, in T. N. Sebeok (ed.), *How animals communicate*, Bloomington: University of Indiana Press.
Bartlett, F. C. (1932) *Remembering*, Cambridge: Cambridge University Press.
Bastock, M. (1956) A gene mutation which changes a behaviour pattern, *Evolution*, 10, 421–39.
Beck, A. T. (1967) *Depression: clinical, experimental and theoretical aspects*, New York: Harper & Row.
Bender, L. (1955) Twenty years of research on schizophrenic children with special reference to those under twenty years of age, in G. Kaplan (ed.) *Emotional problems of early childhood*; New York: Basic Books.
Bem, D. J. (1967) Self-perception: an alternative interpretation of cognitive dissonance phenomena, *Psychological Review*, 74, 183–200.
Bem, S. L. (1983) Gender schema theory and its implications for child development: raising asthmatic children in a gender-schematic society, *Signs: Journal of Women in Culture and Society*, 8, 598–616.
Bentall R. P., H. F. Jackson and D. Pilgrim (1988) Abandoning the concept of 'schizophrenia': some implications of validity arguments for psychological research into psychotic phenomena, *British Journal of Clinical Psychology*, 27, 303–24.
Berk, L. E. (1989) *Child development*; London: Allyn & Bacon.
Berkowitz, L. (1965) Some aspects of observed aggression, *Journal of Personality and Social Psychology*, 2, 359–69.

Berkowitz, L. (1969) The frustration–aggression hypothesis revisited, in L. Berkowitz (ed.), *Roots of aggression: a re-examination of the frustration–aggression hypothesis;* New York: Atherton.

Berne, E. (1968) *Games people play;* Harmondsworth: Penguin.

Bernstein, B. (1965) A sociolinguistic approach to social learning, in J. Gould (ed.), *Penguin survey of the social sciences,* Harmondsworth: Penguin Books.

*Bernstein, D. A., E. J. Roy, T. K. Srull and C. D. Wickens (1988) *Psychology;* Boston: Houghton Mifflin.

*Best, J. B. (1986) *Cognitive psychology;* West Publishing.

Bettelheim, B. (1989) *Freud and Man's soul;* Harmondsworth: Penguin.

Binet, A. and T. Simon (1911) *A method of measuring the development of the intelligence of young children,* Lincoln, Illinois: Courier Company.

*Birch, A. and T. Malim (1988) *Developmental psychology: from infancy to adulthood;* Intertext Bristol.

*Birchwood, M., S. E. Hallett and M. C. Preston (1988) *Schizophrenia: an integrated approach to research and treatment;* London: Longman.

*Blakemore, C. (1988) *The mind machine;* London: BBC Books.

*Blakemore, C. and S. Greenfield (1987) *Mindwaves;* Oxford: Blackwell.

Bleuler, E. (1911) *Dementia praecox, or the group of schizophrenia;* New York: International Universities Press.

Bleuler, E. (1911/1950) *Dementia praecox or the group of schizophrenia,* New York: International Universities Press.

Boring, E. G. (1957) *A history of experimental psychology* (2nd ed); New York: Appleton-Century-Crofts.

Borke, H. (1975) Piaget's mountains revisited: Changes in the egocentric landscape, *Developmental Psychology,* 11, 240–3.

Bornstein, M. H. and M. E. Lamb (1988) *Perceptual, cognitive and linguistic development;* New Jersey: Lawrence Eribaum.

Bower, T. G. R. (1974) *Development in infancy;* New York: W. H. Freeman.

Bowlby, J. (1965) *Child care and the growth of love* (2nd edn); London: Pelican.

Bowlby, J. (1971) *Attachment and loss: volume 1: Attachment;* Harmondsworth: Penguin.

Bowlby, J. (1980) *Attachment and loss: volume 3: Loss: sadness and depression;* London: Pelican.

Bradley, B. S. (1989) *Visions of infancy;* Oxford: Polity Press.

Brehm, J. W. (1966) *A theory of psychological reactance;* New York: Academic Press.

*Bremner, J. G. (1988) *Infancy;* Oxford: Blackwell.

Bretherton, I. and M. D. S. Ainsworth (1974) Responses of one-year-olds to a stranger in a strange situation, in M. Lewis and L. A. Rosenblum (eds.), *The origins of fear;* New York: Wiley.

Brewin, C. R. (1985) Depression and causal attributions: what is their relation?, *Psychological Bulletin,* 98, 297–309.

Broadbent, D. E. (1958) *Perception and communication;* London: Pergamon.

Broadbent, D. A. (1982) Task combination and selective intake of information, *Acta Psychologica,* 50, 253–90.

Broadhurst, P. L. and S. Levine (1963) Behavioural consistency in strains of rats selectively bred for emotional elimination, *British Journal of Psychology,* 54, 121–5.

Bromley, D. B. (1988) *Human ageing;* London: Pelican.

Brown, G. and C. Desforges (1979) *Piaget's theory: a psychological critique*; London: Routledge & Kegan Paul.

Brown, G. W. and T. Harris (1978) *Social origins of depression*; New York: The Free Press.

Brown, J. A. C. (1961) *Freud and the post-Freudians;* London: Pelican.

Brown, R. (1965) *Social psychology*; London: Macmillan.

Brown, R., C. Cazden and U. Bellugi (1969) The child's grammar from I–III, in J. P. Hill (ed.), *Minnesota symposia on child psychology, vol. 2*; Minneapolis: University of Minnesota Press.

Bruner, J. S., R. D. Busiek and A. L. Minturn (1952) Assimilation in the immediate reproduction of visually perceived figures, *Journal of Experimental Psychology*, 44, 151–5.

Bruner, J. S. (1964) The course of cognitive growth, *American Psychoanalytic Association Journal*, 19, 1–15.

Bryant, P. (1974) *Perception and understanding in young children: an experimental approach*, London: Methuen.

Bryant, P. (1982) Piaget's questions, *British Journal of Psychology*, 73, 157–61.

Buck, R. (1988) *Human motivation and emotion* (2nd edn); Chichester: Wiley.

Byrne, D. and D. Nelson (1965) Attraction as a linear function of proportion of positive reinforcements, *Journal of Personality and Social Psychology*, 1, 659–63.

Carlsmith, L. (1964) Effects of early father absence on scholastic aptitude, *Harvard Educational Review*, 34: 3–21.

Carmichael, L. (1926) The development of behaviour in vertebrates experimentally removed from the influence of external stimulation, *Psychological Review*, 33, 51–8.

Cherry, E. C. (1953) Some experiments on the recognition of speech, with one and two ears, *Journal of the Acoustical Society of America*, 25, 975–9.

Chomsky, N. (1957) *Syntactic structures*; The Hague: Mouton.

Cialdini, R. B., J. E. Vincent, S. K. Lewis, J. Catalan, D. Wheeler and B. L. Darby (1975) A reciprocal concessions procedure for inducing compliance: the door in the face technique, *Journal of Personality and Social Psychology*, 21, 206–15.

Clarke, E. (1979) Building a vocabulary: words for objects, actions and relations, in P. Fletcher and M. Gorman (eds), *Language acquisition*; Cambridge: Cambridge University Press.

*Cohen, D. (1988) *Forgotten millions*; London: Paladin.

Cohen, G., M. W. Eysenck and M. E. LeVoi (1986) *Memory: a cognitive approach*; Milton Keynes: Open University Press.

Collins, A. M. and E. F. Loftus (1975) A spreading activation theory of semantic processing, *Psychological Review*, 82, 407–28.

Collins, A. M. and M. R. Quillian (1969) Retrieval time from semantic memory, *Journal of Verbal Learning and Verbal Behaviour*, 8, 240–7.

Comfort, A. (1971) The likelihood of human pheromones, *Nature*.

Coolican, H. (1990) *Research methods and statistics in psychology*; London: Hodder & Stoughton.

Craik, F. I. M. and R. S. Lockhart (1972) Levels of processing: a framework for memory research, *Journal of Verbal Learning and Verbal Behaviour*, 11, 671–84.

Craik, F. I. M. and M. J. Watkins (1973) The role of rehearsal in short-term memory, *Journal of Verbal Learning and Verbal Behaviour*,12, 598–607.

Crowder, R. G. (1982) The demise of short-term memory, *Acta Psychologica*, 50, 291–323.

Crutchfield, R. S. (1955) Conformity and character, *American Psychologist*, 10, 191–8.

Cumming, E. and W. Henry (1961) *Growing old: a process of disengagement*; New York: Basic Books.

Curtiss S. (1977) *Genie: A psychological study of a modern-day wild child*; New York: Academic Press.

Dane, B. C. and W. G. Van der Kloot (1964) An analysis of the display of the goldeneye duck (Bucephala clangula), *Behaviour*, 22, 282–328.

Darwin, C. (1872) *The expression of the emotions in man and animals*; London: Murray.

Davidson, E. S., A. Yasuna and A. Power (1979) The effects of television cartoons on sex-role stereotyping in young girls, *Child Development*, 50, 597–600.

Dawkins, R. (1986) *The blind watchmaker*; Harmondsworth: Penguin.

*Deaux, K. and L. S. Wrightsman (1984) *Social psychology in the 80s* (4th edn); Monterey, California: Brooks/Cole.

Deutsch, M. and H. B. Gerard (1955) A study of normative and informational social influence upon individual judgement, *Journal of Abnormal and Social Psychology* 51, 629–36.

Donaldson, M. (1978) *Children's minds*; London: Fontana Paperbacks.

Eagly, A. H. and R. Warren (1976) Intelligence, comprehension and opinion change, *Journal of Personality*, 44, 226–42.

Ebbinghaus, H. (1885) *Memory* (In translation in London: Dover Publications, 1964).

Ehrlich, D., I. Guttman, P. Schönbach and J. Mills (1957) Post-decision exposure to relevant information, *Journal of Abnormal and Social Psychology*, 54, 98–102.

Eron, L. D. (1987) The development of aggressive behaviour from the perspective of a developing behaviourism, *American Psychologist*, 42, 5, 435–42.

Eron, L. D., L. R. Huesmann, M. M. Lefkowitz and L. O. Walder (1972) Does television violence cause aggression? *American Psychologist*, 27, 253–63.

Erikson, E. H. (1968) *Identity: youth and crisis*; New York: Norton.

Eysenck, H. J. (1965) *Fact and fiction in psychology*, Harmondsworth: Penguin.

Fagot, B. I. (1978) The influence of sex of child on parental reactions to toddler children, *Child Development*, 49, 459–65.

Fagot, B. I. (1985) Beyond the reinforcement principle: another step toward understanding sex role development, *Developmental Psychology*, 21, 1097–104.

Festinger, L. (1957) *A theory of cognitive dissonance*; Evanston, Illinois: Row, Petersen.

Festinger, L. and J. M. Carlsmith (1959) Cognitive consequences of forced compliance, *Journal of Abnormal and Social Psychology*, 58, 203–10.

Fidell, L. S. (1970) Empirical verification of sex discrimination in hiring practices in psychology, *American Psychologist*, 25, 1094–8.

Fiske, S. T. and S. E. Taylor (1984) *Social cognition*; New York: Random House.

Flavell, J. H. (1963) *The developmental psychology of Jean Piaget*; Princeton, NJ: Van Nostrand.

Freedman, J. L. and S. C. Fraser (1966) Compliance without pressure: the foot-in-the-door technique, *Journal of Personality and Social Psychology*, 4, 195–202.

Freud, S. (1900) *The interpretation of dreams* (PFL4)

*Freud, S. (1915) *Papers on metapsychology* (PFL11)

*Freud, S. (1933) *New introductory lectures on psychoanalysis* (PFL2)

Freud, S. (1963) Introductory lectures on psychoanalysis, in J. Strachey (ed.), *The standard edition of the complete works* (vols 15 and 16); London: Hogarth Press.

Frisch K. von (1967) *The dance language and orientation of bees;* Cambridge, Mass: Belknap Press.

*Frosh, S. (1987) *The politics of psychoanalysis*; London: Macmillan.

Frosh, S. (1989) *Psychoanalysis and psychology*; London: Macmillan.

Furrow, D., K. Nelson and H. Benedict (1979) Mothers' speech to children and syntactic development: some simple relationships, *Journal of Child Language*, 6, 423–42.

Galton, F. (1869) *Hereditary genius*, London: Macmillan.

Gardner, R. A. and B. T. Gardner (1978) Comparative psychology and language acquistion, *Annals of the New York Academy of Sciences*, 309, 37–767.

*Garton, A. and C. Pratt (1989) *Learning to be literate*, Oxford: Blackwell.

Geschwind, N. (1965) Disconnexion syndromes in animals and man: parts I and II, *Brain*, 88 (parts 2 and 3) June and September.

Geosell, A. and H. Thompson (1929) Learning and growth in identical twins, *Genet. Psychol. Monogr.*, 6, 1–124.

Gewirtz, J. L. (1965) The cause of infant smiling in four child-rearing environments in Israel, in B. M. Foss (ed.), *Determinants of infant behaviour (vol 3)*; London, Methuen.

Gilhooly, K. J. (1983) *Thinking: directed, undirected and creative*; New York: Academic Press.

Ginsburg, H. and S. Opper (1969) *Piaget's theory of intellectual development: an introduction;* Englewood Cliffs, NJ: Prentice-Hall.

Glanzer, M. and A. R. Cunitz (1966) Two storage mechanisms in free recall, *Journal of Verbal Learning and Verbal Behaviour*, 5, 351–60.

Glover, J. (1988) *I: The philosophy and psychology of personal identity;* London: Pelican.

Goffman, E. (1959) *The presentation of self in everyday life*; Garden City, New York: Doubleday Anchor.

Goffman, E. (1961) *Asylums*; Harmondsworth: Penguin.

Goodall, J. (1978) Chimp killings: is it the man in them?, *Science News*, 113, 276.

Gordon, H. (1923) Mental and scholastic tests among retarded children, *Education pamphlet no. 44*, London: Board of Education.

Gould, S. J. (1984) *The mismeasure of man*; London: Pelican.

Greenberg, B. S. (1972) Children's reactions to TV blacks, *Journalism Quarterly*, 50, 5–14.

Greene, J. (1972) *Psycholinguistics*; Harmondsworth: Penguin.

Gregory, R. L. (1986) *Odd perceptions*; London: Routledge.

Griffin, D. R. (1976) *The question of animal awareness: evolutionary continuity of mental experience*, New York: Rockefeller University Press.

Grohmann, J. (1938) Modification oder Funktionsregung? Ein Beitrag zur Klärung der wechselseitigen Beziehungenzwischen Instinkthandlung und Erfahrung, cited by W. H. Thorpe (1962) *Learning and instinct in animals*; Cambridge: Cambridge University Press.

*Gross, R. (1987) *Psychology: the science of mind and behaviour*; London: Hodder & Stoughton.

Gross, R. D. (1990) *Key studies in psychology*; London: Hodder & Stoughton.

Guiton, P. (1959) Socialization and imprinting in Brown Leghorn chicks, *Animal Behaviour* 7, 26–34.

Hall, K. R. L. and I. DeVore (1965) Baboon social behaviour, in I. DeVore (ed.), *Primate behaviour*; New York: Holt.

Hamilton, W. D. (1964) The genetical evolution of social behaviour: parts 1, 2. *Journal of Theoretical Biology*, 7, 1–52.

Hampson, S. E. (1982) *The construction of personality*; London: Routledge & Kegan Paul.

Hargreaves, D. J., C. G. Molloy and A. R. Pratt (1982) Social factors in conservation, *British Journal of Psychology*, 73, 231–4.

Harlow, H. F. (1962) The heterosexual affectional system in monkeys, *American Psychologist* 17, 1–9.

Harris, M. and M. Coltheart (1986) *Language processing in children and adults*; London: Routledge & Kegan Paul.

Havighurst, R. J. (1964) cited in D. B. Bromley (1988) *The psychology of human ageing*; London: Pelican.

Hayes, K. H. and C. Hayes (1951) Intellectual development of a house-raised chimpanzee, *Proceedings of the American Philosophical Society*, 95, 105–9.

*Hayes, N. and S. Orrell (1987) *Psychology: an introduction*; Longman: London.

Hayslip, B. and P. E. Panek (1989) *Adult development and aging*; New York: Harper & Row.

*Hearnshaw, L. S. (1987) *The shaping of modern psychology*; London: Routledge & Kegan Paul.

*Heather, N. (1976) *Radical perspectives in psychology* (chapter 4: Psychiatry and anti-psychiatry); London: Methuen.

Hebb, D. O. (1949) *The organization of behaviour*; New York: Wiley.

Hess, E. H. (1959) Imprinting, *Science*, 130, 133–41.

Hess, E. H. (1964) Imprinting in birds, *Science N.Y.*, 146, 1128–39.

*Hewstone, M., W. Stoebe, J-P. Codol and G. M. Stephenson (eds) (1988) *Introduction to social psychology* Oxford: Blackwell.

Hinde, R. A. (1954) Factors governing the changes in strength of a partially inborn response, as shown by the mobbing behaviour of the chaffinch (Fringilla coelebs) Parts I and II, *Proceedings of the Royal Society*, series B, 142, 306–58.

Hinde, R. A. (1974) *Biological bases of human social behaviour*; New York: McGraw-Hill.

Hinde, R. A. (1982) *Ethology*; London: Fontana Paperback.

Hinde, R. A. and E. Steel (1966) Integration of the reproductive behaviour of female canaries, *Symp. Soc. Exp. Biol*, 20, 401–26.

Hirst, W., E. S. Spelke, C. C. Reaves, G. Caharack and U. Neisser (1980) Divided attention without alternation or automaticity, *Journal of Experimental Psychology: General*, 109, 98–117.

Hofling, C. K., E. Brotzman, S. Dalrymple, N. Graves and C. M. Pierce (1966) An experimental study in nurse–physician relationships, *Journal of Nervous and Mental Disorders*, 143: 171–80.

Hollander, E. P. and R. G. Hunt (1972) *Classical contributions to social psychology*; Oxford University Press.

Horland, C., I. Janis and H. H. Kelley (1953) *Communication and persuasion*; New Haven, Conn: Yale University Press.

*Horowitz, M. J. (1988) *Introduction to psychodynamics: a new synthesis*; London Routledge & Kegan Paul.

Howes, M. B. (1990) *The psychology of human cognition*, New York: Pergamon Press.

*Howitt, D., M. Billig, D. Cramer, D. Edwards, B. Kniveton, J. Potter and A. Radley (1989) *Social psychology: conflicts and continuities*; Milton Keynes: Open University Press.

Hubel, D. H. and T. N. Wiesel (1962) Receptive fields, binocular interaction and functional cytoarchitecture in the cat's visual cortex, *Journal of Physiology*, 160, 106–54.

Hughes, M. (1975) Egocentrism in pre-school children, cited in M. Donaldson (1978) *Children's minds*; Fontana: London.

Huxley, J. S. (1914) The courtship habits of the great crested grebe (Podiceps cristatus), *Proceedings of the Zoological Society of London*, 2, 491–562.

Inhelder, B. and J. Piaget (1958) *The growth of logical thinking* (Trans. A. Parsons and S. Milgram); London: Routledge & Kegan Paul.

Insko, C. A. (1965) Verbal reinforcement and attitude, *Journal of Personality and Social Psychology*.

Insko, C. A. and J. Schopler (1967) Triadic consistency: a statement of affective–cognitive–conative consistency, *Psychological Review*, 74, 361–76.

Jacklin, C. N. (1989) Female and male: issues of gender, *American Psychologist*, 44, 2, 127–33.

James, W. (1890) *The principles of psychology*, New York: Henry Holt.

James, W. (1890) *The principles of psychology (vols 1 and 2)*; New York: Henry Holt & Company.

Janis, I. L., and Feshbach, S. (1953) Effects of fear-arousing communications, *Journal of Abnormal and Social Psychology*, 48, 78–92.

Jaroslovsky, R. (1988) What's on your mind America?, *Psychology Today*, 8, 54–9.

Johnson-Laird, P. N. (1983) *Mental models*; Cambridge University Press.

Johnston, A., D. DeLuca, K. Murtaugh and E. Diener (1977) Validation of a laboratory play measure of child aggression, *Child Development*, 48, 324–7.

Johnston, J. and J. S. Ettema (1982) *Positive images: breaking stereotypes with children's television*; California: Sage.

Johnston, W. A. and V. J. Dark (1986) Selective attention, *Annual Review of Psychology*, 37, 43–75.

Jones, M. C. (1957) The later careers of boys who were early or late maturing, *Child Development*, 28, 113–28.

Joyce, C. (1988) This Machine Wants to Help You, *Psychology Today*, 2, 44–50.

Jung, C. G. (1964) *Man and his symbols*; London: Picador.

Kahneman, D. (1973) *Attention and effort*, Englewood Cliffs, NJ: Prentice-Hall.

Kamin, L. J. (1968) 'Attention-like' processes in classical conditioning, in M. R. Jones (ed.) *Miami Symposium on the Prediction of Behaviour: Aversion stimulation*, Miami; University of Miami Press.

Kandel, D. B. (1978) Similarity in real-life adolescent friendship pairs, *Journal of Personality and Social Psychology*, 36, 306–12.

Kandel, D. B. and G. S. Lesser (1972), *Youth in two worlds*, San Francisco: Jossey-Bass.

Karlins, M. and H. I. Abelson (1970) How opinions and attitudes are changed (2nd ed.); New York: Springer.

Katcher, A. (1955) The discrimination of sex differences by young children, *Journal of Genetic Psychology*, 87, 131–43.

Kelley, H. H. (1950) The warm–cold variable in first impressions of persons, *Journal of Personality*, 18, 431–9.

Kelly, G. A. (1955) *The psychology of personal constructs*; New York: Norton.

Klaus, M. and J. Kennell (1976) *Maternal–infant bonding*; St Louis: Mosby.

Klopfer, P. H. (1975) Evolution, behaviour and language, in M. E. Hahn and E. C. Simmel (eds), *Communicative behaviour and evolution*, New York: Academic Press.

Klopfer, P. H., D. K. Adams and M. S. Klopfer (1964) Maternal 'imprinting' in goats, *Proceedings of the National Academy of Sciences, USA*, 52, 911–14.

Klüver, H. and P. C. Bucy (1939) Preliminary analysis of functions of the temporal lobes in monkeys, *Archives of Neurology and Psychiatry*, 42, 979–1000.

Kohlberg, L. (1966) A cognitive developmental analysis of children's sex role concepts and attitudes, in E. E. Maccoby (ed.), *The development of sex differences*; Stanford: Stanford University Press.

Kohn, A. (1988) Make love, not war, *Psychology Today*, 6, 35–8.

Kraepelin, E. (1896) *Lehrbuch der psychiatrie* (5th edn); Leipzig: Barth.

Kuffler, S. W. (1953) Discharge patterns and functional organisation of mammalian retina, *Journal of Neurophysiology*, 16, 37–68.

Kuhn, D., S. C. Nash and L. Brucken (1978) Sex role concepts of two- and three-year-olds, *Child Development*, 49, 445–51.

Lack, D. (1943) *The life of the robin*, London: Witherby.

Laing, R. D. (1960) *The divided self*; London: Pelican.

Larsen, K. S. (1974) Conformity in the Asch experiment, *Journal of Social Psychology*, 94, 303–4.

Lenneberg, E. H. (1967) *Biological foundations of language*; New York: Wiley.

Leventhal, H. (1970) Findings and theory in the study of fear communications, in L. Berkowitz (ed.), *Advances in experimental social psychology (vol 5)*; New York: Academic Press.

Light, P. H., N. Buckingham and A. H. Robbins (1979) The conservation task as an interactional setting, *British Journal of Educational Psychology*, 49, 304–10.

Lindsay, P. H. and D. A. Norman (1972) *Human information processing*; New York: Academic Press.

Lloyd, P., A. Mayes, A. S. R. Manstead, P. R. Meudell and H. L. Wagner (1984) *Introduction to psychology*; London: Fontana.

Loftus, E. F. (1975) Leading questions and the eyewitness report, *cognitive psychology*, 7, 560–72.

Loftus, E. F. (1979) *Eyewitness testimony*; Cambridge, MA: Harvard University Press.

Loftus, E. F. (1981) Eyewitnesses: essential but unreliable, *Psychology Today*, 22–8.

Lorenz, K. (1935) Der Kumpen in der umwelt des vogels, *Journal of Ornithology*, 83, 137–213, 289–413.

Lorenz, K. (1937) The companion in the bird's world, *Auk*, 54, 245–73.

Lorenz, K. Z. (1941) Vergleichende Bewegungsstudien an Anatinen, *Journal of Ornithology*, Leipzig, 89, 194–293.

Lorenz, K. Z. (1958) The evolution of behaviour, *Scientific American*, 199 (6), 67–78.

Lorenz, K. Z. (1974) Analogy as a source of knowledge, *Science*, 185, 229–34.

Luchins, A. S. (1957) Primacy-recency in impression formation, in C. I. Horland (ed.), *The order of presentation in persuasion*; New Haven: Yale University Press.

Maccoby, E. E. and C. N. Jacklin (1974) *The psychology of sex differences*; Stanford, Calif.: Stanford University Press.

McGarrigle, J. and M. Donaldson (1974) Conservation accidents, *Cognition*, 3, 341–50.

McGuire, W. J. (1969) The nature of attitudes and attitude change, in G. Lindzey and E. Aronson (eds), *The handbook of social psychology vol. 3*, (2nd edn.); Reading, Mass: Addison-Wesley.

McNeill, D. (1966) Developmental psycholinguistics, in F. Smith and G. A. Miller (eds), *The genesis of language*; Cambridge, Mass: MIT Press.

Manning, A. (1961) The effects of artificial selection for mating speed in Drarophila melanogaster, *Animal Behaviour*, 9, 82–92.

Manning, A. (1967) *An introduction to animal behaviour*, London: Edward Arnold.

Mark, V. and F. V. Ervin (1970) *Violence and the brain*; New York: Harper & Row.

Marr, D. C. (1982) *Vision*; Oxford: Freeman.

*Matlin, M. W. (1989) *Cognition* (2nd edition); New York: Holt Rinehart & Winston.

Mayer, R. E. (1984) *Thinking and problem solving: an introduction to human cognition and learning*; New York; W. H. Freeman.

Mead, G. H. (1934) *Mind, self and society*; Chicago: University of Chicago Press.

Mead, M. (1935) *Sex and temperament in three primitive societies*; New York: Morrow.

Mednick *et. al.* (1975) cited in R. D. Gross (1987) *Psychology: the science of mind and behaviour*; Edward Arnold: London.

Mendel, G. J. (1866) *Experiments in plant hybridization*, translated by R. A. Fisher; Edinburgh: Oliver & Boyd (1965).

Menzel, E. (1975) Human Language – who needs it?, in G. Ferry (ed.), *The understanding of animals: a New Scientist guide*; Blackwell: Oxford.

Merton, R. K. (1957) *Social theory and social structure*; New York: Free Press.

Michael, R. P. and E. B. Keverne (1968) Pheromones in the communication of sexual status in primates, *Nature*, 218, 746–9.

Michaels, J. W., J.M. Blommel, R. M. Brocato, R. A. Linkous and J. S. Rowe (1982) Social facilitation and inhibition in a natural setting, *Replications in Social Psychology*, 2, 21–4.

Milgram S. (1963) Behavioural study of obedience, *Journal of Abnormal and Social Psychology*, 67, 371–8.

Milgram, S. (1974) *Obedience to authority*; New York: Harper & Row.

Miller, G. A. (1967) *The psychology of communication*; London: Pelican.

Miller, N. and R. Bugelski (1948) Minor studies in aggression: the influence of frustrations imposed by the in-group on attitudes expressed toward out-groups, *Journal of Psychology*, 25, 437–42.

Miller, N. E. and L. V. DiCara (1968) Instrumental learning of systolic blood pressure responses by curarized rats, *Psychosomatic Medicine*, 39, 489–94.

Mills, J. and E. Aronson (1965) Opinion change as a function of communicator's attractiveness and desire to influence, *Journal of Personality and Social Psychology*, 1, 173–7.

Milner, B. (1966) Amnesia following operation on the temporal lobes in C. W. M. Whitty and O. L. Zangwill (eds), *Amnesia*; London: Butterworth.

Mischel, W. (1970) Sex-typing and socialization, in P. H. Mussen (ed.), *Carmichael's manual of child development, vol. 1*; New York: Wiley.

Money, J. and A. A. Ehrhardt (1972) *Man and woman, girl and boy*; Baltimore: Johns Hopkins University Press.

Moray, N. (1959) Attention in dichotic listening: affective cues and the influence of instructions, *Quarterly Journal of Experimental Psychology*, 11, 56–60.

Murphy, J., M. John, and H. Brown (eds) (1984) *Dialogues and debates in social psychology*; New Jersey: Lawrence Erlbaum, Open University Press.

Murstein, B. I. (1972) Physical attractiveness and marital choice, *Journal of Personality and Social Psychology*, 22, 8–12.

*Mussen, P. H., J. J. Conger, J. Kagan and A. C. Huston (1984) *Child development and personality* (6th edn); New York: Harper & Row.

Mussen, P. H. and M. Jones (1957) Self-conceptions, motivations and interpersonal attitudes of late and early maturing boys, *Child Development*, 28, 243–56.

Nahemow, L. & M. P. Lawton (1975) Similarity and propinquity in friendship formation, *Journal of Personality and Social Psychology*, 32, 205–13.

Nelson, K. (1973) Structure and strategy in learning to talk, *Monographs of the Society for Research in Child Development*, 38, (1–2, no. 149).

Nelson, K. E. (1989) Strategies for first language teaching, in M. L. Rice and R. L. Schiefelbusch (eds), *Teachability of language*; Baltimore: Brookes.

Neugarten, B. L. (1968) Adult personality: toward a psychology of the life cycle, in B. L. Neugarten (ed.), *Middle age and aging*; Chicago: University of Chicago Press.

Newell, A. and H. A. Simon (1956) The logic theory machine: A complex information processing system, *IRE Transactions on Information Theory*, IT-2(3), 61–79.

Newell, A. and H. A. Simon (1961) GPS: A program that simulates human thought, in H. Billing (ed.), *Lernende Automaten*; Munich: R. Oldenbourg.

Newson, J. and E. Newson (1965) *Patterns of infant care in an urban community*, Harmondsworth: Pelican.

Norman, D. A. and D. G. Bobrow (1975) On data-limited and resource-limited processes, *Cognitive Psychology*, 7, 44–64.

Oates, J. and S. Sheldon (eds) (1987) *Cognitive development in infancy*; Lawrence Erlbaum/Open University Press.

Osgood, C. E., G. J. Suci and P. H. Tannenbaum (1957) *The measurement of meaning*; University of Illinois Press.

Osofsky, J. D. (ed.) (1987) *Handbook of infant development* (2nd edn); New York: Harper & Row.

Parsons, T. (1951) *The social system*; New York: Free Press.

Patterson, G. R., R. A. Littman, and W. A. Bricker (1967) Assertive behaviour in children: a step toward a theory of aggression, *Monographs of the Society for Research in Child Development*, serial no. 113, 32:5.

Pavlov, I. P. (1927) *Conditioned reflexes*, translated and edited by G. V. Anrep; New York: Dover Publications.

Petty, R. E. and T. C. Brock (1976) Effects of responding or not responding to hecklers on audience agreement with a speaker, *Journal of Applied Social Psychology*, 6, 1–17.

Petty, R. E., G. L. Wells and T. C. Brock (1976) Distraction can enhance or reduce yielding to propaganda: thought disruption versus effort justification, *Journal of Personality and Social Psychology*, 34, 874–84.

Piaget, J. (1929) *The child's conception of the world*; Harmondsworth: Penguin.

Piaget, J. (1932) *The moral judgement of the child*; London: Routledge & Kegan Paul.

Piner, K. E. & J. H. Berg, (1988) Instant intimacy, *Psychology Today*, 2, 13.

Posner, M. I. and S. J. Boies (1971) Components of attention, *Psychological Review*, 78, 391–409.

Premack, D. (1971) On the assessment of language competence in the chimpanzee, in A. M. Schrier and F. Stollnitz (eds), *Behaviour of non-human primates, vol. 4*; New York: Academic Press.

Rachman, S. (1974) *The meanings of fear*; Harmondsworth: Penguin.

Radford, J. and E. Govier (eds) (1980), *A textbook of psychology*; London: Sheldon Press.

Reber, A. S. (1985) *The Penguin dictionary of psychology*; Penguin Books: Middlesex.

Rice, M. L. (1989) Children's language acquisition, *American Psychologist*, 44, 2, 149–56.

Richardson, K. and S. Sheldon (eds) (1988) *Cognitive development to adolescence*; Lawrence Erlbaum/Open University Press.

Rips, L. J., E. S. Shoben and E. E. Smith (1973) Semantic distance and the verification of semantic relations, *Journal of Verbal Learning and Verbal Behaviour*, 12, 1–20.

Rosenham, D. L. (1973) On being sane in insane places, *Science*, 179, 250–8.

Rosenthal, R. and L. F. Jacobson (1968) *Pygmalion in the classroom: teacher expectation and pupils' intellectual development*; New York: Holt, Rinehart & Winston.

Rumbaugh, D. M. (1977) *Language learning by a chimpanzee: the Land project*; New York: Academic Press.

Sampson (1971) cited in E. Shaw and R. Davies, *Psychology for GCSE* (1987), Casdec Books.

Sandford, R. N. (1936) The effects of abstinence from food on imaginal processes, *Journal of Psychology*, 2, 129–36.

Schachter, S. (1959) *The psychology of affiliation*; Stanford, California: Stanford University Press.

Schank, R. C. and R. Abelson (1977) *Scripts, plans, goals and understanding*; Hillsdale, NJ: Lawrence Erlbaum.

Seligman, M. E. P. (1975) *Helplessness: on depression, development and death*; San Francisco: W. H. Freeman.

Shallice, T. and E. K. Warrington (1970) Independent functioning of verbal memory stores: a neurophysiological study, *Quarterly Journal of Experimental Psychology*, 22, 261–73.

Shaw, L. and R. Davies (1988) *Psychology for GCSE*; Durham: Casdec.

Sherif, M. (1935) A study of some social factors in perception, *Archives of Psychology*, 27, (187), 1–60.

Sherif, M., O. J. Harvey, B. J. White, W. Hood and C. Sherif (1961) *Intergroup conflict and cooperation: the robbers cave experiment*; Oklahoma: University of Oklahoma Institute of Intergroup Relations.

Shiffrin, R. M. and W. Schneider (1977) Controlled and automatic information processing II: perceptual learning, automatic attending, and a general theory, *Psychological Review*, 84, 127–90.

Skinner, B. F. (1957) *Verbal behaviour*; New York: Appleton-Century-Croft.

Slater, A. and G. Bremner (1989) *Infant development*; Lawrence Erlbaum.

*Smith, P. K. and H. Cowie (1988) *Understanding children's development;* Oxford: Blackwell.

Snyder, M., E. D. Tanke and E. Berscheid (1977) Social perception and interpersonal behaviour: on the self-fulfilling nature of social stereotypes, *Journal of Personality and Social Psychology*, 35, 656–66.

Van Sommers, Peter (1988) *Jealousy;* London: Pelican.

Sorenson, R. C. (1973) *Adolescent sexuality in contemporary America*; New York: World Publishing.

Spalding, D. (1873) Instinct: with original observations on young animals, *Macmillan's Magazine*, 27, 282–93 (reprinted in *British Journal of Animal Behaviour*, 2, 1–11 (1954)).

Spearman, C. (1904) General intelligence objectively determined and measured, *American Journal of Psychology*, 15, 201–92.

Sperling, G. (1960) The information available in brief visual presentations, *Psychological Monographs*, 74.

Stafford-Clark, D. (1967) *What Freud really said*; London: Pelican.

Stein, A. H. and L. K. Friedrich (1975) Impact of television on children and youth, in E. M. Hetherington, J. W. Hagen, R. Kron and A. H. Stein (eds), *Review of child development research (vol. 5)*; Chicago: University of Chicago Press.

Stephan, W. G. (1978) School desegregation: An evaluation of predictions made in Brown v. the Board of Education, *Psychological Bulletin*, 85, 217–38.

*Storr, A. (1988) *Solitude*; London: Fontana.

Sutherland, N. S. and V. Holgate (1966) Two-cue discrimination learning in rats, *Journal of Comparative and Physiological Psychology*, 61, 198–207.

Sweet, W. H, F. Ervin and V. H. Mark, (1969) The relationship of violent behaviour to focal cerebral disease, in S. Garattini and E. Sigg (eds), *Aggressive behaviour*, New York: Wiley.

*Sylva, K. and I. Lunt (1982) *Child development: a first course*; Oxford: Blackwell.

Tajfel, H. and C. Fraser (eds) (1978) *Introducing social psychology*; Harmondsworth: Penguin.

Terrace, H. S. (1979) *Nim*; New York: Knopf.

Thompson, R. (1968) *The Pelican history of psychology*; London: Pelican.

Thoulness, R. H. and C. R. Thoulness (1990) *Straight and crooked thinking*; Dunton Green: Hodder & Stoughton.

Tinbergen, N. (1948) Social releases and the experimental method required for their study, *Wilson Bull.*, 60, 6–52.

Tinbergen, N. (1951), *The study of instinct*; London: Oxford University Press.

Tinbergen N. and D. J. Kuenen (1939) Uber die auslösenden und die richtungge-
benden Reizsituationen der Sperrbewegung von jungen Drosseln, *Z. Tier-
psychol*, 3, 37–60.

Treisman, A. (1960) Contextual cues in selective listening, *Quarterly Journal of
Experimental Psychology*, 12, 242–8.

Treisman, A. (1964) Monitoring and storage of irrelevant messages in selective
attention, *Journal of Verbal Learning and Verbal Behaviour*, 3, 449–59.

Trevarthen, C. (1974) Conversations with a two-month old, *New Scientist*, 2 May.

Tryon, R. C. (1940) Genetic differences in maze learning ability in rats, *Thirty-
ninth yearbook of the National Society for Studies in Education*, part I, 111–19.

Turing, A. M. (1950) Computing machinery and intelligence, *Mind*, 59, 433–60.

Ullman, L. P. and L. Krasner (1969) *A psychological approach to abnormal
behaviour*; Englewood Cliffs, NJ: Prentice-Hall.

Vernon, P. E. (1960) *Intelligence and attainment tests*; London: University of
London Press.

Vernon, P. E. (1961) *The Structure of Human Abilities*; London: Methuen.

Wade, C. and C. Travis (1990) *Psychology* (2nd edn); New York: Harper & Row.

Walker, S. (1984) *Learning theory and behaviour modification*, London:
Methuen.

Walster, E. (1965) The effect of self-esteem on romantic liking, *Journal of
Experimental Social Psychology*, 1, 184–97.

Walster, E., V. Aronson, D. Abrahams, and L. Rottman (1966) Importance of
physical attractiveness in dating behaviour, *Journal of Personality and Social
Psychology*, 5, 508–16.

Watson, J. B. and R. Raynor (1920) Conditioned emotional reactions, *Journal of
Experimental Psychology*, 3, 1–14.

Welford, A. T. (1958) *Ageing and human skill*; Oxford: Oxford University Press.

Wicker, A. W. (1969) Attitudes versus actions: the relationship of verbal and
overt behavioural responses to attitude objects, *Journal of Social Issues*, 25,
41–78.

Wilder, D. A. (1977) Perception in groups, size of opposition and social
influence, *Journal of Experimental Social Psychology*, 13, 253–68.

Wilson, E. O. (1975) *Sociobiology: the new synthesis*; Cambridge, MA: Harvard
University Press.

Wilson, E. O. (1978) *On human nature*; Cambridge, MA, Harvard University
Press.

Wishner, J. (1960) Reanalysis of 'impressions of personality', *Psychological
Review*, 67, 96–112.

Wolpe, J. (1958) *Psychotherapy by reciprocal inhibition*; Stanford, Calif: Stanford
University Press.

Wood, D. (1988) *How children think and learn*; Oxford: Blackwell.

Woodward, W. M. (1971) *The development of behaviour*; Harmondsworth:
Penguin.

Yates, F. A. (1984) *The art of memory*; ARK.

Zajonc, R. B. (1965) Social facilitation, *Science*, 149, 269–74.

Zimbardo, P., C. Hancy and C. Banks, (1973) Interpersonal dynamics in a
simulated prison, *International Journal of Criminology and Penology*, 1,
69–97.

Glossary of terms

ACCOMMODATION – In Piaget's theory, the process whereby individuals alter their existing ways of thinking in order to interpret and deal with new information (see also assimilation).

ACTION POTENTIAL – The brief change in the state of a nerve cell when a nerve impulse is activated.

ALTRUISM – Virtually the opposite of selfishness, the tendency to place others' welfare before that of oneself. In some cases this may even involve endangering one's life in order that others may benefit.

ASSIMILATION – In Piaget's theory, the process whereby the individual is able to use existing ways of thinking for interpreting and dealing with new information (see also accommodation).

ATTACHMENT – An emotional bond between individuals (usually infant and adult) such that the infant is comforted by the other's remaining close, but is distressed by separation from them.

AXON – A part of the *neurone* which conducts information away from the cell towards the *synapse*.

BEHAVIOURISM – An approach to psychology which proposes that a true understanding of behaviour can only come from studying that which can be directly observed and measured.

BIOFEEDBACK – The feeding back into the system (i.e. the body) of information regarding physiological or bodily changes. As a therapeutic technique, for example, patients can be taught to control their pulse rate.

CASE STUDY – A method of investigation which is based upon detailed accounts of an individual's (or small group's) life history, using records, files and the subject's own recollection of events.

CLASSICAL CONDITIONING – Stemming from the work of Pavlov, a type of learning which arises from two stimuli being paired together so that the automatic response to the original stimulus is learnt in connection with a second, previously neutral, one.

CLINICAL INTERVIEW – A technique for gathering information in which the subject is encouraged to respond freely to situations and questions with which they are presented: that is, the discussion is 'unstructured' (see the work of Piaget).

COGNITION – Generally taken to refer to all mental processes such as thinking, decision-making, problem-solving, remembering, and so on. Studied by cognitive psychologists.

COGNITIVE DEVELOPMENTAL THEORY – A perspective which concerns itself with explaining behaviour in terms of the changes that occur (over time) in processes such as thinking and reasoning (see also Psychoanalytic theory and Social learning theory for a contrast).

COMPARATIVE PSYCHOLOGY – A branch of psychology concerned with making comparisons between different animal species.

CORRELATION – A method of investigation which looks at the degree to which two variables are related. However, if a relationship is found to exist, it does not allow the conclusion that one thing causes the other (e.g., depression and rainfall).

CRITICAL PERIOD – A label used with reference to certain kinds of behaviours or responses, the implication being that unless the behaviour takes place within a specific time period, then it never will. Some researchers, though, have shown that the acquisition period can be extended, and so the term 'sensitive period' is often preferred.

CROSS-CULTURAL STUDY – A method of investigation which involves comparing the practices of different cultural groups with regard to such aspects as child-rearing styles and language acquisition.

CULTURE-FAIR – Used in the context of testing and assessment, the view that questions and items should be designed for universal use, and should not penalize people from other cultures or be biased against them in any way (sometimes known as culture-free).

DEPENDENT VARIABLE – That variable in an experiment which the researcher sets out to measure, such as the time taken to complete a task (see also Independent variable).

ECT – or *e*lectro-*c*onvulsive *t*herapy, involves the sending of electrical current through electrodes attached to the scalp of mentally-disturbed patients. Used most often as a treatment for depression.

EGOCENTRISM – The inability to see things from another perspective. According to Piaget, this is one of the features which limits the thinking of pre-operational children.

EMPIRICISM – The school of thought which maintains that knowledge stems from experience and learning.

ENVIRONMENTAL PSYCHOLOGY – A branch of psychology which studies people in the context of their surroundings (e.g., how people interact in crowds, factors in the environment which induce stress, etc.).

ETHOLOGY – The study of animal behaviour in natural settings (as opposed to laboratory studies).

EXPERIMENT – A method of investigation in which the researcher studies the affects of one variable upon another, whilst at the same time attempting to exercise control over 'outside' influences which may affect the results.

GENERALIZATION – Essentially the principle of going from the particular to the general, and applying specific findings on a broader scale; the intention of researchers is to generalize their findings from a (small) sample of subjects to the wider population.

GESTALT **PSYCHOLOGY** – A school of thought which proposes that behaviour can only be fully understood in terms of the 'whole' aspect, and that breaking down behaviours into smaller unit detracts from their appreciation. Exemplified in the statement, 'the whole is greater than the sum of all the parts' (e.g., a crowd is more than a collection of individuals).

HALO EFFECT – In impression formation, the tendency to use on particular characteristic of a person as the basis for an overall view, such as assuming that an attractive person is also intelligent, humorous, good-natured, and so on. It can operate both positively and negatively.

HYPOTHESIS – A clearly defined prediction which a researcher makes at the start of an investigation, and then proceeds to test. The results of the investigation enable the researcher either to support or to reject the hypothesis.

IDENTIFICATION – The process in which an individual adopts the characteristic behaviours and views of another person (or group) inan effort to be like them (e.g., a child identifying with the same-sex parent).

IMPRINTING – The phenomenon associated with early-maturing animals, whereby shortly after birth they follow the first distinctive object (usually the parent) with which they come into contact.

INCIDENTAL LEARNING – Learning which occurs without any specific effort or deliberate intent by the learner at the time.

INDEPENDENT VARIABLE – That variable in an experiment which the researcher alters or deliberately changes in an attempt to see how it affects the dependent variable.

INSTRUMENTAL CONDITIONING – A procedure whereby an animal (or person) learns to associate a specific action with a specific outcome: that is, the action is 'instrumental' in bringing about the outcome.

IQ – Intelligence quotient: the unit of measurement which reflects an individual's performance score on an intelligence test.

LATENT LEARNING – A type of learning which reveals itself some time after it actually took place. It provides evidence for the notion that 'learning' itself can never be directly measured, only performance.

MATURATION – The process by which certain developmental changes occur in an individual's physical make-up as a result of in-built genetic factors, rather than learning. These, in turn, lead to new patterns of behaviour.

MENTAL AGE – A term used in intelligence testing to define an individual's level of intellectual capacity (e.g., 'a bright' child with an actual, or chronological, age of 7 may have the mental age of a 9 year old).

MODEL – As used in social learning theory this refers to an individual whose behaviour sets a standard which is observed and imitated by others.

MOTHERESE – A simplified form of language used by adults (and older children) when speaking to young children. Key words tend to be emphasized and sentences are generally much shorter than in adult speech.

NATIVISM – The school of thought which stresses the role of inborn, biologically-determined influences upon behaviour, (see also Empiricism and the Nature–nurture debate).

NATURE–NURTURE DEBATE – A term used to describe the opposing view-points held on several issues in psychology such as language, intelligence and perception. The 'nature' side supports the influence of inborn factors, while the 'nurture' side argues in favour of learning and experience.

NEGATIVE REINFORCEMENT – A procedure whereby a response is streng-thened by removing an unpleasant stimulus immediately after the (desired) response occurs.

NEONATE – Newborn.

NEURONE – Nerve cell (the basic unit of the nervous system).

NEUROPSYCHOLOGY – A branch of psychology which investigates the impor-tant relationship between the nervous system and behaviour.

NEUROTRANSMITTER – A substance involved in communicating the signal between adjacent cells in the nervous system.

OBSERVATIONAl STUDY – A method of investigation in which subjects' behaviour is observed and recorded, usually with as little interference as possible by the researcher.

PEER – A member of the same age-group.

PERCEPTION – The 'active' process by which information from the senses (such as vision) is interpreted, using past experience and knowledge.

PERCEPTUAL SET – A state of readiness or predisposition to perceive something in a particular way.

POSITIVE REINFORCEMENT – A procedure whereby a response is strengthened by presenting a reward immediately after it occurs.

PRIMACY EFFECT – (a) In impression formation, the tendency to be influenced by the early or first information received about a person; (b) in memory research, the tendency to recall the first items of a list better than those in the middle.

PROSOCIAL BEHAVIOUR – Behaviour which results in a favourable outcome for others (e.g., helping, sharing and cooperating).

PSYCHIATRY – A branch of medicine which specializes in the study and treatment of mental disorders.

PSYCHOANALYTIC THEORY – A perspective, usually linked with the work of Sigmund Freud, which concerns itself with explaining behaviour in terms of unconscious influences said to cause it.

PSYCHOMETRICS – The use of tests and other forms of assessment to measure aspects of behaviour.

PUNISHMENT – A procedure whereby a response is weakened or decreased by presenting an unpleasant stimulus immediately after the response occurs.

RECENCY EFFECT – (a) In impression formation, the tendency to be influenced by the last information received about a person; (b) in memory research, the tendency to recall the later items of a list better than those in the middle.

REHEARSAL – The repetition of previously-learnt information in order to aid remembering it on a later occasion.

REINFORCEMENT A procedure which strengthens or increases the likelihood of a response.

ROLE – That aspect of individuals which leads them to behave in certain ways when interacting with others, and which in turn leads other people to have expectations about their behaviour.

SCHEMA – A term used in cognitive psychology to refer to a mental plan or framework which is used when interpreting objects and events, planning and guiding actions.

SELF-FULFILLING PROPHECY – The tendency for a prediction to come true because of subsequent behaviour which makes it more likely to happen (e.g., people who presume that they will fail an interview may behave in certain ways which in fact bring this about).

SENSATION – The receiving and processing of information by the sense organs (as distinct from perception, which is the actual interpretation of this information).

SOCIAL LEARNING THEORY – A perspective which concerns itself with explaining behaviour in terms of processes, such as the observation and imitation of models.

SOCIAL NORMS – The acknowledged codes of conduct and standards which govern behaviour in a society.

STEREOTYPE – A means of categorizing people on the basis of certain assumptions made about the behaviour of the group to which they belong.

SUPERNORMAL STIMULUS – A term used in ethology for a feature which produces an exaggerated response from an animal (i.e., one that is stronger than normal).

SURVEY METHOD – A method of investigation in which the researcher collects information from a large number of people, either by questionnaire or interview.

SYNAPSE – In the nervous system, the gap between two adjacent nerve cells.

TRANSDUCTION – The process by which incoming sensory information (such as light or sound) is translated into nerve impulses thereby allowing analysis and interpretation.

UNCONDITIONED RESPONSE (UCR) – A term used in classical conditioning for the unlearnt response (usually a reflex) given when presented with a certain stimulus. NB: The *learnt* response is called the CR.

UNCONDITIONED STIMULUS (UCS) – A term used in classical conditioning for the stimulus which elicits an unlearnt response.

Index

A

accommodation   149–50, 281
action potential   225–6, 281
activity theory   13
adolescence   7–10
adulthood   11–13
ageing   12–13, 144
aggression
  cross-cultural studies of   28
  definitions of   21
  sex differences in   27–8
  television and   24–5
  theories of   21–7
agraphia   233
AIDS   9, 57–8
Ainsworth, M.   4–5
alexia   233
altruism   209–10, 281
amenorrhoea   9
American Sign Language (ASL)   178
animism   152
anorexia nervosa   9, 205
anti-depressants   218–19
anti-Semitism   70
aphasia   233
artificial intelligence   145–146
assimilation   149–50, 161, 281
Atkinson, R. C. and Shiffrin,
    R. M.   120–4
attachment   3–5, 207, 281
attention
  automatic and conscious
      processing   118–19
  cocktail party effect   110
  divided   116–18
  methods of studying   110–11
  selective   111–16
attenuator model   114–16
attitudes
  behaviour and   52–4
  changing of   56–1
  consistency theory of   61–3
  definitions of   49
  development of   54–6
  measurement of   50–2
attraction   75–80
audience effect   31, 32

authoritarian personality   71
autism   191, 194, 217
autokinetic effect   33
aversion therapy   190–91
axon   224–7, 281

B

babbling   168–9
Bandura, A.   14, 16
Bandura, A., Ross, D. and Ross,
    S. A.   23–5
Bartlett, F.   124–5
behaviour
  abnormal   212
  evolution and   200–1
  genetics and   203–5
  maturation and   205–6
  modification   191
  rituals   201–2
  therapy   191
behaviourism   275, 281
biofeedback   194, 281
blind spot   88
Bobo doll   23
bottom-up approach   124
Bower, T.   161
Bowlby, J.   3–4
brain
  language and   233
  laterality of function and   272
  plasticity of function and   235
  split-brain studies   233–5
  structure of   228–33
British Psychological Society   263, 267
Broca's area   233–4, 272
Bruner, J.   165
bystander effect   32

C

case study   19, 247, 281
castration complex   19, 246
catatonic schizophrenia   215
central traits   65–6
cerebellum   228, 229
cerebral cortex   90–2, 228, 231–3
Chomsky, N.   176

chromosomal abnormalities 15
chromosomes 14–15
chronological age 134–5
classical conditioning 54, 180–2, 189–91, 281
clinical interview 161, 281
clinical psychology 263
clinical studies 106, 222
cocktail party effect 110
cognition 61, 148, 165, 281
cognitive developmental theory 14, 20, 150, 281
cognitive dissonance 61–3
collective unconscious 249
comparative psychology 198, 281
compensation 237–8
complementarity 79
compliance 40–2
computer simulation 262
concrete operational stage 151, 154–7
concurrent validity 137
conditioned response 181–2, 189
conditioned stimulus 180–2, 189
cones 86–9
conformity 32–40
conservation 153–6, 164
control 252–3
corpus callosum 228, 234
correlation 24, 253, 261–2, 282
counter-stereotyping 73
counter-balancing 256–7
CQSW 266
criminological psychology 265
critical period 15, 173, 207, 282
cross-cutural study 18, 28, 106, 282
culture-fair (tests) 136, 282

D

Darwin, C. 268, 274
debriefing 46
decision time 12
defence mechanisms 245–6
dendrite 224–7
dependent variable 253, 255, 282
depression 216, 219–222
developmental theory 14, 20, 148, 241
deviation 137–8
dichotic listening 110–11, 116
discrimination,
    animal learning and 182
    causes of 69–72
    prejudice and 67–9
    reduction of 72–5
displacement 201, 244
dissonance 61–3
divided attention 116–18

dopamine 217–18
drosophila 204–5
drugs 216–20
DSM 213, 214
dualism 270
dysgraphia 233
dyslexia 233
dysphasia 233

E

Ebbinghaus, H. 273
echoic memory 120
echolalia 168
ECT 216, 219, 282
educational psychology 264–5
ego 242–3, 245
egocentrism 152, 161–4, 282
Electra complex 18–19, 246, 248
electromagnetism 84–5
emergent properties 270
empiricism 81, 106, 282
endocrine system 8, 230–1
environmental psychology 32, 282
epistemology 148
Erikson, E. 9–12
ethnocentrism 70–1
ethogram 199
ethology 22, 197–200, 282
evolution (and behaviour) 200–2
expectancy effects 102
experiment 252, 282
experimental design 256–8
experimental hypotheses 254–5
expert system 131
extraversion 65, 241
eyewitness testimony 125
Eysenck, H. 241

F

facilitation 30–2
Fantz, R. 2
FAP 199–200
filter model 112–13
fixation 246
flooding 190
formal operational stage 157–8, 165
free association 248
Freud, S.
    defence mechanisms 245–6
    methods 247–8
    personality theory of 241–5
    socialization perspective 14
frontal lobe 232
frustration–aggression hypothesis 25–6
F-scale 71

G

Galton, F.   139, 274
Gardner, R. A. and Gardner, B. T.   178
gender   14–16, 145
gender constancy   20
general intelligence   139–40
generalization   46, 75, 181, 282
Genovese, Kitty   32
genital stage   247
Gestalt psychology   82, 106–8, 282
Gregory, R. L.   94, 96
GSR   250
Guilford, J. P.   140

H

halo effect   66–7, 282
hebephrenic schizophrenia   217
hemispheres (of brain)   232, 234–5, 272
holophrase   170
hormones   8, 15, 230–1
Hubel, D. H. and Wiesel, T.N.   90
Humanism   240
hydraulic model   26, 201
hypothalamus   228, 230
hypotheses   254–6, 282

I

ICD   213
iconic memory   120
id   241–2, 244
identification   18–19, 21, 283
identity crisis   7, 9–10
idiographic approach   237, 240
imitation   19, 22, 24
implicit personality theory   67
implosion therapy   190
impression formation   64–7
imprinting   206–9, 283
incidental learning   125, 283
inclusive fitness   210
independent groups design   257–8
independent variable   253, 283
innate   3, 210
instinct   22, 26, 241
instrumental conditioning   182–9, 191–4, 283
intelligence
  artificial   131, 145–6
  current research in   147
  IQ and   135–7, 147, 283
  reliability and   137
  testing, development of   133–6
  test performance, determinants of   141–5
  tests, construction of   136–8

theories of   138–41
validity and   137
interviews   50, 284
introspection   247, 253
introversion   65, 241, 250
intuitive stage   152
invariant order   150
IQ   135–7, 147, 283

J

James, W.   116
jigsaw classroom   74
jnd   272
Jung, C. G.   248–51

K

Kahneman, D.   116, 119
kinship   210
Klinefelter's syndrome   15
Kohlberg, L.   20, 160
Kraepelin, E.   212, 215

L

LAD   176
language
  animal studies and   177–9
  impaired development of   172–3
  one-word stage of   169–70
  overregularization in   171
  pre-linguistic stage of   168–9
  questions, phrasing of   172
  structure of   166–8
  theories of   173–7
  two-word stage of   170–1
LaPiere, R.   52–3
large-scale research   261
latent learning   195–6, 283
laterality of brain function   272
law of effect   182
learned helplessness   220–2
learning
  aggression and   22
  classical conditioning   180–2
  instrumental conditioning   182
  latent   195–6
  pro-social behaviour and   25
  reinforcement   183–9
  sex roles and   19
  theory, applications of   189–94
levels of processing   125–9
libido   241–2
life events   11
Likert scale   51
Little Albert   189–90
Little Hans   19

lobes of brain 232–3
localization of brain function 232, 234–5
Loftus, E. 125
Lorenz, K. 22, 198–202
low-ball effect 42
LTM 121–3

M

MAP 199–200
matched subjects design 257–8
matching hypothesis 77
maternal deprivation 3
maturation
  behaviour and 205–6
  definition of 283
  intelligence and 144
  Piaget and 149
  rates, effects of 8–9
Mead, G. 239
Mead, M. 18, 28
memory
  Atkinson–Shiffrin model of 120–4
  eyewitness testimony and 125
  levels of processing and 125–9
  semantic 129–31
  sensory 120
  serial position effect and 122
  studies, criticisms of 124
menarche 8, 205
mental age 134–5, 283
mental illness 212–15
Milgram, S. 42–6
MLU 171
modelling 14, 19–20, 23, 283
moral realism 159
moral relativism 160
morality 158
Morgan's canon 274
morpheme 167
motherese 171, 175, 283
Motor cortex 234
Müller–Lyer illusion 93

N

Nativism 106, 176, 283
nature–nurture debate 104–6, 176, 268, 283
Naughty Teddy 164
negative reinforcement 184, 283
neonate 106, 283
nervous system
  brain, structure of 228–35
  spinal cord 229
  synapse 226–7
neuron 224–7, 283
neuropsychology 224, 269, 283

neuroses 213
neurotransmitter 217, 226, 283
nomothetic approach 237, 254
norm
  age 136
  social 71, 284
normal distribution 138
null hypothesis 255

O

obedience 42–8
object permanence 151, 161
observational study 253, 258–9, 283
occipital lobe 232
occupational psychology 264
Oedipus complex 18–19, 246
ontogeny 197
operant conditioning 54, 182–9, 191–4
operational definition 255
oral stage 247
order effects (control of) 256–7
overextensions 170
overgeneralization 171
overlearning 273
overregularization 171

P

paranoid schizophrenia 215
parietal lobe 232
Parkinson's disease 216, 218
participant observation 253, 259
Pavlov, I. 112, 180–2
Penfield, W. 232
penis envy 246
perception
  definition of 283
  features of 100–5
  Gestalt theory of 106–8
  nature–nurture debate and 105–6
  sensation and 92
  visual illusions and 93–101
  visual system and 85–92
perceptual set 102, 284
personality
  Freudian theory of 241–8
  Humanism and 240
  Jungian theory of 248–51
  Psychoanalytical theory and 237–8
  Role theory of 238–40
  type and trait approaches to 240–1
persuasive communication 56–61
PGCE 265
pheromone 231
phobia 189–90
phonemes 166–7
photoreceptors 86–9

phylogeny 197
Piaget, J.
    alternatives to 165
    criticisms of 160–5
    educational implications and 160–1
    moral development and 158–60
    stage theory of 14, 148, 150–8
pituitary gland 228, 230
plasticity (of brain) 235
play 6–7, 25, 151, 255, 259–60
populations 253–4
positive reinforcement 24, 54, 183–4, 284
pre-conceptual stage 152
prejudice
    causes of 69–72
    definition of 68
    racism 68–9
    reduction of 72–5
    sexism 69
pre-operational stage 151–4
primacy effect 65, 284
primary reinforcement 185
prison experiment 47–8
prison psychologist 265
programmed learning 191
projection 245
prosocial behaviour 24–5, 284
psychiatry 212, 216, 222, 284
psychoanalytical theory
    aggression and 26–7
    sex roles and 18–19
    personality and 237–8
psychology
    careers in 263–7
    historical account of 271–5
    nature–nurture debate and 268–9
psychometrics 51, 136, 147, 274, 284
psychosexual stages 247
psychoses 213
psychosocial stages 9–10
punishment 184–5, 284
pygmalion effect 143–4

Q

questionnaire 43, 50, 53
questions
    eyewitness research, leading 125
    language, appearance in 172
quotient (of intelligence) 135

R

racism 68–9, 72
random sampling 253
recall 122
recency effect
    impression formation and 64–5

memory and 122, 284
receptive fields 89–90
reciprocity 3
Reductionism 269–70
reflex 2, 229
regression 246, 250
rehearsal 284
reinforcement
    definition of 284
    negative 184, 283
    positive 183, 284
    primary 185
    schedules of 185
    secondary 185
    social learning theory and 20, 22–4
reliability 137
repeated measures 256–8
repertory grid test 240
repression 245
resource allocation 116–18
reticular formation 230
retina 85–90
rituals 201–2
Robber's Cave study 74–5
rods 86–9
role 238, 284
role theory 239
Rutter, M. 4

S

sample 253–4
scapegoating 70
Schachter, S. 75
schema
    Bartlett 124–5
    definition 284
    Piaget 149–50
schizophrenia
    causes of 217–19
    treatment of 191
    types of 215–17
secondary reinforcement 185
self-actualization 250
self-fulfilling prophecy 67, 284
semantic differential 51
semantic memory 129
semantics 167–8
sensation 81–2, 273, 284
sensitive period 209, 282
sensori-motor stage 151, 161
separation anxiety 3–4
serial position effect 122–4
set 102, 284
sex reassignment 17–18
sex role typing
    acquisition of 14–18
    cognitive approach to 20–1

cross-cultural studies and 18
  psychoanalytic theory of 19, 21
  social learning theory of 19–21
sexism 69, 72–3
shadowing 110–11, 112, 115
shaping 174, 194
Sherif, M. 33, 74–5
sign stimulus 198–9
simulation
  computer 262
  prison 47–8
Skinner, B. F.
  language, approach to 174
  reinforcement and 183–5
  schedules and 185–8
Skinner box 183–5
sleep 230
social cognition 165
social facilitation 30–2
social learning theory
  aggression and 22–5
  attitudes and 55–6
  definition of 284
  language and 174
  sex role typing and 19–20
  socialization and 14
social norm 71, 284
social releaser 198–9
socialization 14
sociobiology 209–10
Spearman, C. 139–40
split-brain studies 233–5
spreading activation theory 130
stage theory
  Erikson 9–10
  Freud 247
  Piaget 150–1
standard deviation 137–8
standardization 136
stereotyping 15, 67–8, 73, 80, 94, 284
STM 121–3
strange situation 5
Stroop effect 103–4
subjects 253
superego 243
supernormal stimulus 199, 284
survey 50, 54, 252–3, 261, 284
synapse 123, 285
syntax 167–8, 171, 179
systematic desensitization 190
systematic observation 253, 259–60

T

Tchambuli 18
telegraphic speech 170
television and aggression 24

temporal lobe 232
territorial aggression 21
testosterone 230–1
test-retest method 137
thalamus 87, 89
Thanatos 26–7, 242
Thorndike, E. L. 140, 182, 183
Thurstone, L. L. 51, 140
Thurstone Scales 51
time sample 259
Tinbergen, N. 22, 199, 268
token economy system 193
Tolman, E. C. 195–6
top-down approach 124
trait 64, 65, 240–1
tranquillizers 216–18
transduction 85–6, 224, 285
transitivity 157
Treisman, A. 114–16
trial and error learning 182
Triplett, N. 30
Turner's syndrome 15
twin studies 139
two-process model (of memory) 116, 121–4
two-word utterances 170–1

U

unconditioned response 189, 190, 285
unconditioned stimulus 180–2, 189, 190, 285
unconscious
  collective 249
  personal 248
underextensions 170
unemployment 70, 219, 264

V

validity 136, 137
visual system 85–92, 234
Von Frisch, K. 166

W

Washoe 178
Watson, J. B. 275
Watson, J. B. and Rayner, R. 189
Welford, A. T. 12
Wernicke's area 233–4
World Health Organization 213
Wundt, W. 81, 273

Z

Zajonc, R. B. 31–2
Zimbardo, P. G. *et al.* 47–8